AMERICAN EDUCATION:
YESTERDAY, TODAY, AND TOMORROW

AMERICAN EDUCATION:
YESTERDAY, TODAY, AND TOMORROW

Ninety-ninth Yearbook of the
National Society for the Study of Education

PART II

Edited by

THOMAS L. GOOD

Editor for the Society

MARGARET EARLY

20 NSSE 00

Distributed by THE UNIVERSITY OF CHICAGO PRESS • CHICAGO, ILLINOIS

The National Society for the Study of Education

The National Society for the Study of Education was founded in 1901 as successor to the National Herbart Society. It publishes a two-volume Yearbook, each volume dealing with a separate topic of concern to educators. The Society's series of Yearbooks, now in its ninety-ninth year, contains chapters written by scholars and practitioners noted for their significant work on the topics about which they write.

The Society welcomes as members all individuals who wish to receive its publications. Current membership includes educators in the United States, Canada, and elsewhere throughout the world—professors, researchers, administrators, and graduate students in colleges and universities and teachers, administrators, supervisors, and curriculum specialists in elementary and secondary schools.

Members of the Society elect a Board of Directors. Its responsibilities include reviewing proposals for Yearbooks, authorizing the preparation of Yearbooks based on accepted proposals, and appointing an editor or editors to oversee the preparation of manuscripts.

Current dues (for the year 2000) are a modest $35 ($30 for retired members and for students in their first year of membership). Members whose dues are paid for the current calendar year receive the Society's Yearbook, are eligible for election to the Board of Directors, and are entitled to a 33 percent discount when purchasing past Yearbooks from the Society's distributor, the University of Chicago Press.

Each year the Society arranges for meetings to be held in conjunction with the annual conferences of one or more of the national educational organizations. At these meetings, the current Yearbook is presented and critiqued. All members are urged to attend these meetings. Members are encouraged to submit proposals for future Yearbooks.

American Education: Yesterday, Today, and Tomorrow is Part 2 of the 99th Yearbook. Part 1, published simultaneously, is entitled *Constructivism in Education*.

For further information, write to the Secretary, NSSE, 5835 Kimbark Ave., Chicago, Illinois 60637.

ISSN: 0077-5762

Published 2000 by
THE NATIONAL SOCIETY FOR THE STUDY OF EDUCATION
5835 Kimbark Avenue, Chicago, Illinois 60637

First Printing
Printed in the United States of America

v

Acknowledgments

In the last year of the twentieth century the Board of Directors of the National Society for the Study of Education recognized the need for a yearbook that would address the evolution of educational beliefs, courses of study, and teaching practices through the foregoing hundred years. They called upon Thomas L. Good, editor of the *Elementary School Journal*, to prepare this yearbook, and he graciously agreed to do so while pointing out the need for limiting the scope to elementary and middle school education and selecting reading, mathematics, and social studies as the school subjects to receive particular attention. In this way, important chapters could be devoted to the role of teachers, to students' motivation to learn, to achievement testing, and to the linkages between education and society from 1900 to 2000. Because the span is great, the chapters on each topic would be long and therefore the number of chapters would be fewer than in other NSSE yearbooks.

Accordingly, Dr. Good assembled a team of authorities to identify the issues, decide the order in which they would be presented, and to write the seven chapters that constitute *American Education: Yesterday, Today, and Tomorrow*. Over a year's time, members of the Board reviewed drafts of the chapters, authors revised them, and Dr. Good—to borrow his metaphor—rounded up straying manuscripts, and eventually we got them into the printer's corral.

In addition to Dr. Good and the eleven authors who so freely shared their energies and expertise to produce this end-of-the-century review of American schooling, I must thank Kenneth Rehage, who continues to guide my editorial efforts even while he pretends to have stepped down from editing in order to attend to the many responsibilities of the Society's executive secretary. I am grateful also to Elizabeth Salvetti, who deciphered nearly unreadable squiggles to correct disks for both Part One and Part Two of the 99th Yearbook and prepared the extensive Name Index for both volumes.

MARGARET EARLY
Editor for the Society

Editor's Preface

Where have we been and where are we headed?

It is an honor to edit one of the NSSE Yearbooks published in 2000. In this volume, we address the evolution of educational beliefs, curriculum content, and classroom practices in several important educational areas including reading, mathematics, social studies, measurement, the work of teachers, and conceptions of motivation. These thematic explorations are preceded by a brief sketch of the evolving relationship between education and society from 1900 to 2000.

In the initial chapter, Sharon Nichols and I describe a changing society and draw some linkages between education and the broader culture it serves. It is seen that education is not a linear trend of progress and refinement, as many popular ideas about how to teach quickly appear, recede, and are eventually replaced by new conceptions in practice only to be replaced again by the "original" idea two or three decades later. In addition to outlining the cyclical nature of educational reform efforts, we provide (a) selected "snapshots" of education and society at both the beginning and end of the century, and (b) a discussion of some of the molar debates evident in both 1900 and today through a content and frequency analysis of the *New York Times*. Media interest in education has experienced a dramatic surge over the past hundred years, while the key issues have remained similar. Nichols and Good describe three issues which appear relatively constant: the debates over school control, educational equality, and issues of teacher quality.

In his chapter on reading in the twentieth century, P. David Pearson provides an authoritative review of the enactment of reading instruction throughout the century. In particular, he reviews in depth the dominant materials and the pedagogical practices used for reading instruction across time. Rather than simply summarizing these observable surface features as a basis for analysis, he derives and reports his understanding of the underlying assumptions about the nature of reading that motivate dominant practices. He organizes his review by dividing the century into thirds (1900-1935, 1935-1970, and 1970-2000). Among his many points of analysis, one especially intriguing contribution is his explanation of the various "reading wars."

Doug Grouws and Kristin Cebulla in their chapter on school mathematics at the crossroads note that as we end the century, there is considerable debate both in the popular press and scholarly journals about the value and quality of mathematics instruction. They describe these debates as reminiscent of the rancorous ones in the late 50s and 60s when the United States was thought to be behind in the space race and American students were deficient in mathematical ability.

In Chapter VI, Jere Brophy, Janet Alleman, and Carolyn O'Mahony provide a comprehensive discussion of various positions on how social studies should be taught including traditions located in transmission of the cultural heritage, social science, reflective inquiry, informed social criticism, and personal development. These authors describe the evolution of the social studies curriculum, including reforms suggested for elementary social studies, the expanding community framework (and associated criticism thereof), values and moral education, needed research, especially on students' knowledge and thinking, curricular integration, and teaching for understanding.

In her chapter on teachers' work Dee Ann Spencer places a human face and a social context on teachers who struggle with competing definitions of how to teach reading, mathematics, and social studies and how to measure or understand student growth in these areas. Her history of teaching provides a review of the pressures that teachers (primarily women) faced early in the century. Although the conditions then were difficult, there is considerable evidence to show that many contemporary women teachers also teach under difficult circumstances. Spencer comments as well upon the serious teacher shortage predicted for the next decade and suggests some strategies for dealing with this issue.

Writing on achievement testing in America, Jerome D'Agostino provides a rich historical context for explaining current measurement problems. He provides a description of a pioneering study conducted in Boston in 1847 that in large measure illustrates most of the same dilemmas and opportunities that measurement specialists face today. Indeed, many of the arguments that have evolved in the measurement literature over time were initially identified (although not solved) in this early pioneering study. From the earliest beginnings, he notes the uses of achievement tests were not only conflicting in terms of purposes but were also a political tool employed by opposing forces to maintain their definition of curriculum and instruction.

Mary McCaslin and Eleanor DiMarino-Linnen's chapter, "Motivation and Learning in School," is a review of conceptions of motivation as depicted in articles published in the *American Psychologist* from 1946 to 1995 (publication began in 1946). This fifty-year review and analysis examines motivation for learning in school within the context of extant social policies and cultural beliefs in each decade. In particular, their intent is to better understand educational conceptions of student motivation by interrelating conceptions from society generally and psychology in particular. McCaslin and DiMarino-Linnen selected the *American Psychologist* because of its broad mission to bring psychology to bear on social issues. They intend the chapter for teachers, curriculum theorists, and educational psychologists who are interested in exploring the relations among psychology, societal context, and educational practice.

It has been a privilege to work with this talented and insightful group of authors. I was pleased that this distinguished group would address an ambitious task—describing and analyzing an important dimension of education in both a historical and contemporary perspective—and accomplish it within such a short time period.

It has been a rewarding experience to work with Ken Rehage and Margaret Early in developing the volume. Their wisdom, editorial experience, and editing greatly enriched the volume. I would like to thank Lyn Corno, who initially encouraged me to submit a proposal to the NSSE board of directors for the 99th Yearbook. Her belief in this endeavor, and her support throughout are gratefully recognized. Finally, I would like to thank the reviewers for their helpful critique of authors' initial drafts: Hilda Borko, Robert Calfee, Lyn Corno, Barbara Dougherty, Barbara McKean, Tom Payzant, Ken Rehage, and Sam Stringfield.

THOMAS L. GOOD

Table of Contents

CHAPTER I

Education and Society, 1900-2000: Selected Snapshots of Then and Now

SHARON L. NICHOLS AND THOMAS L. GOOD

Introduction

This yearbook addresses various aspects of public education (curriculum, teachers, and students) and their evolution in this century. This chapter discusses the general relation between education and society at the start and end of this century. As we move into a new millennium it is important to take stock of American education: to discuss where we've been, where we are, and to present informed guesses about where we're headed. In some areas indisputable progress has occurred in American education; however, in other areas, it is arguable that the field has moved in relatively wide recurring circles. Entering the twenty-first century, we face many new issues and conundrums; however, ironically, some long-standing and major issues that educators faced in 1900 still remain.

Describing the relationship between society and education is difficult. Yet policymakers often posit simplistic "cause-effect" relations between schooling and societal outcomes. In 1983 the National Commission for Excellence in Education, published *A Nation at Risk*,[1] a scathing critique of public education, and argued in another publication:

Our nation is at risk. Our once unchallenged preeminence in commerce, industry, science, technology, and innovation is being overtaken by competitors throughout the world . . . if an unfriendly foreign power had attempted to impose on America the mediocre educational performance that exists today, we might have well viewed it as an act of war. As it stands, we have allowed this to happen to ourselves. We have even squandered the gains in student achievement made in the wake of the Sputnik challenge.[2]

Thomas L. Good is a Professor of Educational Psychology at the University of Arizona, Tucson. He also edits the *Elementary School Journal*, which is published by the University of Chicago Press. Sharon L. Nichols is a doctoral student in the Department of Educational Psychology at the University of Arizona.

Today, the American economy is running at high speed and unemployment rates are very low. The dynamic triple combination of high production, low interest rates, and low unemployment functions at a high-octane level—a level that many economists had asserted on theoretical grounds was unobtainable. Further, the federal budget has been balanced—an achievement that most economists had labeled an impossible dream. Yet despite the strength of the American society, many citizens still claim that our current public school system is inadequate and assert that it must be improved if our leadership in science, health, economics, and the military is to be maintained. Although we do not think it appropriate to equate the quality of one's educational system ipso facto with the quality of its economy, it is important to note that the American public school system was blamed for the economic difficulties encountered in the early 1980s. However, the American public education system in the late 1990s is not credited for the success of the economy. In contrast, public education is seen by many to be woefully inadequate.

The tenacity with which policymakers associate economic conditions—both present and future—with education clearly illustrates that education has become a salient public policy point in our society. There is wide consensus that education is a critical area for continued economic growth and political survival.

Citizens today see college education as essential; however, advocates for the importance of college education (for men) can be found in 1900 as well. President Thompson of the Ohio State University wrote in 1900:

The college-bred man gets into his position ten years earlier than the uneducated man and the young college men are becoming more and more leaders of the country. A college education is an absolute guarantee against poverty and distress.[3]

Thompson noted, "In 1896, of the 9 members of the Supreme Court 8 were college graduates, while 6 out of the 9 Cabinet Officers, 105 members of the lower house, and 70 United States Senators were graduates of some college or university."[4] What is perhaps different today is that most citizens—not just a small elite group—argue for the importance of high-quality education and encourage their daughters and sons to pursue college degrees.

The increased societal interest in education is reflected in the amount of media attention given to education. In 1900, the news media paid scant attention to education. Today stories on education appear daily in newspapers, on television newscasts, in magazine articles, and even in movies. If media attention indicates the importance of a topic, it is clear that today's society sees education as a vital issue. Virtually everyone places education on their list of top political issues as is evidenced by the support of both political parties for increased educational funding.

However, we know that many Americans and their political leaders are not satisfied with American schools, and indeed, much media attention on education is negative. Further, there is no consensus on what distinguishes high-quality from low-quality education. Indeed, educators and policymakers have debated whether quality of education is measured by "inputs" (e.g., resources, quality of teachers, number of library books) or "outputs" (e.g., student achievement, graduation rates). Recently, much attention has been focused on educational outputs as debates of student achievement in terms of standards and accountability have seen renewed media attention.[5] Further, many argue that charter schools and voucher programs are needed if public schools are to be reformed.

In this chapter, we attempt to contrast American society in 1900 and 2000. First, we illustrate ways that society and education today are markedly different than in 1900. Second, we explore the saliency of education in the broader society through a systematic investigation of the media including (a) the frequency with which education articles are published in the beginning and end of the century, and (b) the major themes that threaded the debates at these times. Third, based on our media analysis, we note three broad themes that marked the interface of education and society in 1900 and which continue to do so today. These enduring themes are: (1) debate about the use of public monies to support private schools (especially religious ones), (2) debate on equal access to high-quality education for minority children and those from low-income homes, and (3) debate on the quality of teachers and schools. Although media coverage of education is more extensive today, much of what is discussed focuses on the same issues discussed by the media at the start of the century.

COMPARISON POINTS

In the first half of this chapter, we describe various "snapshots" of society and education in 1900 and compare them with current pictures. Before we present our analysis, however, it is useful to make disclaimers. First, there are countless dimensions upon which century-long comparisons could be made, and accordingly our selection of themes is necessarily incomplete. Second, in making selected comparisons, we merely "proxy" more complex issues when we provide averages and estimations. For example, when gathering annual income data for physicians in 1900, one medical historian from the National Library of Medicine noted that reporting general information is a "meaningless" endeavor given that such information varies on many dimensions, including if and where they received medical training and whether they practiced in a large metropolitan area or in a small rural town. Given that medical care was only in its infancy in 1900 (e.g., antibiotics weren't in general use until the 1920s and there were few safe surgical procedures), physicians in 1900 were seen merely as moderately successful tradespeople and not as specialists who hold unique and vital health information. Further, there was no way of evaluating or standardizing medical education, and therefore physicians gained medical information through a variety of methods. One doctor might pick up the trade by observing a more experienced doctor, while another might attend a formal, six-month lecture course. To avoid shallow or oversimplistic interpretations, we emphasize that our "snapshots" are not meant to provide analyses of any issue, but to posit general pictures that allow for a degree of comparison to be made over time. Such pictures can be very useful as we will demonstrate later in the chapter when we examine the comparative status of teachers and physicians then and now.

    To further complicate comparisons, the original broad format used for categorizing information in 1900 makes it difficult to provide adequate modern-day comparisons. This can be illustrated in the 1999 update to the six-decade-old Standard Industry Classification System of businesses. This update dramatically altered an accounting system that had not been changed since the 1930s. For example, at its inception, it was noted that "data on haircuts and brain surgery were all dropped in the same statistical pot" (because both were included in the general service-industry category).[6] Indeed, an increase in haircuts during the 30s could easily have been interpreted as an increase in the number of frontal lobotomies being performed! Today, the new system differentiates businesses into many more categories, thus allowing for the classification of more modern-day jobs such as "fiber-optic cable manufacturing, cellular telephone service, telemarketing, weight-reducing centers, pet supply stores, bed-and-breakfast inns, oil-change and lube shops, and casino hotels."[7] However, this system will probably be inadequate for characterizing and comparing jobs in 2000 with those in 2050. In this chapter, we face the dilemma that "snapshots" provide only broad generalizations and thus fail to describe complexities of the issues.

A third caveat is that 1900 data are not precise, as methods of gathering various data were in their infancy. As a case in point, the practice of registering individual deaths was just being formalized in 1900 and not all states were required to do so. Despite the availability (in most cases) of categorical definitions for the statistics we cite, we feel it unnecessary for the purpose of this essay to present all appropriate qualifications. (Reader, please consult cited source for detailed information on any reported statistic.) Finally, despite our attempt to collect and report accurately, we acknowledge that we are not historians (some of whom espouse the ambiguities and difficulties associated with historical reporting). For example, on the issue of describing life in the Middle Ages, Barbara Tuchman writes:

It may be taken as axiomatic that any statement of fact about the Middle Ages may (and probably will) be met by a statement of the opposite or a different version. Women outnumbered men because men were killed off in the wars; men outnumbered women because women died in childbirth. Common people were familiar with the Bible; common people were unfamiliar with the Bible. Nobles were tax exempt; no, they were not tax exempt. French peasants were filthy and foul-smelling and lived on bread and onions; French peasants ate pork, fowl, and game and enjoyed frequent baths in the village bathhouses. This list could be extended indefinitely.[8]

As Tuchman shows, the act of reporting on historical events can assume very divergent perspectives and, therefore, we acknowledge that our account represents a single perspective. However, our "snapshots" are sufficient to suggest that going to first grade in 1900 was not the same experience that it is in 2000.

Societal Snapshots: Then and Now

HEALTH

In 1900, we were a smaller nation and arguably a less healthy one. Then, the total population of the United States was 76.1 million, whereas now our population exceeds 271.1 million.[9] (See Table 1 on page 10.) The life expectancy in 1900 was 47.3 years for both males and females, whites and nonwhites. As of 1995, the average life expectancy was 75.8 (73.4 for white males and 79.6 for white females; 65.4 for black males and 74.0 for black females). For the year 2000, life expectancy is projected to go up to 74.2 for white males, 80.5 for white females, 74.7 for black females, and it is expected to decrease slightly to 64.6 for black males.[10] We have made notable progress this century in health care and in extending the human life span.

Despite the large medical and technological strides in extending average life expectancy, American citizens' quality of life varies notably. For example, at present the United States does not look terrific on cross-national comparisons of quality-of-life measures. Too many Americans—including children and youth—are living in below-average conditions.[11] As of 1995 13.8% of all adults were living in poverty while 20% of all children (in families and under 18 years old) were living in poverty. Indeed, the percentage of children living in poverty has fluctuated in the last 30 years with the lowest percentage being 14.9 in 1970.[12] (It is instructive to note that, according to some current critics of public education, in 1970 students' achievement scores peaked when child poverty rates reached their low point.) Additionally, despite many medical and societal advances, the health status of the youngest and oldest Americans is tenuous. For example, the United States ranks 19th in the percentage of low-birth-weight infants, behind Japan, Germany, and France;[13] one-third of the elderly living in the Appalachian states are toothless.[14] Perhaps in the next century we can learn how to increase the quality of life for more citizens.

In 1900, the top five major causes of death were major cardiovascular and renal diseases, influenza and pneumonia, tuberculosis, gastritis, and all accidents excluding motor accidents. However, today the top major cause of death remains major cardiovascular disease, but death from pneumonia and influenza, a second leading cause in 1900, has dropped drastically to fifth place. Malignancies, which weren't in the top five in 1900, are now our second most frequent cause of death. The growing dominance of cancer and our increased ability to treat influenza and pneumonia certainly suggest marked environmental, lifestyle, and medical changes since 1900.

The evolution of types and treatments of cancer provides one way to illustrate where we've been and where we are today in the medical field. In 1900, men mostly suffered from prostate, lung, and colon cancer while women mostly suffered from breast, colon, and lung cancer. Today, men and women continue to suffer from these and other forms of cancer. However, what has marked the evolution in cancer's history are the medical and political strides made to treat cancer.

After a century in which research has received billions of tax dollars and attracted the talents of top scientists, the situation is little less bleak than before. Lung, colon, liver, pancreas and other major cancers continue to have appalling fatality rates, with fewer than one in five alive after five years from diagnosis (survival in uterine and stomach cancer has improved).[15]

Politically, this century saw a dramatic increase in spending for cancer research (e.g., 500 million dollars in 1971; one billion in 1976). With the discovery of chemotherapy (aided in part by these large investments), cancer patients' lives are modestly extended and cancer diagnoses are less bleak than was the case in 1900. Additionally, the discovery of the link of smoking to lung cancer in the 1950s has impacted the tobacco industry and the health of individuals worldwide.

Advances in technology and health treatment have dramatically increased the ability to provide wide-reaching medical and disaster aid to individuals around the world. For example, it was only in 1900 that Congress chartered the first chapter of the American Red Cross. Today, the American Red Cross plays a pivotal role in aiding victims of natural disasters locally, nationally, and internationally.

[The American Red Cross is a] volunteer-led humanitarian service organization [that] annually provides almost half the nation's blood supply, certifies more than 8.5 million people in vital life-saving skills, mobilizes relief to victims in more than 689,000 disasters nationwide, provides direct health services to 2.8 million people, assists international disaster and conflict victims in more than 40 countries, and transmits more than 14 million emergency messages to members of the Armed Forces and their families.[16]

The presence of the American Red Cross in the late 1990s is dramatic. As of February, 1999, the Red Cross reported receiving nearly six million volunteer blood donations over the year and had provided services for over 3,000 hospitals nationwide.[17] The American Red Cross also played a major role in aiding victims of Hurricane Hugo in South America, earthquake victims in Columbia, and more than 550,000 Kosovo refugees through facilitating the availability of food, shelter, and clothing and by helping to trace and reunite families who have been separated during this crisis.

DIVERSITY

Over the course of the past one hundred years, the numbers of new immigrants from many countries and cultures have progressively increased. During 1891-1901, an estimated 3.7 million new immigrants reached this country.[18] Approximately 30,428,029 new immigrants arrived during the decades between 1901-1980[19] and an additional 7.3 million new immigrants, it is estimated, arrived in the period between 1981 and 1990. Immigration was mostly from European countries in the earlier part of the century, but more recently its composition has changed to include a larger proportion of individuals of Hispanic descent.

In the early 1900s, immigrants of various ethnicities (Polish, Scandinavian, German) largely wanted to be integrated into both schools and society. During the time period of 1871-1920 when vast numbers of immigrants established themselves in the United States, one historian noted, "the most immediately striking feature of the migration to the United States is its great size, more than six times the number who went to the second-place receiver, Argentina."[20] In 1900, 27% of the total foreign-born population in the United States were from Germany, 16% were from Ireland, and 9% were from England and Wales.[21]

In 1900 Hispanics and Asians were but an infinitesimal part of our population. Indeed, data on the proportion of Hispanics among the total foreign-born population in 1900 differ. One report suggests that there were approximately 78,000 Mexicans living in the United States (or approximately one-tenth of 1% of the total foreign-born population),[22] while another reference suggests that approximately 1% of the foreign-born population at this time were of Hispanic descent.[23] Indeed, in one source of population statistics, persons of Hispanic/Mexican heritage were included in the white category (a practice continued from the 1900 census to the 1930 census).[24] Finally, and unfortunately, the United States has also provided a homeland to many involuntary immigrants, especially African Americans who constituted 12% of the 1900 population[25] and were largely denied the chance to enter society or education in any meaningful way.

There is debate as to whether immigrants reaching our shores around 1900 were coming here in search of land or career opportunities. For example, many believed that immigrants who came before 1900 were mostly land-seekers and those who came after 1900 were mainly wage-seekers in pursuit of employment in the industrial/trade sector. However, despite the industrial advances our country made after the turn of the century, some argued that immigrants still viewed America as a rich agricultural nation which offered many opportunities.

Yet it is less often realized that more homesteads began *after* 1900 than before. Hundreds of thousands of people poured into the western Great Plains, Washington State, and California, particularly from 1901 to 1903, and many were foreign-born. (emphasis added)[26]

Despite those who looked to the United States for opportunities to own land, many continued to flow into America for promises of money and career advancement:

> . . . the economic attractions of the United States were real. Success eluded many, native as well as foreign, but an agricultural ladder did exist, at least in the Midwest and West through World War I. Railroads still had no land to sell and the government had homesteads to give. For the many who lacked the cash and credit to begin as owner-operators, the first rung of the ladder could be tenancy or wage-labor, with the reasonable expectation that, unlike in Europe, one could reach the top of the ladder eventually.[27]

As we enter the twenty-first century, these groups are a major part of America. Now America's population has a greater percentage of Hispanics and Asians than blacks, whereas in 1900, the population was basically white, black, and Native American. By the year 2000, it is estimated that of our entire population, 11.4% will be of Hispanic origin, 71.8% will be white, 12.2% will be black, .7% will be Native American, Eskimo, and Aleut, and 3.9% will be Asian/Pacific Islander.[28] Today, to complicate the issues further, racial intermarriage defies the census bureau's standard ways of reporting race (black, white, and other). Juan Williams describes the situation:

> As I am writing this in 1998 there is an unparalleled rush of immigrants entering the United States. As a result there is a growing nativist backlash based on the new arrivals' reluctance to fully assimilate into American culture. This has led to calls to make English the nation's official language and sparked complaints that immigrants are taking jobs and seats in the universities, while also occupying a larger percentage of welfare rolls.[29]

In debating issues of segregation and desegregation, Williams notes:

> It is true that this generation of immigrants is not leaping aboard the bandwagon of assimilation; they want to live with people from their native land and often want to build schools and churches that will allow them to retain their ethnic and racial identities despite the heat of the great American melting pot.[30]

Ironically, although Americans think of themselves as largely historically formed of immigrants, many do not realize that the number of immigrants entering the country now is greater than it was then. Further it appears that we continue to find it difficult to balance the rights and needs of new immigrants with the broader society. Given that the American population is much more diverse today than it was in 1900, there are pervasive—and growing—numbers of debates surrounding the education of those from other countries. Should schools emphasize the ideals of the old "melting pot" image through assimilationist approaches, or should they instead foster more of a "tossed salad" approach, embracing diversity through multicultural education? Debates surrounding issues of multicultural education have grown tremendously in scope and complexity over the century. (We return to this topic later.)

TABLE 1

COMPARISON OF THE TURN OF THE CENTURIES: YESTERDAY AND TODAY

	1900[1]	MODERN DATA[2]
Population	76.1 million	exceeds 271.1 million
Male	38,816,000 (51%)	129,810,000 (49%)
Female	37,178,000 (49%)	135,474,000 (51%)
White	66,809,000 (88%)	219,749,000 (82%)
Black	8,834,000 (12%)	33,503,000 (12%)
American Indian	NA	2,288,000 (1%)
Asian and Pacific Islanders	NA	9,743,000 (4%)
Hispanic Origin	NA	28,269,000 (10%)
Life expectancy	47.3	75.8
Males	46.6	72.6
Females	48.3	78.9
Top five major causes of death	Major cardiovascular disease Influenza and pneumonia Tuberculosis, all forms Gastritis All accidents	Major cardiovascular disease Malignancies (cancer) Chronic pulmonary disease Accidents and adverse effects Pneumonia and influenza
Death rates		
5-14-year-olds	3.9/1,000	22.5/100,000
15-24-year-olds	5.9/1,000	95.3/100,000
GNP	17.3 billion	7,567 billion
Personal income estimates	14.3 billion	6,449.5 billion
Farms		
Number	5,737,000	1,925,000
Acres	838,583,000	945.5 million

[1] Note: 1900 data taken from U.S. Bureau of the Census (1960). *Historical Statistics of the United States, Colonial Times to 1957.* Washington, DC: US Government Printing Office.

[2] Note: The source for modern data was taken from U.S. Bureau of the Census (1997, October). *Statistical Abstract of the United States: 1997.* (117th edition). Washington, DC. The figures varied by report data (e.g., the major causes of death were estimates from 1995 whereas GNP estimates were from the year ending 1996, the number of farms data stems from 1992, and the population demographic estimates are from 1996).

WEALTH

Stock Growth. The Dow Jones Industrial Average (DJIA), the most widely known index of American economic trends, was established by

Charles Dow in 1882 as an index of stock trading calculated by averaging stock prices (a calculation that continues today, with minor adjustments for market trends). In the late 1800s, there was no way to understand the fluctuations in Wall Street stock prices until the DJIA provided a way to compare economic growth and loss. As one historian states, the opening of the DJIA had powerful advantages for investors:

[It] was like turning on a powerful new beacon that cut through fog. The average provided a convenient benchmark for comparing individual stocks to the course of the market, for comparing the market with other indicators of economic conditions, or simply for conversation at the corner of Wall and Broad Streets about the market's direction.[31]

Similarly, the Dow was seen as a way to monitor the progress and evolution of businesses:

In the century since it was established, the Dow Jones Industrial Average has become more than merely a chart of stock prices. It is also a biography of American businesses, chronicling the shift from a nation of farmers and fledgling industrialists to an economy dominated by service and technology companies.[32]

Originally, the Dow included twelve companies, eleven of which have subsequently dissolved or been absorbed into newer companies, with only General Electric remaining from the original group.

Even though Charles H. Dow called his list an industrial average, many of the original twelve stocks he picked paint the picture of an agrarian economy. The companies grew cotton, sugar and tobacco, and provided cattle feed. To be sure, the original list also included gas, electric and chemical companies, along with streetcar and railroad companies.[33]

By 1916, the industrial average expanded to 20 stocks and by 1928 it expanded again to 30 stocks which reflected the "rising importance of the technology, entertainment and service industries."[34] Today, it remains at 30 companies and represents "about a fifth of the $8 trillion-plus market value of all United States stocks and about a fourth of the value of stocks listed on the New York Stock Exchange."[35]

Finally, as indexed by the DJIA, it is interesting to note where we were then, where we are now, and what has occurred on the way. The first average on May 26, 1896 was 40.94. Since then, the Dow has seen many historic moments including reaching important 1,000 mark milestones, which are indicative of a nation's economic growth. It took 76 years for the DJIA to reach the 1,000 mark on November 14, 1972 and another 14 years to reach the 2,000 mark on January 8, 1987. Over the course of the next 11 years, the DJIA steadily increased over each 1,000 incremental mark with a peak 1,000 mark high of 11,031.59 in April of 1999. The DJIA has also experienced record one-day percentage jumps both up and down. The largest one-day gain of 15.34% occurred on March 15, 1933 which coincided with the first day after Franklin Roosevelt's bank holiday ended.

The biggest [one-day percentage loss] was the historic crash that brought the industrials down 22.61% on October 19, 1987. Among the causes of the 1987 crash were rising interest rates, the United States bombing of Iranian oil platforms, friction with United States trading partners, rampant speculation in the futures markets, and loss of investor confidence after the Dow industrials skidded in September and early October.[36]

In the 1980s, the DJIA had seen one of its most dramatic years since its inception. One of the most impressive surges—44%—occurred during 1987 (this dramatic increase eventually peaked on August 25, 1987). For two months after this peak in August, the Dow dropped nearly 1,000 points and bottomed out on October 19, the day on which it endured a 25% crash—the worst one-day crash in history.

Although American business has devised a way to quantify the health of the economy (GNP, Dow, etc.) such inventories teach us that over time (despite some acute and occasionally prolonged dips) the economy has grown and that society is wealthier. Unfortunately, no such common educational barometer exists to suggest whether we are wiser (or more civil) now than then, although, as we shall see later, educators continue to seek national (and international) tests to measure educational growth.

Sources of Wealth. America has become a formidable international agricultural and industrial presence. As of 1900, with the invention of the McCormick reaper, the United States was by far the world's largest agricultural producer. Many major oil fields were just beginning to be tapped, and we were the largest steel producer in the world, turning out 10,000,000 tons a year.[37] The age of the automobile was just underway as the first gasoline engine car was built in 1892, the world's first auto race occurred in 1896, and the Ford Motor Company was founded in 1903. (Few Americans then considered the many trade-offs that gasoline engineers would introduce to our society such as pollution and issues of mass transportation.)

Gross Wealth. In terms of American trends in production, the annual average gross national product for the time period 1897-1901 was 17.3

billion dollars, whereas in the single year of 1996, the gross national product was 7,567 billion dollars. The annual average gross personal income was estimated from 1897 to 1901 at 14.3 billion contrasted with 6,449.5 billion dollars in 1996. For the time period of 1897-1901, the disposable personal income per capita was estimated at $231 in current dollars; whereas in 1996, it was $20,979.[38] There are many ways to generate income and we have seen Americans move from land (and inherited wealth) and natural resources such as gold and oil to small businesses, large industries, and investments in corporate stocks as represented in the Dow Jones average, which in April, 1999 broke the 11,000 barrier! Indeed, we have become a much richer nation.

Individual Wealth. Andrew Hacker noted that in 1980, 13,505 American households had annual incomes of one million dollars or more whereas by 1995, 68,064 families fell in this bracket.[39] Between 1975 and 1995, Hacker estimates that those in the highest earning brackets experienced a greater proportionate increase in average annual income than those from the lower earning brackets: the richest 5% experienced a 54.1% increase, the top 20% a 35.4% increase, the second 20% a 13.0% increase, the middle 20% a 6.7% increase, the fourth 20% a 4.4% increase, and the bottom 20% a mere 1.5% increase.[40] On international comparisons, the United States ranks 18th in the size of the income gap between its richest quintile and poorest and 16th in the living standards of the poorest 20% of children.[41] Indeed, the gap between the rich and the poor in this country has been acknowledged for some time, but what is relatively new is the growing gap between the rich and the rest of us.

Whereas the median United States family income grew by 37 percent from 1949 to 1959 and by 41 percent in the 1960s, it grew by only 6.8 percent over the next two decades, with 97 percent of the increase since 1979 going to the top 20 percent of families.[42]

Many Americans—including children—live at or below the poverty level (defined for the individual living alone as $150 or less per week, or for a single parent with two children as about $236 per week). Poverty strikes both male and female Americans of all ages: 20.8% of children under 18; 9.5% of men aged 18-64; 13.3% of women aged 16-64; 6.2% of men 65 and over; and 13.5% of women 65 and over. Another statistic shows that 8.5% of whites, 29.3% of blacks, 30.3% of Hispanics, and 14.6% of Asians live in poverty.[43] Despite the increased wealth and productivity of our nation, many individuals continue to live in deplorable conditions. Although many say, "money isn't everything," lack of money in a nation where wealth is so unevenly shared is sufficient to diminish the quality of life for many Americans.

AGRICULTURE

Agriculture has changed dramatically not only in terms of the numbers of farms, but also in terms of ownership and the value attached to farming as a way of life. In 1900, the invention of the McCormick Reaper revolutionized farming and allowed for a more efficient way of harvesting crops on the 5,737,000 farms then in existence, which covered approximately 838,583,000 acres of land (an average of 146 acres per farm). In 1992, the total number of farms had *decreased* dramatically to 1,925,000 while the number of acres these farms covered *increased* to approximately 945.5 million in 1992 (an average of 490 acres per farm). Thus, a major decline in family farm ownership has occurred in this century, and not unexpectedly, with a major shift from more Americans living in rural areas to more living in metropolitan areas.[44]

Tobacco. In 1900, the two most important crops were cotton and tobacco. The role of tobacco growth and consumption has evolved in dramatic ways over the course of the last three centuries. During the 1700s, with the effects of tobacco relatively unknown, it was a commonly accepted practice for children to engage in smoking. George Redway noted in 1886:

It was the custom in England, about the middle of the seventeenth century, for children going to school to carry in their satchel with their books a pipe of tobacco, which their mother took care to fill early in the morning, it serving them instead of breakfast.[45]

During the last century, cigarette sales increased from 4.4 billion in 1900 to a peak of 640 billion in 1981. Indeed, the tobacco industry has been a mainstay for many Americans as over the course of the century more and more individuals smoked, thus affording a modest way of life for farmers and big profits for tobacco companies and advertisers (and, of course, big increases in the Dow Jones average). The influence and importance of smoking in the lives of Americans grew most noticeably during the first and second World Wars. According to one physician in 1913:

[Tobacco] is generally supplied to soldiers on the theory that it keeps them contented in camp, enables them to better withstand the fatigue of long marches, and in a limited sense supplies the lack of food. But most, if not all, of these claims are imaginary. They are made, as a rule, by slaves of the habit, and as a justification of their folly.[46]

One historian wrote that virtually "an entire generation returned from the war addicted to cigarettes."[47] By World War II, cigarettes had become a staple of military life and tobacco companies sent millions of free cigarettes to GIs.

The second half of the century saw increases in deaths from lung cancer and beginning with three landmark studies in 1950, many scientific studies linked tobacco to cancer. These data created a pronounced demand for information to be available to the public through warning labels. In light of this evidence, it is ironic that in the initial push for adding warning labels to cigarette cartons and advertisements, the American Medical Association (as recently as 1964) opposed such labels, arguing that they would have negative effects on the tobacco industry.

More than 90 million persons in the United States use tobacco in some form, and, of these, 72 million use cigarettes . . . the economic lives of tobacco growers, processors, and merchants are entwined in the industry; and local, state, and federal governments are recipients of and dependent upon many millions of dollars of tax revenue.[48]

Starting in the 50s the tobacco industry experienced a relentless attack. The first tobacco liability suit was filed in 1954. Despite this suit and many that followed, no real effects were seen until the 70s when the enforcement of public warning labels began. In 1971, cigarette advertisements were banned from television and radio (a loss that cost the broadcast industry an estimated 220 million dollars). During the 80s, smoking bans were extended to airplanes and restaurants. In 1987, Congress first banned smoking on domestic flights of less than two hours; the ban has now been extended to all flights both national and international. In 1994, McDonald's banned smoking in its 11,000 restaurants, and New York City passed the Smoke Free Air Act banning smoking in dining areas of all restaurants with more than 35 seats.

Throughout the 90s, tobacco giants continued to experience an increase in liability suits, and in a landmark case, one tobacco giant testified to the industry's knowledge of the health risks associated with smoking. In the first settlement of its kind in 1998, the tobacco companies agreed to pay 206 billion dollars over 25 years to cover the cost of tobacco-related illness. Additionally, the effects of these liability claims have reached the advertising sector, and as of April, 1999 (as a part of this 206 billion claim) billboards advertising cigarettes were mandated to be brought down. Tobacco companies agreed to hand over these advertising spaces to states, with some to be used for anti-smoking messages. For example, in Arizona, in place of the highly visible and rugged Marlboro Man advertisements are billboards of cowboys who confess, "I've got emphysema."[49] Now, fewer Americans (especially men) are suffering from lung cancer than before. However, despite the recent drop in cases, lung cancer remains the nation's top cancer killer and experts predict that until more youth are successfully influenced by anti-smoking campaigns, this trend will persist.[50]

Cigarette advertisers have been criticized for promoting the idea that "smoking is cool"—a message received by thousands of teenagers daily. Only recently have laws been created that ban cigarette billboard advertisements from school boundaries. Tobacco companies, however, are not alone in their promotion of mixed messages to adolescents. Indeed, our culture is replete with advertisements which promote normative cultural values—a practice, argue some people, which has notable pejorative effects on students and their capacity to enjoy healthy and safe academic experiences.[51] Now these ambiguous messages have infiltrated schools through the increased presence of big businesses that advertise and promote their products. One critic argues:

At a time when poor children have been killed for their shoes, they are forced to watch advertising messages for high-priced sneakers. At a time when American children are increasingly overweight and at risk of coronary disease, they have been taught how the heart functions from a poster advertising junk food and then served high-fat meals by the fast-food concessionaires that run their school cafeterias. At a time when too many children abuse alcohol they are taught history by a brewery.[52]

Students today are bombarded with ambiguous messages and are pressured to fit certain cultural norms. Given the growing presence of business interests in the school,[53] today's schools need to rethink partnerships with business to be sure that such arrangements benefit children. It is likely that students in 1900, with the absence of TV commercials, MTV, and other fast-paced sound bytes, endured different types of pressures and, therefore, going to school in 1900 was a dramatically different experience than is going to school today.

GOVERNMENT

In 1900, there were 46 states in the union (yet to join were Alaska, Arizona, Hawaii, and New Mexico). The 56th Congress, serving 1899 through 1901, counted 391 representatives of whom 185 were Republicans, 163 Democrats, and 9 "others." Of the 87 members of the Senate, 53 were Republicans, 26 Democrats, and 8 "others." Interestingly, an examination of the Democratic[54] and Republican[55] platforms adopted in 1896 shows no mention of education. Among other things, the Democratic platform, standing behind Presidential hopeful William Jennings

Bryan, expressed opposition to the Gold Standard, opposition to the issue of bonds, support of an income tax that would ensure that the wealthy would pay their share of government expenses, a reduction in the number of "useless government offices," opposition to life tenure in the public service, and opposition to allowing a President to serve for a third term. Bryan stood for "Western radical agrarian interests . . . and favored easier credit and 'free silver.'" Republicans, supporting Presidential hopeful William McKinley supported the existing Gold Standard, advocated restoring the capacity of the merchant marine and the probability that products of American labor would be shipped by vessels flying the Stars and Stripes, favored increasing the size of the Navy, and encouraged all "legitimate efforts to lessen and prevent the evils of intemperance and promote morality."[56]

In 1999, the composition of the 106th Congress is drastically different. Of the 435 members of the House (including four delegates, and one resident commissioner), 222 are Republicans, 211 Democrats, one Independent. Among today's one hundred Senators, 55 are Republicans and 45 Democrats. Whereas no women served in Congress in 1900, today 58 women serve in the House and nine in the Senate. Racial and ethnic diversity in today's Congress is demonstrated by its 468 white, 38 African American, 19 Hispanic, and five Asian members. Despite the increasing diversity of its membership, the Republican party and white males, both at the beginning and end of the twentieth century, held a majority of the Congressional seats.

Political platforms in 1996 differed in many ways from those in 1896, a major difference being that both the Democratic and Republican platforms in 1996 included a resonant cry for education reform. Today's politicians agree that the quality of education needs to be improved and that affording more flexibility for school choice will aid in this goal; however, more Republicans argue for school vouchers, whereas more Democrats want charter schools. Vouchers permit qualified students to attend the school of their choice even if it is out of their district. Charter schools are public schools created by state legislation that affords more flexibility and autonomy in designing curriculum and building school programs. Indeed, charter schools are freed from most state regulations except for the most basic requirements (e.g., child safety). To date, there are no data to suggest that either vouchers or charter schools lead to improved student performance. Indeed, research indicates so wide a variation among schools across the nation that the effects of school choice on student learning are difficult to measure or to predict.

TECHNOLOGY

America has experienced massive changes in technology and industry in the past one hundred years. For example, in 1900, only one out of every seven households had a bath and even fewer had showers. Similarly, there were only 144 miles of hard-surfaced roads. Today, many households have more than one bathroom (and some have Jacuzzi and steam rooms), and countless miles of hard-surfaced roads span the continent. Indeed, travel from Tucson, Arizona, to Perth, Australia, which used to be exceedingly difficult, is today a mere minor inconvenience. In the field of genetic science, 1900 marked the year in which Mendel's genetic discoveries were first accepted after much philosophical debate. Since then, genetic science has seen revolutionary "progress." Today we are able to clone animals making the possibility of cloning human beings a potential riddled with serious moral challenges and ethical dilemmas.

Communications technology has evolved over the century at a tremendous pace. From the Pony Express, which operated between Missouri and Sacramento in 1860-61 when regular mail delivery took up to three weeks to cross the continent, to the telegraph, automatic wire and wireless radio-wave transmission, to the modern-day fax. Now, through the Internet and the World Wide Web, messages can be sent around the world in a matter of seconds.[57]

In the world of television, the first conceptualization of electronic TV was put forth in 1922 and the first transmission of a still picture was conducted in 1925. In 1928, the first mechanical color television was constructed, and in 1948 the first cable TV appeared in rural areas of the United States. Now most Americans own at least one television and broadcasts can be seen over the Internet. By 1995, sound and pictures were able to be sent in "real time" over the Internet and by 1998 digital broadcasts began.[58] Of course, this century has seen advances in other forms of technology, too, but examination of these changes goes beyond the scope of this chapter. We will, however, discuss the role of computers and technology in education in a later section.

YOUTH

Over the course of the century, death rates among youths have declined to some extent. The death rate for 5-to-14-year-olds in 1900 was about .4% and for the same age span in 1995, the rate was about .02%. Similarly, the death rate for youth from 15 to 24 years of age in 1900 was about .6% and in 1995, it was about .1%.[59] The main causes of death among youth were not available in 1900 (recall that death rates for all populations were somewhat under-reported in 1900); however, today we know that the leading causes of death among 5-to-14-year-olds are accidents, cancer, and homicide, and for youth aged 15 to 24, accidents, homicide, and suicide.[60] Some estimate that children growing up in American inner cities experience violence on a level similar to those living in war-torn countries.[61] Although not a common occurrence, the trend of students killing students in the school environment is a modern phenomenon not experienced by many schools in 1900.

Media Representation. In 1900, the media, as represented by the press, paid scant attention to youth as we found in a search of topics in the *New York Times Index* for 1900; in that search for articles, we did not find any headings for "teenagers," "youth," or "adolescents." Today, the media play a pivotal role in framing how youth are portrayed. For example, one columnist recently contended that television news programming has been instrumental in creating an inaccurate image "making America appear to be under siege by armies of teenagers."[62] The media's bias toward youth was illustrated in a report by the Berkeley Media Studies Group, which analyzed roughly 8,000 television newscasts from 26 different stations in California during the fall of 1993. It was found that 68% of the stories that focused on violence concerned youth violence. Further, 84% of those studies focused on only the "salient event" (the blood and gore) and provided no contextual information about the crime or any societal issues possibly related to youth crime such as the easy availability of guns and alcohol and the absence of after-school programs.[63] Unfortunately, this same phenomenon occurs in educational reporting with the media reporting bad news boldly and often ignoring good news.[64]

Employment. Although there are many ways to compare youth of 1900 with youth of 2000, we chose to consider the phenomena of youth employment. In 1900, of the total labor force (representing about 53.7% of the population and including both men and women aged 14 to 65 and over), approximately 10% were males aged 14 to 19, while approximately 4% in the same age span were female.[65] Most teenagers and young adults worked in family businesses and held jobs in trade or industry. Typically, work was seen as a way to help out with family finances. Hence, many youth left schools to enter the workforce. Today, more adolescents are staying in school longer while simultaneously being employed. It is reported that since 1940, 16-year-old males are five times more likely to combine work with school than to quit school;

the statistic for 16-year-old females is 16 times.[66] Indeed, nearly 3 in 10 high school students ages 15 and over had a job during the month of October, 1996.[67] Moreover, high school seniors are estimated to work more than 20 hours a week outside of school.[68] Research has indicated that "students who work more than 10 hours per week are more likely to have problems with substance abuse and poorer school performance than students who work less or not at all."[69]

Adolescents today work for many different reasons. Some work because their income is critically needed to sustain their family; others to save money for college; yet others work to buy the latest "trinkets" (e.g., tattoos, sound equipment, concert tickets) or to support drug use. Research suggests that the reasons youth work have changed in recent years as more suburban, middle class students are working for self-gratification and to buy "trinkets," replacing those in early decades of this century who worked to supplement family income.[70] Unfortunately, today too many minority teenagers have inordinate difficulty in obtaining part-time work. This is especially unfortunate because, as some researchers have argued, a reasonable amount of employment is associated with keeping students in school.[71]

Diversity. Diversity among the youth population has changed dramatically over the century, and it is expected to increase by 2020 when the number of white students will, it is estimated, decline by about 27%, the number of Hispanic children will triple from 6.8 million in 1988 to 18.6 million, and the population of black youth will increase 9%.[72] Additionally, enrollment patterns in colleges have seen notable changes. Now the majority of youth pursue schooling beyond high school, whereas at the beginning of this century, only a fraction of the population obtained a college degree and most of those youth were of Anglo/European descent. Now, however, those who obtain higher education degrees come from a variety of backgrounds. As of 1994, 10% of the total college enrollment were black, 7% were Hispanic, 5% were Asian, and .1% were American Indian.[73]

However, as much as things have changed for youth in this century, some things have not changed. As a case in point, there were then, and continue to be now, vast numbers of young immigrants coming to America *alone*—without their parents—in pursuit of employment and promises for a new and better way of life than the one they left behind. Today, many immigrant teenagers from Africa, China, and Bangladesh, for instance, come to pursue dreams of a better education. However, many young people, today as in the past, enter the United States without

their parents or other adults and are forced to work at menial jobs for
long hours while also trying to learn the English language and attend
school.[74] Their experiences prove far different from their original dream
of "making it" in America.

Education: Then and Now

We started the first section by noting that the health of American
citizens, at an aggregate level, has improved in this century. Although
there are concerns about quality of life for some individuals, this
seems a safe conclusion. As we will see, the health of the educational
system is better in some respects as education is more available now
for women and minorities than in 1900. It seems, however, that the
current health of the American educational system is questioned by
many citizens. Peter Applebone, writing in the *New York Times*, contended that seemingly since the country has lost the menace of the
Soviet Union, it has created a new political enemy—the public school.[75]
We will come back to this theme at the end of the chapter, but suffice
it to say that the role of public education in serving a democracy is a
much more contentious issue now than it was then.

Education, like the broader society, has changed dramatically in
many respects over the course of the twentieth century. The composition of school and college populations, the role and value of schooling,
and issues of teacher training have changed since 1900. For example,
in 1900, teaching was only beginning to be viewed as a profession.
Most teachers at the beginning of the century were required to hold
only a high school diploma. Indeed, one stipulation was that teachers
enter the profession only one or two years after high school. As noted
by James Russell, the Dean of Teachers College in 1900:

Professional training, of whatever kind, must adjust itself to the mental equipment of those who take it . . . in this sphere economic conditions set as the
extreme limit of academic training the completion of a high-school course of
study. It may be lamentable that standards are no higher; but it is a fact, nevertheless, that the rank and file of the teaching profession must take the field
within a year or two after leaving the high school.[76]

However, at the same time, universities were beginning to take
responsibility for educating teachers, and Dean Russell began to argue
for the role of the university in this endeavor:

No one will deny that the interests of public education are as great and as
urgent as the interests of law, medicine or engineering. The university is true to

itself, therefore, when it undertakes the professional training of teachers. University departments of education have as their special function the investigation of educational foundations, the interpretation of educational ideals, the invention of educational methods and the application of educational principles.[77]

The development of Horace Mann High School in New York City marked an important step in creating an environment in which students pursuing teaching careers could learn. In 1902, Russell, now the president of Teachers College at Columbia, described the origins of the ideals of the Horace Mann School in the first volume of the *Teachers College Record*:

A school was needed in which the college professors of education might experiment in curricula and methods of teaching, as professors of science experiment in a laboratory. It was important, too, to have a school in which to illustrate the approved educational principles and to demonstrate the worth of certain new theories in the training of children.[78]

Although the founding of Horace Mann School provides only a glimpse at the fabric of teacher training and research, it suggests the philosophical mindset of the times.

Today, educational reform, teacher training, and teacher accountability are pervasive themes addressed by media, educators, and policymakers. In his 1999 annual State of American Education address, Secretary of Education Richard Riley argued for a *renewed* attention to teacher quality, recommending that states adopt "more thorough licensing systems to screen new teachers and reward experienced teachers with special designations and extra pay."[79] Still, it is the case that despite efforts both then and now, teachers, including even those trained at prestigious universities, are not seen as professionals. One major indicator that teachers (and the university programs that have educated them) have not been afforded professional status is that in some states teachers who teach in special charter schools are not required to have a teaching certificate and, unlike many areas such as medicine and science, federal support for research on educational practice is essentially unavailable. Thus, both then and now, teaching is not considered a profession although some people (both then and now) argue that it needs to become one.

SCHOOL ENROLLMENT

School enrollment data compiled in 1900 were broken into public and private schools. (See Table 2.) A public school was defined as "one operated by publicly elected or appointed school officials in which the program activities are under the control of these officials and which is supported by public funds."[80] A nonpublic school was defined as "one established by an agency other than the State or its subdivisions, primarily supported by other than public funds, and the operation of whose program rests with other than publicly elected or appointed officials."[81]

Now public and private school distinctions are largely based on religious influences. There are three main sectors of private elementary and secondary education. The first and largest sector of private schools is built on the Roman Catholic tradition. It is estimated that 55% of student enrollment in private education is in schools supported by the Roman Catholic Church. The second sector is constituted by other religious schools including fundamentalist Protestant, Lutheran, Jewish, Seventh-day Adventist, and Episcopalian, attended by an estimated 30% of private school students. The third sector of private schools is made up of the independent or nonsectarian schools that have no religious affiliation, enrolling approximately 15% of the total private school population.[82]

For the school year ending in 1900, the total enrollment in public day schools was 15,503,110.[83] Approximately 95% of the students were enrolled in kindergarten through grade 8, and 4% were enrolled in grades 9 to 12 and post-graduate education. Roughly 92% of the student enrollment was in public schools with 8% in nonpublic schools. By the end of 1900, there were approximately 94,883 high school graduates. The percentage of 17-year-olds who were high school graduates has increased dramatically and steadily over the past hundred years. In 1900, only 6.4% of all 17-year-olds were high school graduates; in 1990, 72.4% were.[84]

As of 1995, enrollment in public schools (K-12) was estimated at 50,362,000 (an increase of 34,858,890 students from 1900). There were 32,085,000 students through grade 8 and 12,576,000 in grades 9 to 12 (an increase from 1900 of 17,101,141 and 12,056,749 respectively).[85] The increased enrollment in grades 9 to 12 is especially significant since 1900 estimates include post-graduates and 1995 estimates do not. In the fall of 1999, student enrollment exceeded 55 million. Another interesting difference is that now more children are enrolled in either nursery school or kindergarten (nearly half—48%—of 3- and 4-year-olds). Today, more students are in school, begin school at an earlier age, and stay in school longer than was the case in 1900.

TABLE 2

COMPARISON OF EDUCATION FACTS: YESTERDAY AND TODAY

	1900	MODERN DATA	PROJ 2000
Public School Enrollment[1]	15,503,110	50,362,000	53,668,000
K-8	14,983,859	32,085,000	38,852,000
9-12	519,251	12,573,000	13,804,000
Non Public	1,351,722	5,700,000	6,012,000
High School Graduates[2]	94,883	2,599,000	N/A
Female	N/A	52%	
Male	N/A	48%	
No. of Colleges/universities	977	3,706	N/A
(Includes 4- and 2-year)			
College Degrees (total)[3]	29,375	2,247,000	2,287,000
Female	81%	54.9%	54.7%
Male	19%	45.1%	45.3%
Number of Teachers[4]			N/A
Primary/Secondary Schools	423,062	5.6 million	
Male	30%	26%	
Female	70%	74%	
Average Salary	$325	$36,600	N/A

[1] 1900 data taken from the U.S. Bureau of the Census (1960). *Historical Statistics of the United States, Colonial Times to 1957*. Washington, DC: US Government Printing Office; modern projected data from U.S. Bureau of the Census (1997, October). *Statistical Abstract of the United States: 1997* (117th edition), Washington, DC.

[2] Total number of high school graduates for modern data is from the preceding 12 months of year ending 1995 including persons receiving GED found in U.S. Bureau of the Census (1997, October). *Statistical Abstract of the United States: 1997* (117th edition). Washington, DC.

[3] Modern data based on year ending 1994, found in U.S. Bureau of the Census (1997, October). *Statistical Abstract of the United States: 1997* (117th edition). Washington, DC.

[4] All teacher statistics found at U.S. Census Bureau: The Office of Statistics. Available at http://www.census.gov/Press-Release/cb98-ff.09.html. For 1900, statistics came from U.S. Bureau of the Census (1960). *Historical Statistics of the United States, Colonial Times to 1957*. Washington, DC: US Government Printing Office.

TEACHERS

In 1900, of an estimated 423,000 elementary and secondary school teachers, approximately 70% were female. Census Bureau data indicated that as of 1996 there were 5.6 million teachers (up from 4 million in 1983) and approximately 74% were women.[86] The average annual salary for teachers in 1900 was $325,[87] for farm labor, $247, for federal employees, $1,033, for postal employees, $925, and approximately $2,000 to $3,000 for physicians. In 1930 physicians' average annual net income was $4,870 while teachers were earning $1,420.[88] Salaries for teachers in public elementary and secondary schools in 1996 averaged about $37,700 (with a range from $26,300 in South Dakota to $50,300 in Connecticut),[89] while salaries for postal clerks averaged $24,599 to $36,551, and for postal handlers, from $21,979 to $34,135. Data from 1994 indicated that the median income for farm workers was $30,809,[90] and the mean net annual income for all physicians was $182,400.[91]

It is a cruel century-long theme that teachers have consistently been afforded low status and low pay. At the beginning of the century, teacher qualifications and responsibilities were only beginning to be placed in focus; now, in spite of an incredible push for higher achievement by America's students, teachers are still blamed, devalued, and underpaid for their efforts. The comparative figures for salaries at the start and end of the century make this point poignantly. Teachers' salaries have caught up with postal workers' but are still behind physicians'. It is significant to note that medical professionals have not always enjoyed the prestige afforded them today. In 1900, physicians, although paid more than teachers, were generally seen as no more than common tradespeople. Over the course of the century, with technological advances, availability of specialized degrees, increased funding for research, and the instantiation of rigid academic standards for medical accreditation, the medical profession has seen a dramatic increase in value, as partly reflected by their income levels. Perhaps, if policymakers invested more resources in teacher training, certification, and educational research, teaching might enjoy a higher professional status.

SPENDING ON EDUCATION

Educational spending greatly expanded over the course of the century. In 1902 only a half of 1% of the total direct federal expenditure went to education, whereas 25% was spent on national defense, 22% on postal services, 25% on veteran services, 5% on general interest on debt, 4% on non-highway transportation, .7% on public welfare, and .4% on hospitals.[92] Today, based on estimates for the school year ending in 1994, of a total 265.3 billion dollars spent on public elementary and secondary schools, 45% or $119.8 billion came from state sources, 45% from local sources, only 7% ($18.7 billion) came from federal sources, and 3% ($7.1 billion) from all other sources. Federal dollars in 1994 were allocated such that 2.6% was spent on education, 23% on interest on the general debt, 1.3% on hospitals, 6.3% on public welfare, .9% on police protection, and .3% on correctional facilities.[93] Education continues to be devalued, if the amount of monies government is willing to invest is an indicator of what society values.

In the first decade of this century, the growth of schooling was unparalleled, and for a time spending on schools surpassed spending on defense and public welfare.

Between 1890 and 1918 there was slightly more than one public high school built each day of the calendar year. Enrollments increased 700 percent. Between 1902 and 1913 public expenditure for education more than doubled; between 1913 and 1922 it tripled. More public funds were invested in education during these decades than in national defense and public welfare combined. By 1920 only four groups of wage earners were larger than the pool of public educators.[94]

Still, there is a tremendous difference in investments which are made to accommodate the increasing numbers of students attending and staying in schools and an investment which is made to improve the quality of America's schools.

One of the fundamental characteristics of American education is its inherently unequal funding. Some states spend more money than do other states, and within states there is also notable variation in the amount of money that is spent per pupil from one district to another. It is beyond the scope of this chapter to enter the debate on the relationship between spending and educational performance. Fortunately, there is a rich literature that illustrates both the substantive conclusions and methodological complexities embedded in this issue. Part of the issue obviously depends upon what the money is spent for, and no one would argue that more money per se is important, but many would argue (and we are among them) that targeted money is an important condition for appropriate schooling.

Bruce Biddle recently studied the relationship between child poverty rates, state spending for education, and performance on the 1996 National Assessment of Educational Progress (NAEP) and noted that state funding and students' NAEP performance were correlated at .43. States spending more money on education were associated with higher student performance on the NAEP mathematics test. Further, an astonishing correlation of -.70 was obtained between child poverty rates and NAEP performance; that is, high poverty rates were associated with low NAEP results.

Elsewhere, Sharon Nichols, Tom Good, and Darrell Sabers[95] studied the 1996 NAEP scores in mathematics, reading, and science and the 1998 scores in reading and compared student performance across these four measures with the average state spending per pupil. Their findings showed a substantial positive correlation between resources and performance.

HIGHER EDUCATION

In 1900, about 977 colleges enrolled 238,000 undergraduate (97%) and graduate (3%) students (or less than 1% of the total population).[96] In contrast, as of October 1995, an estimated 14,715,000 students were enrolled in college (or about 7% of the total population), and of these, approximately 54% were female. Twelve percent of the 1995 college population were black, and 88% were white, with 8% of either race identified as Hispanic. Classified by age, 22% were 15 to 19 years old, 20% were 20- and 21-year-olds, 17% were 22 to 24 years old, 23% were in the 25-34 age span, and 18% were 35 and older.[97] As of 1995, more than 450,000 foreign students (nonimmigrants) were enrolled in American colleges and universities, up from 180,000 in 1975.[98]

In 1900, 29,375 higher education degrees were conferred, including bachelor's, master's, or doctor's or equivalent. Only 19% of all the bachelor's degrees were awarded to females. Similarly, 19% of master's degrees and only 6% of doctor's degrees were awarded to females. As of 1995, 2,247,000 higher education degrees were conferred (an increase of 2,217,625 since 1900), and in 1995, women earned 55% of the bachelor's degrees, 52% of the master's degrees, and 37% of the doctor's or equivalent degrees. Further, among 25- to 29-year-olds in 1996, women at 87% of the total were more likely to hold a high school diploma and a bachelor's degree (28%) than men of similar age.[99]

Today, women outnumber men on many college campuses.[100] For example, at the University of North Carolina, Chapel Hill, over 60% of the student body is female, and at Seattle Pacific University it is 65%.[101] Indeed, this trend has been evolving for the last 50 years. "This year [1997] women are expected to earn just over 57 percent of all bachelor's degrees, compared with 43 percent in 1970 and under 24 percent in 1950. The U. S. Department of Education now projects that by 2008 women will outnumber men in undergraduate and graduate programs by 9.2 million to 6.09 million."[102]

Faculty female-to-male ratios have also dramatically changed over this century. In 1900, there were 23,868 faculty members at all four-year institutions and 20% of the faculty were female. In contrast, in the fall of 1992, 32.5% of all faculty and staff members at four-year institutions were female and by 1996 these figures rose to 44%.[103] In 1900 it was customary for women to stay home and take care of the children; now women play substantial societal roles in society, teaching at all levels (not just elementary school) and holding political offices.

Teaching Practice and Faddism

From 1900 to 2000 we have seen the rise and fall of many educational practices.[104] Teachers use strategies viewed as essential which are discarded for new strategies in a few years—and then these strategies are rediscovered years later! The rapid movement of educational practice from one fad to another is likely one reason for the low status of teachers and teacher educators. For example, the Soviet's launching of Sputnik created advocacy for "new math"—and the belief that mathematics should be taught more abstractly using set theory as a building block. Within a decade, educators were recommending more individualized instruction and the need to make mathematics as relevant as possible to the learner. In a short period of time, new recommendations appeared, this time for less individualized instruction and more whole-class instruction. In a short period of time, advocacy for whole-class instruction was replaced by recommendations to let students use their rich experiential knowledge of life and construct their own knowledge. In addition to well-worn educational "fads," there are teaching practices and tools in existence today that weren't present in 1900. One example is the use of standardized testing for evaluating the effectiveness of schools, teachers, and students. In 1900, with the foundation of the College Board, standardized tests were in their infancy and were heralded as a tool for screening college applicants.

HOMEWORK

The issue of homework is one example of the cyclical nature of some reform efforts. For most of the 1800s, homework was in its heyday and served as one vital component in student learning. As chronicled by Steven Gill and Steven Schlossman, homework back then involved constant parroting and intense rote memorization.[105] However, in 1893, a report submitted by Joseph Mayer Rice attacked this constant grind of rote memorizations and recitations, thus sparking an anti-homework movement which lasted until as recently as 1983. In the first half of the century, the strain of two world wars and the vehement attacks by parents against homework and the time it took away from families led to many states adopting a "no homework" policy in elementary schools. The launch of Sputnik in the 50s and the publication of *A Nation at Risk* in 1983[106] renewed interest in homework as an important vehicle to promote learning and excellence in education.

Today, homework is once again in its heyday as policymakers push for longer and more difficult homework assignments. However, although students at every level are experiencing higher homework demands, children in lower grades are experiencing the most dramatic change. With the increasing popularization of standardized testing, more and more school districts are raising standards and increasing the load of homework assignments in earlier grades to prepare students for these examinations. Indeed, first graders in some districts take home twenty minutes' (or more) worth of homework each night when just fifty years ago, it was unheard of for elementary students to have any homework.[107]

PHONETICS VS. MEANINGFUL READING

Although educators bear most of the responsibility for faddism, it should be recognized that other groups—especially state legislators— also bear part of the blame. The California legislature provides a prime example of the political arena's contribution to educational faddism. In less than a decade, the California legislature went from banning phonetics-based instruction in reading (in favor of the whole language approach) to restoring it. Bill Lucia, the executive director of the California board of education, in commenting upon the previous mandate for whole language, said, "We performed a heinous experiment."

NEW MATH AND NEW NEW MATH

As noted earlier, new math was seen as a solution in the 60s. However, math educators quickly moved from the formal presentation of mathematics as set theory to encouraging more use of the natural mathematical understandings that students bring to the classroom. For the past decade, teachers have been encouraged by the National Council of Teachers of Mathematics (NCTM) to do less traditional teaching and to allow students to engage in more cooperative work. However, once again the pendulum has swung too far, and Tom Good and Jere Brophy have noted that many in the mathematical community have made cautionary remarks. In particular, critics of NCTM standards have argued that they (1) overemphasize process relative to ultimate products, (2) overemphasize concepts and understanding relative to skills, (3) overemphasize class discussion and peer collaboration in small groups relative to teacher explanation and teacher-led content development, and (4) are overconfident in the belief that key understandings and skills do not have to be taught directly but will emerge through engagement in authentic activities.[108]

COMPUTERS AND TECHNOLOGY IN SCHOOLS

In 1900, some students completed homework by candle light using only paper and rudimentary writing tools. There was no telephone to call a peer for help and no homework hot line for reaching the teacher on call. The nearest classmate in rural areas often lived three or four miles away. In stark contrast, by the 80s, students were increasingly using computers as tools for learning and for producing homework, and today many students have cell phones and fax machines with which to contact peers for help. In 1984, 27.3% of students used computers at school; by 1993, that percentage increased to 59%.[109] By 1996, 35% of public elementary and secondary schools were equipped with interactive videodisk players, 47% had modem access, 38% were connected with networks, 54% had CD-ROMs, 19% had satellite dishes, and 76% had cable.[110] (Despite these advances, many teachers still teach in classrooms without telephones!)

Today, the impact of technology on education is far reaching. As one example, the format for taking standardized tests is being changed. Specifically, as of April 1999, students have seen the last use of the pencil-and-paper form of the Graduate Record Examination. All future GREs will be taken on a computer screen. John H. Yopp, a vice president with Educational Testing Service, claims that one benefit of taking the GRE on computers is that it will be fairer for more students. "Students will also get their scores immediately instead of having to wait several weeks for notice by mail . . . And while the paper exams were offered four times a year, usually in crowded auditoriums, the computer tests are being offered on about 150 days and are taken in private computer enclosures."[111] Despite this technological advance in test-taking formats, some argue that making the GRE available only through computers may disadvantage those who are more comfortable with reading text on paper than on the computer screen. It is doubtful that test-taking technology benefits everyone equally.

The Internet has also made an impact on students' lives by eliminating the need for typewriters to fill out college applications. College Edge, a division of Snap Technology created to facilitate the college application process, reported processing over 500,000 applications for Fall 1999 college admissions. Although part of the reason for this increase in applications is that there are more high school graduates than ever, another factor is the impact of the Internet. Of course, no innovation is without challenges. One potential problem is that "painless applications" encourage students to apply to more colleges simultaneously,

making it difficult for colleges to determine the seriousness of applicants' choices.[112]

The Internet and the World Wide Web also impact education
through on-line education or virtual universities. Students can now
collect certificates and diplomas without ever setting foot in a classroom.[113] Although the concept of distance education is not new, as cor-
respondence schools attest, the radical surge in technological advances
allows students to experience electronically text, images, data, video,
and even audio in ways that are profoundly new. Unfortunately, despite the wide-reaching potential of Internet education, there is evidence to suggest that virtual universities are forging a divide between
the "haves" and "have nots." Indeed, computer access is stratified by
socioeconomic status and income.

Three-quarters of households with incomes over $75,000 have a computer,
compared to one-third of households with incomes between $25,000 and
$35,000, and one-sixth with incomes below $15,000 . . . white households are
twice as likely as black and Hispanic households to have access to computers
and online services. Those with a B. A. degree or higher are about four times
as likely as those with only a high school education to have online access.[114]

Internet access while offering opportunities never imagined in 1900
are also serving to create new challenges for educators and policymakers in the late 1990s. Equity issues are of notable concern.

Communication through technology is abundantly more present in
schools and society now than at the start of the century. Still, it
remains to be seen if technology per se will enhance the fundamental
quality of students' thinking and learning. Current technology provides citizens and students with immediate and comprehensive access
to vast amounts of information. However, in the past, educators have
responded enthusiastically to various technological advances claiming
that there would be a revolution in learning associated with telephones, movies, overhead projectors, telegraph, television, tape recorders, hand-held calculators, phonographs, ditto machines, Xeroxing,
and language laboratories. Despite the enthusiasm with which technological innovations have been greeted in the past, their impact on
fundamental learning has proved to be relatively minor. For example,
the use of language laboratories has not revolutionized the learning of
foreign languages. Some students use them productively and others
appear not to benefit as much from these experiences as from other
types of learning activities (e.g., face-to-face tutorials and conversations).

Not only have educators articulated the dramatic potential of computers and modern technology, President Clinton and state governors have also advocated for technology.[115] Despite such enthusiasm, there are many who question the impact of technology on students' basic ability to learn and to integrate information creatively. Indeed, some especially harsh critics have suggested that educators have been sold a bill of goods and that much of the technological programs in use have little if any educational benefit.[116] We will leave to authors of future NSSE Yearbooks the task of evaluating the impact of technology on education in the twenty-first century. Perhaps modern technology will revolutionize levels of thinking and integration of topics in important ways; however, it may be that modern technology will become only what the telephone has become, that is, not an important learning tool, but only a valuable mechanism for accessing and integrating information. How (and if) human minds and computers team to synthesize knowledge is a twenty-first century issue. Similarly, how technology is (and will be) used to harness educational goals and instructional techniques will have to be closely monitored. Until policymakers invest in research to evaluate the impact of technology, its use in the classroom may simply become just another fad that results in doing meaningless assignments more quickly.

STANDARDIZED TESTING

In 1900, the SAT College Examination Board was first established thus marking the instantiation of the first four-hour, pen-and-paper standardized test of its kind used as a way of gauging high school students' preparedness for college. The first board consisted of professors, deans, and presidents from thirteen colleges and preparatory schools. The function of this board was to conceptualize the purposes and procedures of a general college entrance examination. For example, as noted in a November, 1900 *New York Times* article:

The board has the power, from time to time, to adopt and publish a statement of the ground which should be covered and of the aims which should be sought by secondary school teaching in each of the following subjects, and a plan of examination suitable as a test of admission to college: botany, chemistry, English, French, German, Greek, history, Latin, mathematics, physics and zoölogy.[117]

Costing $5 in 1900, the SAT today costs $23 and includes questions designed to measure students' verbal and math reasoning skills (a marked change from the broad range of specialized topics initially included on the exam).[118] Clearly, in terms of structure and content, this type of entrance exam has seen notable changes.

Students today take standardized tests not only for college applications, but also for obtaining college credit waivers by taking advanced placement examinations. A recent College Board press release announced that one-fifth of American students now entering college were eligible for credit through advanced placement.[119] Academic opportunities have been greatly expanded over the century. In 1900, many high school graduates didn't have the choice of going to college at all, and those who did were unable to study for and take tests to give them a leg-up on their college course work.

Over the century, standardized testing in secondary and elementary schools increasingly have become popular ways to evaluate and criticize the conditions of public education. Despite a storm of concern about the usefulness of standardized tests, the rapid increase in the use and cost of testing in American education continues.[120] The number of tests that are administered in some schools causes administrators to complain that too much curriculum time is given to testing; if students were tested less, there might be ample time for new learning. But standardized testing has become the barometer for comparing the effectiveness of state educational programs. For example, whether states mandate tests for high school graduation or participate in the National Assessment of Educational Progress (NAEP), some type of standardized protocols are used as indicators to grade the accountability and effectiveness of states' programs.

However, it is time to give standardized tests a careful look as instruments of national policy. Are the scores on tests like The International Mathematics and Science Study (TIMMS), NAEP, and the Iowa Test of Basic Skills (ITBS) truly measures we want to represent what counts most in schools? If such tests are to be more than devices for claiming that some schools are better and more popular than others, education must make better use of testing results. How, for example, can testing be used to improve the thinking and performance of teachers and students?

One recent report graded each state in the areas of achievement, school climate, teacher effectiveness, and resources.[121] As a part of the assigned grade for achievement and accountability, states which had instituted statewide standardized tests for graduation were given higher grades than those that did not. Thus, it appears that evaluation of school performance for all educational participants (students, teachers, schools, administrators) has become both more acute and more public. Still, it is important not to underrepresent the fervor with which schools in 1900 were examined. There is ample evidence that some Americans were concerned about schools at the turn of the century; it's just that the situation by now has been greatly amplified. In 1900, some parents and a few citizens were concerned about education; today, education is everybody's business.

Education in the Media: Then and Now

The characterization of education in media reports then and now would seemingly provide important clues about the relationship between society and education. We studied educational reporting at the beginning and the end of the twentieth century to assess newspapers' coverage of education (both frequency and types of stories reported). Specifically, we conducted a frequency analysis of stories reported in the *New York Times* during the period of 1900-1903 and from 1995 through 1998 as a means of showing media interest and trends at the beginning and the end of the century.

MEDIA ATTENTION TO EDUCATION

In an archival search, we counted articles on educational themes in 1900, 1901, 1902, and 1903 recorded in the *New York Times Index*. The *Index* uses a variety of headings related to educational themes; however, to structure our search systematically, we chose to count only articles listed under the heading of "education." For the first four years of the twentieth century, we found only a handful of articles, editorials, and advertisements: in 1900, 15 articles; in 1901, 22 articles; in 1902, 10 articles; and in 1903, 11. Within these 58 articles we noted various themes pertaining to the state and quality of education.[122]

The number of articles on education published in 1995-1998 was dramatically higher. Consequently, we restricted our article count for this time period to the month of September. We found in September 1995, 232 articles; in September 1996, 237 articles; in September 1997, 252; and in September 1998, 151. Instead of the total of 58 articles published during the entire years of 1900 to 1903, there was a total of 1,008 articles printed in the four Septembers alone of 1995 to 1998.

To look for trends over time, we also counted the number of *Times* articles dealing with education which appeared in September of the years 1920, 1940, 1960, 1980, and 1990. Five articles were printed in September 1920, 61 in 1940, 182 in 1960, 122 in 1980, and 195 in 1990.

Thus, much like the increased use of standardized testing over the century, media coverage of education reflects an incredible increase in information about education available to the public. Interest in education and attempts to measure student learning has steadily grown over the century.

In addition to a frequency search, we attempted to cluster the major themes addressed in educational reporting during 1900-1903. A general coding scheme was constructed and eight broad topics were identified to describe the overall themes of these articles. Eight topics were identified; however, in this chapter we discuss only three themes which also are key issues today: (a) the separation of church and state and issues of school control, (b) equality of education (in part as reflected by college admission practices), and (c) the quality of teachers and schools, and teacher salaries. As noted earlier, it is both instructive and ironic that despite the many changes in American society, core concerns about education are remarkably similar at the beginning and the end of the twentieth century.[123]

Religion, Funding, and School Control. At the beginning of the century, debates surrounding the control of education, the role of religion, and use of public funds for education were popular themes in the *Times.* Three articles over the span of 1900 to 1903 discussed religion and education. In all three of these articles (including one editorial) the debate was centered on the issue of public funding for Catholic (religious) schools.

Given that schooling prior to this century was, in part, formulated and transformed by religious groups, it follows that religion continued to be an important theme. Indeed, from medieval times through the 1800s, the responsibility for education rested mainly with religious denominations. However, by the turn of this century, and through the influence of educators like John Dewey, schools, in the search for equality for all, came under the auspices of government control and funding. In the early 1900s, the Catholic church continued to fight for public funds to support private religious schools. For example a 1900 article in the *Times* quoted a Father Lavelle as saying:

There is a vague idea abroad that it is disloyal to the country to demand what we consider our rights. It is the birthright of every American citizen to demand everything the heart can desire, and if he cannot get it he must organize and insist on having it. We want our share of the public school money for our own schools, and we will get it in time.[124]

Control over education has seen dramatic changes over the last two centuries. James Russell, Dean of Teachers College in 1900, comments on the nature of this change in education and its ideals:

The ideals which determine the growth of educational systems, however, never remain long fixed: they change from age to age, to conform to the development of the political, economic and spiritual life of a people. So long as the Roman Church was the dominant force in European civilization, so long the schools of Christendom were ecclesiastical institutions; but the Reformation emphasized the need of religious instruction for all men; hence the rise of Protestant schools to satisfy that need . . . Within the present century we have seen the grasp of the church on the schools everywhere weakened and in many countries finally removed. State after state has assumed the direction of its school affairs—not for religious ends first of all, but primarily for the purpose of promoting civil order and social stability.[125]

On the brink of the third millennium, public schools are once again fighting to keep religion out of the schools and to keep public monies out of religious schools. Changes in state laws and favorable state supreme court decisions have opened the way for use of private monies to support religious education in some states. For example, the Wisconsin legislature recently passed legislation allowing public dollars to be spent on private schools including private religious schools. The legislation in Wisconsin was upheld by the Wisconsin Supreme Court, and recently the United States Supreme Court decided not to review the decision. Even more recently, in April 1999, Florida passed legislation to authorize giving vouchers to students in low-achieving schools that can be used in private schools.

Arizona legislation has also strengthened the possibility of using state funds to support private education. In 1998, the Arizona legislature passed a law allowing citizens to take a $500 tax credit for an equal $500 contribution to a private school (including religious schools). Further, and importantly, this decision was upheld in 1999 by the Arizona Supreme Court. This legislation with its judicial support is especially important because the Arizona constitution has an explicit clause prohibiting the use of public funds to support private education.

Another dramatic illustration of political influence in the debate about school choice and vouchers is Chancellor Rudy Cruz's threat to resign as chief of New York City schools because of Mayor Rudolph Giuliani's interest in pushing through an experimental program which would spend public tax dollars to allow children to go to private schools. Cruz has strongly asserted that public money should not be used to pay for private education, especially given the acute shortage of funds for the extant public school system.[126] Recently, the New York School board sided with the mayor's proposal to decrease a budget initially outlined by Chancellor Cruz to build more classrooms and reduce class size. With this decision Cruz renewed his promise to resign if the mayor resumed efforts to push a school voucher plan.

Advocates for school choice have garnered a political victory as choice plans (including the distribution of public monies for instruction in religious schools) have gained an educational foothold. However, as Good and Braden have argued, vouchers have not won the educational battle as extant data do not show any reliable relationship between voucher programs and increases in student achievement.[127] Additionally, concerns about the funding of voucher plans have been directed towards the fear that they may erode the common heritage of American schools which allows students from diverse backgrounds to be united in shared experiences. In the words of a recent article in *Time Magazine*, "Cleveland's voucher programs threaten to replace the single-heritage credo of public schools with a system that teaches one faith in one school and a competing faith in another. That's because the hard truth of the city's voucher program is that the choice it offers parents is mainly a choice of religious schools."[128]

As the twentieth century ends, separation of church and state remains as critical an issue as it was at the beginning. Given the strong actions that have started to validate the use of public funds in schools sponsored by religious organizations, Father Lavelle's 1900 prophecy may be fulfilled by legislation and judicial action in the early 2000s.

EQUALITY IN EDUCATION

The *Brown vs. Board of Education* decision by the Supreme Court in the 1950s marked a three-decade-long movement toward more integrated schooling. However, the 90s has seen a trend toward reversal of this movement with an increase in segregation of learners along racial and social class lines. For example, studies of charter school populations suggest such an increase in segregation, and as noted above, some believe that vouchers also allow for more segregated education.[129]

Arguments made in the early 1900s focused mainly on equal education for blacks and whites in Southern schools. In one article, Dr. Charles Dabney, President of the University of Tennessee, asks:

Who are the people about whose education we are speaking? In 1900, these states south of the Potomac contained in round numbers 16,400,000 people,

10,400,000 of them white and 6,000,000 black . . . What is the South doing for these children? In 1900 only 60% of them were enrolled in the schools, over 2,500,000 of them being out of school. In that year the average daily attendance was only 70 percent of those enrolled. Only 42 percent are actually at school. One-half of the negroes get no schooling whatever. One white child in five is left wholly illiterate. . . . in the whole South the average citizen gets only three years of schooling of all kinds in his entire life; and what schooling it is![130]

Equality in education continues to be an important issue. Some argue that continued segregation is at its core a financial issue. For example, Juan Williams notes that immigrants who have money can move into the best neighborhoods, but that immigrants (and other Americans) who do not have education, skills, and money have little hope of advancing in society. "This new divide in America still falls heavily on blacks and other people of color who are disproportionately poorer than whites. This division is not based solely on race or immigrant status: The dividing line now is access to education and professional opportunities."[131]

Issues of busing and the demise of affirmative action are once again sparking the racial debates. In Boston in 1974, explosive tensions surrounding the segregation of students sparked debates over how to desegregate its inner-city students. Busing students to different schools across town was one strategy used to address this issue. The debate over busing has been recently rekindled as some Bostonians argue that students would be better served by staying in their own neighborhoods. Some parents are arguing that money should be invested in their local schools thereby shifting the focus from "desegregation to adding and improving schools."[132] The issue becomes increasingly complex as more and more ethnic minorities are seemingly arguing for equality through autonomy not just integration.

As we noted earlier, some Americans, especially new immigrants, appear to be arguing for their own schools.[133] Hence, equality of opportunity is harder to conceptualize now than then. Some have argued that the establishment of schools that cater to one ethnic group threatens the traditional role of cultural pluralism in American schools. Neil Postman argues that historically cultural pluralism has been important for three reasons: (1) no culture was excluded, (2) the American creed was not threatened even though abuses were noted, and (3) narratives of immigrant experiences were not introduced in the curriculum to create divisiveness. Postman strongly rejects some current efforts to move beyond cultural pluralism:

It would seem that certain versions of what is now called "multiculturalism" reject all three of these ideas, and this rejection, I will soon argue, seriously threatens the future of *public*, as opposed to private, schools. Here I will say only that the idea of public education depends absolutely on the existence of shared narratives *and* the exclusion of narratives that lead to alienation and divisiveness. What makes public schools public is not so much that the schools have common goals but that students have common gods. The reason for this is that public education does not serve a public. It *creates* a public. And in creating the right kind of public, the schools contribute toward strengthening the spiritual basis of that American Creed. That is how Jefferson understood it, how Horace Mann understood it, how John Dewey understood it. And, in fact, there is no other way to understand it.[134]

To further complicate comparisons of equality now and then are recent attempts to turn back affirmative actions plans. Such plans are invoked in the spirit of creating integrated college and workplace settings. Since the passage of Proposition 209 in California, the freshman minority population at the University of California has been cut in half. As a result, California schools and those elsewhere (e.g., the University of Texas) have been trying to devise ways in which they can assure a diverse student population without overrelying on standardized tests. In essence this means that the weight in the admissions formula that is given such tests is being lowered so that other issues can be considered.

Although some conservatives have questioned this practice, Robert Laird, the Director of Admissions at the University of California, Berkeley, noted, "When you look at the difference between high-achieving and low-achieving high schools, they might as well be in two different worlds."[135] However, some argue that eliminating race completely from student applicant profiles is unrealistic:

No good university does that. Each considers what the applicant is and may be: the obstacles she has overcome, her potential for growth, her skill at sports and music and other things. A good university considers, also, the educational value of diversity.[136]

A new and powerful argument advanced by the administrators at the University of Michigan is that more diverse student bodies better prepare students for life. As our nation embodies a more diverse population, students will need skills and attitudes to work with a wide range of individuals. A University of Michigan research study has presented data to show that "five years after graduation, people who were exposed to a diverse student body while in college are more likely to work in integrated settings, live in integrated neighborhoods and have friends of another race."[137] University of Michigan President Lee Bollinger argued, "Encountering those who are different allows our students to learn about each other's similarities and differences and to destroy stereotypes."[138] Indeed, in one poll of registered voters on issues of diversity, 90% of respondents said that promoting a diverse student body is worthwhile even though most believe that students tend to segregate themselves on campuses.[139] Still, it is important to note that these data are correlational and hence will be accepted or rejected depending upon one's political and philosophical beliefs.

We believe that in 1900 the standardized test represented a potential tool for allowing students from diverse social classes more opportunity for college acceptance. As we end the century, the political pressure for using standardized testing appears to move in the opposite direction—to reduce the diversity of the student body.

TEACHING AS A PROFESSION

Articles printed in the first four years of the century addressed the low status of the teaching profession as evidenced by low salaries. Debates over teacher salaries were embedded in calls for higher quality in teaching. Interestingly, a letter to the editor during this period argued that teachers of the lower grades are not as valued nor as well paid for their efforts as teachers of higher grades. The letter writer noted that class sizes in the lower grades are much larger and more complex than classes at the higher grades (since many students leave without finishing school). The argument was that "the training of teachers, the grading of them and their pay are so devised that, broadly speaking, the least competent teachers are provided for the most numerous class, who also need the best instruction."[140] Higher financial incentives for teaching higher grade levels reduce the value and importance of teaching students in the lower grades, who are at least as much, if not more, in need of competent instruction.

We say but little here about the current debate on the need to make teaching a profession because these arguments were made in last year's NSSE Yearbook, *The Education of Teachers*, edited by Gary Griffin.[141] However, we do want to note that this Yearbook makes the point that, despite the extreme interest in teacher education and professional development during the last two decades, there has been little if any change in the structure and content of teacher education programs.[142] Ironically, despite the calls from teacher educators for reforming American schools, there has been little zeal to change teacher education and to study how such changes impact the public schools.

We believe that as long as educators approach teacher education, and its reform, as if they were participants in a debating society, it is unlikely that they will have much effect on policymakers. Informed opinion has impact only if the source has professional credibility. To have a profession it is necessary to have codified evidence, and as long as teacher educators are unwilling to research their own programs and their effectiveness, it seems likely that the struggle for professional identity will continue to be unsuccessful.

Other themes surrounding issues of teacher quality have not changed much over the last one hundred years. For example, arguments making comparisons among teachers and students on an international scale were present in 1900. In a *New York Times* article in 1900, Professor Munsterberg of Germany praised the quality of American teachers claiming that they were far better prepared than their German counterparts. However, his claims were challenged by James Russell and other Americans, who suggested that perhaps it was the case that Germans were such "masters of their art that they knew how to conceal it."[143] Hence, even in 1900 some were playing the international card—European education was better.

Reflections

The role of education in improving student achievement will continue to provide unique challenges to future educators, policymakers, and citizens. As societal and cultural influences become more complex, diverse, and challenging, so will the search for effective strategies to improve the quality of education for America's children. As there were many changes during the past hundred years, there will be many changes ahead. It is expected that by the year 2008, the total number of public and private elementary and secondary enrollments will increase 6%, enrollment at institutions of higher education will increase 12%, the number of high school graduates will increase a dramatic 20%, the number of doctoral degrees awarded to women will increase 34%, and the number of classroom teachers will increase 14%.[144] The composition of our nation and indeed of our youth attending schools is projected to change dramatically over the next fifty years. By 2050 approximately 24.5% of our population will be individuals of Hispanic origin and the white, non-Hispanic majority will be approximately 50% of the entire population. These changes will impact education for students from diverse backgrounds. How will diversity be handled?

Although one way to accommodate diversity is through home schooling and schools restricted to students from a single religion or ethnic group or social class, we believe neither of these strategies is acceptable. If this nation is to survive as a democracy, we believe it imperative that we find ways to continue the tradition of the public schools in which diverse children come together for a common purpose. To do otherwise is to provide the seeds for civil rebellion and religious polarization that we see in Serbia and Kosovo.

The political battle over vouchers and charter schools has the capacity for changing the face and meaning of public education in America. If the balance of political forces should move the conception of schools more sharply to the view of serving the needs of individual group and beliefs, the "publicness" of schools will be weakened. We believe there is ample room to improve American schools, but to do so in a way that erodes the public nature of schooling seems a perilous and short-sighted strategy.

SOCIETY

We have provided brief snapshots of where we have been and where we are now, but it is difficult to make predictions for where our nation and our nation's schools are headed. For example, the past one hundred years have seen tremendous progress in areas of health care, life expectancies, and general health, and it is likely that by the turn of the next century, Americans will be enjoying even longer and healthier lives. However, in light of the evidence of increased wealth and prosperity of our nation, the quality of life for many—particularly the 20% of our children living in poverty—remains at a deplorable level. As individual wealth grows so does the discrepancy between the wealthy elite and the rest of the population.

The landscape of industry and farming is also strikingly different now from what it was then, and we are presently on a technological path with seemingly limitless possibilities. As technology advances and the influences of the Internet grow, future educators will need to determine the impact of these advances on student learning and educational environments.

The culture of youth will continue to evolve with a changing society. Presently, youth violence is receiving a tremendous amount of media attention. The effects of violence as it permeates our culture through video games, movies, television shows, and news media are now receiving heightened attention as citizens continue to search for answers to why some youth engage in violent acts. Although youth violence is not a new phenomenon, the face of violence is changing and forcing educators and policymakers to reconsider the role of schools in preparing students for lives beyond academic accomplishments. Perhaps future educators and policymakers will invest in the idea that, in addition to learning environments, schools also foster social environments where youth negotiate complex issues that transcend academic pursuits.[145]

Perhaps the biggest issue society faces is how to coordinate the tremendous fight for control of schooling. It is clear that education has become everybody's business. Local school boards fight state legislatures for control of the curriculum just as states resist federal impositions on educational policy. How can disparate beliefs about control be linked to securing sufficient educational funds for schools to provide high-quality education? If the American society is not careful, its zeal for political accommodation may spread resources so thin that schools do not have sufficient resources to do an adequate job. If public schools lose large amounts of money to schemes like voucher plans and charter schools, they may well decline rapidly. Without the presence of public schools, it is reasonable to believe that the costs of private education would skyrocket.

EDUCATION

We have provided brief snapshots of schooling in 1900 and the late 1990s. In providing these comparisons we discussed educational and societal relationships and noted that teachers, although believed by many to be an important resource for our children, are devalued by a society that gives low salaries and little prestige to the profession. One poignant illustration of this is the comparison of the teaching and medical professions. In 1900 both professions had little status and, although doctors were paid relatively more than teachers, their role was not seen as unique or special. However, one hundred years later, the discrepancy in value placed on doctors versus teachers is large. Because of technological advances and increased spending on research, among other things, doctors are generally afforded salaries that support very high standards of living. In contrast, teachers in general fail to benefit from high salaries or even moderate prestige. As policymakers continue to place education on their list of priorities, perhaps teachers, teacher education, and students will benefit in certain ways.

However, educators will have to do their share as well. If the status of educators is to improve, more attempts to codify knowledge (in particular contexts) must be achieved. Educators must continue to document the impact of teacher education and knowledge of educational practice on teachers' effectiveness in the classroom.

One of the more persistent educational themes we have discussed involves issues of equal education. Today, through debates over affirmative action sparked by lawsuits throughout the country, we continue to define and redefine what "equal" represents. One dimension of the struggle for equality is how to give students from very diverse backgrounds similar chances of obtaining college degrees without regard to income, ethnicity, race, or gender. The dilemmas of affirmative action are spreading to the public schools, and an increasing number of parents—of mostly white students—are bringing lawsuits against schools which admit minority students alleged to be less qualified. As one student said on this issue:

I don't think any students even know about the quota, so they never judged each other . . . now they are aware of it, and in some ways it brought down some people's sense of value of how well they do. I don't believe that they gave me some slack on the test. I'd rather not think about that because it would really bring down my self-esteem and how I rate myself as a student.[146]

Future educators will need to evaluate these unintended outcomes of efforts to provide equal access to schooling. In the process of redistributing the weight of admission decisions from an emphasis on demographic characteristics to evidence of achievement, schools need to assess what impact this has on students' sense of competency and motivation to achieve.

Finally, states have expressed considerable zest for influencing educational policies and practices and have in some instances enacted strong legislation that, whether intended or not, sharply curtails the capacity of local school districts (and their teachers, principals, and parent-controlled school boards) to make decisions about curriculum and how educational funds are best spent. For example, in New York City, high school students by 2003 will have to pass a stringent examination to graduate from high school. Although only one of every five students in New York City is passing the current exam, the expectation is that more students will pass a tougher exam in 2003. The columnist Bob Herbert expressed his astonishment at this contention and Mayor Giuliani's general approach to educational reform:

Right now the schools are being treated cruelly. The latest mantra is higher standards. The people chanting the loudest (Mr. Giuliani foremost among them) must get a perverse kick out of conning the city's 1.1 million students, because anybody with a brain would know that we don't provide the system with anywhere near the resources necessary to meet existing standards . . . The tough work of preparing children to meet higher academic standards requires a huge long-term commitment and lots and lots of money. Neither Mr. Giuliani nor anyone else will say how that commitment is to be carried out and from where that money will come.[147]

Although the history of education is replete with political struggle for the control of the educational curriculum, it seems that the battlefield is much more explosive today than it was in 1900. Perhaps this is the case because more citizens today believe in the importance of education than did so then.

In addition to the intense political struggle for control of school curricula, a conflict has flared between policymakers and the citizens they represent over what schools should emphasize. For example, most citizens, unlike policymakers and especially state legislators, want more from their children and school experience than simply high grades and test scores. David Berliner and Bruce Biddle reported that Americans believe children should have a wide variety of experience (e.g., participation in little league sports and theater groups), and should gain experience in handling their own money. Further, they noted:

Again, Americans like their children to be creative, to be spontaneous, to be socially responsible and friendly, and to challenge unreasonable authority. Visitors to our country often comment with pleasure on these qualities in America's young people. But if school experiences in this country are designed to promote these qualities, it may also be that the schools downplay stress on the subservient conformity that generates high levels of subject-matter achievement in some countries.[148]

Mary McCaslin and Tom Good have argued that educators need to understand and respond to students as social beings as well as academic learners.[149] Indeed, they contend that to ignore social needs of students is to undermine efforts to provide the needed support and encouragement from teachers that makes subject-matter achievement possible. As we noted earlier, there are no agreed-upon conventions for measuring students' success in schooling; however, it is apparent that Americans have diverse expectations and that although student achievement is an important one, it is not the only lens that citizens use for gauging the success of schools and youth.

MEDIA

We discussed the role of media in describing the interface between education and society throughout the century. Indeed, as evidenced by the increase of media attention toward youth and education, it is clear that issues of schooling have become important topics for modern-day citizens, policymakers, and educators. In fact, there is evidence to suggest that how Americans think about schools in general (as opposed to their local school) is heavily impacted by media accounts. Unfortunately, most reporting is generally undifferentiated and negative. Given the widespread and increasing attention to youth and education, we hope that the media will become more aware of the complexity and variation in educational settings and will provide more differentiated and responsible "snapshots" of educational topics in the twenty-first century. One-sided stories and overly simplistic accounts of education need to be reduced. For example, in 1993, the *Wall Street Journal* published a table showing how states ranked based on NAEP and SAT results and state per-pupil spending. The story implied that state spending does not make a difference in student achievement outcomes. However, in a reaction to the journal article, Howard Wainer argued that these data are misleading and his subsequent analysis indicates that spending does have a relationship to student achievement.[150] Wainer's careful analysis is much harder to find than the *Wall Street Journal* story. As a societal lens for understanding the relationship between education and society, the media need to provide a more balanced and constructive analysis of educational news.

To provide more responsible coverage, the media must view students as more than academic learners and schools as more than environments which foster only traditional achievement. Students live busy, complex lives and schools are social environments which, in part, mirror societal influences. Future "snapshots" of education and society will require more integrated and complex coverage.

The authors would like to thank Michelle Kirmse for her research help with this chapter.

NOTES

1. National Commission for Excellence in Education, *A Nation at Risk* (Washington, DC: United States Department of Education, 1983, April).

2. National Commission for Excellence in Education, "A nation at risk: The imperatives for educational reform," *Elementary School Journal* 84 (1983): 113-130.

3. "Value of college education: President Thompson says it is a guarantee against poverty," *New York Times*, 4 October 1900, p. 1-3.

4. Ibid.

5. "Quality Counts '99: Rewarding results, punishing failure," *Education Week*, 18 (January 1999): 1-206.

6. Dave Skidmore, "Government updates business categories dating from 1930," *Arizona Daily Star*, 21 March 1999, p. D3.

7. Ibid.

8. Barbara Tuchman, *A Distant Mirror* (New York: Balantine Books, 1978), xvii.

9. Population statistics for 1900 taken from U. S. Department of Commerce, *Historical Statistics of the United States Colonial Times to 1957: A Statistical Abstract Supplement* (Washington, DC: United States Government Printing Office. 1960). Population statistics for modern data are taken from Bureau of the Census, *Statistical Abstract of the United States:* 1997, 117th ed. (Washington, DC, 1997 October), 88.

10. All 1900 life expectancy data taken from U. S. Department of Commerce, *Historical Statistics.* All modern life expectancy data taken from Bureau of the Census, *Statistical Abstract of the United States:* 1997, 117th ed., 88.

11. Angela Taylor, "Conditions for American children, youth, and families: Are we 'world class'?" *Educational Researcher* (1996): 10-12.

12. Bureau of the Census, *Statistical Abstract of the United States*, p. 75.

13. United Nations Children's Fund (UNICEF), *The State of the World's Children* (Oxford, England: Oxford University Press, 1993).

14. "A third of Appalachia's old are toothless, study says," *Arizona Daily Star,* 19 March 1999, p. 6A.

15. For an excellent review of the history of medicine see Ray Porter, *The Greatest Benefit to Mankind* (New York: Harper Collins Publishers, 1997).

16. Available online: [http://www.redcross.org/news/inthnews/99/4-2b-99.html] (20 April 1999).

17. Available online: [http://www.redcross.org/] (20 April 1999).

18. Bureau of the Census, *Statistical Abstract of the United States*, p. 475.

19. *Education Week* (27 January, 1991): 26-30.

20. Walter Nugent, *Crossings: The Great Transatlantic Migrations, 1870-1914* (Bloomington, IN: Indiana University Press, 1992), 150.

21. Ibid., 151.

22. U. S. Department of Commerce, *Historical Statistics of the United States Colonial Times to 1957.*

23. Nugent, *Crossings*, p. 150.

24. U. S. Department of Commerce, *Historical Statistics of the United States Colonial Times to 1957.*

25. Ibid., p. 8.

26. Nugent, *Crossings*, p. 152.

27. Ibid., p. 153.

28. Bureau of the Census, *Statistical Abstract of the United States Colonial Times to 1957*, p. 19.

29. Juan Williams, *Thurgood Marshall: American Revolutionary* (New York: Random House, 1998), 403.

30. Ibid., p. 403.

31. Dow Jones Industrial Average. Available online: [http://averages.dowjones.com/abtdjia.html] (13 April 1999), 1.

32. "Industry composition of the Dow average mirrors changes in the United States." Available online: [http://average.dowjones.com/ddmirror.html] (13 April 1999), 1.

33. Ibid.

34. Ibid.

35. Dow Jones Industrial Average. Available online: [http://averages.dowjones.com/abtdjia.html] (13 April 1999), 2.

36. "Market Crash? What's that?" Available online: [http://average.dowjones.com/ddcrash.html] (13 April 1999), 1.

37. Available online: [http://rs6.gov./papr/introess.htm] (April 1999).

38. Bureau of the Census, *Statistical Abstract of the United States*, p. 458.

39. Andrew Hacker, *Money: Who Has How Much and Why* (New York: Scribner, 1997), p. 23.

40. Ibid., p. 10.

41. Children's Defense Fund, *The State of America's Children:* Yearbook 1996 (Washington, DC: Author, 1996).

42. Jack Beatty, "Against inequality," *Atlantic Monthly* (1999, April): 105.

43. Hacker, *Money: Who Has How Much and Why*, p. 63.

44. U. S. Department of Commerce, *Historical Statistics of the United States*.

45. Quote by George Redway in "A history of tobacco use," Available online: [http://www.trail.com/~coco/a_history_of_tobacco_use.html] (29 March 1999), p. 4.

46. Quote by Joseph G. Richardson, M. D. in "A history of tobacco use." Available online: [http://www.trail.com/~coco/a_history_of_tobacco_use.html] (29 March 1999), p. 2.

47. Gene Borio, "The history of tobacco Part III." Available online: [http://www.historian.org/bysubject/tobacco3.htm] (29 March 1999), p. 4.

48. Ibid., p. 14.

49. Laura Brooks, "Cigarette billboards now touting a different message," *Arizona Daily Star* (23, April 1999): 4B.

50. "Fewer Americans are getting cancer, experts say," *Arizona Daily Star* (14 April 1999): 12A.

51. Mary McCaslin and Thomas L. Good, "Moving beyond management as sheer compliance: Helping students to develop goal coordination strategies," *Educational Horizons* (1998):169-176.

52. Alex Molnar, *Giving Kids the Business: The Commercialization of American Schools* (New York: Westview Press, 1996), p. 49.

53. Clinton Boutwell, *Shellgame: Corporate America's Agenda for Schools* (Bloomington, IN: Phi Delta Kappan, 1997).

54. "The democratic platform." Available online: [http://jefferson.village.virginia.edu/seminar/unit8/demplat.htm] (17 March 1999).

55. "The republican platform." Available online: [http://jefferson.village.virginia.edu/seminar/unit8/repplat.htm] (17 March 1999).

56. Information on Presidential candidates available online: [http://rs6.loc.gov/papr/introess.htm] (March 1999).

57. *Encarta Desk Encyclopedia*, Microsoft.

58. Chris Taylor and Unmesh Kher, "How we've become digital," *Time* (1999): 141-142.

59. U. S. Department of Commerce, *Historical Statistics of the United States*; Bureau of the Census, *Statistical Abstract of the United States*.

60. Bureau of the Census, *Statistical Abstract of the United States*.

61. James Gabarino et al., *Children In Danger: Coping with the Consequence of Community Violence* (San Francisco: Jossey-Bass,1992).

62. Derrick Jackson, "TV exaggerates juvenile crime scaring public," *Arizona Daily Star* (12 September 1997): A17.

63. Lois Dorfman, Katie Woodruff, Vivian Chavez, and Lawrence Wallack, "Youth and violence on local television news in California," *American Journal of Public Health* (1997): 1311-1316.

64. Thomas L. Good, Sharon L. Nichols, and Darrell L. Sabers, "Underestimating youth's commitment to schools and society: Toward a more differentiated view," *Social Psychology of Education: An International Journal* (1999): 1-39.

65. U. S. Department of Commerce, *Historical Statistics of the United States*, p. 71.

66. S. F. Hamilton, *Apprenticeship for Adulthood* (New York: Free Press, 1990): p. 20.

67. Gerald Bracey, *The Truth about America's Schools: The Bracey Reports, 1991-1997.* (Bloomington, IN: Phi Delta Kappa Educational Foundation, 1997).

68. Peter Freiberg. "Teens' long work hours detrimental, study says," *APA Monitor*, 22 (6): 19-20.

69. Mary McCaslin and Thomas L. Good, "Compliant cognition: The misalliance of management and instructional goals in current school reform," *Educational Researcher* 21 (1992): p. 5.

70. Mary McCaslin and Thomas L. Good, "The informal curriculum," in *Handbook of Educational Psychology*, eds. David Berliner and Robert Calfee (New York: MacMillan), p. 624.

71. J. Kaufman and J. Rosenbaum, "The education and employment of low-income black youth in white suburbs," vol. 14 (1992): pp. 229-240.

72. Thomas L. Good and Jere Brophy, *Looking in Classrooms*, 7th ed. (New York: Longman, 1997): p. 310.

73. Bureau of the Census, *Statistical Abstract of the United States*, p. 181.

74. Somini Sengupta, "Young Immigrants find a hard new land," *New York Times*, 14 March 1999: 1, 31.

75. Peter Applebone, "Scold war: Yelling at the little red menace," *New York Times*, 14 September 1997, 4, pp. 1-5.

76. James Russell, "The function of the university in the training of teachers," *Teachers College Record* 1 (1900): 7.

77. Ibid., 10.

78. James Russell, "The Horace Mann School," *Teachers College Record* 3 (1902): 1.

79. Frank Bruni, "A new focus on teachers is suggested," *New York Times*, 17 Feb. 1999.

80. U. S. Department of Commerce, *Historical Statistics of the United States Colonial Times to 1957*, p. 202.

81. Ibid., 202.

82. Based on figures from Joseph W. Newman, *America's Teachers: An Introduction to Education*, 3rd ed. (New York: Longman, 1998).

83. U. S. Department of Commerce, *Historical Statistics of the United States Colonial Times to 1957*, p. 202.

84. Lynn Olson, "Lessons of a century: Opening the doors," *Education Week* 18 (27 Jan. 1999): 30.

85. U. S. Department of Commerce, *Historical Statistics of the United States Colonial Times to 1957*, p. 202; Bureau of the Census, *Statistical Abstract of the United States*.

86. "Census Bureau facts for features," 14 Aug. 1998, U. S. Census Bureau: The Office Statistics. Available online: [http://www.census.gov/Press-Release/cb98-ff.09.html] (19 Jan. 1999).

87. U. S. Department of Commerce, *Historical Statistics of the United States Colonial Times to 1957*, p. 208.

88. Ibid.

89. "Census Bureau facts for features," 14 Aug. 1998, U. S. Census Bureau: The Office Statistics. Available online: [http://www.census.gov/Press-Release/cb98-ff.09.html] (19 Jan. 1999).

90. Statistics for income averages and median estimates for 1994 and 1996 from John Wright, *The American Almanac of Jobs and Salaries: Newly Revised and Updated,* 1997-1998 Edition (New York: Avon Books, 1996).

91. Bureau of the Census, *Statistical Abstract of the United States*, p. 125.

92. U. S. Department of Commerce, *Historical Statistics*, p. 725.

93. Op cit. Note: These figures include nursery schools, kindergartens, and special programs when provided by the school system. Distribution is estimated.

94. John O'Donnell, T*he Origins of Behaviorism: American Psychology,* 1870-1920 (New York: New York University Press, 1995): p. 229.

95. Sharon Nichols, Thomas Good, and Darrell Sabers, "Students' achievement performance on National Assessment of Educational Progress Test and State Spending for Education," A working paper, University of Arizona.

96. U. S. Department of Commerce, *Historical Statistics of the United States Colonial Times to 1957*, p. 211.

97. Ibid., p. 190.

98. "Census Bureau facts for features," 14 Aug. 1998, U. S. Census Bureau: The Office Statistics. Available online: [http://www.census.gov/Press-Release/cb98-ff.09.html] (19 Jan. 1999).

99. Bureau of the Census, *Statistical Abstract of the United States.*

100. Brendon I. Koerner, "Where the boys aren't." *United States News and World Report,* 126 (5), 46-55.

101. Ibid.

102. Ibid.

103. U. S. Department of Commerce, *Historical Statistics of the United States Colonial Times to 1957*, p. 202. Bureau of the Census, *Statistical Abstract of the United States.*

104. Thomas L. Good, Sally N. Clark, and Donald C. Clark, "Reform efforts in American schools: Will faddism continue to impede meaningful change?" in Bruce Biddle, Thomas Good, and Ivor Goodson, eds., *International Handbook of Teachers and Teaching* (Netherlands: Kluwer, 1997).

105. Brian Gill and Steven Schlossman (1996). "'A sin against childhood': Progressive education and the crusade to abolish homework, 1897-1941," *American Journal of Education* 105 (1996): 27-66.

106. National Commission for Excellence in Education, *A Nation at Risk.*

107. Michael Winerip, "Homework Bound," *New York Times Magazine* (3 Jan. 1999). For additional information on the history of homework, the reader is directed to Note 105.

108. Thomas Good and Jere Brophy, *Looking in Classrooms*, 8th ed. (New York: Longman, 2000).

109. 1995 figures are taken from the Bureau of the Census, *Statistical Abstract of the United States.*

110. Ibid., 173.

111. Pamela Mandels, "No more pencils for G.R.E." *New York Times* (14 April 1999): A 25.

112. William Honan, "U. S. Colleges inundated by freshman applicants," *New York Times* (17 Feb. 1999).

113. Lawrence Gladieux and Watson Swail, "The virtual university and educational opportunity: Issues of equity and access for the next generation," April 1999 (Washington, DC: The College Board).

114. Ibid., 17.

115. National Education Summit, March 1996, [http://www.summit96.ibm.com].

116. Douglas D. Noble, "A bill of goods: The early marketing of computer-based education and its implication for the present moment," eds. Bruce Biddle, Thomas Good, and Ivor Goodson, *International Handbook of Teachers and Teaching* (The Netherlands: Kluwer): pp. 1321-85.

117. "College Entrance Board," *New York Times* (13 Nov. 1900): p. 6-3.

118. SAT information available online: [http://www.collegeboard.com/] (9 March 1999).

119. "Almost one-fifth of students entering four-year colleges are eligible for credit through advanced placement," August 1996, College Board Press Release, [http://www.collegeboard.org/press/arch9697/960822c.html] (21 July 1998).

120. See Walt Haney, George Madaus, and Robert Lyons, *The Fractured Market Place for Standardized Testing.* (Boston: Kluwer, 1993).

121. "Quality counts '99: Rewarding results, punishing failure," *Education Week*, 18 (27 Jan. 1999): 206.

122. An appendix of all 1900-1903 *New York Times* article titles with corresponding categories is available through the first author.

123. Other general themes were identified in this set of articles; however, they represented topics that were either (a) addressed in only one or two of the articles, or (b) specific to the time period and/or the context of New York City schools.

124. "Catholics and school money," *New York Times* (28 Nov. 1900): 8-3.

125. Russell, "The function of the university in the training of teachers."

126. Dan Barry, "Schools' chief drawing a line over vouchers," *New York Times* (4 March 1999): A1, 20.

127. Thomas L. Good and Jennifer Braden, *The Great School Debate: Choice, Vouchers, Charters, and American Education* (New York: Lawrence Erlbaum) in press.

128. Adam Cohen, "A first report card on vouchers," *Time* (26 April 1999): p. 38.

129. Casey Cobb and Gene Glass, "Ethnic segregation in Arizona charter schools," *Education Policy Analysis Archives* (1999), Available online at [http://olam.ed.asu.edu/epaa/v7n1/].

130. "Schooling in the South," *New York Times* (10 Jan. 1903): 5-1.

131. Williams, *Thurgood Marshall.*

132. Steven Holmes, "Debate rekindled as Boston moves beyond busing," *New York Times* (14 March 1999): p. 16.

133. Ibid.

134. Neil Postman, *The End of Education: Redefining the Value of School* (New York: Knopf, 1995), 19.

135. James Traub, "How diversity serviced prop 209 in California," *New York Times Magazine* (2 May 1999): p. 78.

136. Anthony Lewis, "Whiter than white," *New York Times*, 23 May 1997, [http://www.nytimes.com/comment/] (30 March 1999).

137. Steven Holmes, "A most diverse university's new legal tack," *New York Times* (11 May 1999): A1, A20.

138. Ibid.

139. "National Survey of Voters, Autumn 1998," The Ford Foundation campus diversity initiative, conducted by DYG, INC., Fall 1998. [http//www.inform.umd.edu/EdRes/Topic/Diversity/Response/Web/NewsRoom/polloverview.html] (11 May 1999).

140. "Concerning 'higher' education," *New York Times* (5 Jan. 1901): 8-2.

141. *The Education of Teachers: Ninety-eighth Yearbook of the National Society for the Study of Education*, Vol. 1, ed. Gary Griffin (Chicago: University of Chicago Press, 1999).

142. Mark A. Smylie, Mary Bay, and Steven E. Tozer, "Preparing teachers as agents of change," in *The Education of Teachers*, pp. 48-49.

143. "Pedagogy past and present," *New York Times* (21 July 1900): 496-3.

144. Debra Gerald and William Hussar, "Projections of Education Statistics to 2008," *National Center for Education Statistics* (NCES 98-016), (Washington, DC: United States Department of Education, OERI, June 1998).

145. McCaslin and Good, "The informal curriculum."

146. Tamar Lenin, "Affirmative-action dilemma spreads in public schools," *New York Times* (29 November 1998).

147. Bob Herbert, "The biggest problem," *New York Times* (6 May 1999): A31.

148. David Berliner and Bruce Biddle, *The Manufactured Crisis: Myth, Fraud and the Attack on America's Public Schools* (New York: Addison-Wesley, 1995).

149. Mary McCaslin and Thomas L. Good, *Listening in Classrooms* (New York: Harper Collins, 1996).

150. Howard Wainer, "Does spending money on education help? A reaction to the Heritage Foundation and the *Wall Street Journal*," *Educational Researcher* 22 (1993, December): 22-24.

CHAPTER II

Teachers' Work: Yesterday, Today, and Tomorrow

DEE ANN SPENCER

This chapter reviews teachers' work in historical and contemporary times and forecasts their work in the future. Teachers and their work are the best documented of all occupations. This vast literature fills large sections of libraries and ranges from federal documents to scholarly works to first-hand accounts by teachers. Teachers have also been the central characters in novels, short stories, films, and television series. In some accounts teachers are depicted as heroes and heroines, and in others as Ichabod Crane types or as persnickety spinsters, comedians, or fools whom students can manipulate, or tough characters capable of getting the roughest of inner-city students under control. None of these characterizations bears much resemblance to typical teachers.

In this chapter I focus on descriptions of and research on "real" teachers and the major influences on their work in the past, on their social characteristics, social status, and working conditions in the present, and on the relationship between the past and present as reflected in the influence of reform movements on teachers' work. The chapter closes with my own predictions about the future of teachers' work.

Yesterday: An Historical Overview of Teaching in the United States

By 1860, teachers in the United States were predominantly female, a pattern that has continued until the present time. The transition of teaching to a female-dominated occupation occurred as the result of the interrelationship of social, economic, demographic, and political factors which affected the relationship between the supply and demand for teachers. There were variations in male and female domination of teaching by geographic region, the extent to which the region was

Dee Ann Spencer holds a senior research position in the College of Education at Arizona State University. She conducts research and evaluation projects in public schools and has published in the areas of school reform and teaching as an occupation and has compared teachers' work in the United States and Mexico.

rural or urban, and by whether the setting was elementary schools or high schools.[1] It is useful to review the historical transition towards the feminization of teaching because of the significant impact it has had on the social status of teachers.[2]

In the United States during the seventeenth and eighteenth centuries, teaching was a male-dominated occupation. Generally, men taught episodically to supplement their incomes.[3] In the Colonial period teachers were typically ministers who had been well educated in England. Later, they were trained locally by the church, a practice that some felt diminished the status of teaching. As the demand for teachers grew, so did the Colonists' willingness to accept less well-educated and qualified men to fill teaching positions. In fact, in some instances they hired indentured servants as teachers.[4] During this period women's place was thought to be in the home and not in the classroom, or for that matter, in the workforce at all. Further limitations on women teaching were the result of barriers to their admission to colleges where they might gain the qualifications necessary for teaching positions. As a result, it was not until the early 1800s that women began to enter the teaching force. Their entry into teaching was not due to changing acceptance of women in the workforce, but rather to a need for teachers that could not be filled by men. This need was a reflection of the demographic growth and change in the country as a result of rapid industrialization, a flood of immigrants, and exploration and expansion to the West. Accompanying these changes was the need for a more highly educated workforce which, in turn, led to mass public education and compulsory school attendance.

Support for mass public education was accompanied by both supportive and resistant reactions from different factions, and within these factions complex and conflicting stances were taken. For example, there was support from the working class and from unions who believed that free public education was a route to breaking the social class system. At the same time, they pushed for child labor laws because children were taking jobs from adults.[5] From the perspective of the middle and upper classes, a trained labor force was crucial for further industrial development (and increased capital), but to support public schooling would be costly to them. Further debate centered on the role of state and federal governments in establishing and supporting public schools and on how funds could be equitably distributed. Various factions supported the idea that schools should be avenues for assimilating the growing immigrant population through "Americanizing" them to adopt their new country's values.

Schools were established throughout the states and territories, creating a need for teachers even in the most isolated rural locations. Teachers typically taught a few months a year, their salaries were low, and they frequently moved from one school to another depending on changing needs of local schools and available funds for teachers. At the end of the Civil War, men who had left teaching to join the armies were attracted to more lucrative jobs in the industrial workforce. These events created a tremendous need for teachers and opened the door for women to fill that need. The fact that women were still quite limited in their choices of jobs in most fields drew them to teaching. In the prevailing patriarchal society of the time resistance to hiring women was eased through promoting the idea that teaching was a "suitable job for a woman" because it enhanced their "natural" abilities of caring for children. As a result of rationales like this one, even the poorest of school districts could fill their teaching positions.

Young women teachers were expected to be "paragons of virtue." Despite the pristine view of women held at that time, the historiographical literature is filled with examples of women who left their families and headed westward to unknown territories to take teaching jobs under adverse conditions as much for the adventure as to earn a living.[6] Sandra Myers provides many such examples:

Teachers not only had to contend with cold buildings and lack of supplies, but they often had to cope with other hazards peculiar to the frontier. One Oklahoma woman described her problems when the creek overflowed and flooded her schoolroom; another recalled that her horse had been attacked by a wild stallion as she rode the seven miles to her district school. Yet another frontier teacher wrote of her fear of a herd of wild Texas steers near her school and her attempts to reach her schoolhouse "without coming in contact with those ferocious beasts." Frontier teachers battled rattlesnakes, tarantulas, scorpions, and other insects. Sometimes they even had to protect themselves and their pupils from marauding Indians, outlaws, or drunken cowboys and miners. One teacher, whose school was threatened by a man who "suddenly appeared, drew a pistol, and began shooting," fled with her students to the woods, then armed herself with a pistol. "I'm not going to run off from this school," she declared. "I'm going to protect myself and those children. I'm going to be a second Belle Starr."[7]

The economic necessity of hiring women teachers was accompanied by a deep reluctance on the part of male school boards to give up control over women's roles as wage earners in their schools. Control was gained through the creation of strict regulations about teachers' behaviors. Teachers' lives were carefully monitored through such means as having them board with local families where their every movement was observed and monitored and through imposing strict rules about their social activities (no dancing, card playing, swearing, smoking, or drinking), what they wore, and how they acted. Most closely monitored were teachers' sexual behaviors. Even the merest gossip that would suggest "improper" sexual behavior was the basis for dismissal. To further ensure women teachers' morality and virtue, they were forbidden to marry. Prohibitions on marriage were based on the notion that if teachers married they would then quit teaching, leaving their schools in need of another teacher. At the same time it was considered to be improper for school districts to hire a woman away from her duties as a wife and potential mother. Restrictions on women teachers marrying persisted in some areas until after World War II, when the postwar baby boom gave rise to a tremendous need for teachers.

Today: The Social Characteristics and Working Conditions of Teachers

At the turn of the last century about three-fourths of all teachers were women, and by 1920, 86 percent were women.[8] These numbers declined over the following decades because men were again attracted to teaching as a way of gaining entry into school administration. By 1961, women comprised two-thirds of the teaching force, a proportion that has stayed relatively stable until the present (e.g., in 1991 the proportion rose to about 72 percent).[9] Over recent decades, women teachers have comprised about 85 percent of elementary teachers and 50 percent of high school teachers, while the percentage of male teachers has slowly declined.[10]

In 1991, the typical teacher was 42 years old, a white married woman with two children and a graduate degree, and had taught about 15 years.[11] A survey of these characteristics over the past century shows a marked change in teachers' *age*. The earlier demand for teachers necessitated hiring of women, but these were actually uneducated girls as young as 15 or 16 years old. As requirements for teachers increased, their age also increased because their entry into teaching was deferred until after they had attended normal school. Once women were allowed to marry, it was common for them to enter teaching after college, quit when they married and raised their children, and then return to teaching after several years. The demand was so great for teachers during the 1950s and 1960s that it was relatively easy to leave and re-enter teaching. In the 1990s, only 20 percent of teachers left teaching to work in their homes and to raise children before returning to teaching.[12]

The "older" returning teachers who stayed in teaching resulted in an "older" teacher population. By 1961 the average age of a teacher was 41 years, thirty years later, in 1991, it was nearly identical at 42 years, and in 1996 it increased to 44 years.[13]

The *race/ethnicity* of teachers has been predominantly white because of restrictions on the employment of African Americans in white schools as well as restrictions on entering white colleges.[14] By 1900 only 5 percent of the teaching force was African American. This figure increased very little by 1996 when 7.3 percent of the public school teaching force was African American. Furthermore, African Americans, as well as other minority teachers, are under-represented in all schools, whether urban, suburban, or rural.[15]

Teachers' *educational levels* have risen sharply since the turn of the century. At that time, girls could begin teaching if they finished high school and often taught students with whom they had attended school. Public pressure for more education, training, and credentials for teachers was reflected in the development of normal schools throughout the country. After attending normal schools teachers often worked sporadically on their bachelor's degree, that is, in the summers or on the weekends, while also teaching. The requirement of a bachelor's degree, however, was not uniform across the country until the supply and demand for teachers stabilized, in some cases as late as the 1970s. In 1961, about 23 percent of teachers had a master's or specialist degree, and by 1981, about 50 percent had attained these degrees. The figure had reached 56 percent in 1996.[16]

The predominance of women in teaching, as is true of other female-dominated occupations, has had a profound effect on the social status of teachers. For example, for the past fifty years, teaching has ranked below most other professions on the National Opinion Research Center rating system. The most significant impact of teachers' low social status (relative to other professions requiring college degrees), however, has been on their *salaries*. Comparisons of teachers' salaries from 1976 to 1997 showed that their salaries fluctuated during the 1970s, increased during the 1980s and early 1990s, and reached a peak in 1991. Since 1991, however, teachers' salaries have decreased somewhat. When beginning teachers' salaries were adjusted for inflation, salaries in 1997 were only slightly higher than in 1976, and had dropped each year since 1992.[17]

There are considerable differences in teachers' salaries depending on the geographical area where they teach. In 1997 teachers who taught in urban fringe schools earned the highest average salaries ($43,529), those in central city schools the next highest ($39,377), and those in rural or small town schools, the least ($35,176).[18] In each of the three areas, there were differences in teachers' salaries by the percentage of minority students enrolled in the schools. In urban fringe schools having higher percentages of minority students (20 percent or more), teachers earned less than those in schools with lower percentages of minorities, or than teachers in rural and small town schools. However, in central city schools, teachers in schools with the highest proportion of minority students earned more than teachers in other central city schools. Data for 1993–1994 (adjusted to 1997 constant dollars) showed that teachers at all steps on salary schedules earned more in the Northeast, followed by the West, the Midwest, and the South.

Studies of teachers' salaries have shown that they are not only lower than those of other professions, but that teachers are no better off than those in occupations that do not require a college degree.[19] Comparisons of the starting salaries of college graduates by their major field of study show that between 1977 and 1993, education majors had considerably lower starting salaries than those of all other graduates, and female education majors made 7.5 percent less than male education majors. Because of their low pay, about half of all public school teachers earn some type of supplemental income related to their teaching job, and 25 percent earn incomes from outside sources during the summer or from a second job held during the school year.[20]

The system of using a salary schedule to determine teachers' pay was developed to equalize pay between elementary and secondary teachers, males and females, and whites and African Americans.[21] However, because they were developed independently by each school district, salary schedules and increments, whether school systems have such incentives as career ladders, merit pay, or other forms of remuneration which differ from traditional systems, vary widely from one school district to another within states, as well as between states. The extreme disparities in teachers' salaries from state to state are seen in Table 1, which compares data from 1939-40 to 1996-97 for states paying the highest and lowest average annual salaries. In 1939-40, teachers in New York, the highest-paying state, of the 48 contiguous states, earned salaries that were five times that of teachers in Mississippi (the lowest-paying state). By 1959-60, the highest-paying states paid teachers salaries that were about twice those in the lowest-paying states, a difference that has stayed constant through 1996-97.

During the early decades of this century, secondary teachers were paid more than elementary teachers because teaching in a high school

TABLE 1

AVERAGE ANNUAL SALARY OF INSTRUCTIONAL STAFF IN 48 CONTIGUOUS STATES, 1939 TO 1997

	HIGHEST PAYING STATE	LOWEST PAYING STATE
1939-1940	New York ($2,604)	Mississippi ($559)
1949-1950	District of Columbia ($3,920)	Mississippi ($1,416)
1959-1960	California ($6,600)	Arkansas ($3,295)
1969-1970	New York ($11,240)	Mississippi ($5,959)
1979-1980	District of Columbia ($23,027)	Mississippi ($12,274)
1989-1990	District of Columbia ($43,637)	South Dakota ($22,120)
1994-1995	Massachusetts ($49,860)	South Dakota ($26,037)
1995-1996	Massachusetts ($52,663)	North Dakota ($27,153)
1996-1997	Massachusetts ($54,244)	South Dakota ($27,767)

Source: U.S. Department of Education, National Center for Education Statistics, *Digest of Education Statistics 1997* (Washington, DC: U.S. Government Printing Office), Table 80, p. 87.

required more education. When requirements for elementary teaching changed, salaries between the two levels were more closely matched, although differences remain. When elementary and secondary teachers' annual salaries from 1960 to 1997 are compared in 1997 constant dollars, it can be seen that secondary teachers have consistently earned about $2,000 more than elementary teachers. However, a recent study showed that the reason this discrepancy occurs can be largely attributed to the kinds of "extra duty" for which secondary teachers can be paid (coaching and other extracurricular activities).[22]

Teachers' salaries have shown the greatest variation by gender. The fact that high school teachers earn more than elementary teachers has both attracted males to high school teaching and perpetuated the gender-linked differences in the salaries of male and female teachers. During the nineteenth century, however, the difference in the pay of male and female teachers was extreme, with males typically earning about three times as much as females. This gap has nearly closed, but not entirely. Although some have estimated that male teachers still earn 10 to 13 percent more than females,[23] in 1993-1994 this difference was true only of *base* salaries. However, when their total earned income was compared, male teachers' incomes ($41,031) were 18 percent higher than female teachers' salaries ($34,781).[24]

A much greater gap has always existed between the salaries of teachers and those of administrators. In 1997-98, for all school districts, teachers' salaries were only 40 percent of superintendents', 44.5 percent of assistant superintendents', 62 percent of elementary principals', and 54 percent of secondary principals' salaries.[25] As seen in Table 2, salaries

TABLE 2

AVERAGE ANNUAL SALARIES OF ADMINISTRATORS AND TEACHERS, 1997-98,
IN SCHOOL DISTRICTS OF DIFFERENT SIZE

	25,000 AND OVER	10,000 TO 24,999	2,500 TO 9,999	300 TO 2,499	AVERAGE SALARY OVERALL
Superintendents	$126,631	$106,457	$97,842	$84,563	$101,519
Assistant Superintendents	92,353	90,252	86,755	68,054	90,226
Principals, Elementary	64,490	64,818	66,689	60,841	64,653
Principals, Secondary	74,313	75,488	77,431	67,841	74,380
Teachers	37,565	39,299	42,257	39,083	40,133

Source: Educational Research Service, 1998, *Measuring Changes in Salaries and Wages in Public Schools* (Arlington, VA: ERS), Tables 2, 6, 7, 8, and 9, pp. 11, 16, 17, 18, and 19.

varied by size of school district, with secondary principals earning more than elementary principals across all groups.

In a publication designed by the Educational Research Service to counter the argument that when compared to teachers, administrators are paid too much, the authors point out that most administrators' contracts are for longer work years than teachers, and they generally have more training and experience.[26] However, if the total earned income of teachers who typically work nine to ten months ($36,498) is compared to those of principals who work ten months or less ($50,103), there remains a marked difference in their salaries. The difference is even greater if principals' salaries are compared to teachers' base salary ($34,153). The first comparison shows that teachers earn 73 percent of principals' salaries, but the second comparison drops the figure to only 68 percent of principals' salaries. Looking at the claim of principals' greater experience, we find that teachers who have twenty or more years of experience still earn only 82 percent of the average principals' salaries.

The gap between teachers' and administrators' salaries also reveals significant differences in the salaries of men and women in school districts. In 1993-94 women comprised about 35 percent of principalships when elementary and secondary levels are combined, but when these levels are separated, most female principals are at the elementary level, and a very small percentage of superintendencies are filled by women (only 5 percent in 1984-85).[27] Because the highest salaries in school districts go to superintendents, followed by secondary principals, a very large gender gap exists in the distribution of salaries.

Despite the ongoing negative effects of our society's low regard for teaching as women's work, men continue to enter teaching, but almost solely at the high school level. Few males become elementary teachers. What effects have these factors had on male elementary teachers? Christine Williams has studied male elementary teachers as well as men in some other sex-segregated occupations.[28] She found that once male elementary teachers entered the profession they were "tracked" into administrative or other supervisory positions that were considered more prestigious and better paying. Whereas women have been shown to encounter "glass ceilings," or barriers to reaching the top levels of organizations, she found that the men she studied moved forward in their jobs as though on a "glass escalator." This result occurred primarily because of special mentoring male teachers received from male administrators.

One might think that the social status of teachers in our society would deter some people from entering teaching. That is not the case, however, as evidenced by the fact that in 1996-97 there were 3.1 million teachers in the United States (in both public and private schools), representing 2.1 percent of the total workforce.[29] A major reason women and men are attracted to teaching is that they had positive experiences when they were in school, and they have strong beliefs about the value of education in society; moreover, they were students who liked learning or a particular subject. A more powerful reason for entering teaching, however, is the intrinsic rewards many find in working with children or young people. Recent polls have shown that teachers like their jobs and are satisfied with their working conditions. Although many say that they have considered leaving teaching at some time in their careers, two-thirds say they would go into teaching if they were choosing a career again.[30]

Despite teachers' positive attitudes toward teaching, a study of "stayers" (teachers who stayed in the same school from one year to the next), "movers" (teachers who moved from one school to another), and "leavers" (teachers who left the profession) showed that in 1994-95, 6.6 percent of teachers left.[31] The most frequently cited reasons for leaving were retirement (22.3, 30.4, and 27.4 percent for each time period respectively), followed by pregnancy or child-rearing (18.9, 10.9, and 14.3 percent). In 1994-95, only 5.3 percent reported leaving teaching because they were dissatisfied with teaching as a career.

Of all "leavers," those of most concern are teachers who are in their first years of teaching. In the last decade, comparisons of three school years showed that from 1987-88 to 1988-89, 11.6 percent of teachers with less than one year of experience left teaching; from 1990-91 to

1991-92, 17.2 percent left, and from 1993-94 to 1994-95, 9.3 percent left.[32] Rates of around 7 percent to 9 percent persisted through the third year of teaching for the three time periods. About one-half of beginning teachers leave teaching during the first five years of their careers. These high exit rates have been attributed to many factors which impinge on new teachers' time and energies. Bullough identified several of these factors: beginning teachers are often assigned students of the lowest ability groups, they are asked to teach classes outside their specialty areas, they are not given reduced teaching loads, they are asked to sponsor extracurricular activities, and they don't have their own rooms.[33] In addition, they may experience discipline and management problems while trying to fit their instructional practices to the pedagogical knowledge they learned in college classes. Other difficulties emanate from teachers' efforts to understand and assimilate their particular school's culture, while discovering their role within a team, department, or faculty. As a result of all of these factors, Bullough writes, the first year of teaching poses a "daunting challenge" to a beginning teacher. While most teacher education students leave their student teaching experience with an optimistic attitude, their overwhelming and exhausting experiences during the first year of teaching drain them of much of their optimism. Beginning teachers survive through a trial-and-error method, although, as reviewed above, an inordinate number leave during the first five years. (The implications for teacher shortages will be discussed at a later point.)

Teachers' *working conditions* are dependent on the same factors which affect their salaries: the fiscal resources of the school districts in which they work. Not surprisingly, teachers in less affluent schools not only teach in substandard buildings, but have fewer teaching materials, resources, and opportunities for staff development or professional training than those in more affluent schools. Jonathan Kozol vividly described this range of working conditions, from plush to horrendous and dangerous, in his book, *Savage Inequalities: Children in America's Schools*.[34] Other reports have estimated that as many as 60 percent of public schools are "crumbling" and in need of serious renovation,[35] and conditions in rural school districts are worse than in urban and suburban school districts.[36] The last report pointed out that, although decaying schools in urban areas have attracted more public attention, data suggest that urban school districts have less difficulty raising needed tax monies to build new schools or to renovate old ones, because of businesses in those areas that can help shoulder the costs. Rural school districts, on the other hand, must place the burden on homeowners whose property yields lower taxes. The result of these differences is that while 21 percent of urban school districts built at least one school between 1994 and 1998, only 9 percent of rural districts did so.

The inequality of working conditions has been true throughout the history of American schooling, and teachers in rural schools have typically had the least favorable situations. For example, in 1880 teachers in rural schools on the western frontier (Missouri at that time) had working conditions very similar to those of some rural teachers in the Midwest in the early 1980s. This point is illustrated in the following excerpts from teachers' accounts:

1880: And I must not forget the Schoolhouse which is a log house thirty-five by thirty with four windows & two doors, the south are boarded up & in the four windows of twelve panes each there are ten panes of glass. The cracks are filled with mud plaster & there is no "loft" & the shingles are very holey so that when it rains we take the books up & stand in one place till it begins to drop down & then we move to another spot & then an other.[37]

1980: Julie's classroom was in the worst repair in the school because of a number of leaks. The roof leaked and caused extensive water damage to the ceiling. A steam leak caused the hardwood floor to buckle, forming a triangle three inches high at intervals across the room. Julie was told it could not be repaired until summer, so she wore flat, rubber-soled shoes to keep from tripping. She also brought a large piece of plywood to cover an area that had broken through.[38]

Merging the Past and Present: Reform Movements and Their Effects on Teachers' Work

The effect of school reforms on teachers' work throughout the past century has followed a remarkably predictable pattern. Reforms emanate from multiple sources and take on different meanings and forms in the schools and school districts where they are adopted. For example, one way that school districts survive under the pressure of public criticism is to adopt reforms and then present them to their constituencies as plans for eradicating the old ways and offering solutions to the problems associated with them. More often than not, however, change is only temporary. The diverse contextual features of school organizational settings and the ambiguous nature of innovative policies when translated into everyday situations often lead to failure. That is, reform can be formally adopted by a school, yet never be fully incorporated into the organizational structure so that lasting change takes place. This is due in large part to the fact that the high level of excitement felt in the initial stages of reform is difficult to sustain over the long and often arduous process of implementation. It is also due to the problem of schools adopting ideas for reform from other schools as if they were blueprints for change. When schools assume that "[t]he garment of reform comes in one size that will fit all,"[39] they ignore the social and cultural differences among school communities. When schools adopt multiple reforms simultaneously in their overly innovative zeal, goals become confused and muddled, teachers become exhausted, and change is doomed to failure. As schools become increasingly multicultural in population, this issue becomes even more formidable and unreasonable.

Teachers are the recipients and carriers of school reform but are not often active participants in the selection of those reforms. Judy Randi and Lyn Corno describe teachers' roles in school reform as ambivalent; they are both passive and active participants.[40] Even when reform is "cast upon" teachers from external sources, teachers are creative in synthesizing new ideas with their own instructional practices and teaching context; reforms are "co-constructed and socially derived." Their review of research on the extent to which teachers changed their practices as the result of reforms revealed that little change took place if the reforms were externally defined. However, there was appreciable change in teachers' behaviors as they blended new ideas into the old.

These researchers also found that there are often few long-term effects of reform because of an endless profusion of innovations that appear and reappear in schools. When a new idea appears, old ideas are eliminated regardless of whether they worked or not.[41] And some reforms reappear in new packages. This pattern is captured in the song title, "Everything Old is New Again," although the pattern of school reform would suggest that the inverse is true, "Everything new is old again."[42] Experienced teachers recognize this pattern and take ideas from "innovations," infusing their practical knowledge based on their experiences in ways that best meet the needs of their students.

Particularly influential on this discussion of school reform and its effects on teachers was the work of Larry Cuban.[43] His book, *How Teachers Taught: Constancy and Change in American Classrooms, 1890–1980*, was based on an amazing review of data, including descriptions and photographs of classrooms over the decades from 1890 to 1980 (yielding over 7,000 different accounts), on analyses of large, longitudinal studies in schools, and on his own experiences, observations, and data collection in schools where he was an administrator. It provided a framework for discussing teachers' work in this century as well as for reviewing my own research in schools since 1980. The enduring patterns he found provided strong clues to the future of teachers' work into the twenty-first century. He used a model for analyzing the descriptions and photographs which included the following five dimensions:

1. *Class arrangement* referred to the locations and positions of furniture.
2. *Group instruction* referred to whether the teacher worked with the whole class, small groups, or individuals.
3. *Classroom talk* referred to whether talk was teacher-centered, between teacher and students, or between students and other students.
4. *Class activities* referred to the type of learning activity in evidence and the patterns of interaction involved in them.
5. *Student movement* referred to whether students stayed at their desks or were moving away from them.

Cuban began his work with the period of progressivism from 1890 to 1940 and examined the effects it had on classroom practices. He found that by 1890 schools were similar in several ways; they were graded, they were in session nine months a year, teachers were expected to have had formal training and to have completed school beyond grammar or high school, that there was one teacher for each classroom, desks were placed in rows facing a teacher's desk, there were established curriculums, and grade cards and homework were standard ways of evaluating students' work. On some of these characteristics he found differences between urban and rural schools.

His review of photographs showed that students' desks were commonly bolted to the floor, assuring that the teacher remained the focus of attention and in total control. In this way, teacher-centered instruction became a long-standing and taken-for-granted way that teaching and learning should take place. Rote learning was the common practice, there was a reliance on texts, and class sizes were very large, making both rote learning and reliance on texts necessary, as did the fact that teachers at that time were largely untrained. He summarized schooling at the turn of the century as follows:

Embedded within teacher-centered instruction were a set of assumptions about schools, children, and learning consistent with the profound changes

occurring at the turn of the century in the larger culture. Notions of bureau-
cratic efficiency, organizational uniformity, standardization, and a growing
passion for anything viewed as scientific were prized in the rapidly expanding
industrial and corporate sector of the economy. School officials and teachers
came to share many of these beliefs as well. Harnessed to an infant science of
educational psychology that believed children learned best through repetition
and memorization, these social beliefs, reinforced by the scientific knowledge
of the day about learning, anchored teacher-centered instruction deeply in the
minds of teachers and administrators at the turn of the century.[44]

Cuban added that, although there were variations to teacher-centered instruction due to the early influence of the work of John Dewey,
student-centered classrooms were found primarily only in small private
elementary schools.

Examining descriptions and photographs during the interwar
period, Cuban found that, although in the 1920s and 1930s city
schools were at the forefront of innovation, overall only 25 percent of
elementary and less than that of high school teachers had adopted
progressive teaching practices as a part of a larger movement toward
pedagogical reform. On the whole, teachers continued to use teacher-
centered practices or used a mixed pattern. The reasons for this were
practical yet contradictory. That is, while teachers were amenable to
using progressive teaching methods, they were also expected to maintain order in large classes while preparing students for the workforce
as obedient, respectful of authority, and in command of a common
body of knowledge. He found that for teachers the result of these
dilemmas was:

an uneasy, often fragile configuration. This paradox of progressivism that
grew in the interwar decades is one that has persisted since, creating classrooms where impulses to be efficient, scientific, child-centered, and authoritative beset teachers. Teachers construct patchwork compromises to contain
these competing, often contradictory, impulses . . . at a cost of leaving within
many a vague uneasiness over the aims of teaching, classroom discipline, and
relations with students that seldom goes away.[45]

In the period between 1920 and 1940 Cuban found much diversity
in rural schools in terms of the extent to which progressive methods
were used. As described earlier in this chapter, rural school teachers
received low pay, had less education and experience than teachers in
cities, and often taught in old, isolated buildings with antiquated
equipment. Yet even under these conditions Cuban found evidence of
teachers who "did the best they could with what they had" and were

able to use child-centered methods (e.g., individualized instruction) and allowed students to help other students (i.e., cross-age tutoring).

At the end of the interwar era, Cuban found that progressive teaching practices occurred mostly in elementary schools but never reached the majority of schools in a district. Instead, the dominant pattern was teacher-centered classrooms, with many teachers modifying their teaching methods only slightly and in subtle ways, such as rearranging the furniture. He concluded that between 1900 and 1965, although some changes occurred as the result of the progressive movement, these changes were not widespread and were mostly limited to elementary schools. All in all, teachers relied on traditional teacher-centered practices with a few modifications by some teachers that softened the barriers between teachers and students.

The next period of reform that Cuban examined occurred between 1965 and 1975. During this period, progressivism was revisited through the introduction of open classrooms and alternative schools. This period of reform was triggered by critics' claims that schools had become overly traditional and even prison-like.[46] Students were seen as captives and teachers as controllers and manipulators of knowledge and power. Teachers were seen as frustrated by the complexity of problems they faced each day and, as a result, had become insensitive to the individual needs of their students. The dissatisfaction expressed by critics was shared by many educators as well.

An appealing alternative to traditional teaching practices was found in the philosophy underlying A. S. Neill's *Summerhill*,[47] a book describing his British primary school. Neill believed that it is more important how a child learns than what she or he learns, and that decisions about learning should be made by the child and not enforced by arbitrary goals set by the teacher. It was the task of an open school to provide experiences in the learning environment to capture a child's attention for extended periods thus assuring success, not failure. Teachers played the role of a learning consultant, an understanding and supportive adult, a resource person, and a counselor. They were to become as much a learner as the child. Teachers were to work in close relationships with other teachers, using a team-teaching approach, to prevent isolation from other members of their profession.

Restructuring the physical environment of a school was a key component of this movement. Walls and other structural barriers were viewed as inhibiting children's freedom to move about through learning centers designed to allow students to interact with their environment. Rigid time schedules, seating arrangements with rows of chairs facing the teacher, and other such traditional school configurations were seen as restrictive. As interest grew in the concept of open education, walls were torn down in schools across the country, or new buildings were built without interior walls.

Case studies conducted in open schools vividly described the evolution of the schools in different contexts, as well as the events that led to their demise. Good examples are found in the work of Roland Barth, who studied two inner-city elementary schools; Louis Smith and Pat Keith, who studied Kensington Elementary School in the Midwest; and B. W. Novak, who studied a multiage elementary school in Canada.[48] All three studies were done in public schools, staffed by young, inexperienced, idealistic teachers who were expected by their school systems to set up an innovative program, and were given plentiful resources to accomplish it. Within the first four months of school in each of the studies, however, problems emerged and changes began to be made toward regaining "order" through developing and enforcing rules found in traditional schools. Although the teachers in these case studies changed in some appreciable ways, concerns from parents that their children were not learning the basics, coupled with pressures from district administrators, led to a return to traditional teaching practices. Teachers were unprepared for the noise and chaos which characterized the opening days of these schools and were surprised to find that all children did not have a "natural" ability to guide their own learning. Not only were teachers unprepared for teaching in open schools, but children were not given guidance in how to make good decisions about their learning. As with the pattern of the past, the return to traditional classroom arrangements, organization of schedules, and clearly defined curriculums allowed teachers to deal with large numbers of children with a semblance of order.

From 1978 to 1980, I conducted a study in an open middle school in the Midwest, a new school built in the late 70s.[49] Administrators had heard of the idea of open education at a national meeting, but were not aware of its demise, nor of the literature which delineated the reasons for it. This time lag, characteristic of the spread of reforms across the country, resulted in considerable inconsistency in reform implementation. As with the case studies cited above, very early in the school year, changes were made to gain greater control over the school's one thousand students. The school was built without walls, including the lack of an enclosure around the cafeteria. The noise level was tremendous, particularly during lunch time. One way of gaining control was through issuing rules. Most rules centered on restricting students' autonomous movements around the school build-ing. For example, the restroom was a site of concern. Students were no longer allowed to go to the restroom during class time, but were to use the four minutes between classes.

In addition to new rules, teachers reorganized their classrooms in traditional ways and returned to teacher-centered approaches. Chairs were placed in rows facing the teachers' desk, bulletin boards or partial partitions were used to block off areas from other teachers' areas in the semblance of "real walls," students were expected to sit quietly at their desks and raise their hands to be called on, and traditional assignments and seatwork were given on a group rather than an individual basis. One teacher described the transition toward a traditional form as follows:

I think most of the teachers got real, real strict and it was turned into closed classrooms immediately. The first year was bad news and the teachers decided that it didn't work so we went to traditional teaching in an open school, and that's the way it's been ever since. I wouldn't go so far as to call it a fiasco because the school is well built and very nice and pretty, but we are teaching traditionally in an open situation and that causes some problems.

The open school movement across the country was very short-lived, ending by 1974 in Cuban's estimation. (As I mentioned above, the end came later for schools in some areas of the country). Cuban saw the end of the open school movement as similar to changing the channel on a television set; it was "on" and then "off." Cuban con-cluded that this period did not have the far-reaching and long-lasting effects of the progressive movement because it did not become accepted by most educators through formalized organizational net-works. Instead, it was spread through informal, casual networks which were loosely linked to the educational establishment. As with the ear-lier movement, it was accepted to a much greater extent at the ele-mentary level than at the high school level. Comparing the 1900s and the 1970s, he wrote that despite rearrangements of classrooms—

teachers continued to monopolize classroom verbal exchanges; teachers determined what activities would occur for how long and who would partici-pate. Working alone at a desk while the teacher either supervised or worked with another group continued as a dominant instructional pattern . . . Whole-group instruction, teacher-controlled classroom talk, little student movement, and little variety of tasks captured the high school classroom of the 1970s.[50]

Since Cuban's book was published in 1984, other waves of reform have impacted teachers' work, although none so pervasively as the progressive movement, or even the more short-lived open school movement. Since the late 1980s through the present time, I have conducted a number of studies of school reform in elementary and secondary school in the Southwest and in the Midwest.[51] A central focus of these studies was to trace the process of reform and its outcomes on school organizations, school cultures, students' performance, and the perceptions of teachers, administrators, and students. The schools included three large inner city urban schools (2,000 to 3,000 students) with high minority enrollments in the Southwest; in the Midwest, a medium-sized high school (1,200 students) in a working class community with few minority students, as well as a middle school in a rural area (600 students) and an elementary school in a middle class, medium-sized city (600 students). Additionally, nine combined elementary and middle schools in two school districts with minority populations were studied in a large metropolitan area of the Southwest. A summary of the results across these studies is presented here and then viewed through Cuban's framework to assess the extent to which the enduring patterns he found from 1900 to 1980 continue to exist.

All of the high schools in my studies have had common problems in adopting reforms of the 1980s and 1990s. These problems did not result from a single reform (such as progressive education or open schools), but instead, from the adoption of multiple reforms being advocated by the broader education community, e.g., Coalition of Effective Schools, Accelerated Schools, and Breaking the Ranks. At the same time, multiple instructional strategies were introduced, e.g., the use of block schedules, core student groups, and cooperative learning. This situation was further complicated for teachers by the adoption of other reforms, such as school-based decision making, schools-within-schools, year-round schools, and magnet schools. The simultaneous adoption of multiple reforms was confusing, overwhelming, and exhausting to teachers. As one teacher commented in an interview, "No more projects! Every year has been different from the last four years. I'm burning out!" The changes made to the schools' organizational structures and to decision-making processes did not bring about deep changes in school cultures nor did they affect the expectations that teachers held for students. As a result, none of the schools showed any effect on student outcomes.

An example of a superficial change was the adoption of block schedules in which students were grouped together with one teacher typically for a 90-minute block of time. The rationale for this arrangement was that it offered teachers extended time to explore content areas more thoroughly and to work with students one on one, and it allowed students opportunities to work together more frequently and extensively. In other words, the block schedule would allow for a transition to more student-centered classes. At the end of five years, however, many classes in these schools remained teacher-centered and students sat in rows facing the teachers. The only change was that they sat in this arrangement for up to 90 minutes rather than for the former class period of 45 minutes.

In one of the inner city schools in the Southwest a variant of the block schedule was used in which some ninth grade students were grouped together for the entire day and were required to take a special course on values to presumably "make them more responsible." A small group of teachers across content areas agreed to work together as the students' core teachers. At the end of two years, students in the designated group were compared to the rest of the ninth graders. Across all outcomes measures (standardized tests and district tests, dropout and attendance rates, attitudinal measures, and measures of self-esteem), students in the designated group performed less well. What did change was that close collegial relationships were established among the teachers involved, and teachers could more closely monitor the progress and behaviors of their students than when teaching multiple classes with high student loads. However, the students whom we interviewed said they felt isolated from other students and resented being taught values that had already been taught them by their parents.

In all the schools I studied, both elementary and secondary, cooperative learning was advocated and utilized as a student-centered teaching strategy. However, it was implemented inconsistently and often ineffectively. McCaslin and Good's[52] extensive review of research on cooperative learning is instructive in making sense of this observation. Their work showed that often learning tasks planned for small-group work were poorly designed and implemented because of the misconceptions teachers held about cooperative learning, which is often seen as a panacea. Teachers receive "overly optimistic accounts of the positive effects of small-group instruction and do not receive information about difficult and problematic effects of implementing this model."[53] Little is known, for example, about how small-group learning affects higher-order thinking skills, about the effects on group learning of student-generated goals versus teacher-generated goals (i.e., are the goals of the teachers important to the students?), or about how students actually interact during group sessions and what the interactions mean for students' achievement or affective experiences.

McCaslin and Good suggest that for the successful implementation of cooperative learning teachers must first recognize its limitations and understand that it is more useful for learning some tasks than others, and that much can be gained by using it in conjunction with whole-group instruction. To use cooperative learning effectively requires that teachers have a clear understanding of *why* they are using it. It also requires that teachers monitor students' behaviors in groups to ensure that all students actively participate and that working in groups does not create "extreme social anxiety" for some students. The most effective strategy for understanding what takes place within groups and what effect they are having on students is for teachers to interview their students to ascertain their perceptions and insights into the group process.

Where used effectively, cooperative learning in the high school classrooms I observed resulted in a mixture of teacher-centered and student-centered learning. In this way, as Cuban found, the boundaries between teachers and students were "softened." But more often than not, when students were working in groups the teacher was not paying close attention (or any attention at all) to what their discussions entailed; often they discussed topics far from the intended subject.

The schools using a constructivist philosophy (one in the Midwest and nine in the literacy project in the Southwest) were clearly student-centered. Students moved freely about the classrooms and worked in individual and small group activities. There were differences between schools, however. In the Midwestern school the staff was able to implement the model because they received a large grant for introducing it, although the model was not "institutionalized" through formal channels in the school district nor adopted by any other schools in the district. This created problems quite similar to those experienced in the open school movement; for example, both movements suffered from lack of connectedness to networks, both within the school district as well as to any schools outside the district. Significant amounts of teachers' time were spent in training and in working with external consultants. Time away from their classrooms created a problem of discontinuity of instruction even when permanent in-house substitutes were used. In addition, extraordinarily high teacher turnover necessitated constant training and retraining of teachers. This resulted in teachers teaching at very different levels of understanding of, and expertise in, the program's methods. These differences also created a discontinuity for students as they went from one grade to the next.

At the end of the funding period, few of the teachers who had begun the project were still teaching in the school. Over the five years of the project, measures of student outcomes showed no positive change in students' performance. Indeed, on some measures students not only performed less well than students in other schools in the district, but they did less well the longer they were in the school. Teachers were concerned that what students learned through the depth of knowledge they tried to achieve under the constructivist philosophy (in their words, "hands on, minds on") was difficult to capture through standardized tests that assessed breadth rather than depth of knowledge. However, when multiple assessments were used which were more closely aligned with the program's instructional methods and learning philosophy, they produced the same disappointing results.

Change in the nine schools located in a Southwestern metropolitan area was remarkably different from what I found in the other schools I've just described. Two school districts formed a partnership and adopted a literacy model for their students from kindergarten through the eighth grade. This model, also based on constructivist philosophy, had a much more clearly defined framework for teachers to follow than in the constructivist school in the Midwest. And unlike the Midwestern school, the model was endorsed and supported at all levels of the school districts from the superintendents to the principals to the teachers, all of whom had been trained in the model. This endorsement supported the connectedness and longevity of implementation; also teacher turnover was quite low compared to the Midwestern school. Although all teachers did not have to implement the model in the same way or at the same rate, classroom observations showed that the model was being implemented in similar ways across grade levels and across schools. The model was inculcated into the schools' cultures and a common language was used by administrators, teachers, and students when discussing literacy strategies. Classrooms were student-centered across all of Cuban's dimensions: class arrangements, group discussions, classroom talk, class activities, and student movement. The only break in this pattern was in the seventh and eighth grades where students changed classes throughout the day and teachers had high student loads. As Cuban has pointed out, requiring students to sit in rows is a way for teachers to deal with large numbers of students and movement from class to class, although it limits the possibilities for a truly student-centered class. The school districts found that the most encouraging result of this reform was that students showed good progress on outcomes measures. What remains a question, however, is whether these schools, like open schools of the past, will be able to withstand resistance from parents who may consider the student-centered, noisy classrooms as undesirable and unfocused on teaching their children "the basics." And although most teachers were advocates of the program, there was underlying skepticism. As a teacher recently commented to me, "Well, you know when this idea (reform) goes, like they all do, then at least we'll still have these new materials to work with."

This brief overview of my research suggests that Cuban's model continues to describe how classroom organization and teachers' instructional approaches are influenced by school reforms. As in the past, today's elementary teachers are far more likely to use student-centered instruction than are high school teachers because of the as yet unsolved problems resulting from teaching large numbers of students in several classes during the school day. Pressures to increase students' performance on standardized tests, to keep students in school, and to prepare them for the contemporary workforce also continue to limit the possibilities for student-centered instruction in high schools.

In summary, there are several themes which emerge from a review of teachers' work over the past century. For most of the past one hundred years teachers' social characteristics have remained remarkably consistent. The education of American youth is in the hands of white middle-aged married women who work for male administrators. Teachers today are more highly educated, trained, and credentialed than in previous decades; yet they continue to earn low salaries in comparison to other professionals with the same levels of education. The fact that teaching is a female-dominated profession within our historically sexist society has relegated teachers to lower social status than that of professions employing more men than women. Related to beliefs about "proper" roles for women as caregivers at the turn of the century, the continued use of underqualified substitute teachers and the high rates of out-of-field teaching give support to the misguided notion that teaching is something that anyone can do—that is, it is "a suitable job for a woman."

Another pattern that emerged over the past century is the inequality of teachers' salaries and working conditions between and within states. Some teachers teach for low salaries in school buildings that were built decades ago, with no air conditioning, inadequate lighting, and few or outdated materials, while others teach for high salaries in new buildings designed for optimal learning conditions, and with plentiful materials. Sometimes these schools are in the same geographical region, or even within the same metropolitan area, but in different school districts.

As was clear in Cuban's work and in the review in this chapter of the effects of reform on teachers' work, teachers do change their instructional practices and their relationships with students as the result of reform efforts, but these changes are mitigated by pressures to keep students under control, teach them the basics, and prepare them socially for their places in the workforce. Because a return to the "known" traditional ways of teaching is "safe," these strategies are likely to be used in the future.

Tomorrow: The Future of Teachers' Work

This chapter has looked at the social characteristics of teachers in this century, at working conditions in schools, and on teachers' involvement in reform. Using these topics as a framework, we now ask: what can be projected about the future of teachers' work?

The United States Department of Education is predicting a serious shortage of as many as 2.2 million teachers over the next decade.[54] This shortage will be created from a combination of factors: a population boom of school-aged children, a greater number of teachers approaching retirement, efforts at the national level and in some states to reduce class size, tightened teaching standards which all teacher candidates will not meet, and the continued attrition of new teachers from the field. Although teacher shortages were also predicted for the 1990s, a Schools and Staffing Survey (SASS) report showed that in 1993-94, no school districts were experiencing teacher shortages with any severity, although there were shortages in some areas of the country and in some subject areas—mathematics, science, special education, and bilingual education.[55] A major reason that teacher shortages have not been realized and may not reach the alarming level that is predicted in the future is that at federal and state levels, and in colleges of education and local school districts, steps have been taken to deal with this problem. These steps have included issuing emergency certificates and hiring temporary substitutes (in some cases the requirement for teaching is a high school diploma and no criminal record), placing teachers in areas outside their fields, using more sophisticated recruitment strategies, including recruiting abroad and among retired military, offering incentives and bonuses to teachers,[56] and expanding alternative routes for entry into teaching.

Clearly, some of these strategies are stopgap efforts which do not serve the best interests of students and demean teachers by implying that teaching is something anyone can do, regardless of education, training, or credentials. A good example is the placement of teachers in classes which are out of their field. Richard Ingersoll took an in-depth look at some of the key reasons for there being underqualified teachers in our schools.[57] To do this, he examined SASS data on "out-of-field teaching" and defined an underqualified teacher as one having neither a college major or minor in the subject they were teaching. He found that in well over half of all secondary schools, out-of-field teaching has been widespread from the late 1980s to the mid-1990s, varying by fields with one-third of mathematics teachers, one-fourth of English teachers, one-fifth of science and social studies teachers teaching in a subject for which they had neither a college major or minor. He also found considerable variation in the proportions of underqualified teachers. There were higher levels in schools of high poverty than in more affluent schools, and in small schools than in larger schools. Within schools, students in low-track classes were more likely to have an out-of-field teacher than those in high tracks, and seventh grade students were more likely to have an out-of-field teacher than twelfth graders.

Ingersoll asserts that the reason for this condition is not teachers' lack of education or training in general, but specifically they may lack a degree in the field they are asked (required) to teach. More education, then, will not solve the lack of fit between teachers' college major or minor fields and their teaching assignments in schools. He also argues that despite claims of teacher shortages and despite the difficulties that some schools have in filling positions, few positions remain unfilled at the beginning of school years. For example, in 1993-1994, less than 4 percent of positions were unfilled. The point is that schools can leave no positions unfilled. Out-of-field teaching is legal, expedient, and less expensive for administrators but takes control from teachers over their own teaching assignments and trivializes what they know and do. Such a system, he contends, is not cost free because it leads to the greater probability of teachers leaving the field. To blame teachers for this situation is misguided because the problems lie in "the ways schools are managed and mismanaged and the continuing treatment of teaching as semi-skilled work."[58] Instead, incentives should be given to attract and retain teachers, and principals should cut back on out-of-field assignments for beginning teachers. He concludes that if teachers were paid well and provided with good working conditions, as well as treated as highly respected professionals with expertise and skills, there would be little problem in attracting and retaining qualified teachers.

Another strategy for dealing with teacher shortages has been the development of alternative certification programs in colleges and universities. Emily Feistritzer contends that because of these programs, there is no need for alarm about an impending teacher shortage.[59] She has found the alarm stems from limiting the definition of a "new" teacher to one who is a recent graduate of a teacher education program. She points out that these teachers comprise only 42 percent of newly hired teachers, while people who were engaged in something other than college study immediately before entering teaching and others who had left teaching and then returned comprise the other proportion of new hires. Entry into teaching from other fields has served as a major recruiting method since the early 1980s. Although the idea of alternative certification began as a controversial concept because it was viewed as a shortcut to teacher certification, it has been accepted to the point that in 1997, 41 states plus the District of Columbia had alternative certification programs for a total of 117 programs. Over 75,000 teachers have been licensed through these programs and thousands more through alternative teacher preparation programs in colleges and universities.

Alternative routes to teaching may offset the potential shortage of teachers. At the same time, the demands for more teaching credentials and adherence to state and national standards may either deter or drive some from the field if they do not receive higher pay and other incentives to enter and stay in teaching. Historically calls for more highly credentialed teachers first led to the development of normal schools and colleges of education and eventually to significant increases in teachers' educational level, as well as to requirements for more credentials and certifications for teaching. For example, the *Report on Teaching as a Profession* developed by the Carnegie Forum on Education and the Economy[60] recommended national certification of teachers, a national proficiency examination, master's degrees, and increases in salary as ways of recruiting "the best and brightest" people into the field as well as keeping good or master teachers in schools. Calls for a more highly trained teaching force in the early 1900s,[61] as well as in the 1990s,[62] included similar recommendations. Although these recommendations have led to changes in the qualifications of teachers, they have not led to higher salaries. This discrepancy always has been given recognition by advocates of teacher reform, who often have the power to influence standards for credentialing, but have little power to affect teachers' salaries. Many school districts have meager fiscal resources to increase teachers' salaries, and at the state and national levels, *serious* steps toward increasing teachers' salaries have never been taken.

A decision by one metropolitan school district in the Southwest where I conduct research appeared to be a case of "cutting off one's nose to spite one's face." In the spring of 1999 the district offered attractive incentives for the teachers, certified staff, and administrators to take early retirement. The purpose was to create cost savings by eliminating staff members from the highest steps on the salary schedule (the range of teachers' salaries was from $25,713 at the first step to $56,325 at the top step, and the range for administrators was from $70,515 to $91,018). The offer was so attractive that 10 percent of the district's 2,475 employees left, including 25 percent of administrators, 11 percent of teachers, and 7.4 percent of the classified staff. The district will obviously enjoy tremendous costs savings, but the exit of these highly qualified and experienced staff members means that they will be replaced with less qualified and inexperienced staff members, undoubtedly to the detriment of their high-poverty minority student population.

Smaller class sizes over the past thirty years (from an average of 28 in 1961 to 24 in 1993-94), as well as current federal and state proposals for reductions to a class size of 18, offer more ideal working conditions for teachers. Of course, class size still varies greatly depending on differences within school districts, as well as different criteria for "ideal" size within and between states.

A major influence on teachers and their instructional practices has been the tremendous infusion of technology into schools in recent years—an influence that will take on increasing importance, if not urgency, in the future. While Cuban could not have foreseen this phenomenon in the early 1980s, another dimension of teacher practice might be added to his five which describes the interaction between students and computers. Survey data from 1994-95 indicated that only about one-half (55 percent) of teachers reported using computers and about one-third reported using computers for writing.[63] Most teachers (87 percent) used blackboards or overhead projectors to present materials. These figures do not indicate that computers played a predominant role in instructional practices in the mid-1990s. Further research is needed to better understand to what extent and in what ways teachers and students use computers, and what problems exist to inhibit them.

A common problem across the schools I have studied is that computers were not well integrated into classroom instruction because teachers did not receive adequate training in how to use them effectively. Other problems were schools did not have electrical wiring that could handle the power surges needed for using many computers simultaneously, they did not have technicians who could correct problems as they occurred, and they did not have an adequate supply of software to fit teachers' needs across subject areas. Until problems such as these have been resolved, computers will not be used effectively in schools. This is a deplorable situation considering the central role of technology in the world today.

The fact that most teachers are white monolingual women teaching increasing numbers of students of diverse cultural and linguistic backgrounds has important implications for the future. Working conditions in schools are not only affected by their fiscal resources (or lack of), but of the characteristics of their students. The rapidly changing racial and ethnic composition of school-age children will have a strong impact on teachers and their work. The combination of insufficient resources and the challenge of meeting the needs of students from culturally and linguistically diverse backgrounds is a daunting prospect for already overworked and underpaid teachers.

Tamara Lucas addresses these issues and makes recommendations for teachers' roles when teaching students of cultural and linguistic diversity, especially immigrant students.[64] She writes that despite extensive reforms in school and in teaching practices immigrant students are excluded from the reform efforts because teachers typically do not have adequate training and experience to understand and to meet their needs. Teachers also assume that because these students are enrolled in special programs until they are proficient in English and are assimilated into American culture, they are not a part of the mainstream of the school and therefore do not benefit from reform practices. She recommends that teachers and teaching be reconceptualized through strategies quite similar to those reviewed by Cuban, notably student-centered approaches in which teachers, like their students, become lifelong learners. By engaging in reflective thinking practices and dialoguing with others, teachers can better examine their personal biases and assumptions as well as learn more about their students' varied cultural backgrounds and experiences. This proactive and introspective approach would lead teachers to discover new strategies for educating immigrant students.

Lucas also suggests that teachers collaborate, for instance, in small teams of ESL or bilingual teachers and "mainstream" teachers in order to share information about students, become closer to students and to each other and thereby personalize the school experience for immigrants.[65] Teachers should also serve as facilitators of learning rather than deliverers of instruction, and most important, become cultural and linguistic mediators. Ideally, these mediators would be minority teachers who would serve as the best role models for immigrant children, allowing them to observe people like themselves in positions of authority and to know that their language and culture are valued. Obviously, far more minorities must be recruited into teaching in the future.

Research on the relationship between teachers' social class backgrounds and those of their students has shown that teachers' perceptions of and expectations for students are based in part on students' social class and ethnicity, but are also mediated by the teachers' own social class.[66] These findings indicate that a greater focus needs to be placed on preparing teachers for the diversity they will face in the future. Future teachers must acquire a greater understanding of social class differences and the impact these differences have on teachers' expectations for students and on their teaching practices.

NOTES

1. Geraldine J. Clifford, "Man/Woman/Teacher: Gender, Family, and Career in American Educational History," in *American Teachers: Histories of a Profession at Work*, ed. Donald Warren (New York: Macmillan, 1989): pp. 293-343.

2. Dee Ann Spencer, "Teaching as Women's Work," in *International Handbook of Teachers and Teaching*, eds. Bruce Biddle, Thomas Good, and Ivor F. Goodson (Dordrecht: Kluwer Academic Publishers, 1997); Dee Ann Spencer, "Teachers' Work in Historical and Social Context," in *The Handbook of Research on Teaching, Fourth Edition*, ed. Virginia Richardson (Washington, DC: American Educational Research Association, forthcoming).

3. Robert J. Parelius and Ann P. Parelius, *The Sociology of Education* (Englewood Cliffs, NJ: Prentice-Hall, 1987); Geraldine J. Clifford, "Man/Woman/Teacher: Gender, Family, and Career in American Educational History," in *American Teachers: Histories of a Profession at Work*, pp. 293-343.

4. H. K. Beale, *A History of Freedom of Teaching in American Schools* (New York: Charles Scriber's Sons, 1941).

5. Parelius and Parelius, 1987.

6. Nancy Hoffman, *Woman's "True" Profession: Voices From the History of Teaching* (Old Westbury, NY: The Feminist Press, 1981); Polly W. Kaufman, *Women Teachers on the Frontier* (New Haven, CT: Yale University Press, 1984); Sandra L. Myers, *Westering Women and the Frontier Experience, 1800-1915* (Albuquerque, NM: University of New Mexico Press, 1982); Mary Logan Rothschild and Pamela Claire Hronek, *Doing What the Day Brought: An Oral History of Arizona Women* (Tucson, AZ: University of Arizona Press, 1992); Donald Warren, "Learning From Experience: History and Teacher Education," *Educational Researcher* 14 (1985): pp. 5-12; *American Teachers: Histories of a Profession at Work*.

7. Myers 1982, p. 249.

8. Clifford, "Man/Woman/Teacher," pp. 293-343.

9. U.S. Department of Education, National Center for Education Statistics, *Digest of Education Statistics 1996*, NCES 96-133, by Thomas D. Snyder (Washington, DC: U.S. Government Printing Office, 1996).

10. National Education Association, 1998. "As Teacher Salaries Fall Behind in the United States, NEA Expresses Concern Over Ability to Hire Newcomers," online: [http://www.nea.org/nr/nr980513.html]

11. USDE, *Digest of Educational Statistics, 1996*.

12. U.S. Department of Education, National Center for Education Statistics, *America's Teachers: Profile of a Profession, 1993-94*, NCES 97-460, by Robin R. Henke et.al., Project Office (Washington, DC: U.S. Government Printing Office, 1997).

13. U.S. Department of Education, National Center for Education Statistics, *Digest of Education Statistics, 1997*, NCES 98-015, by Thomas D. Snyder, Charlene M. Hoffman, and Claire M. Geddes (Washington, DC: U.S. Government Printing Office, 1997).

14. Linda M. Perkins, "The History of Blacks in Teaching: Growth and Decline Within the Profession," in *American Teachers: Histories of a Profession at Work*, pp. 344-369.

15. USDE, *Digest of Education Statistics, 1997*, USDE, *America's Teachers: Profiles of a Profession, 1993-94*, 1997.

16. USDE, *Digest, 1997*.

17. U.S. Department of Education, National Center for Education Statistics, *The Condition of Education 1998*, NCES 98-013, by John Wirt et.al. (Washington, DC: U.S. Government Printing Office, 1998).

18. Ibid.

19. P. Anthony, "Teachers in the Economic System," in *Attracting and Compensating America's Teachers*, eds. K. Alexander and D. Monk (Cambridge, MA: Ballinger, 1987): pp. 1-20.

20. USDE, *America's Teachers: Profile of a Profession, 1993-94*, 1997.

21. Joseph W. Newman, *America's Teachers: An Introduction to Education, Second Edition* (New York: Longman, 1994).

22. U.S. Department of Education, Office of Educational Research and Improvement, National Center for Education Statistics, *The Patterns of Teacher Compensation*, by J. Chambers and S. A. Bobbitt (Washington, DC: U.S. Government Printing Office, 1996).

23. Ibid.

24. USDE, *Digest, 1997*.

25. *Measuring Changes in Salaries and Wages in Public Schools: 1998 Edition*, Educational Research Services (Arlington, Virginia, 1998).

26. Nancy Protheroe, 1999, "Disputing the Myths About Public School Administration," Educational Research Services (Arlington, Virginia), online: [http://ers.org/r&i9non.html.]

27. Charol Shakeshaft, *Women in Educational Administration* (Newbury, CA: Sage, 1987); USDE, *Digest, 1997*.

28. Christine L. Williams, "The Glass Escalator:Hidden Advantages for Men in the 'Female' Professions," *Social Problems* 39, no. 3 (1992): pp. 253-267; *Doing "Women's Work"* (Newbury Park, CA: Sage, 1993); and *Still a Man's World* (Berkeley: University of California Press, 1995).

29. USDE, *America's Teachers: Profile of a Profession, 1993-94*, 1997.

30. Ibid.

31. U.S. Department of Education, National Center for Education Statistics, *Characteristics of Stayers, Mover, and Leavers, Results from the Teacher Followup Survey: 1994-95*, NCES 97-450, by Summer D. Whitener et.al. (Washington, DC: U.S. Government Printing Office, 1997).

32. Ibid.

33. Robert V. Bullough, Jr. "Becoming a Teacher: Self and the Social Location of Teacher Education," in *International Handbook on Teachers and Teaching*, pp. 79-134.

34. Jonathan Kozol, *Savage Inequalities: Children in America's Schools* (New York: Crown, 1991).

35. "Schools Crumbling," *The Arizona Republic* (June 26, 1996): p. 1.

36. Anthony DeBarros and Tamara Henry, "Rural Schools Left Wanting," *USA Today* (June 2, 1999).

37. Martha M. Rogers, in *Women Teachers on the Frontier*, ed. Polly W. Kaufman (New Haven, CT: Yale University Press, 1984), p. 184.

38. Dee Ann Spencer, *Contemporary Women Teachers: Balancing School and Home* (New York: Longman, Inc., 1986).

39. Mary Haywood Metz, "Some Missing Elements in the School Reform Movement," *Educational Administration Quarterly* 24, no. 4 (1988): p. 447.

40. Judi Randi and Lyn Corno, "Teachers as Innovators," in *International Handbook of Teachers and Teaching, Part II*: 1163-1221.

41. Ibid.

42. Peter Allen and C. B. Sager, *Everything Old is New Again* (A & M Records, Inc., Beverly Hills, CA, 1977).

43. Larry Cuban, *How Teachers Taught: Constancy and Change in American Classrooms, 1890-1980* (New York: Longman, 1984).

44. Ibid., p. 31.

45. Ibid., pp. 103-104.

46. John Holt, *How Children Fail* (New York: Delta, 1964), *How Children Learn* (New York: Pitman, 1967), and *The Underachieving School* (New York: Pitman, 1969); Herbert Kohl, *36 Children* (New York: Signet, 1967) and *The Open Classroom* (New York: Vintage Books, 1969); Jonathan Kozol, *Death at an Early Age* (Boston: Houghton Mifflin, 1967) and "The Open Classroom: New Worlds For Old Deceptions," *Ramparts*, 11 (July 1972), pp. 38-41; and Charles E. Silberman, *Crisis in the Classroom: The Remaking of American Education* (New York: Vintage Books, 1970).

47. A. S. Neill, *Summerhill* (New York: Hart, 1960).

48. Roland Barth, *Open Education and the American School* (New York: Agathon Press, Inc., 1972); Louis Smith, L. and P. Keith, *Anatomy of Education Innovation: An Organizational Analysis of an Elementary Open School* (New York: John Wiley & Sons, Inc., 1971); and B. W. Novak, *Living and Learning in the Free School: A Case Study*, An unpublished dissertation, York University, Toronto, Ontario, 1973.

49. Dee Ann Spencer and Peter M. Hall, "Processes of Problem Identification and Resolution in Two School Systems," in Norman K. Denzin, ed., *Annual Studies in Symbolic Interaction, Vol. IV* (Greenwich, CT: JAI Press, 1982); and Peter M. Hall and Dee Ann Spencer, "The Social Conditions of the Negotiated Order," *Urban Life* 11, no. 3 (1982): pp. 328-349.

50. Cuban, pp. 200-201.

51. Some results are reported in David L. Altheide and Dee Ann Spencer, "Cultural Maintenance and Narratives of Resistance," in *Studies in Symbolic Interaction, Vol. 23*, ed. Norman K. Denzin (Greenwich, CT: JAI Press, 1999), as well as in progress reports and final reports submitted to school districts and to the Missouri Department of Elementary and Secondary Education.

52. Mary M. McCaslin and Thomas L. Good, *Listening in Classrooms* (New York: HarperCollins, 1996).

53. Ibid., p. 112.

54. USDE, *America's Teachers: Profile of a Profession, 1993-94*, 1997; and Betsy Streisand and Thomas Toch, September 14, 1998, "Many Million of Kids and Too Few Teachers," *U.S. News Online*:
[http://www.usnews.com/usnews/issue/980914/14teac.html].

55. National Center for Education Statistics, *Schools and Staffing in the United States: A Statistical Profile, 1990-91* (Washington, DC: U.S. Government Printing Office, July 1993).

56. Gail Russell Chaddock, "Lots of Students, Not Enough Teachers," September 15, 1998, *The Christian Science Monitor*, Online:
[http://www.csmonitor.com/durable/1998/09/15/p51s.html.]

57. Richard M. Ingersoll, "The Problem of Underqualified Teachers in American Secondary Schools," *Educational Researcher* Vol. 28, no. 2 (March 1999): pp. 26-37.

58. Ibid., p. 34.

59. C. Emily Feistritzer, February 24, 1998, "Teachers Preparation and Classroom Size Reduction," Testimony before the House Committee on Education and the Workforce, online: http://www.ncei.com/Testimony022498.html, and February 1998, "Alternative Teacher Certification: An Overview," The National Center for Education Information, online: http://www.ncei.com/Alt-Teacher-Cert.html.

60. Carnegie Task Force on Teaching as a Profession, *A Nation Prepared: Teachers for the Twenty-First Century* (New York: Carnegie Forum on Education and The Economy, 1986).

61. E. S. Evendon, *Teachers' Salaries and Salary Schedules in the United States, 1918-19* (Washington, DC: The National Education Association, 1919).

62. National Commission on Teaching and America's Future, *What Matters Most: Teaching for America's Future* (New York: Carnegie Corporation, 1996).

63. NCES, 1993.

64. Tamara Lucas, *Into, Through, and Beyond Secondary School: Critical Transitions for Immigrant Youths* (McHenry, IL: CAL and Delta Systems Co., Inc., 1997).

65. Ibid.

66. A. Hemmings and Mary Haywood Metz, "Real Teaching: How High School Teachers Negotiate Societal, Local Community, and Student Pressures When They Define Their Work," in *Curriculum Differentiation: Interpretive Studies in U.S. Secondary Schools*, eds. R. Page & L. Valli (Albany: SUNY Press, 1990): pp. 91-111; Reba Page, "Teachers' Perceptions of Students: A Link between Classrooms, School Cultures, and the Social Order," *Anthropology and Education Quarterly* 18 (1987): pp. 77-99.

CHAPTER III

Motivation and Learning in School: Societal Contexts, Psychological Constructs, and Educational Practices

MARY McCASLIN AND ELEANOR DiMARINO-LINNEN

In this chapter, we present a selective review of articles related to motivational themes published in *American Psychologist* (*AP*) from its inception in 1946 to the present decade. Our goal is to better understand educational conceptions of student motivation in classrooms by studying related conceptions in society in general and psychology in particular throughout the decades. We select *American Psychologist* to represent psychology (rather than the more obviously relevant and narrower *Journal of Educational Psychology* or *Educational Psychologist*, also journals of the American Psychological Association (APA) because of its broader mission to bring psychology to bear on social issues. An historical review of *AP* is uniquely positioned to illuminate the changing arena of public education and citizens' beliefs about personal and social change, progress, and what matters. Psychologists' attempts to bring their work into the equation have direct implications for teachers who enact a curriculum supported by American citizens and who socialize children for our collective future. Hence, this chapter is intended for teachers, curriculum theorists, and educational psychologists who would understand the relations among societal expectations, psychology, and educational practice.

Surprisingly, there is no "motivation" division in either APA or the American Educational Research Association (AERA); thus, our reading erred toward breadth and inclusiveness across various sub-disciplines. In addition to discussing articles specifically focused on motivation, we illustrate the societal and psychological contexts within which motivational conceptions emerge. Contexts are constructed from articles that represent (a) societal perspectives particular to a decade that inform the

Mary McCaslin is an Associate Professor in the Department of Educational Psychology at the University of Arizona. Eleanor DiMarino-Linnen, a licensed psychologist and certified school psychologist, is consultant to the Marple-Newtown School District of Pennsylvania.

broader context of motivational beliefs (e.g., failed social initiatives in the 1970s) and (b) psychologists' perspectives on social issues that also inform motivational themes (e.g., research on stress in the 1980s). Within each decade, societal and psychological contexts give way to analysis of articles that focus more directly on motivation and can be related to motivated student learning in classrooms (e.g., reinforcement theory) and implied "considerations" for educational practice.

Our plan was simple and straightforward. Enacting it was difficult. The decades and the articles that represent them in *AP* become increasingly complex and progressively longer. The average length of the four volumes in the 1940s was 567 pages; in the 1980s, the average length of each of ten volumes was 1366 pages. Thus, our "selective review" appears to be not equally implemented across the decades.

To insure the readability of the chapter and to keep the number of end notes to a minimum, we have inserted a table in the section devoted to each decade, giving author, title, volume, and year of *AP* articles reviewed, and reserving for the Notes on pages 150 to 151 only citations to sources other than the *AP*. When we quote extensively from a particular *AP* article, page references are given in parentheses at the end of the quotation.

Throughout the decades, the general "unit" of motivational interest appears to change. Articles shift from a primary focus on the individual (animal or human) in the 1940s and 1950s, to an interest in group-level phenomena in the 1960s, to a concern with cultural/societal variables in the 1970s. In readings from the 1980s and 1990s we see a return to an individual focus. Societal and psychological belief in the power of the environment to shape, prevent, or cure human motivational phenomena dominates and is challenged in each decade. Reform failures severely test societal commitments and psychological constructs and give rise to changing dynamics of responsibility and accountability—phenomena not unfamiliar to schools. Failed, resistant, or deficient motivation or motivation that is simply different from that desired is a recurring feature of societal initiatives and classrooms.

1946-1949

"The only dogmatism we need today is that of an obstinate refusal to be stampeded into a prematurely closed state of mind."—Raymond Cattell

Don't forget. It is the *AMERICAN Psychologist*. In 1946, both Germany and Japan were defeated and the atomic bomb was ours. Nationalism and pride ruled; however, the sense of power and security were short-lived. By 1949, fear of communism and a grasping USSR, with starving and therefore willing and vulnerable neighbors, was standard fare. The "domino" metaphor dominated; by the time China "fell," Americans were terrified of world communism.

Psychology was busy creating itself and bringing psychologists back into the mainstream. Unity was the goal. In World War II many psychologists had assumed new roles in the military, notably in personnel testing, selection, and training. The military was held in high regard, and many articles published after the war recounted experiences with these new roles. This was also the first and last decade of our analysis in which testing was held in high regard.

Psychology's identity concerns were enduring themes in many articles (e.g., is psychology science or art?) but one in particular is worth noting as it foreshadowed much of what was to come. Lester Guest conducted a questionnaire/interview study, warts and all, that explored public beliefs and opinions about psychologists. With much apology for lack of precision and power, Guest presented data that suggested that many citizens were not sure just what psychologists do, but they did not want their children to be one, nor did they like socializing in the company of psychologists. Even so, every school should have one.

PSYCHOLOGICAL CONTEXT

Intelligence, Testing, and Education. Testing abounds in the 1940s articles. We select two articles relevant to intelligence, its assessment, and its mediation. The first was published in the inaugural issue. Henry Garrett defined intelligence as including "at least the abilities demanded in the solution of problems which require the comprehension and use of symbols." (p. 372) He noted that intelligence began as a practical endeavor and that theory is a follow-up, and asserted that intelligence changes in organization with maturity, evolving from a more unified general ability to a more differentiated profile.

What Garrett would not allow was any role for education in increasing "true" intelligence; it only raised the apparent score. Garrett argued with researchers like Read Tuddenham, whose data illustrated an increase in IQ test performance between soldiers in World Wars I and II that could then be correlated with school attainment. Tuddenham pointed to improved educational quality and opportunity to explain IQ increases. Garrett rejected this reasoning and went so far as to claim that "many soldiers were undoubtedly closer to the elementary school child than to the superior adult," presumably overrepresenting undifferentiated "g" in the result. The debate over "schools do or do not make a difference" has an astonishingly long history in this country, whose citizens believe in the better past if not the better future. This debate comes to a head in the 1980s' *AP* selections.

Motivation and Personality. Conceptions of motivation underlie much of the thinking in post-war articles, indirectly in discussion of relatively abstract constructs like validity in testing, data collection, and psychotherapy and directly in research on motivated behavior, including such topics as tolerance toward ambiguity and prejudice, consumer reactions to the integration of black sales clerks in department stores, social facilitation, and specificity of aspiration and rate of learning. We selected for discussion three APA presidential addresses that explored theoretical issues in motivation. Ernest Hilgard spoke of "Human motives and the concept of self," Carl Rogers of "Significant aspects of client-centered therapy," and John Anderson of "Personality organization in children." Together, these articles frame tensions in the study of motivation and implications for practice that continue for the next 50 years.

Hilgard's opening paragraph is the most compelling and clear call for the study of motivation in our 50-year analysis:

No problems are more fascinating than those of human motivation, and none are more in need of wise solution. To understand the struggles which go on within economic enterprise, to interpret the quarrels of international diplomacy, or to deal with the tensions in the daily interplay between individuals, we must know what it is that people want, how these wants arise and change, and how people will act in the effort to satisfy them. (p. 374)

Hilgard's framework was inclusive: intrapersonal and interpersonal dynamics at the individual and collective level. The underlying theory was as well. Adult motivation was a function of the interaction of culture and biology: "Man is assuredly a mammal as well as a member of society." (p. 374)

The challenge of Hilgard's conceptual breadth of motivational phenomena was considerable. In the next five decades, psychologists may emphasize one feature over another (e.g., the cognitive emphasis in the 1960s-90s), but with few exceptions (notably McClelland), psychologists will not attempt to integrate features and dynamics of human motivation to the same degree. Even fewer present research on motivation unique to the particulars of classroom learning.

Certain themes in Hilgard's analysis of motivational phenomena do metamorphose in interesting ways in future work. For example, Hilgard asserted that defense mechanisms were appropriated by psychologists who were hostile to the theoretical "baggage" of psychoanalysis. One

TABLE 1

AMERICAN PSYCHOLOGIST ARTICLES REVIEWED (1946-1949)

Anderson, John, "Personality organization in children," 3, 1948.
Bayton, James, "Opportunities for Negroes in psychology," 2, 1947.
Bryan, Alice and Edwin Boring, "Women in American psychology: Statistics from the OPP questionnaire," 1, 1946; "Women in American psychology: Factors affecting their professional careers," 2, 1947.
Cattell, Raymond, "Ethics and the social sciences," 3, 1948.
Frankel-Brunswik, Else, "Tolerance toward ambiguity as a personality variable," 1, 1946.

Garrett, Henry, "A developmental theory of intelligence," 1, 1946.
Geldard, Frank and Chester Harris, "Selection and classification of aircrew by Japanese," 1, 1946.
Guest, Lester, "The public's attitude towards psychologists," 3, 1948.
Gurnee, Herbert, "Group interaction in a learning situation," 1, 1946.
Hilgard, Ernest, "Human motive and the concept of self," 4, 1949.

Rogers, Carl, "Some observations on the organization of personality," 2, 1947.
Saenger, Gerhart, "Customer reactions to the integration of Negro sales personnel," 1, 1946.
Tuddenham, Read, "Soldier intelligence in World Wars I and II," 3, 1948.

result was an atheoretical, nonsystematic, laundry-list approach to adjustment mechanisms that was also limited by the extrapolation of animal experiments. Hilgard cited the considerable research on anxiety conducted with rats (a prominent theme in the 1950s). He noted that humans, like rats, feel anxious, but unlike rats, humans also feel guilty. Guilt makes us human (in contrast to shame, which can be observed in dogs). This is not a small point. Hilgard suggested in 1949 that "to feel guilty is to conceive of the self as an agent capable of good or bad choices." These dynamics are core constructs in the attributional approach to achievement motivation and helping behavior published in *AP* in the 1980s and 1990s.

Guilt suggests a conception of self. Defense mechanisms of denial and disguise suggest a need for self-protection. Defining the self and how it might change were core issues for Hilgard, as they were for Carl Rogers. Hilgard distinguished self-*awareness*, which informs self-identity, self-evaluation, and self-criticism, from the *inferred* self that is more inclusive, less open to awareness and more open to socialization. Hilgard claimed that "the search for the self" was an essential task for psychology; our reading of *AP* in the ensuing 50 years suggests the wisdom of his stance.

Rogers' 1947 address illustrated well the tensions between clinical and experimental psychology, "hypothesis" and "insight." He painstakingly argued the improvements in reliability and validity of essentially free form self-report due to improved technology (i.e., recorders) and the technique of clinician noninterference (e.g., unconditional regard). Self-reports were now observations, not introspections. Rogers' central thesis was that "behavior is not directly influenced or determined by organic or cultural factors, but primarily (and perhaps only) by the perception of these elements." Thus, the primary task of psychology was to understand the world as viewed by the individual; laws of interest were those that govern perception.

Rogers asserted that the self was capable of reorganization, particularly in nonthreatening situations. It was the therapist's job to realize nonthreatening conditions: no more fixed labels and psychometrics. Thus, the primary task of clinical practice was to understand another's perception, to see *with* him, which allowed change to occur in perception of self and reality, and therefore behavior. Rogers' emphases on process rather than fixed status orientations, the primary role of perception, the capability of self-reorganization, and the lessened emphasis on direct environmental effects on motivated behavior have much in common with theories of motivation that emerged in the 1960s and essentially dominated thereafter.

John Anderson's address was on the occasion of the newly formed Division of Childhood and Adolescence. Like Hilgard's and Rogers' arguments, Anderson's were organized by (or against) psychoanalytic constructs. Like Rogers, Anderson focused on perception; namely, adult misperceptions of children and how they influence policies for children. Anderson took aim at the need to make children "fit" with adult beliefs about themselves. He challenged prevailing beliefs that children, when normal, are passive and docile, responsive to all stimuli, and unusually vulnerable to shock and trauma. Not only were these beliefs erroneous, they were not good for children. Instead, Anderson detailed "scientific findings" which portray

the child as an energy system with high capacity for self repair and selectivity; the child as a persistent personality system with high capacity to resist deformation, stress, and trauma; and the child as a mechanism that meets life not as a storehouse or filing cabinet, but as an active system engaged in transforming input into outgo. (p. 410)

Anderson addressed in particular the distinction between temporary experiences and those with more permanent effects (e.g., trauma).

He offered a provocative analysis of what he called "repetitive and reiterative" phenomena within a constant stream of stimulation and response that served to keep children's "skills, experiences and memories alive." Anderson included (1) the frequently told family story that fixes behavior and creates expectations; (2) consistent presentation of attitudes and roles in the environment, like gender cues in school readers; (3) the child's own attention-getting devices as in retelling a story because everyone liked it so much the first time; (4) repeated return to incomplete experiences, as when an adult's unsatisfying answer to a child's question causes the child to ask again and again; (5) persistent pattern of adjustment which results in symbolic representation of an underlying problem, for example, in drawings; and (6) group expectations and roles that emerge over time and force conformity and mold personality because of their recurrence. Anderson wrote as one who knows children and how adults relate to them and his repetitive and reiterative strategies readily translate into provocative research questions on classroom interaction. Of the three presidential addresses, however, Anderson's appears to have had the least impact on educational psychology or education. With few exceptions, concern with children and social policy is notably sporadic in *AP*. Articles and Special Issues that appeared in the next 50 years, notably in the 1970s and 1980s, suggest that adults have continued to misperceive children, only this time, in ways that allow their neglect.

1950s
"The truth shall make you free."—Edward Tolman

In national Gallup polls conducted in 1950, 1954, and 1959, respondents were asked, "What do you think is the most important problem facing the country today?" The answer in 1950 was war (40%); in 1954, threat of war (18%) and communism in the United States (17%); and in 1959, keeping the peace (38%).[1] Several events of the 1950s likely contributed to the evolution of these concerns: the Korean Conflict, Senator Joseph R. McCarthy's UnAmerican Activities Committee, threats by the United States against the Soviet Union, and the Supreme Court's school desegregation order, which was followed by civil unrest.

Many *AP* articles in the 1950s reflect a decade torn by the horrors of war and cold war social policies and their impingement on the individual. Citizens feared conformity and the robotic power of subliminal perception. To many people, psychologists were suspect; they were the "engineers of conformity," according to John Marks and his co-authors.

Psychologists feared many of the same things. In *AP* articles, academic freedom, loyalty oaths, conformity, delinquency, authoritarianism, leftists, passivists versus psychologists, and psychology in the military are recurring topics.

A concern for the times pervades "academic" writing as well. Lewis Terman, like several authors in this period, correlated scientific talent with national security. He implied that support of the gifted was as necessary as it was patriotic. Terman's data suggested that stability, not turmoil, underlies success among the gifted; however, he allowed that this might not explain all cases of realized talent, citing Hitler and "possibly" Senator McCarthy as counterexamples. Edward Tolman also went beyond his data to address social problems. He related his research on rat learning, curiosity, and need to rising anti-intellectualism, scapegoating, and fear in the academy. His writing is passionate:

Even rats will learn (and sometimes faster) how to get to food when there are fearful electric shocks along the way. Hence, if our need as human beings for a liberal society be passionate enough, if our demands for freedom, for fair play, for honesty, for open minds, and for simple human decency really be overwhelming (and basically I believe they are), then whatever our fears and distorting mechanisms we men will continue to seek the truth. Our liberal schools and colleges will survive, in spite of the recurring attacks upon them. They shall be neither Communized nor Nazified. For I assert that we, the people, all of us, intellectuals, and nonintellectuals alike, still want the truth and nothing but the truth. For in our hearts the words of the Nazarene still echo: "And ye shall know the truth, and the truth shall make you free." (p. 538)

The anxieties of an uncertain present co-exist with optimistic beliefs in a better future. This is most evident with the appearance of television. Four articles published in 1955 foreshadow enthusiasms for the computer and the Internet. Television was seen as the ultimate societal enhancer and equalizer that would "uplift" a newly informed citizenry; it would transform public interests and public schools. It would humanize the classroom, freeing teachers to be more involved in the personal and psychological tasks of teaching.

Not everyone was ecstatic. In 1955, George Wischner and Ivan Scheier noted that extant data did not support such optimism. The promise of educational TV as they saw it—providing the front-row seat for every student, multiplying the best instructors, and cutting class sizes—must be tempered by noting that TV was particularly suited to the transmission of material involving small parts and their interrelationships. Data suggested that the effectiveness of TV instruction was interactive with subject matter, instructor, and student aptitude; students of lower aptitude performed better than students with average and higher aptitude.

One wonders what other factors might be operative. For example, were there differences in who had access to television outside of school? Television ownership in the 50s was decidedly middle and upper-middle class. Poor families wanted TV but couldn't afford it; upperclass families could afford it but many disapproved. Families with children were the first to buy TVs. Owning a television and watching television were not the same. Persons of low income, education, and occupational status spent more time watching TV and more than half of non-owners watched TV regularly. Early TV was a considerable socializer. As Thomas Coffin put it, "When the TV set arrives in the home, so do the visitors." (p. 634)

Some early concerns about the human costs of television, such as less reading, effect on school performance, exposure to crime and violence, are similar to those today, but some of the benefits perceived are surprising. In addition to making friends and renewing old acquaintances, TV was credited with increasing family cohesion by providing common experiences and interests during more evenings spent at home, even if it decreased family conversation.

The apparent success of advertising on television inspired hypotheses about its potential to promote student learning and effective recall. Coffin predicted that television could mold desirable behavior and habits of citizenship if necessary social mechanisms were in place. Others were more cautious, noting that the role of commercial goals and techniques in the inhibition or enhancement of learning required research attention. Thirty years later, the validity of these concerns is well illustrated by textbook publishers promoting products like Nike shoes and Oreo cookies to facilitate understanding of mathematics (and/or materialism), Pizza Hut fueling reading programs (and food preferences), and Channel One bringing sponsored news into classrooms.

PSYCHOLOGICAL CONTEXT

Conceptions of motivation are embedded in articles on intelligence and learning and in longitudinal research on the gifted. Motivation also is directly addressed in research in the laboratory and the workplace. The focus of each research program is the individual (animal or person). Individual focus extends to arguments about methods for research on individual change (versus statistical representation of group aggregates) in learning theory and intelligence.

Intelligence and Achievement. Many articles appeared on the structure of human intelligence, problem solving, creativity, and non-ability determinants. Especially relevant for our purposes, however, and perhaps surprising to readers, *non-intellective* factors in intelligence were a large part of the debate. In 1950, David Wechsler argued that general intelligence was a manifestation of the personality as a whole. He viewed E. L. Thorndike's trichotomy of social, abstract, and practical intelligences as an unrealized beginning to better understanding the role of emotion and conative factors in intelligence.[2] The stability or instability of intelligence and non-ability factors in achievement were key in two longitudinal studies, Lewis Terman's "Discovery and encouragement of exceptional talent" and Nancy Bayley's "On the growth of intelligence." Both articles, Terman's based on a 30-year study of children identified as gifted, and Bayley's on data from the Berkeley Growth Study that spanned 25 years, challenged popular beliefs about intelligence. Terman targeted the promotion of genius, linking early characteristics with adult achievements and dispositions; Bayley tackled assumptions about the inheritability and stability of IQ by examining individual growth curves of IQ from infancy through adulthood. The decade ends with a decidedly less malleable conception of intelligence: Cyril Burt's "The inheritance of mental ability," published in 1958.

Animals and Learning in School. In contrast to articles on human intelligence, cognition, and successful talent, articles that expressly focused on learning and motivation and its relevance to students, teachers, and classrooms, were based on research on laboratory animals. The irony was not lost on writers of the period. Simply put, educational psychologists were not getting the job done. Psychologists charged that what little research was done was too often fixated on repeating the work of Thorndike without concern for realistic educational situations.

Ernest Haggard, while quite critical of educational psychologists, suggested a reformulation of learning theory that remains refreshingly provocative today:

One method to get us out of our present conceptual maze with respect to learning and related phenomena might be to ask ourselves such questions as: What if we thought of the organism as possessing motivations of its own (rather than only those imposed or aroused by the experimenter), and unique patterns of abilities and interests which change as it grows older (rather than being more or less uniform and constant for all subjects)? What if we thought of learning as involving a modification of motivational (rather than response) systems? What if we concerned ourselves more with learning which is meaningful and important to the learner as a person (and less with the learning of segmental responses or artificial verbal materials)? (p. 542)

Arthur Melton was concerned about the futility of learning theory wars (cognitive vs. stimulus-response) which exploded in the 1960s and continue to this day. Melton was especially critical of educational psychologists' "bizarre" choice of research subjects (white rats and college undergraduates of vaguely defined privilege) and tasks (rote learning of nonsense syllables and conditioned eyelid response). Melton considered such choices obvious failures to develop a scheme for describing learning and problem-solving tasks and the humans engaged in them. Each represents a failure of sampling; neither promotes representation or generalization of human learning.

Calls for more representative research on educational practice and reconceptualizations of learning theory would have to wait. In 1954 Tolman presented the human implications of his work on needs, wants, and learning in rats and chimpanzees, and the decade ended on a similar note.

Tolman maintained that animals express a purely cognitive curiosity need that interacts with more "practical wants" like thirst or fear. He asserted that all new learning involves curiosity. Up to a certain level, a practical want facilitates the arousal of curiosity. At higher levels of want or need, however, curiosity is diminished. Decreased curiosity impoverishes need fulfillment because less attention is paid to potentially useful stimuli and their relationships. Thus, the quality of problem solving is diminished. For example, a somewhat hungry rat finds food more quickly than one that is not hungry. In contrast, a very hungry rat has more difficulty finding food and also may fail to notice the water bowl along the way. These were the data upon which Tolman based his predictions of proactive human behavior in conditions of moderate arousal and the destructive effects of fear on curiosity and discerning truth. Tolman's reasoning suggests a decrease rather than an increase in student learning under such heightened arousal conditions.

The introduction by Harold Schlosberg to the special section in volume 13(3), "Control of behavior through motivation and reward," claimed that learning theory was selected for the inaugural symposium because of its central importance to all psychologists and because "there are some promising signs of real progress in this area after a decade or two of the doldrums." B. F. Skinner, Neal Miller, and Don Hebb were invited; Skinner studied pigeons, Miller white rats, and Hebb dogs. Kenneth Spence also published in this issue; he reported on drive theory and classical conditioning with noxious stimuli in humans.

Skinner's article begins with a serendipitous account of the top floor of a flourmill in Minneapolis, the ubiquitous pigeons, and his attempt to alleviate wartime project fatigue by teaching a pigeon to bowl. The results were two ideas essential to reinforcement as a theory of learning *and* motivation: the acquisition of behavior through shaping successive approximations and the maintenance of behavior through intermittent reinforcement. Skinner extrapolated the integration of schedule and performance in pigeon behavior to the explicit design of social situations and solving practical problems, including school discipline. He called for a return to orderly conduct through positive reinforcement: "a careful husbanding of small reinforcers and the nurturing of proper contingencies." (p. 98) This is, of course, based on the premise that teachers have reinforcers at their disposal. Skinner noted, however, that even in the worst case, a teacher can "at least reinforce a class by dismissing it." The assumption that learning in classrooms is, by definition, aversive is not unique to Skinner.

Miller described the interface of research on organic processes (e.g., pharmacology) and measurement of drives that he asserted is basic to laying the foundation for understanding motivation and reward. He reported on various invasive experiments with rats and cats (e.g., brain lesion) and illustrated the difficulties and the promise of studying individual drives and their interrelationships. Extrapolating from animal experimentation, Miller hypothesized that people differ in strength of innate drives for fear, guilt, and anxiety. Innate differences suggest that people are differentially susceptible to learning strong fears and guilts; thus, fears may be amenable to medication. In addition to medication, Miller speculated that an "unconventional combination" that also includes therapy, training in social skills, and environmental changes may be effective in "emotional re-education." (p. 106) This treatment package is not uncommon in 1999, but also is not mainstream as the sheer volume of pharmaceutical-only (e.g., Ritalin) distribution in schools attests.

Hebb's invited article concerned social intelligence and the detrimental effects of isolation. Hebb studied the physical and mental effects of stimulus deprivation on the social intelligence of dogs (e.g., exploratory behavior, sharing food, response to friendly or threatening situations). His data indicated that dogs reared in isolation exhibited motivational deficits in initial perception and response. While acknowledging the differences between man and dog, Hebb built on these data to address dynamics of human social intelligence, its development in children and loss in adults.

TABLE 2

AMERICAN PSYCHOLOGIST ARTICLES REVIEWED (1950-1959)

Bayley, Nancy, "On the growth of intelligence," 10, 1955.
Burt, Cyril, "The inheritance of mental ability," 13, 1958.
Coffin, Thomas, "Television and impact on society," 10, 1955.
Grace, Harry, "Educational psychology and education," 10, 1955.
Guilford, J. P., "Creativity," 5, 1950; "Three faces of intellect," 14, 1959.

Haggard, Ernest, "The proper concern of educational psychologist," 9, 1954.
Hebb, D. O., "The motivating effects of exteroceptive stimulation," 13, 1958.
Hovland, Carl and Howard Kendler, "The New York University conference on human problem solving," 10, 1955.
Iscoe, Ira, "On harmonious relationships with public schools," 14, 1959.
Jersild, Arthur, "Self-understanding in childhood and adolescence," 6, 1951.

Keesey, Truman, "A new world," 10, 1955.
Kelly, George, "Television and the teacher," 10, 1955.
Marks, John, et al., "Group participation and conformity," 14, 1959.
Melton, Arthur, "Present accomplishment and future trends in problem-solving and learning theory," 11, 1956.
Miller, Neal, "Central stimulation and other new approaches to motivation and reward," 13, 1958.

Ross, Sherman and John Gustad, "Psychology: The science talent search and high school teaching," 9, 1954.
Schlosberg, Harold, "Symposium on control of behavior through motivation and reward: Introductory remarks," 13, 1958.
Skinner, B. F., "Reinforcement today," 13, 1958.
Spence, Kenneth, "A theory of emotionally based drive (D) and its relation to performance in simple learning situations," 13, 1958.
Strong, Edwards, Jr., "Satisfactions and interests," 13, 1958.

Terman, Lewis, "The discovery and encouragement of exceptional talent," 9, 1954.
Tolman, Edward, "Freedom and the cognitive need," 9, 1954.
Wechsler, David, "Cognitive, conative, and non-intellective intelligence," 5, 1950.
Wischner, George and Ivan Scheier, "Some thoughts on television as an educational tool," 10, 1955.

Hebb maintained that motivation was a function of perception, skill, and value: "We want to bring up children with 'democratic' values; if in fact this is to be so, they must know how to put them satisfyingly into effect. It is hardly realistic for the social scientist to concentrate only on establishing desirable motivations—how long can one expect them to survive, not to extinguish, if the corresponding social skills are missing." (p. 110) Hebb anticipated 1980s research on the development of "will and skill" but with a decidedly different emphasis. He looked to skill to enact motivation; modern self-regulated learning theories primarily look to motivation to enact skill or define "skillful motivation" as self-control or volition.[3]

Hebb also studied adult motivation, in particular, the continual need for an informative perceptual environment. Stimulus deprivation research in the United States and Canada was spurred by wartime brainwashing atrocities. Researchers examined the effects of varying degrees and modalities of sensory deprivation. The results frightened Hebb. Perceptual deprivation resulted in acute personality disturbance with alternating periods of apathy and desire—mood swings that maximize the effects of propaganda.

Hebb summarized the work and its more mundane daily implications: exteroceptive stimulation matters and accustomed environments are part of "personal" motivation; without them motivation readily dissipates. Hebb noted the ubiquitous (and futile) phenomenon of taking work on vacation. It seems reasonable to consider as well as the effects on students of long summer vacations.

Finally, Spence studied the effects of aversive stimuli, rather than the aversive absence of stimuli. Working within the drive theory of Clark Hull,[4] Spence foreshadowed 1980s research on stress when he studied the motivational properties of emotionality—defined as fear acquired through classical conditioning—and the moderating influence of preadaptation on emotional response and individual differences in emotionality. Studies with humans ranged from eyelid-conditioning experiments to more complex tasks (i.e., paired associates). Spence detailed work on drive, learning, and performance suggesting that higher drive level facilitates performance, but not learning. Indeed, higher drive initially impedes learning, although if skill increases, higher drive ultimately will facilitate performance. Research by Spence and Tolman, albeit based on animals and contrived tasks, suggests that recent calls for higher standards, mandated "high risk" testing, and the end to social promotion may increase student drive (i.e., acquired fear) just as intended. And it may well backfire since increased fear and impoverished learning do not yield higher test scores. Both research programs suggest that moderation is key and even then what enhances performance may impede learning.

Spence also reports work by Janet Taylor, who developed the Manifest Anxiety Scale (MAS) to measure stable individual differences in reported level of anxiety (which could then be studied in interaction with task difficulty, complexity, and the like). As adapted for students

the MAS assumes, by definition, that the stuff of schooling—the public arena of success and failure—is aversive. Thus, the basic motivation
or "drive" for students is fear acquired through classical conditioning.
The MAS identifies levels of anxiety in response to routine classroom
instruction and testing events and is still commonly used in research
on student motivation today.

Spence and other learning theorists were not unusual in assuming
that classrooms are aversive, that the biggest reinforcement available to
a teacher is dismissal, and that student motivation to learn is acquired
fear. Several authors asserted deplorable school conditions as a given.
Needless teacher-bashing is evident, especially in published commen-
taries. Ira Iscoe addressed these attitudes, noting that much of the
arrogance among psychologists toward teachers was misguided and
self-serving. He reminded psychologists that their work may interfere
with teacher goals, curricula, and school routines. Unfortunately, the
scapegoating of teachers and self-serving intrusions into schools in the
1950s continues in the 1990s.

Characteristics of Successful People. Research on adults and nonintellective factors in successful lives informs a third source of motivational
beliefs in the 1950s. Terman's longitudinal data supported an earlier
review by Wechsler that suggested nonintellective personality factors
were essential to a conception of intelligence. Wechsler hypothesized
that beyond a given point, lack of intellectual ability accounted for relatively few school failures; rather, personality does. The nonintellective personality components of intelligence that Wechsler asserted
were volitional characteristics which he termed "conative" factors of
drive, persistence, will, and perseveration. Each influences the effectiveness of intelligent behavior.

One goal of Terman's research published in 1954 was to demystify
giftedness. Popular beliefs and suspicions about persons of exceptional
talent at the time included the maxim, "early ripe, early rot," with ultimate psychosis. Hence, Terman studied character, interest, and personality traits in addition to intelligence among children. He found
that children of 140 IQ or higher possessed, among other traits, superior social adjustment. Following the children for 30 years, he found
that "early ripe, early rot" did not occur. While IQ scores predict ability to achieve, they show much less about what "direction the achievement will take, and least of all do they tell us what personality factors
or what accidents of fortune will affect the fruition of exceptional ability."

Terman included in his longitudinal study of talented individuals the nonintellective factors of life success, which he defined as the "extent to which a subject made use of his superior intellectual ability" rather than earned income. Terman divided his now adult male subjects into two success groups: those he rated "A" and those "C." He found that after similar childhoods, differences between male adults rated "A" and those rated "C" emerged early in high school. Of the multitude of measures taken in 1922, 18 years before the A and C groups were identified, four conative traits in childhood revealed the most marked adult group differences. The traits were prudence, self-confidence, perseverance, and desire to excel. In 1922, the A's were also rated significantly higher on leadership, popularity, and sensitiveness to approval or disapproval. By 1940, group differences included marriage and divorce rates, which were higher in the C group. (Interestingly, modern research on student academic underachievement reveals similar adult patterns of uneven employment and divorce rates.[5]) In 1940, ratings were taken again. Rater agreements of subject, wife, and parent (if possible) were unanimous on the four conative traits that paralleled those measured 18 years earlier. Groups differed on "persistence in the accomplishment of ends," "integration toward goals, as contrasted with drifting," "self-confidence," and "freedom from inferiority feelings." These last two nonintellective factors, re-emerge as explanatory achievement constructs in the 1980s, when "self-concept" in education is considered an important educational goal for students *independent* of level of excellence or achievement. In the early 1990s, the focus shifts to the first factor, the student's responsibility to persist.

Terman matches these patterns to the findings of Catherine Cox in her 1926 study of 100 leading geniuses (of 300), whose outstanding traits were "persistence of motive and effort," "confidence in their abilities," and "strength or force of character."[6] In summary, Terman noted that the greatest contrasts between A and C groups were in drive to achieve and in all-around mental and social adjustment. In contrast to prevailing beliefs about achievement stemming from emotional tension, Terman's research indicated that stability underlies success.

The work of Wechsler and Terman on adult adjustment foreshadowed much current interest in student "volition" and its enhancement.[7] An article about "satisfactions and interests" in the adult workplace by Edward Strong, Jr., an industrial psychologist, foreshadowed modern motivational work in student "interest," "goal theory," and "goal coordination."[8] In his critique of employee survey research,

Strong delineated interests (which predict choice and direction) from satisfaction (fulfillment or pleasant feeling).

Strong argued, in contrast to reinforcement theory, that the motivational properties of satisfaction are in *dis*satisfaction: the discrepancy between reality and fantasy, aspiration and the expectation that it will be achieved. Thus, Strong argued that rather than asking employees, "How satisfied are you with this and that?" researchers should ask, "What do you want? What do you expect to get? What are the chances you will get what you want?" Motivation, like interest, is expected to indicate direction and choice. Specific goals must be considered in relation to dissatisfaction and anticipated future. Strong defined goals as both emotional and rational, as "phantasies, wishes, daydreams, aspirations, plans," most of which are subject to social pressures. Like modern researchers, Strong assessed goals by their number, motivational contagion, complexity, proximity, and instrumentality. Belief in goal attainment predicts level of satisfaction or dissatisfaction. When there is no chance of goal attainment, personal resentment or withdrawal and goal abandonment or substitution may result. Belief in goal attainment can be expressed in expenditure of effort or resources, or willingness to forego other goals (similar to conative factors described by Wechsler and Terman). The satisfaction/dissatisfaction process is cyclical, but in the long run satisfaction requires a sense of improvement.[9]

Like Terman and Wechsler, Strong considered childhood fantasies the foundation of adult plans. Strong also believed that we are more than our capability: we are what we *can* do and what we *want* to do. What we want to do informs goals and conative strategies to meet them. Modern theorists on goal coordination would agree and add that strategies to coordinate and enact goals, like interests, are acquired and can be taught. Where Strong's writings focused on adults at work, the extrapolation to students in classrooms seems relatively straightforward. In combination with Wechsler's and Terman's, these studies are perhaps the most helpful of the 1950s *AP* offerings for designing a proactive approach to enabling student motivation. Unfortunately, the better known works in educational psychology from this decade are those learning theory studies rooted in a limiting conception of human and animal motivation as simply biological hedonism and acquired (classically conditioned) fear and anxiety. These limitations also undergird popular present-day "get tough" management systems at the classroom and school levels.

Finally, we select one article written at the beginning of the decade, even though it is not representative of the 1950s, because the author is concerned about real children in real classrooms, their self and other understandings, and their empowering relationships with teachers. Arthur Jersild fused psychoanalytic concerns about adult manifestations of childhood trauma with a humanistic belief in education and change. He argued for the ounce of prevention rather than the pound of cure and called for an increased role for child psychology in schools, noting that rather than directly address children's needs, "[m]uch of what we do in education is an evasion rather than a way of facing problems that occur in the lives of children and adolescents." (p. 122)

Jersild called for students learning how to understand self and others in school rather than through subsequent "re-education" in therapy. He noted that teachers in effect teach psychology whether they know it or not because of the very nature of classroom experiences for children. Jersild, unlike other authors considered here, included teachers in the solutions rather than the definitions of problems.

Jersild was refreshingly comfortable with aspects of childhood and personal limitations that make us uneasy, ultimately to the disservice of children. He reminds us that childhood is not the romantic time of life adults seem bent on believing. Children can be cruel, they develop understanding only with difficulty, and troubles seem unending. Children learn that not everyone can be the best or even above average on anything that counts. Children learn to cope more or less with the anxiety that such experiences engender. Schools play a major role in making life difficult for children but also in helping them come to terms with realistic self-appraisals, positive aspirations for self, and appropriate expectations for others.

Jersild's ideas are remarkably contemporary. His expectations that (a) schools do more than transmit "the curriculum," (b) teachers and students should be studied as they engage in learning and relationships that are meaningful to them, and (c) connections between home and school, parent and teacher are important matters well describe much current educational thinking.[10] Finally, we note that Jersild, writing in 1951, worried about the adults children might become, possibly as one result of a decade of wars brought on by adults. In the 1960s and 1970s, we see a society more worried about the adolescents children might become, possibly as one result of children who did not profit from the Great Society and adolescents who would *not* fight wars brought on by adults. In the 1990s, schools, perhaps more than ever, are central to these concerns.

1960s
"Reject nothing, but reorder all"—Karl Weick

A 1965 Gallup poll asked, "What do you think is the most important problem facing the country today?" Civil rights was the answer of 52% of the respondents. Pivotal events in this decade include: Soviets shooting down an American U-2 spy plane, Martin Luther King's "I have a dream" speech, and American troops taking the offensive in Vietnam. This is also the decade of political assassinations, school busing protests, urban riots, and the 1968 Democratic National Convention in Chicago.

American Psychologist articles in the 60s reflect major shifts in the social and political climate in America. The early 60s encompassed feelings of hope, patriotism, and success. The youth generation, the "we" generation, believed they could change the world, improve social conditions, and create equality for all. Political dialogue was one means of trying to achieve these goals. The Space Race was on and the United States had landed a man on the moon. It was a Great Society. *AP* articles illustrate a shift from understanding the individual to understanding and promoting social change. Psychologists were urged to meet the social challenge and to "cure" society's ills. Throughout the 60s, cure was still seen as attainable, even if increasingly difficult. Schools could lead the way to a better future and all learners could be successful given the right resources. Poor student learning was viewed as a function of outdated instructional materials and teaching practices—a problem that could, and would, be fixed.

Arthur Brayfield wrote of the euphoria, the "gigantic tide of rising expectations" at the beginning of the decade that would dissipate by decade's end in the aftermath of political assassinations, increased racial tensions, and the escalation of the Vietnam War. Political dialogues turned into political struggles and an "us" against "them" atmosphere obtained. The emerging women's liberation movement and the push for equality between whites and blacks changed the landscape of society.

PSYCHOLOGICAL CONTEXT

Psychology's interests turned towards groups and gaining a greater understanding of group differences and the motivational dynamics of similarity and conformity within them. Articles included concerns with social unrest and protests; understanding group phenomena would render groups more predictable and, by extension, society safer. Adults and those in positions of maintaining the status quo especially were invested in gaining an understanding of what was happening on college campuses throughout the United States. Causes of unrest and protest were categorized. They ranged from blaming permissive parenting and affluence on the one hand; and on the other, to the individual as a victim and justified crusader against some social or political ill such as the Vietnam War, the draft, and unresponsive university environments.

American psychologists were curious about their own group differences relative to their peers in other cultures. An interest in Soviet educational methods was especially prominent, spurred on in part by Sputnik. Americans feared that the Soviets were "ahead" and the Soviet commitment to the collective "socialist morality" could be an effective weapon against the United States, where commitment to individualism had resulted in fractured parent-child relationships and the entitlement of individuals and subgroups (minorities, women) that were splintering America. In 1963 alone, *AP* published three articles dedicated to Makarenko, a leading Soviet educator who worked with troubled youth in times of rapid social change.

Much was made of Soviet educators' use of *group* competition and recognition to increase *individual* student performance. Individual group members were responsible for helping less able members improve and for doing their personal best so that the entire group was more successful. Principles of group competition to motivate individuals were presented in manuals for training school directors, supervisors, and teachers who were instructed to "activate" the children through competition. The Soviet manipulation of group competition, quite novel in the early 1960s, is commonplace in today's American classrooms. Ironically, we term these competitive group strategies to enhance student performance "cooperative" learning.

Intelligence. Articles on intelligence and achievement in this decade emphasized group differences and the variables believed to account for them. Psychologists attempted to identify major environmental handicaps to intellectual development. Their list of environmental insults was long and varied ranging from physiological and nutritional factors in humans and rats to female dominance in child rearing, irregular education, and teacher expectations. Sensitivity to the effects of environmental factors on intelligence directly affected the structure, content, and timing of school. One result was a federal initiative for large-scale early intervention and compensatory education programs. Schools, especially preschools, were given the task of turning things around and ameliorating the effects of environmental handicaps. There was considerable optimism, until the end of the 60s, that these goals could be reached.

This also was the decade in which Arthur Jensen's article in the *Harvard Educational Review*[11] set off a hailstorm of controversy related to whether heredity or environmental factors contributed to IQ differences between blacks and whites. This controversy fueled ongoing concerns with intelligence testing, ethics, and the use of IQ test results. In November 1965, the *American Psychologist* devoted an entire issue to the controversy over the testing movement. Two Congressional committees had already investigated the use of intelligence tests and personality inventories as well as issues of invasion of privacy. Psychologists were asked to define how much power they had, and citizens wanted to know how they could be protected from abuses of realized power. Popular distrust of psychologists from the 1940s and 1950s had continued to grow in the 1960s.

Active Intelligent Learning. Within the intense activism of the 60s, the behavioral model of man as a passive receiver of and reactor to the environment eroded. As individuals attempted to reshape society, psychology reconceptualized humans as active creators of their environment. In models of behaviorism, man was predictable, a rational transmitter of information who lived in an objective world and was knowable in scientific terms. In contrast, in experiential or phenomenological models, man was unpredictable, an a-rational generator of information, unique from others, living in a subjective world, and essentially unknowable. In classrooms these models differently informed not only the dynamics of learning and instruction, but their management. The behavioral learner who was an empty vessel in a row of other empties, each a passive receiver of objectively sequenced instructional materials and practices, gave way to the experiential learner in the open classroom. The experiential learner was ready to learn and actively shaped the learning environment. Acceptable management policies in the behavioral classroom such as group control procedures, efficiency and compliance goals are antithetical to the experiential model and vice versa.

The 60s moved psychology into a larger and broader context for understanding learning. Group influences, situational variables, and the social/cultural context in which learning and development occurred became integral features of the learning context for many psychologists. If growth of mind occurred from the outside in, as Jerome Bruner suggested, individual learning was restricted by cultural opportunity. Opportunity included access to quality schools and the quality of the instruction within them. The context of traditional schooling

TABLE 3

AMERICAN PSYCHOLOGIST ARTICLES REVIEWED (1960-1969)

Adams, Henry L., "Achievement testing in England," 23, 1968.

Argyris, Chris, "The incompleteness of social-psychological theory: Examples from small group, cognitive consistency, and attribution research," 24, 1969.

Bauer, Raymond, "The obstinate audience: The influence process from the point of view of social communication," 19, 1964.

Brayfield, Arthur, "About special privilege and special responsibility," 20, 1965; "Human effectiveness," 20, 1965.

Bronfenbrenner, Urie, "Soviet methods of character education: Some implications for research," 17, 1962.

Bruner, Jerome S., "The course of cognitive growth," 19, 1964; "The growth of mind," 20, 1965.

David, Henry et al., "Reciprocal influences in international psychology: A summary report of the 1959 APA symposium," 15, 1960.

David, Henry P., and William Swartley, "Toward more effective international communication in psychology," 16, 1961.

Farber, I. E., "The things people say to themselves," 18, 1963.

Garner, Wendell R., "To perceive is to know," 21, 1966.

Grice, Robert G., "Do responses evoke responses?" 20, 1965.

Guilford, J. P., "Intelligence: 1965 model," 21, 1965.

Helson, Harry, "Current trends and issues in adaptation-level theory," 19, 1964.

Hitt, William, "Two models of man," 24, 1969.

Mackinnon, Donald, "The nature and nurture of creative talent," 17, 1962.

McNemar, Quinn, "Lost: Our intelligence? Why?" 19, 1964.

Miller, George, "Psychology as a means of promoting human welfare," 24, 1969.

Miller, Neal, "Analytical studies of drive and reward," 16, 1961.

Mischel, Walter, "Continuity and change in personality," 24, 1969.

Prentice, W. C. H., "Some cognitive aspects of motivation," 16, 1961.

Razran, Gregory, "Growth, scope, and direction of current Soviet psychology: The 1963 All-Union Congress," 19, 1964.

Rosenzweig, Mark, "Environmental complexity, cerebral change, and behavior," 21, 1966.

Rubinstein, Eli, "Paradoxes of student protests," 24, 1969.

Sarason, Irwin, "Verbal learning, modeling, and juvenile delinquency," 23, 1968.

Skinner, B. F., "Operant behavior," 19, 1964.

Solomon, Richard, "Punishment," 19, 1964.

Vernon, Philip, "Ability factors and environmental influences," 20, 1965.

Weick, Karl E., "Social psychology in an era of social change," 24, 1969.

Wickert, Frederic R., "Industrial psychology in Africa," 15, 1960.

Young, Paul T., "Affective arousal," 22, 1967.

that had focused on memorizing facts, finding answers, and solving the problem of what the teacher wanted were limiting opportunities at best. Bruner emphasized the need to promote instead intrinsic commitment to problem solving through a curriculum of "intensiveness and depth over extensiveness and coverage." (p. 1015) Growth of mind required the opportunity to be reflective and to exercise thinking and internally driven problem-solving skills. As the decade came to a close, psychologists would continue to assert the importance of the individual and intrapersonal processes. As the optimism of social engineering and the Great Society faded in the popular culture, human thinking would become the object of psychology, surpassing previous interest in animal and human behavior.

Changing Conceptions of Motivation. Disillusionment with the status quo in society was paralleled in psychology. Theorists turned away from an understanding of humans as being basically motivated to maintain homeostasis towards a view of humans as motivated to seek out positive affective and cognitive experiences. The decade of ideas and idealism led to an intense interest in how ideas activated individuals. By the late 60s, there was a deep interest in how individuals think and how cognitive processes could be motivational influences.

Arguments about what is essentially human pervade the motivational literature of this decade. The notion that humans are *effective* rather than merely *affected* individuals supported non-unidirectional models of causality. In 1964, Raymond Bauer asserted that bi-directional transaction undergirded motivation—the transaction occurring not only between "environment" and the individual but also between individuals, as in social communication. He was especially interested in how individuals remain unaffected by attempts to influence them. Traditionally, research on communication had been defined by the effects of the communicator on the listener. Little was known about the effect of the listener on the communicator. It became important to understand how environmental (physical and social) conditions and incentives functioned as motives. These constructs are well represented in modern educational research, for example, in the dynamics of teacher expectations and differential student vulnerabilities to them.

Humans now were less predictable because they were not simply responders to stimuli. The struggle of the active yet less predictable individual yielded constructs of mental health as "human effectiveness," a measure of effectiveness and adaptability to changing environmental conditions. Mentally healthy persons seek to be effective in their environment. Effectiveness energy is intrinsic and includes the motivation to explore the environment and possibly to affect it. Issues of being effective and competent in the environment are motivational principles, not unlike Tolman's study in 1954 of relations between curiosity and need in rats. Like Jersild in 1951, Brayfield argued that human effectiveness should be the core of education. Like writers in the 1950s, he asserted that, to the detriment of the Great Society, psychologists had failed to study the conditions in schools that promote human effectiveness.

In 1968, Irwin Sarason echoed these beliefs, particularly in the effectiveness of models and role-playing to facilitate desired change. The Soviet harnessing of social learning and modeling, novel ideas earlier in the decade, were taking hold. The issues of curriculum scope, sequence, and relevance with regard to student characteristics had yet to be fully explored. For now, exposure and (hopefully available) modeling were key. Sarason's approach was reflected in judicial decisions and the societal move towards desegregated schools, which attempted to improve the learning and performance of disadvantaged populations by having them attend school with more advantaged learners. Like Soviet parents, citizens were expected to put the collective good above their own individual needs or preferences as their children were bussed or school populations changed. But what resulted from desegregation initiatives was white flight from public to private schools and from the city to the suburbs. White flight reflected, in part, cultural beliefs in, or fears of, the power of social exposure.[12] Currently, "least restrictive environments" for learners with disabilities also are rooted, in part, in social modeling beliefs.

Powerful conceptualizations of cognition as motivation were represented by several theorists of this decade. Cognitive theorists argued that motives were a kind of perceptual event, woefully unstudied. They claimed that what had been studied as motivation was nothing more than a set of techniques with an unsupported conceptual basis in one-dimensional affective (negative to positive) consequences; that is, behaviorists had dominated the study of motivation. Now it was their turn. W. C. H. Prentice in particular argued that historically explanations for human behavior had always attempted to reduce motives to something else rather than understand motives as behaviors carried on for their own sake, such as in play.

Prentice's conceptions of motivation and learning were unique: were there conditions under which fundamental psychological change occurred rather than the mere suppression or activation of responses?

Thus, he argued for greater complexity in understanding motivated learning. Prentice looked at attributes such as level of difficulty and novelty as stemming from interactions between tasks and persons. A student's willingness to be engaged in a task involved how novel and interesting the task was perceived to be and how graded the challenge was in learning how to complete the task. It followed that curriculum tasks could not be generically sequenced and thought to be the same for all students. Instead an "appropriate" learning task, or one in which the student had the most willingness to engage, would involve some assessment of the novelty and challenge of that task relative to that particular learner.

Such complexities of motivated learning did not influence the classrooms of the decade, nor for that matter subsequent decades. In part, this was a function of the dominance of seemingly quite different instructional models, whole-class direct instruction of intellectual skills and individualized or small-group mastery learning of sequential objectives.[13] Each instructional model adhered to a conception of "task" that determined learner engagement and was defined by a curriculum analysis. In each model, learners mentally and physically reproduced instruction rather than actively reconstructed it. This essentially noncognitive approach to instruction included parallel conceptions of management. Teachers managed behavior, not cognition, whether it involved group or individual behavior modification.[14]

Behavior management in classrooms built on the work of behavioral psychologists who were well represented in *AP* in the early 60s. Despite the influence of cognitive theorists, behavioral psychologists writing in *AP* persisted in their attempts to deal with motivation without a reference to cognition. Behaviorists claimed cognitive processes were consequences, not determinants, of behavior. Other traditional behavioral themes continued as well. Neal Miller studied the effects of drive on learning; Robert Grice looked at how responses could evoke further responses. Contiguity was expanded. Rather than looking at learning as simple stimulus-response connections or as the result of contiguity of associations, behavioral psychologists began looking at the impact of early learning on later learning and what kept individuals motivated to continue to learn and behave beyond the initial learning condition.

Skinner believed that intermittent reinforcers, rather than other motivational variables, were usually involved in maintaining behaviors after they had been acquired. He did not believe it was useful to bring in concepts like purpose, intention, or expectancy as motives. Richard

Solomon argued for a more in-depth understanding of punishment rather than positive reinforcements as an easier way to control students. Harry Helson investigated properties of reinforcements, such as timing, frequency, magnitude, intensity, and distinctiveness, and their impact on learning. These reinforcement properties would be considered "state of the art" in educational research on motivation in the 1970s and 1980s.

The behavior-versus-cognition debate in psychology was not paralleled in classroom approaches to managing student motivation. For the most part, 60s psychology was "applied" in classrooms through looking at how reinforcements (token, social, and material) could modify behavior and academic performance. Student motivation in the typical classroom of the era was "known" by the outcome of learning and behavioral compliance. A quietly working student was labeled "motivated to achieve" rather than "obedient" or *maybe* motivated to achieve.

In summary, overall theories of motivation in this decade moved from a behaviorist interpretation of man as a passive receiver of reinforcements to man as actively constructing meaning from his environment. The perception, influence, and interpretation of groups and of how individual motives were influenced by group processes were explored. As the decade ended, motivation theory came to include cognitive, person-centered variables as well as situational, operant influences.

1970s

. . . activism has become agitation and we are bewildered. I think by our inaction, by our feeble solutions to real problems, we have denied the hope that bred that early activism.—George McGovern.

Gallup polls in 1970 and 1975 again asked, "What do you think is the most important problem facing the country today?" In 1970, 27% of respondents said campus unrest and 22% named the Vietnam War; in 1975, 60% identified the high cost of living as the most important problem. Events of this decade include the National Guard killing four students at Kent State University in 1970, the Watergate scandal, the Arab oil embargo of 1973, the 1973-75 recession, the hostage crisis in Teheran, and inflation reaching the highest level in 33 years.

McGovern's comments aptly usher in a decade of *AP* articles that shift from a primary focus on large-scale social reform to greater emphasis on individual processes; from "outer-directedness" to "inner-directedness." In general, psychology's reactionary posture to events in the broader social context that began in the early 60s continued, but with a notable difference. In the 60s, the thrust of much research was to make a new beginning and to effect change; this is not evident in the 70s. Instead, the relevance of social psychology is more questioned than celebrated. Psychology was feeling its limits and was more concerned with studying itself than others. The scientific method as a source of solutions for social problems was in doubt; thus, recommendations and predictions were less tenable. In 1973, Harriet Rheingold wrote that "what marks our times is the painful awareness of not knowing what to do. We seem to drift in lethargy, bewilderment, and near-despair, and we feel powerless to alter events." (p. 43) It is not surprising that the erosion of respect for authority—parental and political—not only continues but strengthens in this decade marked by the resignation of Richard Nixon.

The idea of "too much" emerges. However, rather than research programmatic interventions, psychologists in the 1970s chastised individuals to practice restraint because the depletion of natural resources, pollution, and overpopulation threatened the survival of the planet. So too did nuclear energy and weaponry, television and violence, privilege, and bigotry. William Looft challenged Americans' right to believe they should have "uninterrupted expansion of territory, population, and economic power." He attacked the "psychology of more" embedded in the American way which defined status as unbridled growth and sheer accumulation of things—houses, cars, money, clothes, children, academic degrees, awards, and publications. Looft argued that the "psychology of more" was learned early in life; witness the motivational strategy of encouraging children to compete and compare "who got more As."

In this decade, society was accused of failing children in the areas of mental retardation and mental health. Failure of a child was a societal failure. Jerome Dusek's call for "diversified elementary school curricula responsive to the needs of children" exemplified this orientation. Local schools would serve as the home base for children's health services including mental health practitioners, physicians, dentists, and social workers. Early childhood education would stress the "needs of the child" as well as the "needs of society"—an expansion of the role of the school that continues to fuel social debate.

Understanding differences among groups of individuals also changed in this decade. In the 1960s, views of the individual as a self-actualizing, internally motivated being afforded personal ascriptions for failures of motivation. Rudolf Moos reviewed the first six months of *Psychological Abstracts* and found 82% of the classifiable studies related differences between groups to person-centered variables. In the 70s, psychologists faulted studies that failed to take into account contextual variables, ignoring their role in the inhibition or actualization of personal aspiration. Group differences in the latter models were attributed to environmental constraints and contextual influences.

Psychologists like Herbert Kelman raised concerns about blaming the victim. The emphasis in social research in the early 70s was to view group differences as due to inequities in power, resources, and opportunities rather than to the pathology of deviant individuals and communities. Re-conceptualization of gender in the 70s from inherent biological traits to socialization and opportunity is one example of the power of this shift in perspective in society as well as psychology.

At the close of the decade, David McClelland described disillusionment with psychology. The grandiose plans of transforming society and ameliorating injustice had proved futile. Concerns that "managing motivation" was manipulation of less powerful people and groups had risen. McClelland captured the two interpretations of "psychology's failure." One position stated: "We failed because by and large we tried to change people rather than society. According to this view, man is not responsible for his acts; society makes him what he is. Therefore, if you want to change him, change society. To argue otherwise is to 'blame the victim' when what is needed is a radical change in the conditions that victimized him in the first place." The second position was based on the idea of self-enlightenment and personal responsibility: "You can successfully cultivate your own garden but no one else's." (p. 203)

McClelland postulated a third position which attributed the failure to setting impossibly high and unrealistic goals for social improvement because psychology was *motivated by power* rather than achievement. He argued that the goal of power was simply to have an impact while the goal of achievement was to produce a successful change. He saw America in the 60s as being "power oriented" and compared successful and unsuccessful attempts at intervention. Successful programs were based on a solid understanding of achievement motivation and the development of motivation, not just task competence.

Psychologists were losing ground in helping to right social injustices and inequalities. It was clear that producing change meant managing and changing complex variables encompassing multiple persons and environments. Seymour Feshbach wrote that "it is much easier to tamper with the human body than with the body politic. Social change is especially difficult to effect if . . . it entails modifications in income distribution and social privilege." (p. 453)

The parallels between McClelland's and Feschbach's analyses of the failure of the grand reforms of the 1960s and modern-day calls for educational reform via increased standards are provocative. Critics charge that mandated yet underfunded reforms require all students, and some more than others, to be resilient and self-regulating, to not only "rise above" but to *compensate* for inadequate school conditions, curricula, and lack of fit between school opportunities and a meaningful future.[15] Raising educational standards and implementing high stakes testing without proper investment to enable their achievement raises questions of sheer power motivation. The impact of such reforms may well be powerful, perhaps a resurgence of white flight from cities and public schools; perhaps the continued demise of the public school with corresponding societal willingness to invest public money in private educational enterprises. Each would certainly be a societal impact, but what would each achieve?

PSYCHOLOGICAL CONTEXT

As researchers in the 1970s became more critical of person-centered explanations for motivation, Kurt Lewin and Henry Murray's work was rediscovered.[16] In the early 70s variance in behavior was accounted for by situational and environmental variables and consistency was due to similarity in contexts, not reinforcements, as the behaviorists would have it. By the late 70s, individual processes returned within models of interactionism and reciprocal determinism. In interactionism, individuals who were affected by context in turn generated, selected, or changed the context in which they were immersed. Thus, human interaction was inherently motivational.

Albert Bandura's model of reciprocal determinism at the end of the decade captured how far psychology had come in grappling with person-versus-environment models. Bandura argued that motivation could not be understood by personal determinants such as traits, instincts, and drives nor by environmental determinants such as a description of situational influences. In reciprocal determinism each component was intimately related rather than independent or simply interactive. Individual and environmental variables were defined by each other and could not be described or understood separate from the relationship with each other. In these conceptualizations, environments could have pervasive effects on individuals and individuals could have pervasive effects on environments. Thus, the behavior of an individual both extracted from and created the environment in which the individual was immersed. Reciprocally, the environment effected change in

TABLE 4
AMERICAN PSYCHOLOGIST ARTICLES REVIEWED (1970-1979)

Atkinson, Richard, "Ingredients for a theory of instruction," 27, 1972.

Bandura, Albert, "The self system in reciprocal determinism," 33, 1978.

Bijou, Sidney, "Development in the preschool years: A functional analysis," 30, 1975.

Broadbent, Donald E., "The hidden preattentive processes," 32, 1977.

Bronfenbrenner, Urie, "Toward an experimental ecology of human development," 32, 1977.

Bruner, Jerome S., "Nature and uses of immaturity," 27, 1972.

Buhler, Charlotte, "Basic theoretical concepts of humanistic psychology," 26, 1971.

Caplan, Nathan and Stephen Nelson, "On being useful: The nature and consequences of psychological research on social problems," 28, 1973.

Cole, Michael and Jerome Bruner, "Cultural differences and inferences about psychological processes," 26, 1971.

Dember, William, "Motivation and the cognitive revolution," 29, 1974.

Dillehay, Ronald, "On the irrelevance of classical negative evidence concerning the effect of attitudes on behavior," 28, 1973.

Dirkes, M. Ann, "The role of divergent production in the learning process," 33, 1978.

Dusek, Jerome, "Implications of developmental theory of child mental health," 29, 1974.

Ebel, Robert L., "And still the dryads linger," 29, 1974.

Feschbach, Seymour, "The environment of personality," 33, 1978.

Fischer, Edward, "Birth planning of youth: Concern about overpopulation and intention to limit family size," 10, 1972.

Garner, Wendell R., "The stimulus in information processing," 25, 1970; "The acquisition and application of knowledge: A symbiotic relationship," 27, 1972.

Hamm, Norman, "The politics of empiricism: Research recommendations of the joint commission of mental health of children," 29, 1974.

Haskett, Gary, "Research and early education: Relations among classroom, lab, and society," 28, 1973.

Hoffman, Lois, "Changes in family roles, socialization, and sex differences," 32, 1977.

Kagan, Jerome and Robert Klein, "Cross-cultural perspective on early development," 28, 1973.

Kaplan, Stephen, "The challenge of environmental psychology: A proposal for a new functionalism," 27, 1972.

Kelley, Harold, "The process of causal attribution," 28, 1973.

Kelman, Herbert, "The rights of the subject in social research: An analysis in terms of relative power and legitimacy," 27, 1972.

TABLE 4—*Continued*
AMERICAN PSYCHOLOGIST ARTICLES REVIEWED (1970-1979)

Kendler, Howard, "Environment and cognitive control of behavior," 26, 1971.
Lefcourt, Herbert, "The functions of the illusions of control and freedom," 28, 1973.
Looft, William R., "The psychology of more," 26, 1971.
Lott, Bernice, "Who wants the children? Some relationship among attitudes towards children, parents, and the liberation of women," 28, 1973.
Maehr, Martin, "Culture and achievement motivation," 29, 1974.

McClelland, David, "Testing for competence rather than for intelligence," 28, 1973; "Managing motivation to expand human freedom," 33, 1978.
McGovern, George, "The child's the American future," 25, 1970.
Mischel, Walter, "On the future of personality measurement," 32, 1977.
Moos, Rudolf, "Conceptualizations of home environment," 28, 1973.

Notz, William, "Working motivation and the negative effects of extrinsic rewards: A review with implications for theory and practice," 30, 1975.
Pfaffman, Carl, "The behavioral science model," 25, 1970.
Ramey, Craig, "Children and public policy: A role for psychologists," 29, 1974.
Rheingold, Harriet, "To rear a child," 28, 1973.
Rokeach, Milton, "Long-range experimental modifications of values, attitudes, and behavior," 26, 1971.

Rotter, Julian, "Generalized expectancies for interpersonal trust," 26, 1971.
Segal, Erwin and Roy Lachman, "Complex behavior or higher mental process: Is there a paradigm shift?" 27, 1972.
Sherif, Muzafer, "On the relevance of social psychology," 25, 1970.
Tedeschi, James T., Barry R. Schleuker, and Thomas V. Bonoma, "Cognitive dissonance: Private ratiocination or public spectacle," 26, 1971.
Tiffany, Donald and Phyllis Tiffany, "Social unrest: Powerlessness and/or self-direction?" 28, 1973.
Zigler, Edward and Penelope Trickett, "I.Q., social competence, and evaluation of early childhood intervention programs," 33, 1978.

the individual and motivated selective patterns of responding. The emphasis on humanism and person-centered variables in the 60s and early 70s ended with a capitulation to the environment as the ultimate producer of "internal" motives, or shaper of their expression, via processes of reciprocal determinism. Bandura's model would inform classroom research on achievement motivation in the 1980s and 90s; indeed, Bandura's work dominates conceptions of student learning and motivation today.

Intelligence and Achievement. The heritability debate continued into the 70s and included not only the role of genetics in intelligence, but also in psychopathology and behaviors like aggression. The more dominant theme, however, is the debate over the definition and relevance of intelligence testing. McClelland, for example, criticized the construct of intelligence and objected to the growth of the testing movement throughout the 60s and 70s. He charged that intelligence tests served to discriminate against the lower socioeconomic classes because they prevented access to the mainstream culture, which was necessary in order to perform well on the tests in the first place: a societal Catch-22 in which psychology was a key player.

One part of the intelligence debate that foreshadowed much thinking on the matter in the 1990s was the role of social intelligence in intelligent behavior, not unlike Wechsler's position in the 1950s. Only this time the debate was fueled by challenges to the efficacy of large-scale, federally funded, compensatory education programs. Edward Zigler and Penelope Trickett argued that social competence, defined as successfully meeting societal expectations, should be employed as the measure of success of educational intervention programs like Head Start. Other psychologists argued the issue was more basic. Psychologists continued to recognize the relationship between poverty and educational disadvantage, the impetus for Head Start, and searched for age periods in which intervention would be most successful. Not all psychologists were persuaded. Jerome Kagan and Robert Klein, for example, challenged the notions of "critical periods" for learning, enduring effects of deficient environments, and continuity of abilities.

Continuing a theme of the 60s, psychologists also argued that formal schooling was undoing the gains made in compensatory preschool programs. Gary Haskett, for example, questioned the value of traditional, structured education, especially compared with the more creative and unstructured settings of preschools. He questioned the appropriateness of transitioning preschoolers into elementary schools that required almost the opposite learning methods to which they had been previously exposed—and then measuring for learner continuity.

Changing Conceptions of Environment and Learning. In the 70s, the concept of the "generic" environment faded. The way in which an individual perceived and was oriented to a stimulus determined what the environment was for that individual. Thus, individuals actively "construct" the environment which then determines behavior; they are not simply passive receivers of generic environmental influences that cause them to react in some manner. Stimulus perception or construction of the environment is potentially idiosyncratic and inherently motivational. What a stimulus is for one individual is not necessarily what that stimulus is for another person as was assumed in the 50s. Howard Kendler argued that cognitive characteristics, such as alertness and interest, must be included in trying to understand what motivates individuals towards particular actions. Thus, the action of an individual defining stimulus properties became the subject of study (by, for example, Wendell Garner). The "preattentive process" that described how an individual's attention is caught by one stimulus over another is one example of this research agenda that has influenced classroom instruction. Teachers attempt to orient students to relevant task features within a context that renders such stimuli salient and potentially meaningful, perhaps by cueing prior learning and working within a student's interest domain.

Conceptions of group differences in achievement changed as well. Differences between groups were now viewed as a difference in orientation to and perception of the task at hand. An individual may look less able and motivated and more disadvantaged (a "deficit interpretation") because he or she was not responding to the task in the manner in which the observer had defined it (a "difference interpretation"). Different subcultural groups were predisposed to different interpretations and motivated by different concerns. Thus, cultural differences in performance were a function of orientation to a different set of parameters rather than an incapacity to respond; it was a matter of perspective. Teachers of disadvantaged students were to recognize intellectual difference and seek to transfer skills the child already possessed (i.e., prior "natural" learning) to novel school tasks, rather than assume the child brought neither skill nor context to school. Parallel arguments applied to deviance and alleged lack of motivation. Deviant or deficient motivation was a matter of (whose) goals and (whose) perspective.

Similarly, in contrast to the earlier view that learning is the same whenever, wherever, and with whomever, the specifics of when, where, and with whom became important in understanding what learning was taking place. In the 1970s, much animal research was discarded as irrelevant to human learning. The distinctly human capacity for language and for symbolic representation challenged the behavior models based on drives and needs in animal learning. Unlike humans, animals are unable to use symbolic representation and therefore remain tied to their immediate environment. The study of uniquely human capacities enabled by language such as metacognition, self-direction through self-talk and self-evaluation could not be understood through experiments with rats.

Perception, language, learning, and motivation were interdependent in the "learning theories" of the 1970s. Educational psychologists attempted to integrate these constructs in task research on metacognition and self-regulated learning in the 1980s.[17] Self-talk would become an important learning component in self-regulation theory and the practice of teaching metacognitive strategies. Rather than simply focusing on simply learning content, schools would emphasize helping students understand their own thinking. Self-talk, then, was both a learning and motivational tool.[18] The direct, explicit teaching of learning strategies through the teaching of metacognition would become a focal point of educational reform. Unfortunately, the motivational power of these constructs was not equally realized. Even in the late 1990s, however, self-regulated learning constructs typically are not integrated in teacher education curricula, nor are the effects of social dynamics on them sufficiently examined. Rather, the more dominant interest in teacher preparation has been on the social features, the "with whom" of learning, particularly the effects on student achievement of interpersonal processes within and between small groups— much like the Soviet manipulation of social learning described in *AP* in the 1960s.

Human Motivation. Conceptualizations of motivation predictably emphasized internal processes, stimulus and task properties, and contextual influences. In the beginning of the decade, trait and traditional behavioral models were challenged. Explanations of motivation came to include a sensitivity to what individuals bring to a task as well as an understanding of how the task and the environment structured the individual. By the end of the decade, concepts of reciprocal determinism appeared, emphasizing the co-construction of individuals and the environment.

The locus of motivational influences steadily moved away from the external (where influences impinge on a passive organism) to the internal. Humans are proactive, self-realizing organisms whose natural inclination is to be active and motivated. They are adaptive systems who structure their environments and make them livable through the processes of perception, prediction, evaluation, and action. Even so, context counts. Martin Maehr argued for the importance of context and cultural relativity in eliciting and defining achievement motivation. Teaching practices and curricula should *bring out* a response rather than *establish* a response: Learners must be actively involved in the learning process. Psychologists in the 1970s again argued against what was the dominant instructional model of the decade: direct instruction of facts and skills to passive recipients. Instead, teachers should promote divergent thinking processes to enhance creativity and independent thinking as well as academic learning goals. For example, Ann Dirkes writes that when these goals are formulated, students "use ideas in new ways and become impatient with extensive replication." Thus, new learning goals generate new motivations and therefore create new (and perhaps more) management problems and opportunities.

The development of humanistic psychology, information processing theory, and concepts of intentionality in the 70s all reflected the premise that a motivated state was basic to human nature. Cognitive constructs such as dissonance and imbalance motivated individuals to act in a certain manner. Dissonance motivated individuals to think about why they "didn't feel right." Rather than performing actions to fulfill needs or reduce drives, individuals engaged in behavior to maintain a consistent view of the self. Edward Fischer used internal processes of self-esteem and disposition towards others (interpersonal trust and authoritarianism) to understand and predict overt behavior. Interpersonal trust and the stress of its violation would become major motivational themes in the next decade.

In contrast to the 1950s when the individual had no choice but to respond to a stimulus, in the 1970s the individual was deciding not only to respond or not but also to what. Many internal processes came to be viewed as motivational influences. For example, unobservable cognitive variables like attitudes motivated certain actions. So, too, did beliefs and ideas. Herbert Lefcourt, like Rogers in 1947, found that individuals were more motivated when they were performing under conditions in which they thought they had more control. Locus of control became an important predictor of achievement. William Dember argued that religious and political ideals, for example, could be powerful motivators and even override biological needs.

In classroom research, motivation to learn was the result of the merger between internal characteristics, curriculum materials, and instructional practices. Richard Atkinson advocated computer-assisted instruction to supplement normal classroom teaching. Items to be learned were "response sensitive," that is, selected on the basis of previous performance to optimize achievement and motivation. Parallel to the conceptualization of the individual as adaptive to the environment, optimal instruction was adaptive to the learner. And, of special interest to teachers, adaptive instruction rendered motivation moot because "when the instructional process is truly adaptive the student's progress is sufficient reward in its own right."

The decline of behaviorist interpretations of learning and motivation was also evident in the emergence of research on extrinsic rewards and their impact on intrinsic motivation. Rewards were not generically good and reinforcing. Since individuals were already in a state of being intrinsically motivated it was not necessary, and in fact it could be harmful, to offer rewards. Research on the effects of extrinsic rewards on work motivation by William Notz paralleled research by Mark Lepper and David Greene[19] on children's learning and creativity. Extrinsic rewards lowered motivation for tasks that were intrinsically motivating.

The integration of research on the motivational costs of rewards and Atkinson's response-sensitive model of adaptive instruction had provocative implications for educators. Students had intrinsic motivation to learn and to complete tasks if instructional practices were a good match to their level of skill and development. Intrinsic motivation would propel the student along through increasingly challenging (i.e., response-sensitive) learning tasks. Failure to learn would be due to poor motivation, caused by inappropriate task progression (i.e., response-insensitive) *or* the interference of extrinsic reward. By the late 80s, lack of sufficient intrinsic motivation would be blamed on an overly indulgent society and parenting style that eroded the child's natural motivational state—two culprits that fomented student rebellion in the 1960s. The other 60s culprits—individuals as victim and/or justified crusader—are noticeably absent.

The relationship between interpersonal processes and intrapersonal perception also functioned as motives in the 1970s. Influences of the group on the individual's sense of self were defined as motives in concepts like social approval. Harold Kelley viewed social perception and self-perception as motivational constructs. According to Kelley, the goal of attribution theory was to help explain and predict how individuals would react to their social environment at specific times and places. As the decade progressed, attribution theory also became important in social rules for allocating responsibility, assigning blame, delivering punishment, and withholding redemption.[20]

In summary, in the 1970s psychologists portrayed humans as striving to maintain consistency and adaptability. Curriculum reform called for the student's natural receptivity to certain tasks. Instructional practice, especially in early childhood education, stressed using the child's natural tendencies and motivations to achieve learning. In the face of the complexity and the magnitude of resources needed to make meaningful change, psychology moved toward a theme of self-responsibility and self-efficacy. The question became how to get the individual to thrive and remain motivated despite environmental constraints or in-dulgences. As the 80s approached, concepts of inoculation (hardiness), volition, self-regulation, and prevention would take hold.

1980s

"If you can tolerate high levels of arousal, go for big wins; if you can't, go for small wins"—Karl Weick

Gallup polls taken in 1980 and 1985 again asked, "What do you think is the most important problem facing the country today?" In 1980 the answer was foreign policy (44%) and the high cost of living (39%); in 1985, the threat of war (23%) and unemployment (21%). Events dur-ing the decade include Muslim terrorists in Lebanon killing 240 United States Marines and the first trillion-dollar budget submitted to Con-gress. This is also the decade of increasing concerns about covert in-volvement in international affairs, including the Iran-Contra Scandal.

The *American Psychologist* in the 1980s, with an average volume length of 1,366 pages, offers a diffuse array of social concerns and is replete with competing assertions about what matters and who defines it—popular culture, social policy, practitioners, scientists, or pseudo-scientists. Questions of pervasive personal and social change mark the decade; only this time there is even less optimism than in previous decade. Karl Weick embodies this change, contributing the quotation that captured the spirit of the 1960s ("reject nothing, but reorder all") *and* the one for the 1980s.

In the 1980s, opportunities were just more problems. International problems fueled *AP* debates on arms proliferation, nuclear war, the negotiation of peace in other nations, and the need for Americans to learn more about their world. National and local concerns in *AP* in-cluded increases in crime and homelessness and the viability of work, education, and our standing in the global marketplace.

Senator Edward Kennedy identified three major challenges of the decade: (a) the cost of health care (and unhealthy behavior), (b) con-tinuing high unemployment, and (c) the crisis in education (as evi-denced by cross-national comparisons in mathematics and science achievement). We examine *AP* articles related to health care to illus-trate what seems a typical transformation phenomenon of the decade: from national financial crisis to societal problem, to individual respon-sibility, accountability and, ultimately, blame.

Kennedy asserted that health costs were bankrupting and imperil-ing our society. Health promotion was key to health cost reduction;

holding institutions and individuals accountable for lack of health was part of that package. Just-world thinking permeated conceptions of disease and health promotion. A disease that previously had been a tragedy became a personal responsibility: now lung cancer was your own fault. We argue that this progression from societal cost to individual blame foreshadows the transformation of societal attitudes toward and treatment of students later in the decade to the present, when *failed* students are to blame for failure.

In the 1980s, demands for "wellness" behavior merged with attempts to control individual health-threatening behavior in both physical and mental health domains. One result of the now primary role of life-style in the prevention of (and thus, responsibility for) costly diseases and accidents was that "private" individual behavior was not so private or benign anymore. Social prevention and remediation programs targeting obesity, smoking cessation, and drug and alcohol abuse proliferated and typically failed. Stanley Schachter maintained that the behavior change picture was not as dismal as decades of failed social programs would indicate. "Self-cure" of smoking, drug use, and obesity, he argued, were relatively common: Those who can, help themselves.

Academic psychologists were not totally absent from the self-help scene. Gerald Rosen reported the work of the APA's Task Force on Self-Help Therapies, which concluded that commercial rather than professional standards dominated the self-help market. Rosen named names, contrasting well-known researchers' actual findings with the "absurd," exaggerated, and unresearched claims of their popular do-it-yourself treatment books. Even so, self-help literature, helpful or not, fueled societal demands for personal control: Just do it.

This is the personal control and health belief context in which the Acquired Immune Deficiency Syndrome (AIDS) emerged. AIDS already was considered an epidemic in 1984. A special Issue of *AP* in 1984 was devoted to conceptualizing AIDS in terms of psychological/behavioral factors with a focus on prevention through changing individual and group behavior given the absence of effective treatments or cure. Concerns with sexual exploitation, aggression, sexuality, and "wellness," particularly of adolescents, pervaded the decade. The period of adolescence had lengthened, in part due to an earlier average age of menarche (16 years old 150 years ago, 12 and ½ in 1989) and in part a function of a longer and more complex transition to adulthood. Psychologists studied preventive interventions that might shield adolescents from unhealthy behavior with both near-term damage (e.g., STDs, accidents) and long-term outcomes (e.g., cardiovascular disease) that narrow life options. Programs were designed to restrict adolescent risk-taking (e.g., Drug Abuse Resistance Education, Postponing Sexual Involvement). Like the adult intervention models grounded in social learning theory that preceded them, these programs also would fail.[21]

Ironically, help-yourself extended to learning to be a victim in the 1980s. Unemployment and job uncertainty go hand-in-hand with homelessness and crime. The President's Task Force on Victims of Crime and the report of the first APA Task Force on the Victims of Crime and Violence (1985) conveyed the pervasive and crippling fear among citizens of random yet omnipresent senseless acts of violence. The focus of the special section was on the consequences of crime and how victims overcome the stress of their experience. The Task Force concluded that help was not always helpful; indeed help can make matters worse, creating a "second wound" of revictimization through callous or inadvertent inattention. The government's role in decreasing crime (or unemployment or homelessness) in the first place was not the focus of these reports. Instead, the goal was for citizens to learn how to cope with the *reality* of crime and its effects: Just get over it.

Finally, subgroup interests, demands, and power(lessness) were part of the decade. Along with the organizational power of the AARP (originally "retired persons") and the reality that the boomer generation was getting on in years, their parents were living longer, and women's place was not necessarily at home caring for them, aging emerged as an important area of study. A special section on "Aging in America: Roles for psychology" was included in the Public Forum series. Skinner poignantly noted that the problem in old age is not so much the having of ideas, but having them "when you can use them." He called for the design of a "prosthetic environment," in the spirit of eyeglasses and hearing aids, so that "in spite of reduced biological capacities, behavior will be relatively free of aversive consequences and abundantly reinforced."

In marked contrast to adults' concerns with their own welfare and future, based in part on the international competitiveness of our students, youth were ignored, if not "assaulted," in much public policy. Ruby Takanishi et al. decried the changing mood of the country, the *reduction* in federal expenditures for most social programs since 1979, and the shift in program responsibility to the states, which disproportionately affected youth, the "forgotten constituency." Attempts by the federal government to restrict the rights of adolescents occurred simultaneously with federal attempts in 1982 to "liberalize" child labor laws for 14- and 15-year-olds, allowing younger children and longer hours even as adult unemployment was a continuing national crisis.

Frustration with the seemingly senseless, mean-spirited, and ultimately culturally defeating policies toward children and the adverse effects on them was consistent throughout the decade. Even so, psychologists attempted to integrate research with informed policy for children and families. For example, research on development, working parents, and day care was used to inform suggestions for infant care and workplace policies for parents. Research on adolescent competence and development led to policy statements protecting adolescent autonomy and privacy rights and contextual arguments in understanding adolescent adaptation and mental health. Policy research on school desegregation sought to disentangle beliefs from results, no matter how disappointing, to better design social reforms. Authors struggled to delineate intervention models even if complex and uncertain.

PSYCHOLOGICAL CONTEXT

The "me" decade, as it has come to be known, was complicated. Three themes in the decade exist in parallel form in society in general and psychology in particular. First, the high stakes and immediacy of societal problems raised the level of arousal for psychologists as well as citizens. Psychologists study the detrimental effects of high arousal— for example, decrements in learning and efficacy of problem solving— they do not necessarily escape them. Psychology was ill prepared to "solve" society's problems, let alone in a social context of "benign neglect" and a political context of denied funding.

Second, distrust pervaded psychology as well as society. Psychologists struggled with the apparent limits of the grand theories, the validity of the empirical literature, and the motives of individual researchers and readers. Gone were simple if-then formulations, troika metaphors, and isomorphic artificial intelligence simulations to guide understanding of self and other. Instead, the reader was confronted with theories that challenged what we "think" we know. "New" theories of historical and contextual mediation spoke of "making fact and fables"; elaborations of reciprocal determinism and self-efficacy made it increasingly difficult to locate causes of human behavior; and theories of personal traits, individual interpretation, and chance events delineated why change cannot be understood, let alone engineered.

Analytical complexity does not always inform action; indeed it can render action futile. Timing matters, and the coincidence of intense societal need and heightened theoretical complexity was unfortunate. Intense societal need demands timely action; theoretical complexity demands time to determine action. One effect of this juxtaposition in psychology in the 1980s appears to have been an action paralysis or "collective inefficacy" too easily justified by the relative lack of research funding. A second effect was intense interest in emotion, especially and not surprisingly, stress as one product of unrealized efficacy and daily hassles. The relations among stress and health, pathology, inhibition, and particularly aggression were well represented throughout the 1980s. The considerable interest in aggression also included the more usual suspects: television and real-world violence in the streets and at home.

In addition, "problems" or worse had been found in the empirical literature. Cyril Burt, twice published in *AP* (1958 and 1972), either made "well-intentioned but sloppy mistakes" or deliberately "cooked" his identical twin study data, and J. B. Watson's case of "Little Albert" apparently was more a story than a case. Although Watson's behavior may seem less extreme than Burt's, the off-camera manipulations were not. Franz Samelson raises provocative questions about the failures of the scientific community to monitor, critically review, and replicate research and to recognize the social pressures that impinge on researchers. Perhaps the scientific enterprise was not so objective after all, an observation that raised difficult questions about just what *is* known, because of whom and how.

Personal responsibility emerged as a central construct in psychology as well as society in the 1980s. Some psychologists questioned researchers' motives rather than (or in addition to) their data or interpretation. For example, controversies surrounded the Westinghouse Study of Head Start. Victor Cicirelli charged that critics who advocated educational interventions mostly did not like the findings (somewhat negative) and thus sought to discredit the work. In contrast, others seeking to eliminate Head Start misinterpreted the study, inappropriately claiming it proved Head Start a failure and poor children unaffected by help.

Charges of political motivation in "scientific" research and psychological constructs occur throughout the decade; consider "On the politics of psychological constructs: Stop the bandwagon, I want to get off": So did many educators. Even as educational psychologists were undertaking research more relevant to real children in real schools, the theoretical and contextual complexities of their efforts were swamped by the political realities weighing on educators. Educational politics of the era were about the bottom line, not the idiosyncratic constructions of individual learners engaged in tasks of intrinsic interest. Unfortunately, the mismatch between psychological advances in learning, cognition, and motivation and societal restrictions on what it means to learn would do little to improve "the process of education" for students; some students were denied more than others.[22]

A third theme was a defensive self-reliance that was also confrontational. Milton Rokeach and Sandra Ball-Rokeach documented changes in American values from 1968-1981: the most dramatic changes were a fluctuating but ultimate decrease in the value of social equality and increases in "personal values emphasizing a comfortable life, a sense of accomplishment, and excitement." This pattern is consistent with Spence's argument that the Protestant work ethic (and by extension achievement motivation) had undergone successive permutations in modern America that include intrinsic meaningfulness, material deservedness, self-actualization and, ultimately, unbridled individualism or the preeminence of personal entitlement over the common good. One mantra of the "me" generation emerged in psychology as in society but with a slightly more ironic twist: "Help yourself." Indeed, the presidential address at the APA convention in 1987 argued the benefits of enlightened self-interest and strategic personal responsibility for enhancing personal well-being and thereby contributing to the common good.

Defending Assessment. Psychology also would play an instrumental role in Kennedy's second challenge of the decade, the "crisis" in education, specifically in individual aptitude and achievement testing and school accountability. The Nairn/Nader Report in 1980 attacking the Educational Testing Service fueled the testing debate; *A Nation at Risk* ignited the school quality debate. The Special Issue on Testing: Concepts, Policy, Practice, and Research was in response to continuing societal distrust of conceptions of intelligence, tests, test bias, and their use among those social groups who were not advantaged by them. John Garcia succinctly warned "that logic is often enslaved by motive" in the field of mental testing where professional authority sets the rules. Authority was still suspect and psychology would continue to defend testing practices and refine definitions of intelligence and achievement throughout the decade.

Defending the Public School. Societal challenges to psychological conceptions of student learning, intelligence, and achievement were played out in the popular press. As educational psychologists turned to more-process-than-product orientations of learning, thinking, and intelligence and the learning and motivational implications of the multicultural realities of American schools were explored, society was demanding concrete outcomes to facilitate student and teacher accountability. To many citizens (and educators) psychology was taking the "learning" out of learning in classrooms; for some, psychology also was replacing "American" with "multicultural," but it would be educators and students in American schools who would be held accountable even so.

APA published articles relevant to classroom learning and instruction throughout the 1980s, but attention focused on the politics of education occurred in 1983. APA's response to *A Nation at Risk* was a Special Issue: Psychological Science and Education. Well-known educators and educational psychologists addressed calls for education reform (e.g., career ladders, professional standards, and testing for teachers). Articles spanned behavioral, cognitive, and social aspects of teacher and student learning within the context of "real-world complexity." The study of differences organized the special issue: differences among learners in talent, age, and gender; in type and complexity of learning; in particulars of various subject matter; and in adapting instruction for potential interactions among them. This special issue demonstrated the active attention to learning in schools which had been missing yet called for in earlier decades, although earlier themes are evident as well. For example, the issue includes articles on gifted and talented children, in which Terman and Cox are still the standards of comparison, mathematics learning, science education, and military training. Two articles are of particular note. Thomas Good and Rhona Weinstein argued that schools matter because they make a difference, and Jere Brophy argued that teachers matter because they influence students. That these arguments needed to be made at all provides some insight into the social climate of distrust of institutions and those who work within them that pervaded the decade. It is even more troubling that such arguments needed be made when data on access to quality schools and upper-level courses in mathematics and science were used to explain the gaps between black and white achievement and gender differences in mathematics achievement. In hindsight, perhaps most troubling was the argument that did not occur. Educators did not note the hypocrisy of the government's simultaneous calls for longer and more school days and also longer and more workdays for children. The result was an insidious double bind made even more indecent because of differing vulnerabilities among youth. The lack of integrity in societal care for children in the 1980s that continues to the present is staggering.

Defining Motivation. The work of Erich Fromm, who died in 1980, provides a useful framework to organize selected theoretical arguments on motivation in the 1980s.[23] Fromm conceptualized human freedom as a lifelong dialectical struggle among our human potential, our animal nature, and social forces. The human struggle provokes anxiety and fear; the struggle to understand the human struggle is less dramatic but stressful even so. Mainstream cognitive psychologists in the 1980s, continuing the developments of the 1970s, mostly gave up the three-pronged integration that characterizes neo-psychoanalytic approaches and focused their attention on "uniquely human" characteristics, for example, symbolic representation and self-evaluation, and/or the socialization that affords, hinders, or engineers their expression.

One result was a conceptualization of human motivation that no longer included biological or unconscious motives, which had been fundamental constructs in the behavioral and psychoanalytic traditions. Emotions, wants, and needs became cognitively based: humans think about how they feel and what they want. For Hazel Markus and Paula Nurius, for example, the ego became "possible selves," the cognitive components of "hopes, fears, goals, and threats" that inform how people think about their future. The nature of the (temporal) relationship between cognition and emotion was debated, and cognitive processes unique to humans—values, interests, beliefs, expectancies and the like (measured by parallel cognitive instrumentation)—were presumed to encase human motivation. Biological processes were recast in terms of development and aging within a culture; animal experimentation need not, and for many did not, apply. McClelland argued powerfully, but apparently not persuasively, against the mainstream. His arguments frame the following discussion.

Tracing the basic findings of general behavior theory, McClelland reaffirmed that what an animal can do is not the same as what it does. This distinction is critical because it delineates learning from motivation (which are blurred by Skinner). Clark Hull's original and elaborated formulas are standard fare in educational psychology. The original formula—the tendency to make a response is a function of drive strength (the motive part) times habit strength (the learning part)—was expanded to include environmental incentives. The result: sEr (the tendency to act) = D (motive or drive strength) × sHr (skill or habit strength) × K (incentive in the environment). The particulars of the formula are important. McClelland documents the validity of multiplicative relationships in the formula as asserted by Hull: if *any* of the variables is equal to zero, they predict zero tendency to act.

In 1964, John Atkinson redefined Hull's variables in cognitive terms around achievement tasks and relabeled the entire equation "motivation" so that all the variables were now motivational and cognitive, and there was no longer a term that referred only to aroused motives or needs. One effect of this reformulation was to set in motion decades of motivational research that ironically is much less integrative than Atkinson's programmatic research on motivation and operant behavior and much less interested in the fluidity or stream of motivated activity. Subsequent researchers not only substituted reported attitude for spontaneous behavior but also opted for discrete events rather than motivational movements.

Atkinson's approach to the study of motivation was mostly retained, particularly in the sociocognitive approach that emphasized the individual student's cognitive mediation of achievement events, eventually in real (not simulated) classroom settings. Carol Dweck, for example, studied linkages among students' theories of intelligence ("entity" or fixed and "incremental" or malleable), goal orientations for achievement (performance or learning), personal confidence (high or low), and achievement behavior (mastery-oriented or helpless). Her research model supports the promotion of student belief in incremental intelligence and adoption of learning goals to sustain mastery-oriented behavior in which, independent of personal confidence, students seek challenge and remain persistent. Beliefs about cognition influence cognition. Atkinson's focus on individual differences also provided a common ground for emerging research on multicultural differences in trait motivation (individual, culturally mediated) and state motivation (situational manipulations) and their interactive effects on the achievement behavior of minorities.

Fromm and many others would argue that something essentially human was lost in the cognitive revision of motivation theory. McClelland documented that motivated action was one of the losses. He reported data showing that without an aroused motive human value (or interest or expectancy) does not lead to action. If a need is aroused, however, value then determines in important ways the direction of human action. McClelland's arguments and data have profound implications for motivation in the classroom. For example, let's say that educators hope to motivate students by focusing on things that students value (the incentive part that is most open to environmental manipulation). The Hull formula would suggest that a focus on environmental incentives only promotes the tendency to study (the student action the educator hopes to increase) if the student has the motive or need to learn *and* sufficient knowledge and skill. Several hypotheses could follow. Let's focus first on the motive piece.

Hull's formula predicts students will not study in the absence of motive. One could argue (and many do) that social promotion inhibits students' need to achieve. Many believe that students do not study because they do not fear grade retention; thus, retention could be hypothesized to increase study because it increases fear. Another hypothesis might assert that the lack of a perceived relationship between school learning and meaningful work fails to arouse the motive or need to learn. In this scenario, instantiation of a convincing relationship between high school graduation and ultimate occupation (and income) could be hypothesized to increase the need to achieve and, therefore, increase study behavior. A third hypothesis might focus on the student whose needs are fully met. In this case, increasing the scarcity of satisfaction might trigger motive and thereby increase study behavior. Each hypothesis addresses the absence-of-motive part of the Hull equation and thus the absence of study behavior in the presence of environmental incentives.

A different set of hypotheses emerges, however, if we focus on the "habit" piece. If the habit or skill variable in Hull's formula is deficient, so, too, is the tendency to study *even if* motives and incentives are present. Learning allows motivation. A student who fears retention becomes a more complex (and potentially even more tragic) case. No amount of need to achieve, or acquired fear or anxiety, or desire for the good life can compensate for a "habit" value of zero. Recall as well caveats of an earlier era: too much motive or arousal can be detrimental to learning and thinking. It's a matter of optimal amounts and therein lies the difficulty in implementation. Recall as well that learning is also a matter of opportunity and quality[24] and that absent or deficient instruction requires student compensation if learning is to occur. Increased student tendency to study in itself does not, by definition, equal increased student test scores even in optimal instructional settings, let alone in deficient ones. Our retained student may have failed and have been failed.

Another outcome of the cognitive revolution in motivation was the rise of rational, a-rational, and "boundedly rational" personal constructs and behavior in mainstream research and theory. Daniel Kahneman and Amos Tversky, for example, presented a theory of cognitive and "psychophysical" determinants for human decisions that were not predicted by decision theory, but were nonetheless rational (i.e., predictable) even if wrong. Attributional approaches to understanding motivation were based upon a rational phenomenology in which the meaning of success and failure was logical in theory and in instrumentation: Students feel good about success; bad about failure. Attribution theory of achievement motivation initially was based upon identifying believed causes of success and failure. Discrete beliefs (i.e., ability, effort, task difficulty, luck) were subsequently studied for underlying multidimensional judgments, initially causality, stability, and control. Relationships among cognitive attributional processes, reported affect, and behavior within personal and interpersonal dynamics were explored throughout the decade. In much attributional research at the end of the decade, motivation and judgment became synonymous and civilized. Motivation was now even less about motive and more about cultural rules of personal responsibility and interpersonal exchange, a position we will elaborate in the next section.

The more psychoanalytic writings of the decade apparently did not influence educational psychologists or practitioners. Yet provocative and potentially relevant articles appeared. Anthony Greenwald wrote of the resistance of the "totalitarian ego" to change whether or not change is "good for you." Roy Schafer analyzed undercurrents of motivational dynamics in "The pursuit of failure and the idealization of unhappiness." He reminded readers that not all motivational dynamics are as they appear or "should be" and that personal motivation has a past as well as a present. Similarly, Asher Pacht suggested that perfection can be not only undesirable but detrimental, certainly not a mainstream point of view in cognitive approaches to motivation.

In short, one result of the cognitive revolution in motivation is a focus on the future within an a-historical present juxtaposed with a lessened value of the here and now. It is no wonder that cognitive motivational theories were ineffective in grappling with desires of the flesh, as evidenced in the failed social intervention programs of the decade. Cognitive motivational theories also are difficult to translate into classrooms. Yet, it is in the here and now of classrooms that students build on their past, *and* learn and love, *and* fantasize and plan realistically and optimistically (hopefully) for their future. If we assert that cognition is everything, perhaps we risk becoming too uniquely human, valuing delay of gratification and a future orientation focused on goals and strategic planfulness at the expense of (rather than integrated with) the pleasure and the pain in the here-and-now of life. It seems these motivational struggles are relevant to a more complete, and thus potentially more enabling, understanding of student motivation. That we seek to understand student motivation within societal institutions which we *require them to attend* suggests we work a little harder. Jersild comes to mind.

Maintaining Motivation. The 1970s' questions of how to get the individual to thrive and remain motivated despite environmental constraints or indulgences emerged in the 1980s as questions of apathy and agency. Not surprisingly, each is difficult to define, and there is also the matter of emphasis. For example, Skinner defined apathy as individual satiation and his notion of agency was essentially acting out. His apparent interpretation of the "me decade" was that it was possible to have too many goods—not a small concession. Then he gets to the point:

Where thousands of millions of people in other parts of the world cannot do many of the things they want to do, hundreds of millions in the West do not want to do many of the things they can do. In winning the struggle for freedom and the pursuit of happiness, the West has lost its inclination to act. (p. 572)

Skinner might be disgusted but, characteristically, he located the root of the problem in cultural practices that eroded principles of reinforcement (bifurcating and prioritizing pleasurable over strengthening effects). His top two culprits were practices that alienate workers from the consequences of their work and helping those who could help themselves. Marxist arguments on the first are well known. On the second, Skinner maintained that unwarranted help deprived individuals of reinforcing consequences that would shape and maintain useful behavior and the opportunities to acquire those consequences. Skinner combined the effects of the two practices, alienating work and unwarranted help, to assert:

. . . people who avoid labor and have things done for them escape from many aversive consequences, but beyond a certain point they deprive themselves of strengthening consequences as well . . . The effect can be corrected by restoring more strengthening contingencies. Once that is understood, our problem may be simpler than we think. It is much easier to change contingencies of reinforcement than to restore will, refill a reservoir of psychic energy, or strengthen nerves. (p. 570, 572)

Skinner addressed education and teacher management of student motivation more directly. He asserted that the "task of education is to build a repertoire of behavior that will eventually have reinforcing consequences in the daily and professional life of the student." Teachers are part of student life, either through modeling or reinforcing consequences; historically most of the latter have been negative, "if not the birch rod or cane, then criticism or failure." Skinner described three by-products of punishment: escape (truancy), counterattack (vandalism), and stubborn inaction, and he called instead for teachers to use unconditioned reinforcers of success and progress. In some sense, Skinner's by-products of punishment seem more moderate representations of student behavior that educators find worrisome only a dozen years later. Truancy does not seem as bad as dropping out; vandalism against property is less terrifying than assaults on peers and teachers with deadly weapons, and stubborn inaction sounds thankfully silent. It is ironic that Skinner linked these student outcomes to punishment by authority in the same analysis in which he included Marxist conceptions of worker alienation. Research on work, employment, and unemployment in the same decade noted the motivational dynamics of workers striking against redundancies on the job. The Skinnerian approach to programmed instruction and the reinforcing properties of practice arguably fit under the same umbrella, each even more punitive if not done well.

A second approach to the analysis of apathy and agency emerged from articles more based in social psychology. Social dynamics and interpersonal relationships were consistent themes throughout the decade, including concerns with particular effects of other persons on an individual, issues of social bonding, and interpersonal relations and their developmental significance. Helping behavior, not surprisingly, emerged as a central theme; however, simple acts of altruism were not so simple in the 1980s. Questions raised included the tensions between apathy and altruism, altruism by one and manipulation by another, and the recurring theme of helpfulness or harm even so. For example, the first article of the first volume, "Interpersonal trust, trustworthiness, and gullibility" is all about to be or not to be a chump juxtaposed with the personal and societal costs of distrust.

The dynamics of helping get quite complicated when extending or withholding help is cast as a potential solution to a cognitive representation of a problem. The interaction of multiple variables informs whether helping is appropriate. *AP* articles in the 1980s suggest that others may want to help or to be helped; and help may be deserved or not and helpful or not. The problem solver considers the presence or absence of requests for help with (a) judgments of deservingness or

TABLE 5

AMERICAN PSYCHOLOGIST ARTICLES REVIEWED (1980-1989)

Albee, George, "Preventing psychopathology and promoting human potential," 37, 1982.

Allen, Bem, "After the missiles: Sociopsychological effects of nuclear war," 40, 1985.

Anastasi, Anne, "Evolving trait concepts," 38, 1983.

Atkinson, John, "Studying personality in the context of an advanced motivational psychology," 36, 1981.

Averill, James, "Studies on anger and aggression: Implications for theories of emotion," 38, 1983.

Banaji, Mahzarin and Robert Crowder, "The bankruptcy of everyday memory," 44, 1989.

Bandura, Albert, "The psychology of chance encounters and life paths," 37, 1982a; "Self-efficacy mechanism in human agency," 37, 1982b; "Human agency in social cognitive theory," 44, 1989.

Batchelor, Walter, "AIDS: A public health and psychological emergency," 39, 1984.

Baumrind, Diana, "New directions in socialization research," 35, 1980.

Belmont, John, "Cognitive strategies and strategic learning: The socio-instructional approach," 44, 1989.

Birren, James, "Aging in America: Roles for psychology," 38, 1983.

Blight, James, "Toward a policy-relevant psychology of avoiding nuclear war: Lessons for psychologists from the Cuban missile crisis," 42, 1987.

Brickman, Philip et al., "Models of helping and coping," 37, 1982.

Brophy, Jere, "Teacher influences on student achievement," 41, 1986.

Buss, Arnold, "Personality as traits," 44, 1989.

Carey, Susan, "Cognitive science and science education," 41, 1986.

Carroll, John and John Horn, "On the scientific basis of ability testing," 36, 1981.

Chiles, Lawton, "The federal budget and the new federalism: Trends affecting mental health," 37, 1982.

Cicirelli, Victor, "The misinterpretation of the Westinghouse study: A reply to Zigler and Berman," 8, 1984.

Cohen, Sheldon et al., "Physiological, motivational, and cognitive effects of aircraft noise on children: Moving from the laboratory to the field," 35, 1980.

Cole, Nancy S., "Bias in testing," 36, 1981.

Cook, Stuart, "Experimenting on social issues: The case of school desegregation," 40, 1985.

Deutsch, Francine, "Calling a freeze on 'stress wars': There is hope for adaptational outcomes," 41, 1986.

Dohrenwend, Bruce P. and Patrick E. Shrout, "Hassles in the conceptualization and measurement of life stress variables," 40, 1985.

Dweck, Carol S., "Motivational processes affecting learning," 41, 1986.

Edney, Julian, "The commons problem: Alternative perspectives, 35, 1980.

TABLE 5—*Continued*
AMERICAN PSYCHOLOGIST ARTICLES REVIEWED (1980-1989)

Emery, Robert, "Family violence," 44, 1989.
Eron, Leonard, "Prescription for reduction of aggression," 35, 1980.

Folkins, Carlyle and Wesley Sime, "Physical fitness training and mental health," 36, 1981.
Frijda, Nieo, "The laws of emotion," 43, 1988.
Gagné, Robert, "Learning outcomes and their effects: Useful categories of human performance," 39, 1984.
Garcia, John, "The logic and limits of mental aptitude testing," 36, 1981.
Gerard, Harold, "School desegregation: The social science role," 38, 1983.

Glaser, Robert, "The future of testing: A research agenda for cognitive psychology and psychometrics," 36, 1981; "Instructional psychology," 37, 1982; "Education and thinking: The role of knowledge," 39, 1984.
Glaser, Robert and Lloyd Bond, "Testing: Concepts, policy, practice, and research (Introduction to special issue)," 36, 1981.
Glaser, Robert and Ruby Takanishi, "Introduction: Creating a knowledge base for education: Psychology's contributions and prospects," 41, 1986.

Good, Thomas and Rhona Weinstein, "Schools make a difference: Evidence, criticisms, and new directions," 41, 1986.
Greeno, James, "Psychology of learning, 1960-1980: One participant's observations," 35, 1980; "A perspective on thinking," 44, 1989.
Greenwald, Anthony, "The totalitarian ego: Fabrication and revision of personal history," 35, 1980.
Halff, Henry, James Hollan, and Edwin Hutchins, "Cognitive science and military training," 41, 1986.

Hamburg, David and Ruby Takanishi, "Preparing for life: The critical transition of adolescence," 44, 1989.
Hartup, Willard, "Social relationships and their developmental significance," 44, 1989.
Herrington, Lois Haight, "Victims of crime: Their plight, our response," 40, 1985.
Hobfoll, Stevan, "Conservation of resources: A new attempt at conceptualizing stress," 44, 1989.
Horowitz, Frances and Marion O'Brien, "Gifted and talented children: State of knowledge and directions for research," 41, 1986.

Huston, Aletha, Bruce Watkins, and Dale Kunkel, "Public policy and children's television," 44, 1989.
Interdivisional Committee on Adolescent Abortion, "Adolescent abortion: Psychological and legal issues," 42, 1987.
Jahoda, Marie, "Work, employment, and unemployment: Values, theories, and approaches in social research," 36, 1981.
Janis, Irving, "The role of social support in adherence to stressful decisions," 38, 1983.
Jones, Lyle, "White-Black achievement differences: The narrowing gap," 39, 1984.

TABLE 5—*Continued*

American Psychologist Articles Reviewed (1980-1989)

Kagan, Jerome, "Temperamental contributions to social behavior," 44, 1989.

Kahneman, Daniel and Amos Tversky, "Choices, values, and frames," 39, 1984.

Kelman, Herbert, "Conversations with Arafat: A social-psychological assessment of the prospects for Israeli-Palestinian peace," 38, 1983.

Kennedy, Edward, "The challenges before us," 39, 1984.

Kennedy, Steven, James Scheirer, and Anne Rogers, "The price of success: Our monocultural science," 39, 1984.

Koop, Everette C., "Report of the Surgeon General's workshop on pornography and public health," 42, 1987.

Latane, Bibb, "The psychology of social impact," 36, 1981.

Lazarus, Richard, "Thoughts on the relation between emotions and cognitions," 37, 1982.

Lazarus, Richard et al., "Stress and adaptational outcomes: The problem of confounded measures," 40, 1985.

Lepper, Mark, "Microcomputers in education: Motivational and social issues," 40, 1985.

Lepper, Mark and Jean-Luc Gurtner, "Children and computers: Approaching the twenty-first century," 44, 1989.

Lerner, Barbara, "The minimum competence testing movement: Social, scientific, and legal implications," 36, 1981.

Linn, Robert, "Admissions testing on trial," 37, 1982.

Linz, Daniel, Edward Donnerstein, and Steven Penrod, "The findings and recommendations of the attorney general's commission on pornography: Do the psychological "facts" fit the political fury?" 42, 1987.

Lynn, Michael and Andrew Oldenquist, "Egoistic and nonegoistic motives in social dilemmas," 41, 1986.

Maehr, Martin and Douglas Kleiber, "The graying of achievement motivation," 36, 1981.

Marijana, Benesh and Bernard Weiner, "On emotion and motivation: From the notebooks of Fritz Heider," 37, 1982.

Markey, Edward, "The politics of arms control: A matter of perception," 40, 1985.

Markus, Hazel and Paula Nurius, "Possible selves," 41, 1986.

McAlister, Alfred et al., "Mass communication and community organization for public health education," 35, 1980.

McClelland, David, "How motives, skills, and values determine what people do," 40, 1985; "Motivational factors in health and disease," 44, 1989.

Mednick, Martha, "On the politics of psychological constructs: Stop the bandwagon, I want to get off," 44, 1989.

Melton, Gary, "Toward 'personhood' for adolescents: Autonomy and privacy as values in public policy," 39, 1983.

Melton, Gary and Nancy Russo, "Adolescent abortion: Psychological perspectives on public policy," 42, 1987.

TABLE 5—*Continued*

AMERICAN PSYCHOLOGIST ARTICLES REVIEWED (1980-1989)

Miller, George, "The children's congress: A time to speak out," 38, 1983.
Miller-Jones, Dalton, "Culture and testing," 44, 1989.
Nathan, Peter, "Failures in prevention: Why we can't prevent the devastating effect of alcoholism and drug abuse," 38, 1983.
Nelson, Alan, "Psychological Equivalence: Awareness and response-ability in our nuclear age," 40, 1985.
Nesher, Pearla, "Learning mathematics: A cognitive perspective," 41, 1986.

Pacht, Asher, "Reflections on perfection," 39, 1984.
Packer, Martin, "Hermeneutic inquiry in the study of human contact," 40, 1985.
Patterson, G. R., Barbara DeBaryshe, and Elizabeth Ramsey, "A developmental perspective on antisocial behavior," 44, 1989.
Perloff, Robert, "Self-interest and personal responsibility redux," 42, 1987.
Pepitone, Albert, "Lessons from the history of social psychology," 36, 1981.

Powers, Sally, Stuart Hauser, and Linda Kilner, "Adolescent mental health," 44, 1989.
Rodin, Judith, "Current status of the internal-external hypothesis for obesity: What went wrong?" 36, 1981.
Rokeach, Milton and Sandra Ball-Rokeach, "Stability and change in American value priorities 1968-1981," 44, 1989.
Rook, Karen, "Promoting social bonding: Strategies for helping the lonely and socially isolated," 39, 1984.
Rosen, Gerald, "Self-help treatment books and the commercialization of psychotherapy," 42, 1987.

Rotter, Julian, "Interpersonal trust, trustworthiness, and gullibility," 35, 1980.
Rubinstein, Eli, "Television and behavior: Research conclusions of the 1982 NIMH report and their policy implications," 38, 1983.
Samelson, Franz, "J. B. Watson's little Albert, Cyril Burt's twins, and the need for a critical science," 35, 1980.
Scarr, Sandra, "Constructing psychology: Making facts and fables for our times," 40, 1985.
Schachter, Stanley, "Recidivism and self-cure of smoking and obesity," 37, 1982.

Schafer, Roy, "The pursuit of failure and the idealization of unhappiness," 39, 1984.
Skinner, B. F., "Intellectual self-management in old age," 38, 1983; "What is wrong with daily life in the western world?" 41, 1986; "Whatever happened to psychology as the science of behavior?" 42, 1987.
Siegel, Max, "Crime and violence in America: The victims," 8, 1983.

Singer, Jerome and David Krantz, "Perspectives in the interface between psychology and public health," 37, 1982.
Singer, Jerome and Dorothy Singer, "Psychologists look at television: Cognitive, developmental, personality, and social policy implications," 38, 1983.
Spence, Janet, "Achievement American style: The rewards and costs of individualism," 40, 1985.

TABLE 5—*Continued*
AMERICAN PSYCHOLOGIST ARTICLES REVIEWED (1980-1989)

Sternberg, Robert, "Testing and cognitive psychology," 36, 1981.
Stipek, Deborah and Jacquelyn McCroskey, "Investing in children: Government and workplace policies for parents," 44, 1989.

Strickland, Bonnie, "Internal-external control expectancies: From contingency to creativity," 44, 1989.
Takanishi, Ruby, Patrick DeLeon, and Michael Pallak, "Psychology and public policy affecting children, youth, and families," 38, 1983.
Task Force on the Victims of Crime and Violence—Executive summary: Final report of the APA task force on the victims of crime and violence," 40, 1985.
Tharp, Roland, "Psychocultural variables and constants: Effects on teaching and learning in schools," 44, 1989.
Tittle, Carol, "Gender research and education," 41, 1986.

Wagner, Richard, "Psychology and the threat of nuclear war," 40, 1985.
Weick, Karl, "Small wins: Redefining the 'scale of social problems,'" 39, 1984.
Weinberg, Richard, "Intelligence and IQ: Landmark issues and great debates," 44, 1989.
Weiss, Stephen, "The federal role in disease prevention and health promotion," 40, 1985.
Woodhead, Martin, "When psychology informs public policy: The case of early childhood intervention," 43, 1988.

Worthington, Jr. et al., "The benefits of legislation requiring parental involvement prior to adolescent abortion," 44, 1989.
Wright, John and Aletha Huston, "A matter of form: potentials of television for young viewers," 38, 1983.
Wurtzel, Alan, "Television policy research and the social science community: An industry perspective," 38, 1983.
Zajonc, R. B., "Feeling and thinking: Preferences need no inferences," 35, 1980.
Zigler, Edward and Winnie Berman, "Discerning the future of early childhood intervention," 38, 1983.
Zigler, Edward and Susan Muenchow, "Infant day care and infant-care leagues: A policy vacuum," 38, 1983.

exploitation, (b) diagnoses and problem representation, (c) design, selection, and enactment of solutions, and (d) assessment of intended and unintended costs and benefits to the recipient and the help providers. One result is arguably a complexity of problem solving that is cognitively overwhelming and emotionally dysfunctional. In this scenario, "solutions" to the full problem likely are doomed to be inadequate; thus, an easier decision rule may be to help yourself before another and easier still not to help another at all. In this analysis, one could argue that, for many, the me-ness and cultural apathy of the

1980s was a viable strategy with a good enough solution to complex social problems. What appears to be motivational deficiencies were instead information overloads.

Finally, the work better known to educators on the apathy-agency question of the 1980s, which is also influential in the 1990s, is the program of research by Bandura in which self-responsibility and self-efficacy are taken to the next level. As the progression of Bandura's publications on triadic reciprocal determinism (or later, "causation") across the decade illustrates, people progressively are seen as more capable and thus more responsible for self-control. Bandura's early position on power of chance events to render life paths essentially unpredictable is modified to allow for life paths traveled by an individual with an influential self-efficacy. Self-efficacy was believed to lend predictability and consistency to humans. Self-efficacy influenced thought (e.g., decision making and judgment), motivation (e.g., effort and positive emotions like optimism and recovery from failure), affect (e.g., aversive emotions of anxiety, stress, depression and their control) and action (selection and construction of environments) in dealing with the environment.

Later in the decade, Bandura stressed the integration of self-efficacy (which serves as a proximal determinant of thought, motivation, emotion, and action) with the human capacity for forethought, symbolic activity, and goal-setting into a theory of self he termed "human agency." Bandura argued further that through "emergent interactive agency" humans were uniquely able to exercise self-control by effecting change in situations and themselves; thus, the notion of human agency raised fundamental questions of determinism, freedom, and control. Bandura defined freedom as the exercise of self-control.

In contrast to earlier positions, Bandura reduced the power of the environment relative to the individual in the triadic model of reciprocal causation. He also modified earlier conceptions of learning and motivation when he noted that success, especially easily attained success, was not all it is cracked up to be; resiliency required experience in mastering difficulty. These latter arguments on the limits of success were part of the educational debate of the time as researchers encountered successful students who were nonetheless bored and fragile, anything but "adaptive" learners who understood themselves and tasks as malleable.[25]

Bandura's elaborations of reciprocal "causation" in *AP* from 1978 to 1989 were remarkably "in synch" with the general culture of the period. The definitions of person and environment that took some of the pressure off the environment to instill and maintain human behavior *and* off individuals to be totally self-determining initially gave way to relatively greater emphasis on environmental factors and finally on personal influences. Greater personal influence through mechanisms of self-efficacy, *which could be taught*, allowed the expectation that humans could transform the environment, chance events notwithstanding. The ability to transform the environment coupled with the uniquely human capacities of forethought, symbolic representation, and self-evaluation yielded an individual who could *transcend* the environment. In the process, motivation acquired volitional qualities, self-reliance became power, and self-control became freedom: a reenactment of individualism and the American dream not unlike the 1950s.

1990s

"I think that optimism is a mistake, but hope, a necessity"—Alan Boneau

Gallup polls taken in 1990 and 1995 again asked, "What do you think is the most important problem facing the country today?" In 1990, the answer was the budget deficit (21%) and drug abuse (18%); in 1995, it was crime and violence (27%). In this decade, the United States achieved the highest incarceration rate in the world: over one million inmates.

In the first half of the 1990s, society struggled with issues of poverty, educational achievement, violence, and the stress of multiple roles and demands, much of which continues at the close of the decade and century. *AP* articles reflect these concerns. Themes continued from the 1980s included homelessness, violence against women, stress (notably in the workplace), work motivation, and adolescence. Concerns with health care reimbursement, the influence of medical perspectives such as neuropsychology, and prescription benefits emerged.

Themes of vulnerability are apparent. From 1992 to 1995, 17 articles focused on violence, mostly against women and children. Senator Nancy Kassebaum notes that "there were 2 million reports of child abuse in 1987—a 176% increase since 1980." Concerns with homelessness run a gamut from diagnostic issues to social policies. A special issue summarized what was known about homelessness and provided direction for researchers, service providers, and policymakers. Of special concern was the approximately one-third of the homeless who suffer from mental illness. The statistics were staggering: on a given night 567,000 to 600,000 Americans were homeless.

Occupational stress and anxiety also are present. Employees became less likely to view their current employment as permanent and secure. Corporate downsizing resulted in workers doing multiple jobs and worrying nonetheless about their job security—for good reason. In 1995 alone, for example, at a time of record-breaking executive compensation and stock market activity, 3.26 million American workers were fired. Psychologists became even more interested in stress and its effects on the individual, families, society, and productivity. Senator Mark Hatfield called for the development of a comprehensive national strategy to reduce job-related stress because stress-related symptoms accounted for at least two-thirds of all visits to physicians and cost the economy 50 to 150 billion dollars a year. Raymond Katzell and Donna Thompson wrote about work motivation and various theories to raise the level of motivation of workers; definitions of "motive" apparently quite different from the anxiety and fear constructs of the 1950s research.

The growth of small businesses mirrored this trend. Self-reliance was again the prominent message, but unlike the 1980s, there is an added twist of self-protection and some cynicism. Loyalty may be only to oneself, but the goal is survival—the one who is still holding on after the dust settles. Self-interest was no longer just self-enhancing; in the 90s, self-interest was necessary for survival.

Economically, the gap between the haves and the have nots continued to grow. "Lean and mean" stood for efficiency and productivity; failings in business were linked to presumed failures at school. Performance-based assessment became the key to salary increases and job security. Performance objectives for administrators and teachers were based on increased student test scores and for CEOs and managers on increased profit margins. Federally funded educational initiatives like Head Start and Title I were told to prove their worth or prepare not to be funded. Several *AP* articles described the differences between social and economic conditions of the mid-1990s and those of the mid-1960s when Head Start was created. Chaya Piotrkowski et al. described the dramatic changes:

Poverty today wears a different face from when Head Start was first conceptualized. Community-wide epidemics of violence, the advent of crack cocaine, the spread of AIDS, and the explosion of homelessness among families with children have affected poor communities with an intensity that has spared few. These stressors go far beyond the burdens of poverty that Head Start initially was designed to address. (p. 136)

Zigler and Styfco continued to defend Head Start successes, while acknowledging a need for improvement. Senator Kassebaum called for "program accountability," the establishment of "general performance measures [and] more effective enforcement of Head Start policies." Although Kassebaum reportedly supported increased funding, high and low quality programs needed to be differentiated. Teachers again became a convenient target to blame for program quality and low educational outcomes, despite increasing social difficulties like substance abuse, impoverished environments, childhood neglect, domestic violence, and transient populations—the very issues that had proved too complex, unwieldy, and ingrained to tackle in the 1980s.

Help still was not the answer, nor would it be for the remainder of the decade. In Welfare-to-Work programs, for example, the poor now were viewed as "innocent victims" of a misguided government that had done harm by being too helpful, an hypothesis supported by attributional analyses of the time and Skinner's unique integration of Marx and materialism in the previous decade. Welfare had taken away the intrinsic drive of the poor to better themselves. Further, welfare eroded everyone's ability to be self-reliant. Society stopped short of blatantly blaming the poor for their state of deprivation, in part because of the shameful number of poor children involved. Even so, poor children along with their teachers would be held accountable for their lack of achievement in school and failure to profit from Head Start.

Even in the midst of domestic turmoil, the 90s affirmed the role of the United States as an economic and military world leader. The Information Age was here and now, reaffirming beliefs in science and technology and the individualism and self-reliance of the American dream. Society would provide tools and resources but it was up to the individual to create his or her own success. We were back on track.

PSYCHOLOGICAL CONTEXT

The 90s continued the interests in intelligence, testing, cognition, emotion, and attribution that emerged in the 1970s and that characterized much of the social and psychological debates of the 1980s.

Intelligence and Testing. Neuroscience influenced intelligence assessment in the 1990s. Joseph Matarazzo predicted the use of "biological tests of intelligence and cognition that record individual differences in brain functions at the neuromolecular, neurophysiologic, and neurochemical levels." Biology will answer the challenges to intelligence testing that have plagued psychologists for decades because neurological findings will end the validity question. The assumption is that differences among individuals who function differently on measures of neurological structures and processes are more "real," and thus more meaningful, than differences on previous assessments. It is as if one would no longer have to make an inference from a test finding to understand current or predict future performance.

Matarazzo emphasized understanding cognitive processing of information on each individual test item rather than simply documenting level of performance. The new assessment instruments looked at the processes of planning, arousal-attention, and simultaneous and successive processing, much as had been predicted a decade earlier. Matarazzo also was concerned with the use of assessment in legal proceedings and the continuing distrust of the testing movement and expert witnesses in matters of child custody and large financial settlements.

Articles on intelligence and testing questioned earlier influential research in the area. Hamilton Cravens, for example, critiqued Terman's decisions to study longitudinal change at the group rather than individual level, his fixed theory of intelligence, and behavioral view of maturation. He described Terman's views as "locked in time," presumably realizing that his own critique is similarly restricted. Finally, Gerald Barrett and Robert Depinet reviewed McClelland's work from the 1970s and 1980s. They challenged each of McClelland's five criticisms of intelligence testing: (1) grades in school did not predict occupational success, (2) intelligence tests and aptitude tests did not predict occupational success or other important life outcomes, (3) tests and academic performance only predicted job performance because of an underlying relationship with social status, (4) such tests were unfair to minorities, and (5) competencies would be able to predict important behaviors better than would more traditional tests. Barrett and Depinet argued that for all five criticisms research had shown that McClelland's 1973 propositions, methods, and conclusions were either not compelling (e.g., mono-method bias) or were wrong. Clearly, disagreement still rules within the field of intelligence assessment and competency testing. Where psychologists disagree, sometimes strongly, citizens distrust.

Learning and Instruction. In the climate that brought "Goals 2000" educational standards were raised and instructional objectives became more demanding. Self-regulation continued to be a key component in student learning. Thus, it was the responsibility of the teacher to present objectives, but it was also the responsibility of the student to "get it." Earlier learning theory debates were now cast between advocates of knowledge compilation and specific skill acquisition versus proponents of global metacognitive strategies across content and skills areas.

Kent Johnson and T. Joe Layng argued against structuralist models of instruction and advocated selectionist models in which skills are built until fluency is achieved. They argued that higher complex skill attainment is dependent on mastery and fluency of all hierarchical subskills. In addition to repetition and practice to automaticity (as in overlearning), selectionist models were concerned with the rate of performance and practice skills until a certain number of accurate responses occur within a given time period. In classroom enactments of procedural skill programs, the student strives for efficiency in a skill and works independently to achieve goals of fluency. The teacher identifies error and provides alternative responses. This model is consistent with a Skinnerian tradition: the teacher controls the learning process, gives immediate feedback, and minimizes errors. The gradual accumulation of skill components reflects the ideas of shaping and successive approximations in the earlier Skinnerian models. Robert Glaser, an advocate of more global, metacognitive strategies, countered this approach, asking:

> whether the extensive practice required to attain reasonable efficiency and automaticity in basic procedural skills might be achieved not only in highly structured environments in which students practice subcomponent procedures, but also in the context of the mature task format of a cooperative learning group. (p. 33)

Glaser advocated a variation of reciprocal teaching in which students take turns in leading a group in the use of knowledge acquisition strategies. In classroom enactments of metacognitive programs, students have intrinsic motivation to understand the world around them and to extend their knowledge. They are self-regulated in their learning and profit from small-group learning opportunities. The teacher (or peer) provides expert scaffolding. So, too, can texts. Walter Kintsch argued that instructional materials also reflect different learning orientations. He advocated writing texts consistent with the metacognitive approach that would require readers to participate actively in the comprehension process by providing them with "opportunities to use their knowledge" rather than those that "spell everything out." Gaps are good; they are invitations for the reader to "fill in." Research on student perceptions of such texts seems an important next step!

Finally, Glaser encouraged the "return of learning theory within instructional research." Learning theory, which was emphasized in the 1950s and early 1960s, had focused on the acquisition and transfer of knowledge. It had been nudged out by three decades of cognitive science that had focused more on performance and competence. It appears that at least some educational psychologists in the early 1990s were closer to societal conceptions of educational outcomes than they had been a decade earlier.

Feeling motivated: Intrapersonal and interpersonal dynamics. Following the considerable interest in emotion in the 1980s, motivational principles became intertwined with theories of emotional development and expression in the 1990s. For some theorists, motivation now was viewed as affective and cognitive. David Geary, for example, viewed motivation as the affective component that induced individuals to engage in activities that served to build and strengthen cognitive structures that were primarily biological. He differentiated biologically primary abilities (e.g., the ability to use language, which is found throughout the world) from biologically secondary activities (e.g., the ability to read, which is found in some cultures but not all). For Geary, the function of schools was to provide opportunities to develop secondary abilities valued by that particular culture. Emotion motivates students to engage in primary biological activities because they find them inherently enjoyable; however, as Geary points out, many biologically secondary activities that improve performance, such as practice, are not inherently enjoyable. Thus, students pursue these activities for cognitive reasons: because they believe them worthwhile or instrumental to another goal that is affectively pleasing, such as a teacher's approval.

Discussing the cognitive-motivational-relational theory of emotion, Richard Lazarus stated that "the motivational concepts now being used, such as values, goal commitments, intentions, and plans, are fused with cognitive activity in contrast with earlier concepts such as instincts, drives, and needs which implied innate biological forces without cognitive referents." (p. 819) Lazarus takes these concepts one step forward: motivation means the acute emotions and moods attached to the status of goals and everyday encounters.

Peter Lang considered motivation and emotion somewhat differently. Emotions were what happened when a person was prevented from completing a behavior (recall Strong on motivation as *dis*satisfaction). Lang viewed emotions as "motivationally tuned states of readiness." He proposed that two motive systems existed in the brain—one

TABLE 6

AMERICAN PSYCHOLOGIST ARTICLES REVIEWED (1990-1995)

Anastasi, Anne et al., "Centennial observations," 47, 1992.
Anderson, John R., "Problem solving and learning," 48, 1993.
Barrett, Gerald V., and Robert Depinet, "A reconsideration of testing for competence rather than intelligence," 46, 1991.
Boneau, Alan C., "Observations on psychology's past and future," 47, 1992.
Cravens, Hamilton, "A scientific project locked in time: The Terman genetic studies of genius, 1920s-1950s," 47, 1992.

Eccles, Jacquelynne et al., "Development during adolescence: The impact of stage-environment fit on young adolescents' experiences in schools and in families," 48, 1993.
Glaser, Robert, "The reemergence of learning theory within instructional research," 45, 1990.
Geary, David C., "Reflections of evolution and culture in children's cognition: Implications for mathematical development and instruction," 50, 1995.
Hatfield, Mark O., "Stress and the American worker," 45, 1990.
Johnson, Kent R. and T. Joe Layng, "Breaking the structuralist barrier: Literacy and numeracy with fluency," 47, 1992.

Jones, James M., Irene S. Levine, and Allison A. Rosenberg, "Homelessness research, services, and social policy," 46, 1991.
Kassebaum, Nancy L., "Head Start: Only the best for America's children," 49, 1994.
Katzell, Raymond A., and Donna E. Thompson, "Work motivation: Theory and practice," 45, 1990.
Kintsch, Walter, "Text comprehension, memory, and learning," 49, 1994.
Lang, Peter J., "The emotion probe: Studies of motivation and attention," 50, 1995.

Lazarus, Richard S., "Cognition and motivation in emotion," 46, 1991; "Progress on a cognitive-motivational-relational theory of emotion," 46, 1991.
Levine, Irene S., and Debra J. Rog, "Mental health services for homeless mentally ill persons: Federal initiatives and current service trends," 45, 1990.
Matarazzo, Joseph D., "Psychological testing and assessment in the 21st century," 47, 1992; "Psychological assessment versus psychological testing: Validation from Binet to the school, clinic, and courtroom," 45, 1990.

Piotrkowski, Chaya S. et al., "Strengthening mental health services in Head Start: A challenge for the 1990s," 49, 1994.
Takanishi, Ruby and Patrick H. DeLeon, "A Head Start for the 21st century," 49, 1994.
Weiner, Bernard, "Metaphors in motivation and attribution," 46, 1991; "On sin versus sickness: A theory of the perceived responsibility and social motivation," 48, 1993.
Zigler, Edward and Sally Styfco, "Head Start: Criticisms in a constructive context," 49, 1994.

which was appetitive and one which was aversive. These systems were subcortical neurophysiological circuits in the brain activated by primary reinforcement. For Lang, the aversive and appetitive motivational systems played a fundamental role in organizing emotional expression. Motivation/emotion theorists of individual behavior in the 1990s reviewed here, like their earlier counterparts in the 40s and 50s, tried to delineate primary from secondary (or acquired) drives, and the processes of respondent and operant conditioning, to better understand the role of biology and emotion *with* cognition in human motivation. In the first decade of the twenty-first century, perhaps individuals will become a little less uniquely human and, in the process, more fully motivated.

Motivational research in the early 1990s also included the study of *inter*personal processes. Jacquelynne Eccles and colleagues directly studied motivation in school as a function of person-environment fit. They looked at the impact of change in teacher efficacy, teacher-student relationships, and degree of decision-making opportunities in classrooms on early adolescents' achievement-related beliefs, motives, values, and behavior. They proposed that motivation and doing well were dependent on the degree to which the environment matched, rather than mismatched, students' developmental and psychological needs.

Specifically, these researchers were concerned with the transition between elementary and middle or junior high school. They concluded that an adolescent's motivation was positively related to teacher efficacy and classrooms that provided greater opportunities for student decision making, choice, and self-management. They suggested that the general decline in motivation ascribed to adolescents may be due to new school environments that, when compared with previous school experiences, consisted of greater emphasis on teacher control and discipline, less personal and positive teacher-student relationships, and practices such as whole-class task organization, between-classroom ability grouping, and public evaluation of the correctness of work. These aspects of junior high classrooms were especially detrimental when considered with adolescent developmental needs. The authors were persuasive:

The environmental changes often associated with transition to junior high school seem especially harmful in that they emphasize competition, social comparison, and ability self-assessment at a time of heightened self-focus; they decrease decision making and choice at a time when the desire for control is growing; they emphasize lower level cognitive strategies at a time when the ability to use higher level strategies is increasing; and they disrupt social networks at a time when adolescents are especially concerned with peer relationships and may be in special need of close adult relationships outside of the home. (p. 94)

Finally, attribution theory thrived in the early 1990s. Attribution research had focused primarily on achievement motivation in the 1980s; by the 1990s, the model also was influential in the social realm and interpersonal processes. Attribution researchers explored inferences about intentionality, responsibility, and blame and their effect on interpersonal emotion and behavior. The attribution model of helping behavior asserted that attributional judgments of why an individual needs or seeks help influence emotion, which in turn motivates behavior.

A decade earlier, attributional dynamics of helping behavior were directly studied in classroom management. In this research program, teachers were considered helping agents and social models and classmates were potential agents or bystanders.[26] Judgments of perceived controllability and intention were particularly informative in understanding why teacher strategies differed with individual students. For example, if a teacher judges a student to need extra help on an assignment because the student was sick and missed the appropriate class experience (a cause over which the student is perceived to have no control), the teacher will feel sympathy and provide the student extra supports. In contrast, if a teacher judges that a student who seeks extra help missed appropriate class experience because of fooling around (a cause over which the student is presumed to have control and thus can be held responsible), the teacher will feel annoyed or angry and withhold help. Anger can also lead to additional punishment and control attempts.

Students can predict and understand attributional rules, affect, and behavior implemented by their teacher as early as first grade if teachers explain their reasoning. Students also use attributional rules to negotiate fair interpersonal behavior with their classmates. Mary McCaslin argues that school and classroom management policies must at least be as sophisticated as students' attributional knowledge if authority is to be respected as a potential source of meaningful learning (and Skinner's three by-products of punishment—escape, counterattack, and stubborn inaction—are not to follow).[27]

Retrospection, Contemplation, and Possibilities. As the 90s began, several *AP* articles reflected on the state of psychology as a field. We choose two to discuss here. Alan Boneau presents the perspectives of some senior psychologists, and Anne Anastasi and colleagues present a more optimistic outlook. Boneau surveyed senior psychologists about the field today relative to the expectations they held 25 years ago. The most frequently reported change was the shift from experimental psychology and behaviorism to cognitive theory. The most unanticipated change was psychology's current orientation towards health delivery.

Many of Boneau's respondents expressed concern that the field was "splintering and eclipsing." For many, the inclusion of so many voices had threatened the needed framework and direction afforded by one unifying voice. In the past two decades, psychology had entered into an identity crisis with various factions elbowing for primacy. Interdisciplinary approaches were viewed by some as a threat to the future of the field where "many of the scientific problems on which we work are increasingly seen as a proper domain of other disciplines." Cynicism and disappointment permeate the comments of Boneau's respondents. Psychology's failure to make progress was noted:

The biggest surprise to me has been how little has been accomplished. In 1962 I was full of hopes that the scientific study of behavior and its neural underpinnings would lead in 10 years, or at most 15, to a fundamental understanding. . . . In hindsight, I think I shouldn't have been so surprised. . . . Yet, the failure to remember and build on the factual discoveries of the past has, nevertheless, been a sore disappointment. (p. 1588)

As psychologists continued forced-choice debate and argument amongst themselves (e.g., behaviorism versus cognition; psychology as a science versus psychology as a mental-health, practice-oriented field; biology versus environment) rather than study the problems of the "real world," society listened less and psychology's perceived relevance declined.

More optimistic predictions for psychology's future rested on hopes for integration and synthesis. Anne Anastasi saw the rise of life-span developmental psychology and cross-cultural psychology as promising examples of the movement towards integration and synthesis. Rather than demise, Anastasi et al. believed that "psychology as a scientific discipline is coming of age." For these authors, the hope for unification came from learning theory which, despite the discordance among its researchers, offered "a promising route to unification across *all* fields of psychology" and a source of optimism for some in the 1950s as well.

Epilogue

As psychology begins a new century and educators look for informed support to help achieve their goals for children, we join in Boneau's urgent appeal:

Will we not always need to have a science of humanity; a discipline concerned with understanding and explaining the human individual coping in a social-cultural-environmental context? I must point out that that is not what psychology is now, but perhaps it should be. If psychology is something else now, what can we do to bring about needed change? And what changes are needed? These are not easy questions. We can expect no easy answers. I believe that they are worth raising, however, in the hope that somewhere, someone or some group may attempt to formulate a programmatic answer. Is anyone out there? (p. 1596)

We are. So are millions of students and their teachers, most of whom participate in the public schools. Haggard's call to educational psychology in 1954 reverberates: educational psychologists owe it to their discipline and to society to study things that matter to the education of our children. Our review suggests that psychology need not be reactive to cultural events and understandings, but it likely will remain so if researchers only get interested in education after national or world events have created a problem or after policymakers have found and framed the "problem with education." Educational psychologists and educators must work together to *anticipate* issues. We agree with Marie Jahoda, who wrote in 1981, that to "study in the here and now what may be a major issue in the future requires more solid historical perspective—and collaboration."

One benefit of writing this chapter has been the getting of an education. Hopefully, one benefit of reading this chapter has been an appreciation of the interplay of the cultural and the psychological in coming to define motivation and what that might mean for educational practice. We believe that advances in knowledge in educational psychology come from an appreciation of interrelated domains of inquiry, recognition of the legitimacy and limits of a variety of theory and research methods, and an appreciation of the cultural embedding of the practice of psychology and the work of the public school. We suggest that the ability to ask new questions whose pursuit may promote the viability of the public school and the well-being of its participants rests upon better communication and collaboration between psychology and education.

More than fifty years ago, Carl Rogers wrote of the need to see with, rather than simply evaluate or label, another. This seems good advice. The suspicion that has at times characterized exchange (or lack thereof) between psychology and education has prohibited genuine collaboration that just might serve the purported goal of each: enhancement of the education and well-being of children. If educational psychology is to meaningfully influence education, it must be committed not only to the challenges that confront educators daily, but to anticipate those which may confront them tomorrow. If education is to understand the learning, motivational, developmental, and identity implications of being a student, one of the multiple and potentially competing roles that a child assumes, it must be committed to adopting multiple lenses through which one can see *with* a child, as well as recognizing those *through which* society will evaluate and label her. Our children deserve nothing less than such commitments.

The authors are indebted to the research assistance of Helen Infanti, who located and reproduced much of the critical material we reviewed for this chapter. The authors also wish to acknowledge and thank the critical eye and sustained helpfulness of Sharon Nichols.

NOTES

1. "The Nation: What's the Problem?" *New York Times*, 1 August 1999, sec. 4, p.4. If reported concerns ranking first and second are within 5 percentage points, both concerns are listed. This source and decision rule applies to Gallup poll data and decade events for each decade.

2. Edward Thorndike, *The Measurement of Intelligence* (New York: Teachers College, Columbia University, 1926).

3. Mary McCaslin and Thomas L. Good, "The informal curriculum," in David Berliner and Robert Calfee (eds.), *Handbook of Educational Psychology* (New York: Macmillan, 1996): 622-672.

4. Hull, Clark, *Essentials of Behavior* (New Haven, CT: Yale University Press, 1951).

5. McCall, Robert, "Academic underachievers," *Current Directions in Psychological Science*, 3 (1994): 15-19.

6. Catharine C. Cox, "The early mental traits of three hundred geniuses," in Lewis Terman (ed.), *Genetic studies of genius* (Stanford: Stanford University Press, 1926).

7. Lyn Corno, "The best-laid plans: Modern conceptions of volition and educational research," *Educational Researcher*, 22 (1992): 14-22.

8. Ann K. Renninger, Suzanne Hidi, and Andrea Krapp (eds.), *The role of interest in learning and development.* (Hillsdale, NJ: Lawrence Erlbaum Associates, 1992); Carole Ames, "Classrooms: Goals, structures, and student motivation," *Journal of Educational Psychology*, 84 (1992): 261-270-271; Kenneth Dodge, Steven Asher, and Jennifer Parkhurst, "Social life as a goal-coordination task," in Carole Ames and Russell Ames (eds.), *Research on motivation in education: Vol. 3. Goals and cognition* (New York: Academic Press, 1989): 107-135; McCaslin and Good, "The informal curriculum."

9. See also, Heinz Heckhausen, *Motivation and action* (P. Leppmann, Trans.) (Berlin: Springer, 1991).

10. Nel Noddings, *The challenge to care in schools* (New York: Teachers College Press, 1992).

11. Arthur R. Jensen, "How much can we boost IQ and scholastic achievement? *Harvard Educational Review*, 39 (1969b): 1-123; Arthur R. Jensen, "Reducing the Heredity-Environment uncertainty," in *Environment, Heredity, and Intelligence. Harvard Educational Review* (Reprint, no. 2, 1969a): 211.

12. In July 1999, the Boston School Committee (voting 5 to 2) dropped race as a factor in pupil assignments to schools, reportedly to avoid a pending lawsuit by parents who charge the system discriminates against white children (currently 15% of Boston public school students) by giving them less choice in the school they attend. The rhetoric of giving all children, regardless of race, color or creed, equal access to successful schools has given way to "choice." (See Carey Goldberg, "Race-based busing ends in Boston," *New York Times* (18 July 1999), sec. 4, p. 2; and "A change of course in Boston," *New York Times* editorial (17 July 1999), p. A24.

13. David Berliner and Barak Rosenshine, "The acquisition of knowledge in the classroom," in Richard Anderson, et al. (eds.), *Schooling and the Acquisition of Knowledge* (Hillsdale, NJ: Lawrence Erlbaum, 1977): 375-413; Benjamin Bloom, "Time and learning," *The American Psychologist*, 29, no. 9 (1976): 682-688; and Carl Bereiter and Siegfried Engelmann, *Teaching Disadvantaged Children in the Preschool* (Engelwood Cliffs, NJ: Prentice-Hall, 1966), respectively.

14. Walter Doyle, "Academic work," *Review of Educational Research*, 53 (1983): 159-199; J. Kounin, *Discipline and group management in classrooms* (New York: Holt, Rinehart and Winston, 1970); and Lee Canter, "Assertive discipline: A response," *Teachers College Record*, 90 (1989): 631-638 respectively.

15. McCaslin and Good, "The informal curriculum."

16. Kurt Lewin, *Field Theory in Social Science* (New York: Harper, 1951); Henry Murray, *Explorations in personality* (New York: Oxford University Press, 1938).

17. Lyn Corno and Ellen Mandinach, "The role of cognitive engagement in classroom learning and motivation," *Educational Psychologist*, 18 (1983): 88-108.

18. Mary McCaslin Rohrkemper, "Self-regulated learning and academic achievement: A Vygotskian view," in B. Zimmerman and D. Schunk (eds.), *Self-regulated Learning and Academic Achievement: Theory, research, and practice* (New York: Springer, 1989): 143-168.

19. Mark Lepper and David Greene, *The hidden costs of reward: New perspectives on the psychology of human motivation* (Hillsdale, NJ: Lawrence Erlbaum, 1978).

20. J. S. Carroll and J. W. Payne, "Judgments about crime and the criminal: A model and a method for investigating parole decisions, in B. D. Sales (ed.), *Prospectives in Law and Psychology. Vol. 1: The Criminal Justice System* (New York: Plenum, 1976).

21. Constance Yowell and Mark Smylie, "Self-regulation in democratic communities," *Elementary School Journal*, 99 (1999): 469-490.

22. Jerome Bruner, *The Process of Education* (New York: Vintage Books, 1963); and McCaslin and Good, "The informal curriculum."

23. Erich Fromm, *The Heart of Man* (New York: Harper and Row, 1964).

24. John Carroll, "A model of school learning," *Teacher's College Record*, 64 (1963): 723-733.

25. Mary Rohrkemper and Lyn Corno, "Success and failure on classroom tasks: Adaptive learning and classroom teaching," *Elementary School Journal*, 88 (1988): 299-312.

26. Mary Rohrkemper, "The influence of teachers' socialization style on students' social cognitive and reported interpersonal classroom behavior," *Elementary School Journal*, 85 (1984): 245-275; Mary Rohrkemper, "Individual differences in students' perceptions of routine classroom events," *Journal of Educational Psychology*, 77, 29-44; Mary Rohrkemper and Jere Brophy, "Teachers' thinking about problem students," in J. Levine and M. C. Wang (eds.), *Implications of Learning* (Hillsdale, NJ: Lawrence Erlbaum Associates, 1983).

27. Mary McCaslin, "The problem of problem representation: The Summit's conception of student," *Educational Researcher*, 25 (1996): 13-15.

CHAPTER IV

Reading in the Twentieth Century

P. DAVID PEARSON

This is an account of reading instruction in the twentieth century. It will end, as do most essays written in the final year of any century, with predictions about the future. My hope is to provide an account of the past and present of reading instruction that will render predictions about the future transparent. Thus I begin with a tour of the historical pathways that have led us, at century's end, to the rocky and highly contested terrain we currently occupy in reading pedagogy. After unfolding my version of a map of that terrain, I will speculate about pedagogical journeys that lie ahead of us in a new century and a new millennium.

Even though the focus of this essay is reading pedagogy, it is my hope to connect the pedagogy to the broader scholarly ideas of each period. Two factors render this task easier for the first two-thirds of the century than for the last third. First, the sheer explosion in the number of educational ideas and movements in the last thirty years makes these connections more difficult. Second, because I have lived through this last third as a member of the reading profession, I am too close to examine current practices with the critical eye of historical distance. That realization, of course, compels me to work harder at the contextualization and to be as open and as comprehensive as possible in considering alternative explanations of recent events in the history of reading instruction.

The developments in reading pedagogy over the last century suggested that it is most useful to divide the century into thirds, roughly 1900-1935, 1935-1970, and 1970-2000. This division yields two periods of enormous intellectual and curricular activity (the first and third) and a relatively quiet period at mid-century.

To guide us in constructing our map of past and present, we will need a legend, a common set of criteria for examining ideas and practices in

P. David Pearson is the John A. Hannah Distinguished Professor of Education at Michigan State University. He also co-directs the Center for the Improvement of Early Reading Achievement.

each period. Several candidates suggest themselves. Surely, the *dominant materials* used by teachers in each period will be relevant, as will the *dominant pedagogical practices*. Both materials and pedagogy are relatively easy to witness because they lie on the surface of instruction where they are easy to see. Other important points of comparison, such as the *role* of the *teacher* and the *learner* in the process of learning to read, lie beneath the instructional surface and require deeper inferences, greater interpretation, and more unpacking for observation and analysis. Finally, for each set of practices, the most difficult task will be to understand the underlying assumptions about the *nature of reading* and *learning to read* that motivate dominant practices in each period.

The Reading Scene at Last Turn of the Century

The rhetoric of the reformers of the mid and late nineteenth century, intellectual giants such as Horace Mann and Colonel Francis Parker,[1] would lead us to conclude that the demons of drill and practice on isolated sounds and letters had been driven out of our pedagogical temples by the year 1900. So strong was their indictment, so appealing their alternative methods of reason and meaning, that one could hardly imagine the continuation of a method as painful to both student and teacher alike as was the alphabetic approach. Yet in spite of the wonderful accounts of innovative language experience activities and integrated curriculum in the laboratory schools at Columbia and the University of Chicago,[2] alphabetic approaches still dominated the educational landscape in the United States at least through World War I. These were classic synthetic phonics approaches (learn the parts before the whole) in which, at least in the earliest stages of learning to read, students encountered, in rapid succession, letter names, then letter sounds, then syllable blending activities that were organized into tight drill and practice sequences. The synthetic phonics traditions established much earlier in the century by Noah Webster's *Blue Back Speller* and McGuffey's *Eclectic Readers* were still strongly in evidence.[3] Once the code had been cracked, students were expected to move right into works of literature, most of which were written for adults rather than children. Drill and practice continued after the primer level, but moved from letter names and sounds into other aspects of the language arts, including grammar, rhetoric, and elocution.

Taking Stock: 1

The role of the learner in this period was to receive the curriculum provided by the teacher and dutifully complete the drills provided. The role of the teacher was to provide the proper kinds of drill and practice. In this period being able to read meant being able to pronounce the words on the page accurately, fluently, and, for older students, eloquently.[4] The prevailing view of reading as a cognitive process was what we have come to call the simple view of reading. In the simple view, reading comprehension is thought of as the product of decoding and listening comprehension (RC = Dec * LC), and the major task of instruction is to ensure that students master the code so that comprehension can proceed more or less by "listening to what you read."[5]

Developments in the First Third of the Century

From 1900 to 1935 many new ideas emerged in the psychology and pedagogy of reading. These ideas had important and long-lasting consequences for reading instruction; many, in fact, are still with us on the cusp of a new century. I review several of these ideas in some detail because they provide a useful framework for understanding the reforms of later periods.

EARLY READING REFORMS

Words to letters. Several types of reform emerged (re-emerged may be a more accurate term for there are earlier iterations of each in the historical literature) to counter the evils of what most educators regarded as the mindless drill and practice of the alphabetic approach to beginning reading instruction. Despite the flurry of reform attempts, only two gathered enough momentum to survive. The first, dubbed the words-to-letters approach by Mitford Mathews,[6] introduced words in the very earliest stages and, for each word introduced, immediately asked children to decompose it into component letters.[7] Words-to-letters is the obverse of the alphabetic, or letters-to-words, approach. However, with the alphabetic approach, it shares the goal of ensuring that children learn the sound correspondences for each letter and the same set of underlying assumptions about the nature of teaching, learning, and reading. Today we would call it analytic (whole to part) phonics.

Words to reading. The second reform, which Mathews dubbed words-to-reading, later came to be known as the look-say or whole word method of teaching reading. Here, no attempt was made to analyze words into letter-sounds *until* a sizable corpus of words were learned as sight words. Contrary to popular opinion, which would have us believe that phonics was never taught in the look-say approach,[8] some form of analytic phonics (a modified version of words-to-letters) usually kicked in after a corpus of a hundred or so sight words had been learned. It was different from a strict word-to-letters approach, though, because the strict requirement for decomposing each word into its component letters was dropped in favor of what might be called focused analysis. For example a teacher might group several words that start with the letter f (e.g., *farm, fun, family, fine,* and *first*) and ask students to note the similarity between the initial sounds and letters in each word. As it turned out, this approach (a combination of look-say with analytic phonics) persevered to become the "conventional wisdom" from 1930-1970.

A potpourri. Beyond these, there were a host of specialized programs described by various scholars at the turn of the century.[9] For example, no less than six specialized alphabets appeared in this period, each designed to make the task of learning to read easier by employing a temporary alphabet that created a one-to-one letter-sound match for young readers. George Farnham designed what may have been the first truly meaning-based approach to beginning reading; it was a whole sentence approach in which a series of single pictures were matched directly to a sentence describing its content (e.g., There are three eggs on the table). Finally, numerous examples of the use of group-composed language experience stories as young readers' first texts appeared, though this approach did not gather much momentum until after World War II.[10]

OTHER INFLUENTIAL DEVELOPMENTS

Testing and the scientific movement. Reading was influenced by a host of developments during this period. For example, reading performance, like most other educational phenomena, became the object of scientific examination and systematic testing relatively early in the twentieth century.[11] Starting with the work of Edward L. Thorndike and William S. Gray, the period from roughly the first to the second World War witnessed the development of numerous reading assessments.[12] The first published reading assessment, circa 1914, was an oral reading assessment created by Gray (who eventually became a pre-eminent scholar in the reading field and the senior author of the country's most widely used reading series). However, most reading assessments developed in the first third of this century focused on the relatively new construct of silent reading. Unlike oral reading, which had to be tested individually and required that teachers judge the quality of responses, silent reading comprehension and rate could be tested in group settings and scored without recourse to professional judgment (only stop watches and multiple choice questions were needed). Thus it fit the demands for efficiency and scientific objectivity, themes that were part of the emerging scientism of the period. Significant developments in reading comprehension would occur in the second third of the century, but assessment would remain a psychometric rather than a cognitive construct until the cognitive revolution of the early 1970s. When comprehension was implemented in school curricula, the same infrastructure of tasks used to create test items was used to create instructional and practice materials—finding main ideas, noting important details, determining sequence of events, cause-effect relations, comparing and contrasting, and drawing conclusions.[13]

Text difficulty and readability. Text difficulty, codified as readability, emerged as an important research area and curricular concept in the first half of this century. Unlike the developments in testing, readability was grounded in child-centered views of pedagogy dating back to theorists such as Pestalozzi, Froebel, and Herbart and championed by the developmental psychology emerging in the 1920s and 30s.[14] The motive in developing readability formulas was to present children with texts that matched their interests and developmental capacities rather than to baffle them with abridged versions of adult texts. The first readability formula, created to gauge the grade placement of texts, appeared in 1923, and it was followed by some 80 additional formulas over the next forty years until the enterprise drew to a close in the late 1960s.[15] Irrespective of particular twists in individual formulas, each more or less boiled down to a sentence difficulty factor, typically instantiated as average sentence length, and a word factor, typically codified as word frequency. These formulas were critical in the production of commercial reading materials from the 1920s through the 1980s. For reasons that will become apparent later in this chapter, readability formulas did not survive the cognitive revolution in reading instruction in the 1970s and 1980s, although there are signs of their recovery in the 1990s.

Readiness. The third important curricular construct to emerge in the first third of the century was readiness. Like readability, it was grounded in developmental psychology rather than the scientific movement in education.[16] In research, the readiness movement was a search for the behavioral precursors to beginning reading acquisition: What skills or capacities must be in place before reading instruction can begin in earnest? What skills predict early reading success? The typical candidates for readiness skills were alphabet knowledge, auditory discrimination, visual discrimination, color and shape discrimination, following directions, language development, and, from time to time, kinesthetic and motor activities.[17] Despite the inclusion of a wide array of cognitive, perceptual, and linguistic variables in elaborate predictive studies, time and again knowledge of the names of the letters of the alphabet emerged as the best predictor of later reading achievement.[18] Scholars conducted studies with titles like "When Should Children Begin to Read?" and "The Necessary Mental Age for Beginning Reading."[19] Even though there was considerable controversy between those who wanted to delay formal instruction until maturation had a chance to do its work and those who wanted to nudge it along with specific and explicit skills instruction, both sides shared the assumption that a formal stage of readiness preceded the acquisition of reading.

Reading skills. A fourth key curricular construct was "reading skills"—that discrete unit of the curriculum which ought to be learned by students and taught by teachers. An important related construct was the notion of a scope and sequence of skills, a linear outline of skills that if taught properly ought to lead to skilled reading. While skills have always been a part of reading instruction (witness all the bits and pieces of letter sounds and syllables in the alphabetic approach), the skill as a fundamental unit of curriculum and the scope and sequence chart as a way of organizing skills that extend across the elementary grades are twentieth century phenomena, nurtured, I would add, by the rapid expansion of commercial basal reading programs and standardized reading tests.[20]

The basal experience with skills led quite directly to two additional curriculum mainstays—the teachers' manual and the workbook. Throughout the nineteenth century and at least up through the first three decades of the twentieth century, basal programs consisted almost entirely of a set of student books. Teachers relied on experience, or perhaps normal school education, to supply the pedagogy used to teach lessons with the materials. Occasionally, for students who had progressed beyond the primer to one of the more advanced readers, questions were provided to test understanding of the stories in the readers. In the early 1900s, publishers of basals began to include supplementary teaching suggestions, typically a separate section at the front or back of each book with a page or two of suggestions to accompany each selection. In one common practice of the period, publishers provided a model lesson plan for two or three stories; for later stories, they referred the teacher back to one of the models with the suggestion that they adapt it for the new story. By the 1930s, the teachers' manuals had expanded to several pages per selection.[21] The other significant development in the 1930s was the workbook, often marketed with titles like *My Think and Do Book* or *Work Play Books*.[22]

Both of these developments were symptomatic of the expansion of scope and sequence efforts: the more skills included, the more complicated the instructional routines and the greater the need for explicit directives to teachers and opportunities for students to practice the skills. From the 1930s until at least the 1980s, this approach to skills development increased in intensity and scope. It was gradually extended beyond phonics to include comprehension, vocabulary, and study skills.[23] As I indicated earlier, the comprehension skills that made their way into basal workbooks and scope and sequence charts were virtually identical to those used to create comprehension tests. Each expansion resulted in heftier and more complex teachers' manuals and workbooks, another trend that has continued virtually unchecked since it began in the 1930s.

Remediation. Strictly speaking, remediation is a medical or psychological construct rather than a curricular construct. I have elevated it to the status of a curricular construct in this chapter for the simple reason that it has exerted such a powerful influence on reading pedagogy over the past century. Beginning in the waning days of the nineteenth century and reaching its peak in the 1960s, the medical model has been a dominant force in our quest to meet the needs of those who struggle to learn to read. The hope is, and always was, that if we could just find the peaks and valleys in each child's profile of reading skills, we could offer focused instruction that would remedy the weaknesses and bring him or her (mostly *hims*, as our actuarial data suggest)[24] into a kind of skill equilibrium that would enable normal reading. It was, until recently, our sole approach to meeting individual needs.

Even in the classroom, the medical model, with its emphasis on diagnosis and prescription, has been the backbone of much of our instruction. After all, if filling in the valleys in children's instructional profiles works for those most in need, why wouldn't it work just as well for those less needy of instructional intervention? Don't all children deserve this sort of attention to individual needs? Note also that this diagnostic-prescriptive approach was a comfortable, maybe even a perfect, fit with the increasing emphasis on skills and scope and sequence charts in each succeeding edition of basals of this period; it is, after all, in the various skills that the performance peaks and valleys show up.

Professional Consensus. That Colonel Parker and Horace Mann felt the need to rationalize their child-centered approaches with rhetoric detailing the evils of the dreaded alphabetic approach suggests that debate was alive and well at the beginning of the century. My account of developments in the first third of the century implies a level of consensus that is not justified. Even though most scholars accepted the new emphasis on silent reading and comprehension without much debate, they found less agreement on matters of early reading. The ubiquity of the words-to-reading approach notwithstanding, a vocal phonics lobby, complete with their own published materials, remained active throughout this period. And the concept of readiness was hotly debated, with maturationists and interventionists lining up on opposite sides.[25] That said, it must be acknowledged that the rhetoric of this period was no match for what was to come later on; the metaphor of a smoldering fire seems an apt description of the recurring curricular debate during this period. Blazes would erupt later in the century.

Developments at Mid-Century

THE SCENE IN THE 1960s

The period that spans roughly 1935 to 1965 is best viewed as a time in which we engaged in fine-tuning and elaboration of instructional models that were born in the first third of the century. Most important, the words-to-reading approach that had started its ascendancy at the turn of the century gained increasing momentum throughout the century until, as has been documented in survey research conducted in the 1960s, over 90 percent of the students in the country were taught to read using one commercial variation of this approach or another.[26] So common was this approach that Jeanne Chall in her classic 1967 book, *Learning to Read: The Great Debate*, felt comfortable describing the then prevailing approach as a set of principles, which can be roughly paraphrased as follows:[27]

- The goals of reading, from the start in grade one, should include comprehension, interpretation, and application as well as word recognition.
- Instruction should begin with meaningful silent reading of stories that are grounded in children's experiences and interests.

- After a corpus of sight words is learned (somewhere between 50 and 100), analytic phonics instruction should begin. Phonics should be regarded as one of many cueing systems, including context and picture cues, available to children to unlock new words.
- Phonics instruction should be spread out over several years rather than concentrated in the early grades.
- Phonics instruction should be contextualized rather than isolated from real words and texts.
- The words in the early texts (grades 1-3) should be carefully controlled for frequency of use and repeated often to ensure mastery.
- Children should get off to a slow and easy start, probably through a readiness program; those not judged to be ready for formal reading instruction should experience an even longer readiness period.
- Children should be instructed in small groups.

While a few elements in her list are new, such as the early emphasis on comprehension and interpretation and the contextualization of phonics instruction, virtually all of the elements introduced in the early part of the century were included in her description of the conventional wisdom of the 1960s. A few things are missing when one compares Chall's list of principles underlying the conventional wisdom with our earlier account of the key developments through 1935. One is the role of skills in commercial reading programs. While skills did not make it onto her list of principles, it is clear from several chapters (specifically, chapters 7 and 8) in her 1967 book that she was mindful of their importance and curricular ubiquity. By the 1960s, skills lessons in the teachers' manual, accompanied by workbooks allowing students to practice the skills, were much more elaborate than in the 30s, 40s, or 50s. The other missing piece is the elaborate development of the teachers' manual. Earlier, I implied that they got bigger with each succeeding edition of the series. By the middle 1960s, that small teachers' guide section in the back of the children's book we found in the 20s and 30s had expanded to the point where the number of pages devoted to the teachers' guide equaled the number of student text pages in the upper grades and exceeded it in the primary grades.[28]

Taking Stock: 2

The materials of the 1960s were not fundamentally different from the materials available in the early part of the century. Students read stories and practiced skills. Text difficulty was carefully controlled in the basal reading materials published between the 1930s and the 1960s.

In the earliest readers (pre-primer through first reader at least), vocabulary was sequenced in order of decreasing frequency of word usage in everyday written and oral language. Since many of the most frequent words are not regularly spelled (*the, of, what, where,* etc.), this frequency principle provided a good fit with the whole-word or look-say emphasis characteristic of the words-to-reading approach so dominant during this period.

Students were still the recipients, and teachers still the mediators, of the received curriculum. Meaning and silent reading were more important in the 1960s version of reading curriculum than in 1900 or 1935, as evidenced by a steady increase in the amount of time and teachers' manual space devoted to comprehension activities, but it was still not at the core of the look-say approach. When all is said and done, the underlying model of reading in the 1960s was still a pretty straightforward perceptual process; the simple view—that comprehension is the product of decoding and listening comprehension (RC = LC × Dec)—still prevailed. Readers still accomplished the reading task by translating graphic symbols (letters) on a printed page into an oral code (sounds corresponding to those letters) which was then treated by the brain as oral language. In both the look-say approach to learning sight vocabulary and its analytic approach to phonics, whether the unit of focus is a word or a letter, the basic task for the student is to translate from the written to the oral code. This view of reading was quite consistent with the prevailing instructional emphasis on skills. If sight words and phonics knowledge was what children needed to learn in order to perform the translation process, then decomposing phonics into separable bits of knowledge (letter-to-sound, or in the case of spelling, sound-to-letter, correspondences), each of which could be presented, practiced, and tested independently, was the route to helping them acquire that knowledge.

THE LEGACY OF THE SCHOLARSHIP OF THE 1960s

In beginning reading, the decade of the 1960s was a period of fervent activity. In the early 1960s, in an effort to settle the debate about the best way to teach beginning reading once and for all (this time with the tools of empirical scholarship rather than rhetoric), the Cooperative Research Branch of the United States Office of Education funded an elaborate collection of "First Grade Studies," loosely coupled forays into the highly charged arena of preferred approaches to beginning reading instruction.[29] While each of the studies differed from one another in the particular emphasis, most of them involved a comparison of different methods of teaching beginning reading. They were published in a brand new journal, *Reading Research Quarterly*, in 1966. Jeanne Chall completed her magnum opus, *Learning to Read: The Great Debate*, in 1967. It too had been funded in order to put the debate behind us, but Chall would use different scholarly tools to accomplish her goals. She would employ critical review procedures to examine our empirical research base, the content of our basal readers, and exemplary classroom practices. In 1965, Lyndon Johnson's Elementary and Secondary Education Act, one key plank in his Great Society platform, brought new resources for compensatory education to schools through a program dubbed Title I. And Commissioner of Education James Allen would, at decade's end, establish the national Right to Read program as a way of guaranteeing that right to each child in America. The country was clearly focused on early reading, and many were optimistic that we would find answers to the questions about teaching reading that had vexed us for decades, even centuries.

Chall's book and the First Grade Studies had an enormous impact on beginning reading instruction and indirectly on reading pedagogy more generally. One message of the First Grade Studies was that just about any alternative, when compared to the business-as-usual basals (which served as a common control in each of more than 20 separate quasi-experimental studies), elicited equal or greater performance on the part of first graders (and, as it turned out, second graders).[30] It did not seem to matter much what the alternative was—language experience, a highly synthetic phonics approach, a linguistic approach (control the text so that young readers are exposed early on only to easily decodable words grouped together in word families, such as the *-an* family, the *-at* family, the *-ig* family, etc.), a special alphabet (i.e., the Initial Teaching Alphabet), or even basals infused with a heavier-than-usual dose of phonics right up front—they were all the equal or the better of the ubiquitous basal. A second message, one that was both sent and received, was that the racehorse mentality of studies that compare one method against another had probably run its course. By accepting this message, the reading research community was free to turn its efforts to other, allegedly more fruitful, issues and questions—the importance of the teacher quite irrespective of method, the significance of site, and the press of other aspects of the curriculum such as comprehension and writing.[31] With the notable exception of the Follow-Through Studies in the 1970s, which are only marginally related to reading, it would take another twenty-five years for large-scale experiments to return to center stage in reading.[32]

In spite of a host of other important recommendations, most of which had some short term effect, the ultimate legacy of Chall's book reduces to just one—that early attention to the code in some way, shape, or form must be reinfused into early reading instruction. For the record, Chall recommended five broad changes: (a) make a necessary change in method (to an early emphasis on phonics of some sort), (b) re-examine current ideas about content (focus on the enduring themes in folk tales), (c) re-evaluate grade levels (increase the challenge at every grade level), (d) develop new tests (both single component tests and absolute measures with scores that are independent of the population taking the test), and (e) improve reading research (including its accessibility). Each of these recommendations will be discussed later.

The look-say basals that had experienced virtually uninterrupted progress from 1930 to 1965 never quite recovered from the one-two punch delivered by Chall's book and the First Grade Studies in 1967. Given the critical sacking they took from Chall and the empirical thrashing they took from the First Grade Studies, one might have expected one of the pretenders to the early reading throne, documented so carefully in the First Grade Studies, to assume the mantle of the new conventional wisdom in the years that followed. Ironically, it was the basals themselves, albeit in a radically altered form, that captured the marketplace of the 1970s and 1980s. They accomplished this feat by overhauling themselves to adapt to a changing market shaped by these two important scholarly efforts. Basal programs that debuted in the five years after Chall's book appeared were radically different from their predecessors. Most notably, *phonics* that had been relegated to a skill to be taught contextually after a hefty bank of sight words had been committed to memory, was back—from day one of grade one—in the series that hit the market in the late 1960s and early 1970s. Surprisingly, it was not the highly synthetic alphabetic approach of the previous century or the remedial clinics of the 1930s (which one might have expected from a reading of Chall's book). It is better described as an intensification and repositioning (to grade one) of the analytic phonics that had been taught in the latter part of grade 1 and in grades 2 to 4 in the look-say basals of the 1960s.[33] Equally significant, there was a change in *content*, at least in grade one. Dick and Jane and all their assorted pairs of competing cousins—Tom and Susan, Alice and Jerry, Jack and Janet—were retired from the first grade curriculum and replaced by a wider array of stories and characters; by the early 1970s, more of the selections were adaptations of children's literature rather than stories written to conform to a vocabulary restriction or a read-ability formula.

It is hard to determine how seriously educators and publishers took Chall's other three recommendations. For example, in the basals that came out after Chall, the grade 1 books (the preprimers, primers, and readers) were considerably more *challenging* than their immediate pre-decessors, mainly by virtue of a much more challenging grade 1 vocab-ulary—more words introduced much earlier in the grade 1 program.[34] One series even divided its new vocabulary words into words that ought to be explicitly introduced as sight words and those words, which they dubbed *decodable*, that should be recognized by the students by applying the phonics skills they had been taught up to that point in the program.[35] Beyond grade 1, however, changes in difficulty were much less visible, and no appreciable increase in the readability scores of these later levels occurred.

In testing, a major change toward single component tests did occur, although it is difficult to attribute this change solely to Chall's recom-mendation. Beginning in the early 70s and running through at least the late 80s, each successive edition of basal programs brought an increase in the number of single component tests—tests for each phonics skill (all the beginning, middle and final consonant sounds, vowel patterns, and syllabication), tests for each comprehension skill (main idea, find-ing details, drawing conclusions, and determining cause-effect rela-tions) at every grade level, tests for alphabetical order and using the encyclopedia, and just about any other skill one might think of.

But other events and movements of the period also pointed toward single component tests. For one, owing to the intellectual contribu-tions of Benjamin Bloom and John Carroll, the mastery learning move-ment[36] was gathering its own momentum during the late 1960s. Ac-cording to proponents of mastery learning, if a complex domain could be decomposed into manageable subcomponents, each of which could be taught and learned to some predetermined level of mastery, then most, if not all, students should be able to master the knowledge and skills in the domain. Second, criterion-referenced tests were spawned during this same period.[37] The logic of criterion-referenced assessment was that some predetermined level of mastery (say 80% correct), not the average for a group of students in a given grade level, ought to be the reference point for determining how well a student was doing on a test. A third construct from this period, curriculum-embedded assess-ment,[38] held that students should be held to account for precisely what was needed to march successfully through a particular curriculum—no less, no more. If one could specify the scope and sequence of knowledge and skills in the curriculum and develop assessments for each, then it should be possible to guide all students through the curriculum, even if some needed more practice and support than others. One can imagine a high degree of compatibility among all three of these powerful constructs—mastery learning, criterion-referenced assessment, and curriculum-embedded assessment. All three provide comfortable homes for single component assessments of the sort Chall was advocating.

With powerful evidence from mastery learning's application to college students,[39] publishers of basal programs and some niche publishers began to create and implement what came to be called skills management systems.[40] In their most meticulous application, these systems *became* the reading program. Students took a battery of mastery tests, practiced those skills they had not mastered (usually by completing worksheets that looked remarkably like the tests), took tests again, and continued through this cycle until they had mastered all the skills assigned to the grade level (or until the year ended). Unsurprisingly, the inclusion of these highly specific skill tests had the effect of increasing the salience of workbooks, worksheets, and other skill materials on which students could practice in anticipation of (and as a consequence of) mastery tests. Thus the basals of this period were comprised of two parallel systems: (1) the graded series of anthologies filled with stories and short non-fiction pieces for oral and silent reading and discussion, and (2) an embedded skills management system to guide the development of phonics, comprehension, vocabulary, and study skills.

Chall's last recommendation was to improve reading research. Research had been too inaccessible (to the very audience of practitioners who most needed it), too narrow in scope, and too dismissive of its past. All that needed to change, she argued. As I will detail in the next section, reading research changed dramatically, but not necessarily in a direction Chall envisioned.

One other change in basal reading programs in this period worth noting was the technology to place reduced facsimiles of student text pages onto a page where it could be surrounded by teaching suggestions and questions for guided reading. This was hailed as a major advance in the utility of manuals because teachers did not have to turn back and forth from student text to the teacher's section in order to guide the reading of a story.

This was the scene, then, in the early 1970s, just as the reading field was about to embark on a new curricular trek that continues even today.

If the middle third of the century was characterized by a steady, unwavering march toward the ever-increasing prominence of a particular philosophy and set of curricular practices encapsulated in ubiquitous basals that championed a look-say approach,[41] the early 1970s brought major challenges in philosophy and pedagogy—harder texts, more phonics, and a skill development program unlike anything seen before.[42]

Taking Stock: 3

But even with some alterations in the materials available and some new pedagogical twists, the pedagogy of the early 1970s revealed little fundamental change in the underlying assumptions about the role of the teacher and learner or the nature of reading and writing. Teachers, armed with their basal manuals, controlled the learning situation as never before, and students continued to play the role of passive recipient of the knowledge and skills mediated by the teacher. Most important, reading was still a fundamentally perceptual process of translating letters into sounds. If anything, the perceptual nature of reading was made more salient than in the 1950s and 1960s by the return of phonics to center stage.

Developments in the Last Third of the Century

READING AS THE PROVINCE OF OTHER SCHOLARLY TRADITIONS[43]

Somewhere during this period—the exact point of departure is hard to fix—we began a journey that would take us through many new twists and turns on the way to different landscapes than we had visited before. Along the way we confronted fundamental shifts in our views of reading and writing and started to create a variety of serious curricular alternatives to the conventional wisdom of the 1970s. Just beyond the horizon lay even more unfamiliar and rockier territory—the conceptual revolutions in cognition, sociolinguistics, and philosophy that would have such far-reaching consequences for reading curriculum and pedagogy of the 1980s and 1990s.

Reading became an ecumenical scholarly commodity; it was embraced by scholars from many different fields of inquiry. The first to take reading under their wing were the linguists, who wanted to convince us that reading was a language process closely allied to its sibling language processes of writing, speaking, and listening. Then came the psycholinguists and the cognitive psychologists, followed soon by the sociolinguists, the philosophers, the literary critics, and the critical theorists. It is not altogether clear why reading has attracted such interest from scholars in so many other fields. One explanation is that reading is considered by so many to be a key to success in other endeavors in and out of school; this is often revealed in comments like, "Well if you don't learn to read, you can't learn other things for yourself." Another is that scholars in these other disciplines thought that the educationists had got it all wrong, and it was time for another group to have their say. Whatever the reasons, the influence of these other scholarly traditions on reading pedagogy is significant; in fact, the pedagogy of the 1980s and 1990s cannot be understood without a firm grounding in the changes in world view that these perspectives spawned.

Linguistics. In 1962, Charles Fries published a book entitled *Linguistics and Reading.* In it, he outlined what he thought the teaching of reading would look like if it were viewed from the perspective of linguistics. In the same decade, several other important books and articles appeared, each carrying essentially the same message: The perspective of the modern science of linguistics, we were told, would privilege different models and methods of teaching reading. It would tell us, for example, that some things do not need to be taught explicitly because the oral language takes care of them more or less automatically. For example, the three different pronunciations of *–ed* (as in *nabbed, capped,* and *jaded*), need not be taught as a reading skill because our oral language conventions determine the pronunciation almost perfectly. English in its oral form demands the voiced alternative /d/ after a voiced consonant such as /b/. It demands the unvoiced alternative /t/ after an unvoiced consonant such as /p/, and it requires the syllabic version /ǝd/ after either /d/ or /t/. To teach these rules, which are very complex, would likely make things more confusing than simply allowing the oral language to do its work without fanfare.

Another linguistic insight came to us from the transformational generative grammars that replaced conventional structural linguistics as the dominant paradigm within the field during the 60s and 70s. Noam Chomsky published two revolutionary treatises during this period—*Syntactic Structures* in 1957 and *Aspects of a Theory of Syntax* in 1965. With these books Chomsky revolutionized the field of linguistics and paved the way, theoretically, for equally dramatic changes in the way that psychologists thought about and studied the processes of language comprehension and language acquisition.

Chomsky also provided the basis for a nativist view about language acquisition—a view that holds that humans come to the world "wired" to acquire the language of the community into which they are born.

He and others drew this inference from two basic and contrasting facts about language: (a) language is incredibly complex and (b) language is acquired quite easily and naturally by children living in an environment in which they are simply exposed to (rather than taught!) the language of their community well before they experience school. Only a view that children are equipped with some special cognitive apparatus for inferring complex rules could explain this remarkable feat.

Because our prevailing views of both reading comprehension and reading acquisition were derived from the same behavioristic assumptions that Chomsky and his peers had attacked, reading scholars began to wonder whether those assumptions would hold up when we applied similar perspectives and criticisms to analyses of written language comprehension and acquisition.[44]

Psycholinguistics. During the decade after the publication of *Syntactic Structures*, a new field of inquiry, psycholinguistics, evolved. In its first several years of existence, the field devoted itself to determining whether the views of linguistic competence and language acquisition that had been set forth by Chomsky and his colleagues could serve as psychological models of language performance. While the effort to develop a simple mapping from Chomsky to models of language performance waned after a few unsatisfactory attempts, the field of psycholinguistics and the disposition of psychologists to study language with complex theoretical tools had been firmly established.

Particularly influential on our thinking about reading were scholars of language acquisition[45] who established the rule-governed basis of language learning. In contrast to earlier views, these psycholinguists found that children did not imitate written language; rather, as members of a language community, they were participants in language and invented for themselves rules about how oral language worked. This insight allowed researchers to explain such constructions as "I eated my dinner" and "I gots two foots." Roger Brown and his colleagues showed conclusively that children were active learners who inferred rules and tested them out. Much as Kenneth Goodman would later show with written language, "mistakes," especially overgeneralizations, in oral language could be used to understand the rule systems that children were inventing for themselves.

The analogy with oral language development was too tempting for reading educators to resist. Several adopted something like a nativist framework in studying the acquisition of reading, asking what the teaching of reading and writing would look like if we assumed that children can learn to read and write in much the same way as they learn to talk—that is, naturally. What would happen if we assumed that children were members of a community in which reading and writing are valued activities that serve important communication functions? What if we assumed that the most important factors in learning to read and write were having genuine reasons for communicating in these media and having access to a data base in which there was so much print and talk about print that students could discover the patterns and regularities on their own, much as they do when they discover the patterns and regularities of oral language? While the seminal work involved in putting these assumptions to empirical tests would wait for a couple of decades, the seeds of doubt about our perceptually based views of reading acquisition were firmly planted by the middle 1960s.

Two influential individuals, Kenneth Goodman and Frank Smith, led the reading field in addressing these kinds of questions. In 1965, Goodman demonstrated that the errors children made while reading orally were better viewed as windows into the inner workings of their comprehension processes than as mistakes to be eradicated. He found that the mistakes that children made while reading in context revealed that they were trying to make sense of what they read. In another seminal 1967 piece, *Reading: A Psycholinguistic Guessing Game*, Goodman laid out the elements of language that he thought that readers employed as they constructed meaning for the texts they encountered. In reading, he conjectured, readers use three cue systems to make sense of text: syntactic cues, semantic cues, and grapho-phonemic cues. By attending to all of these cue sources, Goodman contended, readers could reduce their uncertainty about unknown words or meanings, thus rendering both the word identification and comprehension processes more manageable.[46]

Smith's revolutionary ideas were first presented in 1971 in a book entitled *Understanding Reading*.[47] In this seminal text, Smith argued that reading was not something one was *taught*, but rather was something one *learned* to do. Smith believed that there were no special prerequisites to learning to read, indeed, that reading was simply making sense of one particular type of information in our environment. As such, reading was what one learned to do as a consequence of belonging to a literate society. One learned to read from reading. The implication, which Smith made explicit, was that the "function of teachers is not so much to *teach* reading as to help children read" (pg. 3). This certainly challenged the notion of the teacher as the individual who meted out knowledge and skills to passively waiting students. For Smith, all knowing and all learning were constructive processes; individuals made sense of what they encountered based on what they already knew.[48] Even perception, he contended, was a decision-making, predictive process based on prior knowledge.

Smith also argued that reading was only incidentally visual. By that, Smith meant that being able to see was necessary but not sufficient to achieve understanding. He identified four sources of information: orthographic, syntactic, semantic, and visual, all of which he claimed were somewhat redundant, and argued that skilled readers made use of the three sources that were a part of their prior knowledge (the orthographic, syntactic, and semantic) in order to minimize their reliance on visual information. In fact, the danger in relying too heavily on visual information is that readers might lose sight of meaning.

The psycholinguistic perspective had a number of influences on reading pedagogy. First, it valued literacy experiences that focused on making meaning. This meant that many classroom activities, particularly worksheets and games, which focused on enabling skills such as specific letter-sound correspondences, syllabication activities, structural analysis skills, specific comprehension activities, or study skills were devalued. Second, it helped us to value texts for beginning readers, such as example 1 (see Table 1), in which authors relied on natural language patterns, thus making it possible for emerging readers to use their knowledge of language to predict words and meanings. This meant that texts that relied on high-frequency words in short, choppy sentences (what we have come to call basalese), as in example 2, or those based upon the systematic application of some phonics element (i.e., a decodable text), as in example 3, were correspondingly devalued.

TABLE 1
SAMPLE TEXTS FOR BEGINNING READING

1. Red Fox, Red Fox, what do you see? I see a blue bird looking at me. Blue Bird, Blue Bird, what do you see? I see a green frog looking at me. 2. Run, John, run. Run to Dad. Dad will run. Run, Dad. Run, John. See them run.	3. Nat can bat. Nat can bat with the fat bat. The cat has the fat bat. The rat has the fat bat. Nat has the fat bat. Bat the bat, Nat.

Third, the psycholinguistic perspective helped us understand the reading process and appreciate children's efforts as readers. Errors were no longer things to be corrected; instead they were windows into the workings of the child's mind, allowing both the teacher and the child to understand more about the reading process and reading strategies. Understanding miscues also helped educators focus on comprehension and appreciate risk-taking.

Fourth, psycholinguists gave us a means (miscue analysis) and a theory (reading as a constructive process) that was remarkably distinct from previous ideas about reading. The perspective made explicit links between oral and written language acquisition and helped us view reading as language rather than simply perception or behavior. In a sense, psycholinguistics continued the changes and traditions begun by the linguistic perspective; however, within the reading field, its influence was deeper and broader than its academic predecessor.

Most important, psycholinguistics affected our views of teaching and learning in a fundamental way. Reading scholars began to rethink ideas about what needed to be taught, as well as the relation between teaching and learning. So, instead of asking, "What can I teach this child so that she *will eventually become* a reader?", we began to ask, "What can I do to help this child *as* a reader?" Some teachers began to welcome all children into what Smith referred to as "The Literacy Club" as an alternative to teaching children so-called prerequisite skills.[49]

Cognitive psychology. If psycholinguistics enabled psychologists to reexamine their assumptions about language learning and understanding by placing greater emphasis on the active, intentional role of language users, cognitive psychology allowed psychologists to extend constructs such as human purpose, intention, and motivation to a greater range of psychological phenomena, including perception, attention, comprehension, learning, memory, and executive control of all cognitive process. All of these would have important consequences in reading pedagogy.

I cannot emphasize too strongly the dramatic nature of the paradigm shift that occurred within those branches of psychology concerned with human intellectual processes. The previous half-century, from roughly the teens through the fifties, had been dominated by a behaviorist perspective in psychology that shunned speculation about the inner workings of the mind. Just show us the surface-level outcomes of the processes, as indexed by overt, observable behaviors. Leave the speculation to the philosophers. That was the contextual background against which both psycholinguistics and cognitive psychology served as dialectical antagonists when they appeared on the scene in the late 60s and early 70s.

The most notable change within psychology was that it became fashionable for psychologists, perhaps for the first time since the early part of the century, to study reading.[50] And in the decade of the 1970s works by psychologists flooded the literature on basic processes in reading. One group focused on text comprehension by trying to ferret out how it is that readers come to understand the underlying structure of texts. We were offered story grammars—structural accounts of the nature of narratives, complete with predictions about how those structures impede and enhance human story comprehension. Others chose to focus on the expository tradition in text.[51] Like their colleagues interested in story comprehension, they believed that structural accounts of the nature of expository (informational) texts would provide valid and useful models for text comprehension. And in a sense, both of these efforts worked. Story grammars did account for story comprehension. Analyses of the structural relations among ideas in an informational piece did account for text comprehension. But what neither text-analysis tradition really tackled was the relationship between the knowledge of the world that readers bring to text and comprehension of those texts. In other words, by focusing on structural rather than the ideational, or content, characteristics of texts, they failed to get to the heart of comprehension. That task, as it turned out, fell to one of the most popular and influential movements of the 70s, schema theory.

Schema theory[52] is a theory about the structure of human knowledge as it is represented in memory. In our memory, schemata are like little containers into which we deposit particular experiences that we have. So, if we see a chair, we store that visual experience in our chair schema. If we go to a restaurant, we store that experience in our restaurant schema, if we attend a party, our party schema, and so on. Clearly schema theory is linked to Piaget's theories of development and his two types of learning, assimilation and accommodation. When we assimilate new information, we store it in an existing schema; when we accommodate new information, we modify the structure of our schemata to fit the new data. The modern iteration of schema theory also owes a debt to Frederic Bartlett, who, writing in the 1930s, used the construct of schema to explain culturally driven interpretations of stories. For Bartlett, cultural schemata for stories were so strong that they prevented listeners, whether European or native Alaskan in background, from adopting the story schema of the other culture to understand its stories. Bartlett's account predates the current constructivist models of cognition and learning by sixty years; and his view is as inherently constructive as those that have succeeded him. In essence, Bartlett was saying exactly what modern constructivists say—that readers and listeners actively construct meanings for texts they encounter rather than simply "receiving" meaning from the texts.[53]

Schema theory also provides a credible account of reading comprehension, which probably, more than any of its other features, accounted for its popularity within the reading field in the 1970s and 80s.[54] It is not hard to see why schema theory was so appealing to theoreticians, researchers, and practitioners when it arrived on the scene in the 1970s. First, it provides a rich and detailed theoretical account of the everyday intuition that we understand and learn what is new in terms of what we already know. Second, it also accounts for another everyday intuition about why we, as humans, so often disagree about our interpretation of an event, a story, an article, a movie, or a TV show—we disagree with one another because we approach the phenomenon with very different background experiences and knowledge. Third, it accounts for a third everyday intuition that might be called an "it's-all-Greek-to-me" experience: Sometimes we just don't have enough background knowledge to understand a new experience or text.

While these insights may not sound earthshaking after the fact, for the field of reading, and for education more generally, they were daunting challenges to our conventional wisdom. Examined in light of existing practices in the 1970s, they continued the revolutionary spirit of the linguistic and psycholinguistic perspectives. Schema theory encouraged us to ask:

What is it that my children already know? And how can I use that to help them deal with these new ideas that I would like them to know?

rather than:

What is it that they do not know? And how can I get that into their heads?

More specifically, with respect to reading comprehension, schema theory encouraged us to examine texts from the perspective of the knowledge and cultural backgrounds of our students in order to evaluate the likely connections that they would be able to make between ideas that are in the text and the schema that they would bring to the reading task. Schema theory, like the psycholinguistic perspective, also promoted a constructivist view of comprehension; all readers must, at every moment in the reading process, construct a coherent model of reading for the texts they read. The most important consequence of this constructivist perspective is that there is inherent ambiguity about where meaning resides. Does it reside in the text? In the author's mind as she set pen to paper? In the mind of each reader as she builds a model of meaning unique to her experience and reading? In the inter-action between reader and text?

Sociolinguistics. Sociolinguistics as a discipline developed in parallel with psycholinguistics. Beginning with the work of William Labov, and Joan Baratz and Roger Shuy, sociolinguists had important lessons for reading scholars.[55] Mainly these lessons focused on issues of dialect and reading. Sociolinguists were finding that dialects were not ill- or half-formed variations of standard English. Instead, each dialect constituted a well-developed linguistic system in its own right, complete with rules for variations from standard English and a path of language develop-ment for its speakers. Speakers of dialects expressed linguistic *differ-ences* not linguistic *deficits*. The goal of schooling was not, and should not be, to eradicate the dialect in the process of making each individual a speaker of standard English. Instead, sociolinguists stressed the need to find ways to accommodate children's use of their dialect while they are learning to read and write. Several proposals for achieving this accommodation were tried and evaluated. The first was to write special readers for dialect speakers. In the early 1960s, several examples of Black dialect readers appeared and, almost as rapidly, disappeared from major urban districts. They failed primarily because African-American parents did not want their children learning with "special" materials; they wanted their children to be exposed to mainstream materials used by other children.[56] The second equally unsuccessful strategy was to delay instruction in reading and writing until children's oral language became more standardized. Teachers who tried this technique soon found out just how resistant and persistent early language learning can be. The third, and most successful, approach to dialect accommodation involved nothing more than recognizing that a child who translates a standard English text into a dialect is performing a remarkable feat of translation rather than making reading errors. So, an African-American child who says /pōs/ when he sees *post* is simply applying a rule of Black English which requires a consonant cluster in ending position to be reduced to the sound of the first consonant. Unfortunately for children who speak a dialect, we, as a field, did not take the early lessons of the sociolinguists to heart. We continue to find schools in which children are scolded for using the oral language that they have spent their whole lives learning. We also continue to find children whose dialect transla-tions are treated as if they were oral reading errors.

Prior to the advent of the sociolinguistic perspective, when educators talked about "context" in reading, they typically meant the print that surrounded particular words on a page. In the 1980s, and primarily because of the work of sociolinguists, the meaning of the word context expanded to include not only what was on the page, but what Bloome and Green referred to as the instructional, non-instructional, and home and community contexts of literacy.[57] From a sociolinguistic perspective, reading always occurred in a context, a context that was shaped by the literacy event at the same time as it shaped the event. The sociolinguistic versions of knowledge and language as socially and culturally constructed processes moved the constructivist metaphor to another plane, incorporating not only readers' prior knowledge in the form of schemata, but also the meanings constructed by peers and by one's cultural ancestors.

The most significant legacy of the sociolinguistic perspective was our heightened consciousness about language as a social and therefore cultural construction. Suddenly, reading was a part of a bigger and more complex world. Sociolinguists examined the role of language in school settings. For example, they pointed out that often success in reading was not so much an indication of reading "ability" per se, but of the success the individual experienced in learning how to use language appropriately in educational settings. Thus success, according to a sociolinguistic analysis, was more an index of how well children learned to "do school" than how well they could read. They contrasted the functions that language serves in school with the functions it serves outside of school and helped us rethink the role of language within the classroom. By studying the community outside of school, sociolinguists made us conscious of social, political, and cultural differences; as a result, we began to rethink our judgments of language and behavior. We saw that any judgment call we made, rather than reflecting the "right" way, simply reflected "our" way—the way we as teachers thought and talked and behaved because of the cultural situation in which we lived outside as well as inside school. By focusing on the role of community in learning, they caused many educators to rethink the competitive atmosphere of classrooms and of school labels and to recommend changes within schools so that children could learn from and with each other. With these contributions from sociolinguists, it was becoming more and more apparent that reading was not only not context-free but that it was embedded in multiple contexts.

Literary theory perspective. One cannot understand the pedagogical changes in practice that occurred in the elementary reading curriculum in the 1980s without understanding the impact of literary theory, particularly reader response theory. In our secondary schools, the various traditions of literary criticism have always had a voice in the curriculum, especially in guiding discussions of classic literary works. Until the middle 1980s, the "new criticism" that had emerged in the post World War II era had dominated for several decades, and it had sent teachers and students on a search for the one "true" meaning in each text they encountered. With the emergence (some would argue the re-emergence) of reader response theories, all of which gave as much, if not more, authority to the reader than to either the text or the author, the picture, along with our practices, changed dramatically. While there are many modern versions of reader response available, the work of Louise Rosenblatt has been most influential among elementary teachers and reading educators. In the 1980s, many educators re-read (or more likely read for the first time) Rosenblatt's 1976 edition of her 1938 text, *Literature as Exploration*, and *The Reader, the Text, The poem*, which appeared in 1978. Rosenblatt argues that meaning is something that resides neither in the head of the reader (as some had previously argued) nor on the printed page (as others had argued).[58] Instead, Rosenblatt contends, meaning is created in the transaction between reader and document. This meaning, which she refers to as the poem, resides above the reader-text interaction. Meaning is therefore neither subject nor object nor the interaction of the two. Instead it is transaction, something new and different from any of its inputs and influences.[59]

THE PEDAGOGICAL CORRELATES OF NEW PERSPECTIVES

While the post-Chall basal tradition continued well into the decade of the 1980s, new perspectives and practices began to show up in classrooms, journal articles, and basal lessons in the early 1980s.

Comprehension on center stage. Comprehension, especially as a workbook activity and a follow-up to story reading, was not a stranger to the reading classrooms of the 30s through the 70s. As indicated earlier, it entered the curriculum as a story discussion tool and as a way of assessing reading competence in the first third of this century.[60] Developments during mid-century were highlighted in an earlier NSSE yearbook devoted to reading;[61] by mid-century, the infrastructure of comprehension had been elaborated extensively and infused into the guided reading and workbook task. It was a staple of basal programs when Chall conducted her famous study of early reading, and had she emphasized reading instruction in the intermediate grades rather than grade one, it would undoubtedly have been more prominent in her account.

During the late 1970s and through the decade of the 1980s comprehension found its way to center stage in reading pedagogy. Just as a nationally sponsored set of research activities (i.e., the First Grade Studies and Chall's book) focused energy on reforms in beginning reading in the late 1960s, it was the federally funded Center for the Study of Reading, initiated in 1976, that focused national attention on comprehension. Although the Center's legacy is undoubtedly bringing schema theory and the knowledge-comprehension relationship into our national conversation, it also supported much research on comprehension instruction,[62] including research that attempted to help students develop a repertoire of strategies for improving their comprehension.[63] This research was not limited to the Center; indeed many other scholars were equally involved in developing instructional strategies and routines during this period, including emphases on monitoring comprehension,[64] transactional strategies instruction,[65] KWL graphic organizers,[66] and, more recently, questioning the author.[67] Many of these new strategies found their way into the basals of the 1980s, which demonstrated substantially more emphasis on comprehension at all levels, including grade one.[68]

Literature-based reading. Even though selections from both classical and contemporary children's literature have always been a staple of basal selections dating back to the nineteenth century (especially after grade 2 when the need for strict vocabulary control diminished), literature virtually exploded into the curriculum in the late 1980s. A short burst in literary content occurred after Chall's critical account of the type of selections and the challenge of basal content; more excerpts from authentic literature appeared, even in the grade one readers. But these selections had two characteristics that had always offended those who champion the use of genuine literature—excerpting and adaptation. Rarely were whole books included; instead, whole chapters or important slices were excerpted for inclusion. And even when a whole chapter was included, it was usually adapted to (a) reduce vocabulary difficulty, (b) reduce the grammatical complexity of sentences, or (c) excise words (e.g., mild profanity) or themes that might offend important segments of the market.

Beyond basals, children's literature played an important supplementary role in the classrooms of teachers who believed that they must engage their students in a strong parallel independent reading program. Often this took the form of each child selecting books to be read individually and later discussed with the teacher in a weekly one-on-one conference. And even as far back as the 1960s, there were a few programs which turned this individualized reading component into the main reading program.[69]

But in the late 1980s, literature was dramatically repositioned. Several factors converged to pave the way for a groundswell in the role of literature in elementary reading. Surely the resurgence of reader response theory as presented by Rosenblatt was important, as was the compatibility of the reader response theory and its emphasis on interpretation with the constructivism that characterized both cognitive and sociolinguistic perspectives. Research also played a role; in 1985, for example, in the watershed publication of the Center for the Study of Reading, *Becoming a Nation of Readers*, Richard Anderson and his colleagues documented the importance of "just plain reading" as a critical component of any and all elementary reading programs.[70] This is also a period that witnessed an unprecedented expansion in the number of new children's books published annually. Finally, a few pieces of scholarship exerted enormous influence on teachers and teacher educators. Perhaps most influential was Nancie Atwell's *In the Middle*. In her account she laid out her story, as a middle school teacher, of how she invited readers, some of whom were quite reluctant, into a world of books and reading. The credibility of her experience and the power of her prose were persuasive in convincing thousands of classroom teachers that they could use existing literature and "reading workshops" to accomplish anything that a basal program could accomplish in skill development while gaining remarkable advantages in students' literary experience.[71]

In terms of policy and curriculum, the most significant event in promoting literature-based reading was the 1988 California Reading Framework. The framework called for reading materials which contained much more challenging texts at all levels. More important, it mandated the use of genuine literature, not the dumbed-down adaptations and excerpts from children's literature that had been the staple of basal programs for decades. Publishers responded to the call of California's framework and produced a remarkably different product in the late 1980s and early 1990s than had ever appeared before on the basal market.[72] Gone were excerpts and adaptations, and with them almost any traces of vocabulary control. Skills that had been front and center in the basals of the 70s and 80s were relegated to appendix-like status. Comprehension questions were replaced by more interpretive, impressionistic response to literature activities. All this was done in the name of providing children with authentic literature and authentic activities to accompany it. The logic was that if we could provide students with real literature and real motivations for reading it, much of what is arduous about skill teaching and learning will take care of itself.

Book Clubs and literature circles are the most visible instantiations of the literature-based reading movement.[73] The underlying logic of Book Clubs is the need to engage children in the reading of literature in the same way as adults engage one another in voluntary reading circles. Such voluntary structures are likely to elicit greater participation, motivation, appreciation, and understanding on the part of students. Teachers are encouraged to establish a set of "cultural practices" (ways of interacting and supporting one another) in their classrooms to support students as they make their way into the world of children's literature. These cultural practices offer students both the opportunity to engage in literature and the skills to ensure that they can negotiate and avail themselves of that opportunity.

Process writing. In the middle 1980s, writing achieved a stronghold in the elementary language arts curriculum that it had never before held. Exactly why and how it achieved that position of prominence is not altogether clear, but certain explanations are plausible. Key understandings from the scholarship of the 70s and 80s paved the way. Functionality associated with the sociolinguistic perspective encouraged teachers to ask students to write for genuine audiences and purposes. The psycholinguistic notion of "error" as a window into children's thinking allowed us to worry less about perfect spelling and grammar and more about the quality of the thinking and problem solving children were producing. The general acceptance of constructivist epistemologies disposed us to embrace writing as the most transparently constructive of all pedagogical activities. All of these constructs allowed us as a profession to take a different developmental view on writing, one consistent with the emergent literacy perspective that was gaining strength in early childhood literacy. We came to view all attempts to make sense by setting pen to paper, however deviant from adult models, as legitimate and revealing in their own right if examined through the eyes of the child writer. Led by Donald Graves and Lucy Calkins, we revolutionized our views of early writing development.[74] Finally, we began to see reading and writing as inherently intertwined, each supporting the other.

Integrated instruction. It is impossible to document the history of reading instruction in the twentieth century without mentioning the ways in which we have attempted to integrate reading with other curricular phenomena. Two stances have dominated our thinking about how to integrate reading into other curricula—integration of reading with the other language arts (writing, speaking, and listening) and integration across subject matter boundaries (with mathematics, science, social studies, art, and music). Like literature-based reading, both senses of integration have long been a part of the thinking about elementary reading curriculum.[75] In fact, a look back to the progressivism of Dewey and other scholars in the first part of this century reveals substantial rhetoric about teaching and learning across curricular boundaries.[76] From that early spurt of energy until the late 1980s, however, integrations assumed a minor role in American reading instruction. In basal manuals, for example, integration was portrayed almost as an afterthought until the late 1980s; it appeared in the part of the lesson that follows the guided reading and skills instruction sections, signaling that these are things that a teacher can get to "if time permits." Things changed in the late 1980s. For one, integrated curriculum fit the sociolinguistic emphasis on language in use—the idea that language, including reading, is best taught and learned when it is put to work in the service of other purposes, activities, and learning efforts. Similarly, with the increase in importance of writing, especially early writing of the sort discussed by Graves and his colleagues,[77] it was tempting to champion the idea of integrated language arts instruction. In fact, the constructivist metaphor is nowhere played out as vividly and transparently as in writing, leading many scholars to use writing as a model for the sort of constructive approach they wanted to promote in readers. The notion was that we needed to help students learn to "read like a writer."[78] Also influential in supporting the move toward integrated instruction was the work of Donald Holdaway, who, in concert with many teacher colleagues, had been implementing an integrated language arts approach in Australia for a few decades.[79]

Whole language. Important as they are, comprehension, literature-based reading, process writing, and integrated instruction pale in comparison to the impact of whole language, which must be regarded as the most significant movement in reading curriculum in the last thirty years.[80] In fact, one might plausibly argue that whole language co-opted all four of these allied phenomena—comprehension, literature-based reading, integrated instruction and process writing—by incorporating

them, problems along with strengths, into its fundamental set of principles and practices. Whole language is grounded in child-centered pedagogy reminiscent of the progressive education movement (the individual child is the most important curriculum informant).[81] Philosophically
it is biased toward radical constructivist epistemology (all readers must
construct their own meanings for the texts they encounter). Curricularly, it is committed to authentic activity (real, not specially constructed, texts and tasks) and integration (both within the language arts
and between the language arts and other subject matters). Politically, it
is suspicious of all attempts to mandate and control curricular decisions
beyond the classroom level; as such, it places great faith and hope in the
wisdom of teachers to exercise professional prerogative in making decisions about the children in their care. Whole language owes its essential character and key principles to the insights of linguistics, psycholinguistics, cognitive psychology, sociolinguistics, and literary theory
detailed earlier. It owes its remarkable—if brief—appearance in the
national limelight of reading instruction to its committed leaders and a
veritable army of committed teachers who instantiated it in their classrooms, each with his or her own unique signature.[82]

When whole language emerged as a movement in the 80s, it challenged the conventional wisdom of basals and questioned the unquali-
fied support for early code emphases that had grown between 1967
and the early 1980s.[83] One of the great ironies of whole language is
that its ascendancy into curricular prominence is best documented by
its influence on the one curricular tool it has most consistently and
most vehemently opposed, the basal reader.[84] As suggested earlier,
basals changed dramatically in the early 1990s, largely, I conjecture, in
response to the groundswell of support within the teaching profession
for whole language and its close curricular allies, literature-based
reading and process writing.

Vocabulary control, already weakened during the 1970s in response to Chall's admonitions, was virtually abandoned in the early
1990s in deference to attempts to incorporate more literature, this
time in unexpurgated form (i.e., without the practices of adaptation
and excerpting that had characterized the basals of the 70s and 80s)
into the grade 1 program.[85] Phonics, along with other skills, was back-
grounded, and literature moved to center stage.

Basal programs appropriated or, as some whole language advocates
have argued, "basalized" the activities and tools of whole language.
Thus in the basals of the early 1990s, each unit might have a writing
process component in which the rhetoric if not the reality of some

version of process writing was presented to teachers and students. In the 1980s, comprehension questions, probably following a story line, might have sufficed for the guided reading section of the manual (the part that advises teachers on how to read and discuss the story), but in the 1990s, questions and tasks that supported deep probes into students' response to literature became more prevalent. Another concession to literature-based reading was the creation and marketing of classroom libraries—boxed sets of books, usually thematically related to each unit, that teachers could use to extend their lessons and units "horizontally" and enrich children's literary opportunities.

Basals also repositioned their "integrated language arts" and "integrated curriculum" strands. Dating back even to the 1920s and 1930s, basals had provided at least a "token" section in which teachers were encouraged to extend the themes or skills of the basal story into related writing (e.g., rewriting stories), oral language (e.g., transforming a story into a play and dramatizing it), or cross-curricular activities (e.g., conducting community surveys, tallying the results, and reporting them), but these forays were regarded as peripheral rather than core. In the basals of the early 1990s, as skills moved into the background,[86] these integrated language arts activities were featured more prominently as core lesson components.[87]

These changes can, I believe, be traced to the prominent position of whole language as a curricular force during this period.[88] Publishers of basals accomplished this feat of appropriation not by ridding their programs of the skills of previous eras, but by subtle repositioning—foregrounding one component while backgrounding another, creating optional components or modules (e.g., an intensive phonics kit or a set of literature books) that could be added to give the program one or another spin. Unsurprisingly, this created bulkier teachers' manuals and more complex programs.

Acceptance of whole language was not universal. To the contrary, there was considerable resistance to whole language and literature-based reading throughout the country.[89] In many places, whole language never really gained a foothold. In others what was implemented in the name of whole language was not consistent with the philosophical and curricular principles of the movement; California, whole language advocates would argue, is a case in point. Whole language got conflated with whole class instruction and was interpreted to mean that all students should get the same literature, even if teachers had to read it to them.[90]

Nor was there a single voice within the whole language movement. Whole language scholars and practitioners differ on a host of issues, such as the role of skills, conventions, and strategies within a language arts program. Some say, if we can just be patient, skills will emerge from meaningful communication activities; others spur things on by taking advantage of spontaneous opportunities for mini-lessons; still others are willing to spur spontaneity a bit.

Even so, it is fair to conclude that by the early 90s, whole language had become the conventional wisdom, the standard against which all else was referenced. The rhetoric of professional articles belies this change. As late as the mid-1980s, articles were written with the presumption of a different conventional wisdom—a world filled with skills, contrived readers, and workbooks. By 1991-92, they were written with the presumption that whole language reforms, while not fully ensconced in America's schools, were well on their way to implementation. The arguments in the 90s were less about first principles of whole language and more about fine-tuning teaching repertoires. The meetings of the Whole Language Umbrella grew to be larger than most large state conventions and regional conferences of the International Reading Association. By 1995, whole language was no longer a collection of guerrilla sorties into the land of skills and basals that characterized it through the mid 1980s. It had become the conventional wisdom, in rhetoric if not in reality.

Taking Stock: 4

Returning to the lenses outlined at the beginning of this chapter (range of materials and practices, role of teacher, role of learner, and the processes of reading and learning to read), in whole language, we finally encounter major shifts in emphasis in comparison to what we found at the beginning of the century. In whole language, teachers are facilitators not tellers. They observe what children do, decide what they need, and arrange conditions to allow students to discover insights about reading, writing, and learning for themselves. Because this is truly child-centered pedagogy, learners occupy center stage. As Jerome Harste puts it, the child is the primary curriculum informant. Students must be decision makers who are involved in choices about the books they read and stories they write. The materials of reading instruction are the materials of life and living—the books, magazines, newspapers, and other forms of print that children can encounter in everyday life are the materials they should encounter in the classroom—no less, no more. Ideally, there is no need for the sort of contrived texts and tasks of the sort found in basal reading programs. Instructional practices focus not on presenting a diet of skills carefully sequenced to achieve mastery but on creating activities and tasks that support the learning students need at a particular point in time. If skills and strategies are taught, they are taught in "mini-lessons," highly focused forays into the infrastructure of a skill or strategy followed up by immediately recontextualizing the skill in a genuine reading or writing situation. In contrast to previous periods, reading was now regarded as a meaning-making, not a perceptual, process. The reader was an active participant in creating, not a passive recipient of, the message in a text. The process of acquiring reading was also markedly different from the "readiness" perspective so dominant in the first eighty years of the century. Emergent literacy, the alternative to traditional reading readiness views, does not specify a "pre-reading" period in which children are prepared for the task of reading. All readers, at all stages, are meaning makers, even those who can only scribble a message or "pretend" read.[91] Thus, at century's end, reading pedagogy finally developed some viable alternatives to the conventional views of teacher, learner, and process that had dominated pedagogical practice for the entire century. As it turned out, the new directions were short-lived.

THE DEMISE OF WHOLE LANGUAGE

At century's end, just when it appeared as if whole language, supported by its intellectual cousins (process writing, literature-based reading, and integrated curriculum), was about to assume the position of conventional wisdom for the field, the movement was challenged seriously, and the pendulum of the pedagogical debate began to swing back toward the skills end of the curriculum and instruction continuum. Several factors converged to make the challenge credible, among them (a) unintended curricular casualties of whole language, (b) questionable applications of whole language, (c) growing dissatisfaction with doctrinaire views of any sort, (d) a paradigm swing in the ideology of reading research, (e) increasing politicization of the reading research and policy agenda, and (f) increasing pressure for educators of all stripes, especially reading educators, to produce measurable results.

Unintended curricular consequences. In its ascendancy, whole language changed the face of reading instruction, and in the process, left behind some curricular casualties, few of which were intended by those who supported whole language. Those, myself included,[92] who supported practices that were discarded in the rise of whole language, had difficulty supporting the whole language movement even though we might have been philosophically and curricularly sympathetic to many of its principles and practices. This lack of enthusiasm from curricular moderates meant that whole language failed to build a base of support that was broad enough to survive even modest curricular opposition, let alone the political onslaught that it would experience at century's turn.

What were these casualties? I see at least four: skills instruction, strategy instruction, an emphasis on text structure, and reading in the content areas. Earlier, I suggested that one of the consequences of whole language was the relegation of skills to the "appendices" of instructional programs. In accepting whole language, we tacitly accepted the premise that skills are better *caught* in the act of reading and writing genuine texts for authentic purposes than *taught* directly and explicitly by teachers. The argument is the same for phonics, grammar, text conventions, and structural elements. These entities may be worthy of learning, but they are unworthy of teaching. This position presents us with a serious conundrum as a profession. Admit, for the sake of argument, that the skills instruction of the 1970s and earlier, with decontextualized lessons and practice on "textoids" in workbook pages, deserved the criticism accorded to it by whole language advocates (and scholars from other traditions). But a retreat from most skills instruction into a world of "authentic opportunity" did not provide a satisfactory answer for teachers and scholars who understood the positive impact that instruction can have. Many young readers do not "catch" the alphabetic principle by sheer immersion in print or by listening to others read aloud. For some it seems to require careful planning and hard work by dedicated teachers who are willing to balance systematic skills instruction with authentic texts and activities.[93]

Strategy instruction was another casualty. This loss was particularly difficult for scholars who spent the better part of the early 1980s convincing basal publishers and textbook authors that the thoughtful teaching of flexible strategies for making and monitoring meaning was a viable alternative to mindless skills instruction, where skills were taught as though they were only ever to be applied to workbook pages and end-of-unit tests. But the strategy lessons that filled our basals in the middle to late 1980s—direct advice from teachers about how to summarize what one has read, how to use text structure to infer relations among ideas, how to distinguish fact from opinion, how to determine the central thread of a story, how to use context to infer word meanings, and how to make and evaluate the accuracy of predictions— were virtually non-existent in the basals of the early-to-middle 1990s. While there is no inherent bias in whole language or literature-based reading against the learning and use of a whole range of cognitive strategies, there is, as with phonics and grammar, a serious question about whether direct, explicit instruction in how to use them will help. The advice is to let them emerge from attempts to solve real reading problems and puzzles, the kind students meet in genuine encounters with authentic text. There may have been reason for concern about the strategy instruction of the 80s. But revision rather than rejection of these strategies was not a part of the rhetoric of whole language.[94]

Structural emphasis was also suspect within whole language. This suspicion extended to formal grammars, story grammars, rhetorical structures, and genre features of texts. As with skills and strategies, whole language reformers do not claim that students should not learn and develop control over these structural tools; they simply claim that, like skills, they are best inferred from reading and writing authentic texts in the process of making meaning. So, the advocates are comfortable in adopting Frank Smith's[95] admonition to encourage kids to read like a writer (meaning to read the text with a kind of critical eye toward understanding the tools and tricks of the trade that the author uses to make her points and achieve her effects on readers), but they would likely reject a systematic set of lessons designed to teach and assess children's control of story grammar elements (such as plot, characterization, style, mood, or theme) or some system for dealing with basic patterns of expository text. As with skills and strategies, many of us see a compromise alternative to both the formulaic approach of the early 1980s and the "discovery" approach of the new reforms—dealing with these structural elements as they emanate from stories that a group is currently reading can provide some guidance and useful tools for students and teachers.

Content area reading also suffered during the ascendancy of whole language and literature-based reading. Content area texts—expository texts in general, but especially textbook-like entries—were not privileged in a world of literature-based reading. This is not an implicit criticism of the literature-based reading movement; rather it is a comment about the reallocation of curricular time and energy that occurs when a movement gains momentum. There is a certain irony in this development, for it is expository reading, not narrative reading, that most concerns middle and high school teachers. The cost here has been very dear. To enter middle school and high school classrooms in order to examine the role of expository text is to conclude that it has none. Occasionally teachers assign expository texts for homework, but when students come to class the next day, clearly having avoided the assignment, teachers provide them with an oral version of what they would have gotten out of the text if they had bothered to read it. Most high school teachers have quite literally given up on the textbook for the communication of any important content. While understandable, this approach is, of course, ultimately counterproductive. There comes a time in the lives of students—either when they go to college or enter the world of work—when others expect them to read and understand informational texts on their own and in printed form rather than through oral or video transformation.[96]

Because whole language did not go out of its way to accommodate any of these curricular practices, those who were sympathetic with whole language but also champions of one or another approach were not available to help whole language respond to the criticism leveled at it in the late 1990s.

Questionable applications of whole language. One of the dilemmas faced by any curricular challenge is sustaining the integrity of the movement without imposing the very sorts of controls it is trying to eliminate. Whole language has not found a satisfying way of managing this dilemma, and it has suffered as a consequence. Many schools, teachers, and institutions appropriated the whole language label without honoring its fundamental principles of authenticity, integration, and empowerment. Basal reader publishers made the most obvious and widespread appropriation, some even positioning their basal series as "whole language" programs. Earlier, I noted another misapplication in which whole language was confounded with whole-class instruction. Nowhere was this conflation more extreme than in the implementation of the California literature framework. The logic that prevailed in many classrooms was that it was better to keep the entire class together, all experiencing the same texts, even if it meant that the teacher had to read the text to those children who lacked the skills to read it on their own. Implicit in this practice are two interesting assumptions: (1) that getting the content of the stories is the most important goal for reading instruction, and (2) that the skills and processes needed to read independently will emerge somehow from this environment in which many students are pulled through texts that far exceed the grasp of their current skills repertoire. Needless to say, whole language had enough on its hands dealing with its own assumptions and practices; these philosophical and curricular misapplications exposed the movement to a whole set of criticisms that derived from practices not of its own making.

One of the primary reasons for misapplication of whole language is, in my view, the lack of an explicit plan for professional development. Whole language gives teachers a wide berth for making curricular and instructional decisions, for whole classes and for individual children. It assumes that teachers who are empowered, sincere, and serious about their personal professional development will be able to tailor programs and activities to the needs and interests of individual children. Such an approach makes sense only when we can assume that teacher knowledge is widely and richly distributed in our profession. To offer these prerogatives in the face of narrow and shallow knowledge is to guarantee that misguided practices, perversions of the very intent of the movement, will be widespread. The puzzle, of course, is where to begin the reform—by ensuring that the knowledge precedes the prerogative, or by ceding the prerogative to teachers as a way of leveraging their motivation for greater knowledge.[97]

Growing dissatisfaction with extreme positions. While it has reached its peak in the last five years, concern about extreme positions, be they extremely child-centered (such as the more radical of whole language approaches) or extremely curriculum-centered (such as highly structured, unswerving phonics programs) is not new. Voices from the middle, extolling balanced approaches or rationalizing the eclectic practices of teachers, began to be heard even in the earliest days of whole language's ascendancy.[98] Scholars and teachers raised a number of concerns about the assumptions and practices of the whole language movement. Most importantly, they expressed concern about the consequences of whole language outlined earlier in this essay. They questioned the assumption that skills are best "caught" during the pursuit of authentic reading activity rather than "taught" directly and explicitly. They also questioned the insistence on authentic texts and the corollary ban on "instructional" texts written to permit the application of skills within the curriculum. They questioned the zeal and commitment of the movement qua movement, with its strong sense of insularity and exclusivity. Finally, they worried that the press toward the use of authentic literature and literature-based reading would eradicate, albeit unintentionally, what little progress had been made toward the use of informational texts and teaching reading in the content areas.[99]

Ironically, in the past few years, these voices from the middle have found themselves responding not to those who hold a radical whole language position, but to those who hold steadfastly to the phonics first position. Even so, the fact that those with centrist positions were not inclined to defend whole language when the political campaign against it began in the middle 1990s undoubtedly hastened the demise of whole language as the pretender to the title of conventional wisdom.

Changing research ideology. Prior to the 1980s, qualitative research in any form had little visibility within the reading research community. Among the array of qualitative efforts, only miscue analysis[100] and some early forays into sociolinguistic and anthropological accounts of literacy had achieved much in the way of archival status.[101] But all that changed in the 1980s and early 1990s. Qualitative research more generally, along with more specific lines of inquiry taking a critical perspective on literacy as a social and pedagogical phenomenon, became more widely accepted as part of the mainstream archival literature.[102] Treatises pointing out the shortcomings of traditional forms of quantitative inquiry, especially experimental research, appeared frequently in educational research journals.[103] In terms of curriculum and pedagogy, it is important to remind ourselves that much of the research that undergirds whole language comes from this more qualitative, more interpretive, more critical tradition. Thus the credibility of this type of research increased in concert with the influence of whole language as a curricular movement.

Somewhere in the mid-1990s, the discourse of literacy research began to take a new turn. Stimulated by research supported by the National Institute for Child Health and Human Development, a "new" brand of experimental work began to appear, beginning in the middle 1980s and gathering momentum that has reached a peak in the past year or two.[104] This is experimentalism reborn from the 1950s and 60s, with great emphasis placed upon "reliable, replicable research," large samples, random assignment of treatments to teachers and/or schools, and tried and true outcome measures.[105] This work does not build upon the qualitative tradition of the 80s and early 90s; instead it finds its aegis in the experimental rhetoric of science and medicine and in the laboratory research that has examined reading as a perceptual process.[106] Although not broadly accepted by the reading education community (at least as of the time when this chapter was put to bed in 1999), this work has found a very sympathetic ear in the public policy arena.[107]

The political positioning of this research is important, but so is its substance. Two themes from this work have been particularly important in shaping a new set of instructional practices—phonemic awareness and phonics instruction.

The absolutely critical role played by phonemic awareness (the ability to *segment* the speech stream of a spoken word and/or to *blend* separately heard sounds into a normally spoken word in the development of the ability to decode and to read for meaning has been well documented in the past decade and a half.[108] Irrespective of mode of instruction, the overwhelming evidence suggests that phonemic awareness is a necessary but not a sufficient condition for the development of decoding and reading. First, children who possess high degrees of phonemic awareness in kindergarten or early in first grade are very likely to be good readers throughout their elementary school careers.[109] Second, almost no children who are successful readers at the end of grade one exhibit a low level of mastery of phonemic awareness. On the other hand, a substantial proportion of unsuccessful end-of-grade-one readers possess better than average phonemic awareness; this evidence is the critical piece in establishing that phonemic awareness is a necessary but not a sufficient condition for reading success. While we can be confident of its critical role in learning to read, we are less sure about the optimal way to enhance its development. Many scholars have documented the efficacy of teaching it directly, but they also admit that it is highly likely to develop as a consequence of learning phonics, learning to read, or especially learning to write, especially when teachers encourage students to use invented spellings.[110] Research in whole language classrooms suggests that writing is the medium through which both phonemic awareness and phonics knowledge develop—the former because students have to segment the speech stream of spoken words in order to focus on a phoneme and the latter because there is substantial transfer value from the focus on sound-symbol information in spelling to symbol-sound knowledge in reading.[111]

The second consistent thread in the new experimentalism of the 1990s is the simple but undeniable emphasis on the code in the early stages of learning to read. Reminiscent of Chall's earlier conclusions, scholars in this tradition tend to advocate phonics, first, fast, and simple.[112] Less well documented, and surely less well agreed upon, is the optimal course of instruction to facilitate phonics development. Even Philip Gough, a classic bottom-up theorist, while arguing that what distinguishes the good reader from the poor reader is swift and accurate word identification, suggests that an early insistence on reading for meaning may be the best way to develop such decoding proficiency. Both Gough and Connie Juel are convinced that students can learn how to read when they have "cryptoanalytic intent" (a disposition to decipher the specific letter-to-sound codes), phonemic awareness, an

appreciation of the alphabetic principle (i.e., regardless of the numerous exceptions, letters do stand for sounds), and "data" (some texts to
read and someone to assist when the going gets tough).[113]

After reviewing available instructional evidence, two of the most
respected scholars in this tradition, Marilyn Adams and Connie Juel, independently concluded that children can and should learn the "cipher"
through a combination of explicit instruction in phonemic awareness
and letter-sound correspondences, a steady insistence on invented
spellings as the route to conventional spellings in writing activities, lots
of opportunity to read connected text (especially when the texts contain
enough decodable words to allow students to apply the phonics information they are learning through explicit instruction). Both of these
reviewers, known for their sympathies toward instruction in the code,
are quick to add that rich experiences with language, environmental
print, patterned stories, and "Big Books" should also be a staple of
effective early reading instruction.[114]

Politicization of the reading research and policy agenda. One of the
great hopes of educational researchers is that policymakers will take
research seriously when they establish policy initiatives at a local, state,
or national level. After all, the improvement of educational practice is
the ultimate goal of educational research, and policy is our society's
most transparent tool for educational improvement. Historically, however, research has been regarded as one among many information
sources consulted in policy formation—including expert testimony
from practitioners, information about school organization and finance,
and evaluations of compelling cases. In the past half decade research, at
least selective bits of research, has never been taken more seriously.
Several laws in California make direct references to research. For example, in 1998 Assembly Bill 1086 prohibited the use of Goals 2000
money for professional developers who advocated the use of context
clues over phonics or supported the use of inventive (sic) spellings in
children's writing. The federally sponsored Reading Excellence Act of
1999, which allocated $240,000,000 for staff development in reading,
requires that both state and local applications for funding base their
programs on research that meets scientifically rigorous standards. The
"scientifically rigorous" phrase was a late entry; in all but the penulti-
mate version of the bill, the phrase was "reliable, replicable research,"
which had been interpreted as a code word for experimental research.
As of early 1999, "phonics bills" (bills mandating either the use of
phonics materials or some sort of training to acquaint teachers with

knowledge of the English sound symbol system and its use in teaching) had been passed or were pending in 36 states.[115]

Policymakers like to shroud mandates and initiatives in the rhetoric of science, and sometimes that practice results in very strained, if not indefensible, extrapolations from research. This has happened consistently in the current reading policy arena. Two examples make the point vividly. First, California Assembly bill 1086, with its prohibition on context clues and invented spelling, represents an ironic application of research to policy. The irony stems from the fact that many of the advocates of a return to code emphasis, such as Marilyn Adams, read the research as supporting the use of invented spellings in the development of phonemic awareness and phonics.[116] Second, the mandate in several states calling for the use of decodable text (usually defined as text consisting of words that could be sounded out using a combination of the phonics rules taught up to that point in the program *plus* some instant recognition of a few highly frequent "sight" words) is based upon the thinnest of research bases. The idea is that children will learn to use their phonics better, faster, and more efficiently if the texts they read permit facile application of the principles they are learning. While it all sounds very logical, there is precious little research evidence to support the systematic and exclusive use of decodable text.[117] This lack of evidence, however, does not seem to have banked the policy fires on this matter.

Professional groups have entered the policy fray in recent years. For example, the American Federation of Teachers has endorsed a particular set of programs as scientifically validated to produce excellent results. Interestingly, each of the programs on their endorsed list is committed to early, systematic, explicit phonics instruction in a highly structured framework. The AFT influence is evident in some other professional movements, such as the Learning First Alliance.[118]

When research moves into the policy arena, one of two outcomes is most likely. If the research is widely accepted by members of the profession from which it comes, widespread acceptance and implementation usually follows. This often occurs in medical, pharmaceutical, or agricultural research. If widespread consensus on what the research says about practice is not reached, then research-based policy initiatives are likely to sharpen and deepen the schisms that already exist, and the whole enterprise is likely to be regarded as a "war" among Balkanized factions within the field. The latter scenario appears to characterize the reading field.[119]

Interestingly, the debate, accompanied by its warlike metaphors, appears to have more life in the public and professional press than it does in our schools. Reporters and scholars revel in keeping the debate alive and well, portraying clearly divided sides and detailing a host of differences of a philosophical, political, and pedagogical nature.[120] Teachers, by contrast, often talk about, and more importantly enact, more balanced approaches. For example, several scholars, in documenting the practices of highly effective, highly regarded teachers, found that these exemplary teachers employed a wide array of practices, some of which appear decidedly whole language in character (e.g., process writing, literature groups, and contextualized skills practice) and some of which appear remarkably skills-oriented (explicit phonics lessons, sight word practice, and comprehension strategy instruction).[121]

Producing measurable results. Evaluation has always posed a conundrum for whole language supporters. First, some oppose the use of any sort of externally mandated or administered assessments as a matter of principle, holding that assessment is ultimately the responsibility of a teacher in collaboration with a student and his or her parents. Second, even those supporters who are open to external forms of accountability, or at least reporting outside the boundaries of the classroom or school, often claim that standardized tests, state assessments, and other external measures of student accomplishment do not provide sensitive indicators of the goals of curricula that are based upon whole language principles. Most appealing would be assessments that are classroom-based and individualized in nature, with the option of aggregating these sorts of data at the classroom and school levels when accountability comes knocking. During the 1990s, many felt that the increased emphasis on performance assessment and portfolios would fill this need.[122] In an age of high expectations, explicit standards, and school and classroom level accountability, none of these options is a good fit with the views and desires of policymakers and the public. Both of these constituents seem quite uneasy about the quality of our schools and our educational system, so uneasy that leaving assessment in the hands of our teachers seems an unlikely outcome. It is not at all clear to me that the proponents of at least the strong versions of whole language can, or will be willing to, hold themselves accountable to the sorts of measures that the public and policymakers find credible.

Who holds the high ground? One other factor, both subtle and speculative (on my part) seems to be an undercurrent in the current rhetoric.

Whole language has always privileged the role of the teacher as the primary curriculum decision-maker. Teachers, the argument goes, are in the best position to serve this important role because of their vast knowledge of language and literacy development, their skills as diagnosticians (they are expert "kidwatchers"), and the materials and teaching strategies they have at their disposal. And in the arguments against more structured approaches, this is exactly the approach whole language advocates have taken: "Don't make these decisions at the state, district, or even the school level. Arm teachers with the professional prerogative (and corollary levels of professional knowledge) they need in order to craft unique decisions for individual children." While this may seem a reasonable, even admirable position, it has recently been turned into an apology for self-serving teacher ideology.[123] The counter argument suggests that the broad base of privilege accorded to teachers may come at the expense of students and their parents. Thus, those who advocate a strong phonics-first position often take the moral high ground: "We are doing this for America's children (and for YOUR child!) so that they have the right to read for themselves." Even if one opposes this rhetorical move, it is hard not to appreciate the clever repositioning on the part of those who want to return to more phonics and skills.

Taken together, these factors create a policy environment in which whole language seems unlikely to flourish as the mainstream approach to teaching reading and writing. In the final analysis, however, I believe that the reluctance to own up to the "measurable results" standards is the Achilles heel for whole language. If whole language advocates were willing to play by the rules of external accountability, to assert that students who experience good instruction based upon solid principles of progressive pedagogy will perform well on standardized tests and other standards of performance, they would stand a better chance of gaining a sympathetic ear with the public and with policymakers. And as long as the criteria for what counts as evidence for growth and accomplishment are vague or left to individual teachers, the public will continue to question the movement; they will continue to wonder whose interests are being served by an unwillingness to commit to common standards.

Looking Ahead: Will We Benefit from the Lessons of History?

So where has this journey left us? And where will it take us next? We are, as Regie Routman suggests, at a crossroads.[124] Many recent developments suggest that we are retreating to a more familiar, more comfortable paradigm in which phonics, skills, and controlled text dominate our practices. Other developments suggest that we are on the verge of a new paradigm, a hybrid that weds some of the principles of whole language (integrated instruction and authentic texts and tasks) with some of the traditions of earlier eras (explicit attention to skills and strategies, some vocabulary control of early readers, and lots of early emphasis on the code) in an "ecologically balanced" approach to reading instruction.[125] The most cynical amongst us might even argue that we are just riding the natural swing of a pendulum that will, if we have the patience, take us back to whole language, or whatever its child-centered descendant turns out to be, in a decade or so. Before making a prediction about the direction the field will take, let me play out the first two scenarios, phonics first and balanced reading instruction.

ONE ALTERNATIVE FOR THE FUTURE

If those who have advocated most strongly for a return to phonics and a heavy skills orientation have their way—if they are able to influence federal, state, and local policy as well as the educational publishing industry—we will experience moderate to substantial shifts on most, but not all, of the criteria I put forward as lenses for tracking changes in reading pedagogy over this century (range of materials, range of pedagogical practices, role of teacher, role of student, underlying theory of reading and reading acquisition). As I read their views about policy and practice, the greatest changes will occur at the very earliest stages of learning to read—kindergarten and grade 1. They suggest explicit instruction on phonemic awareness and phonics, with a strong preference for decodable texts in the early grades. When it comes to writing, literature, response, and comprehension, they seem quite content to cede curricular authority to the practices that emerged during the 80s and early 90s, those associated with whole language, literature-based reading, and process writing.[126] Thus, looking broadly at the entire elementary reading curriculum (the range of materials and the range of pedagogical practices), things might, on the surface, look similar to the early 1990s, with some retreat to the 1980s, especially in terms of skill and strategy instruction.

But beneath that curricular surface, major changes would have occurred. For example, the role of the teacher and the learner would have reverted to what they were at the beginning of the century. The role of the teacher would be to transmit the received knowledge of the field, as reflected in research-based curricular mandates, to students. Students would eventually be regarded as active meaning makers, but only after they had received tools of decoding from their teachers. The greatest changes of all would have taken place in the underlying model of reading and reading acquisition. The simple view of reading (RC = Dec × LC) would have returned in full force, and the job of young readers would be to acquire the decoding knowledge they lack when they begin to learn to read.

A SECOND ALTERNATIVE

If those who are pushing for ecological balance carry the day, the field will experience less dramatic shifts. A balanced approach will privilege authentic texts and tasks, a heavy emphasis on writing, literature, response, and comprehension, but it will also call for an ambitious program of explicit instruction for phonics, word identification, comprehension, spelling, and writing. A balanced approach is likely to look like some instantiations of whole language from the early 90s, but recalibrated to redress the unintended curricular consequences outlined earlier in this chapter. Major differences between a balanced approach and the new phonics are likely to manifest themselves most vividly in kindergarten and grade 1, where a rich set of language and literacy experiences would provide the context from which teachers would carve out scaffolded instructional activities to spotlight necessary skills and strategies—phonemic awareness, letter-sound knowledge, concepts of print, and conceptual development. Thus instruction, while focused and explicit, would also be highly contextualized.

Beneath the curricular surface, balanced approaches seem to share slightly more in common, at least on a philosophical plane, with whole language than with new phonics approaches. The teacher is both facilitator and instructor. The teacher facilitates learning by establishing authentic activities, intervening where necessary to provide the scaffolding and explicit instruction required to help students take the next step toward independence. The student is, as in whole language, an active meaning maker from day one of preschool. Reading is a process of constructing meaning in response to texts encountered in a specific context, and the emergent literacy metaphor, not the readiness metaphor, characterizes the acquisition process.

AN ECOLOGICALLY BALANCED APPROACH

Just in case my personal bias has not emerged, let me declare it unequivocally. I favor the conceptual map of the ecologically balanced approach. There are several reasons for favoring this stance. First, my reading of the research points to the balanced curricular position, not to the new phonics position, both at a theoretical and a pedagogical level. I do not see much support for the simple view of reading under-lying the new phonics; readers do construct meaning, they don't just find it lying there in the text. Regarding pedagogical research, my reading requires me to side with Chall's view that while some sort of early, focused, and systematic emphasis on the code is called for, no particular approach can be singled out. And while I readily accept the findings of the phonemic awareness research, I do not read them as supporting drill and practice approaches to this important linguistic understanding; to the contrary, highly embedded approaches, such as invented spelling, are equally as strongly implicated in the research.[127]

Second, an ecologically balanced approach is more respectful of the entire range of research in our field. It does not have to exclude major research paradigms or methodological approaches to sustain its integrity.

Third, an ecologically balanced approach also respects the wisdom of practice. It is no accident that studies of exemplary teachers, those who are respected by their peers and nurture high student achieve-ment, consistently find that they exhibit a balanced repertoire of instructional strategies. Teachers who are faced with the variations in achievement, experience, and aptitude found in today's classrooms apparently need, and deserve, a full tool box.

Finally, an ecologically balanced approach respects our profes-sional history. It retains the practices that have proved useful from each era but transforms and extends them, rendering them more effective, more useful, and more supportive of teachers and students. And it may represent our only alternative to the pendulum-swing view of our pedagogical history that seems to have plagued the field of reading for most of this century. A transformative rather than a cycli-cal view of progress would be a nice start for a new century.

NOTES

1. See Mitford Mathews, *Teaching to Read* (Chicago: University of Chicago Press, 1996) for an account of the contributions of both these reformers.

2. See Edmund Burke Huey, *The Psychology and Pedagogy of Reading* (New York: Macmillan, 1908) for an extensive account of the methods that prevailed at the last turn of the century.

3. Noah Webster, *The American Spelling Book* (Boston: Isaiah Thomas and Ebenezer Andrews, 1798) was first published a little over two centuries ago. The first of William H. McGuffey's *Eclectic Readers* appeared between 1836 and 1840; for example, William H. McGuffey, *Eclectic Fourth Reader* (Cincinnati: Truman and Smith, 1838). Both were still available for purchase in 1900.

4. Many of the textbooks of the last half of the 19th century explicitly emphasized elocution in the textbooks for the upper elementary grades. See Mathews, *Teaching to Read*.

5. The simple view is a term coined by Philip Gough most probably as a rhetorical counter to the rampant complexity in theories and models of reading developed in the 1970s. See Philip B. Gough and M. L. Hillinger, "Learning to Read: An Unnatural Act," *Bulletin of the Orton Society* 30 (1980): 171-176.

6. Matthews, *Teaching to Read*.

7. Matthews, *Teaching to Read*, documents many cases of this general approach to the reform of reading pedagogy dating back to the 1840s in the United States and to the 17ᵗʰ Century in Germany.

8. For example, in his popular 1955 book, *Why Johnny Can't Read*, Rudolph Flesch argued that the primary cause of low reading performance during the 40s and 50s was the failure of our schools to teach phonics because of the strong grip of the look-say approach on our nation's teachers and textbook authors.

9. The very best description of the "state of the art" in early reading appears in Huey, *The Psychology and Pedagogy of Reading*.

10. A wonderful example of this approach from the University of Chicago laboratory school appears in Huey, *The Psychology and Pedagogy of Reading*.

11. See Daniel P. Resnick, "History of Educational Testing," *Ability Testing: Uses, Consequences, and Controversies, Volume 2*, eds. A. K. Wigdor and W. R. Garner (Washington, DC: National Academy Press, 1982).

12. A useful account of the assessments dominant in the first third of the century can be found in Gertrude Hildreth, *Bibliography of Mental Tests and Rating Scales* (New York: The Psychological Corporation, 1933).

13. This tradition of isomorphism between the infrastructure of tests and curriculum has been a persistent issue throughout the century. See, for example, Dale D. Johnson and P. David Pearson, "Skills Management Systems: A Critique," *The Reading Teacher*, 1975; and Resnick, "History of Educational Testing." Also see Nila Banton Smith, *American Reading Instruction* (Newark, DE, 1966): 180-186, for an account of the expansion of reading comprehension as a curricular phenomenon.

14. See Smith, *American Reading Instruction*, 259-262, for an account of the emergence of child-centered reading pedagogy. Foundational thinkers for this movement were Johann H. Pestalozzi, *How Gertrude Teaches Her Children* (Syracuse, NY: C. W. Barden Publisher, 1898); Freidrich Froebel, *The Education of Man* (New York: D. Appleton and Company, 1887); John F. Herbart, *Outlines of Educational Doctrine* (New York: Macmillan, 1990).

15. Ironically, it was the field's most ambitious effort in readability by Bormuth in 1966 that provided the closing parenthesis on this 40-year enterprise. John R. Bormuth, "Readability: A New Approach," *Reading Research Quarterly* 1 (1966): 79-132.

16. Smith, *American Reading Instruction*, 259-262.

17. Ibid., 355-56.

18. Even as recently as the influential National Academy of Science Report published in 1998, letter-name knowledge once again emerged as the best predictor of later achievement: Catherine Snow, Susan Burns, and Peg Griffith, *Preventing Reading Difficulties in Young Children* (Washington: National Academy Press, 1998).

19. M. V. Morphett and Carlton Washburne, "When Should Children Begin to Read?" *Elementary School Journal* 31 (1931): 496-501. Arthur I. Gates, "The Necessary Mental Age for Beginning Reading," *Elementary School Journal* (1937): 497-498.

20. See also Benjamin Bloom and Ralph Tyler for accounts of the influence of tests on curriculum.

21. Smith, *American Reading Instruction*, 208-209. By the 1940s, they had expanded to more than 500 pages per student book.

22. Smith, *American Reading Instruction*, 208-229.

23. Smith, *American Reading Instruction*, 231-239.

24. The first book on remedial reading was published in 1922: Clarence T. Gray, *Deficiencies in Reading Ability: Their Diagnosis and Treatment* (Boston: D. C. Heath & Company, 1922). One of the most influential scholars of disability was Arthur I. Gates, *The Improvement of Reading* (New York: Macmillan, 1935).

25. Nowhere is this tension better illustrated than in the contrast between Morphett and Washburne, "When Should Children Begin to Read?" and Gates, "The Necessary Mental Age for Beginning Reading."

26. Mary C. Austin and Coleman Morrison, *The First R.* (New York: Macmillan, 1963).

27. This account is taken from Jeanne Chall, *Learning to Read: The Great Debate* (New York: McGraw Hill, 1967): 13-15.

28. Smith, *American Reading Instruction*, 276.

29. Guy L. Bond and Robert Dykstra, "The Cooperative Research Program in First Grade Reading Instruction," *Reading Research Quarterly* 2: entire issue.

30. The reporting of data for students through grade 2 did not receive the fanfare that the first grade report did, an outcome which I find unfortunate because it was, in many ways, even more interesting. It showed stronger effects overall for code-based approaches, and it revealed the most provocative of all the findings in this entire enterprise—the project effect. The project effect was this: using analysis of covariance to control incoming performance, students were better off being in the poorest performing approach in project A than they were being in the best performing approach in Project B. This raises the whole issue of impact of contextual factors on reading achievement. See Robert Dykstra, "Summary of the Second-grade Phase of the Cooperative Research Program in Primary Reading Instruction," *Reading Research Quarterly* 4 (1968): 49-70.

31. If we were focusing on the impact of these studies on research rather than practice, these issues would occupy more of our attention. In a sense the First Grade Studies created an opening for other research endeavors; indeed, the directions that reading research took in the middle 70s—the nature of comprehension and the role of the teacher—suggest that there were groups of scholars ready to seize the opportunity.

32. When large-scale experiments returned in the early 90s, it was not the Department of Education, but the National Institute of Child Health and Human Development, that led the renaissance. For accounts of the development of the NICHD effort, see G. Reid Lyon, "Research Initiatives in Learning Disabilities: Contributions from Scientists Supported by the National Institute of Child Health and Human Development," *Journal of Child Neurology* 10: 120-127, or G. Reid Lyon and V. Chhaba, "The Current State of Science and the Future of Specific Reading Disability," *Mental Retardation and Developmental Disabilities Research Reviews* 2: 2-9. It is also worth noting that one of the likely reasons for the demise of Method A vs. Method B experiments is that scholars in the 1960s were looking for main effects rather than interaction effects. Had they set out to find that methods are uniquely suited to particular populations in this work, they might not have rejected them so completely.

33. The impact of Chall's book, particularly the phonics recommendation, was documented by Helen Popp, "Current Practices in the Teaching of Beginning Reading," *Toward a Literate Society: The Report of the Committee on Reading of the National Academy of Education*, ed. John B. Carroll and Jeanne S. Chall (New York: McGraw Hill, 1975).

34. In an unpublished research study completed in 1978, Hansen and Pearson found two- and three-fold increases in the number of words introduced in the first

200   READING   IN   THE   TWENTIETH   CENTURY

grade books for the popular series published by Scott Foresman and Ginn. Jane Hansen and P. David Pearson, "Learning to Read: A Decade after Chall," unpublished manuscript, University of Minnesota.

35. The teachers' manuals of the Ginn 360 program provide the most notable example of this new trend. See Clymer et al., Ginn 360 (Lexington, Massachusetts: Ginn & Company, 1968).

36. Mastery learning can trace its intellectual roots to works of Benjamin Bloom and John Carroll: Benjamin Bloom, "Learning for Mastery," *Evaluation Comment* 1 (1968): entire issue; John Carroll, "A Model of School Learning," *Teachers College Record* 64 (1963): 723-732.

37. For an account of criterion-referenced assessment as it emerged during this period, see James Popham, *Criterion-referenced Measurement*. (Englewood Cliffs, NJ: Prentice-Hall, 1978).

38. Stanley L. Deno, "Curriculum Based Measurement: The Emerging Alternative," *Exceptional Children* 52 (1985): 219-232.

39. Bloom, "Learning for Mastery."

40. The most popular of these systems was the Wisconsin Design for Reading Skill Development, followed closely by Fountain Valley. Their heyday was the decade of the 1970s, although they remained a staple, as an option, through the 80s and 90s and are still available as options in today's basals. For an account of the rationale behind these systems, see Wayne Otto, "The Wisconsin Design, A Reading Program for Individually Guided Education," *Individually Guided Elementary Education: Concepts and Practices*, eds. Herbert J. Klausmeier, Robert A. Rossmiller, and M. Saily (New York: Academic Press, 1977). For a critique of these programs during their ascendancy, see Johnson and Pearson, "Skills Management Systems."

41. This is not to say that there were no challengers to the conventional wisdom that emerged in the middle of the century. To the contrary, the alphabetic approach, now dubbed synthetic phonics, lived a healthy life as a small guerrilla force throughout the period, as did the language experience approach and a few assorted alternatives. See Chall, *Learning to Read*, and Mathews, *Teaching to Read*, for accounts of these programs.

42. It should be noted that a major child-centered reform movement, the open classroom, was creating quite a wave in educational circles and elementary schools throughout the United States in the early 1970s. It is hard, however, to find any direct impact of the open classroom movement on reading instruction. However, one could make the argument that the open classroom philosophy had a delayed impact in its influence on the whole language movement in the late 1980s.

43. Some portions of the text in this section appeared in modified form in P. David Pearson and Diane Stephens, "Learning about Literacy: A 30-year Journey," *Elementary Reading: Process and Practice 4-18*, eds. Christine J. Gordon, George D. Labercane, and W. R. McEachern (Boston: Ginn Press, 1993). (Sections adapted with the knowledge and permission of the co-author and publisher.)

44. To assert that Chomsky laid the groundwork for an essential critique of behaviorism as an explanatory model for language processes is not to assert that he drove behaviorism out of psychology or education.

45. See Roger Brown, *Psycholinguistics* (New York: Macmillan: 1970) for an account of this view of language development.

46. Kenneth G. Goodman, "A linguistic study of cues and miscues in reading," *Elementary English* 42, 639-643; Kenneth G. Goodman, "Reading: A psycholinguistic guessing game," *Journal of the Reading Specialist* 4: 126-135.

47. Frank Smith, *Understanding Reading: A Psycholinguistic Analysis of Reading and Learning to Read* (New York: Holt, Rinehart, & Winston, 1971).

48. In all fairness, it must be admitted that this contribution was not exclusively Smith's. As we shall point out in later sections, many other scholars, most notably David Rumelhart and Richard Anderson, championed constructivist views of reading. It is fair, however, to say that Smith was the first scholar to bring this insight into the reading field. David Rumelhart, "Schemata: The Building Blocks of Cognition," *Theoretical Issues in Reading Comprehension*, eds. Rand J. Spiro, Bertram C. Bruce, and William F. Brewer (Hillsdale, NJ: Erlbaum, 1980). Richard C. Anderson and P. David Pearson, "A schema-theoretic view of basic processes in reading comprehension," eds. P. David Pearson, Rebecca Barr, Michael L. Kamil, and Peter Mosenthal, *Handbook of Reading Research* (New York: Longman, 1984).

49. Frank Smith, "Reading Like a Writer," *Language Arts* 60, 558-567 (1983).

50. During this period, great homage was paid to intellectual ancestors such as Edmund Burke Huey, who as early as 1908 recognized the cognitive complexity of reading. Voices such as Huey's, unfortunately, were not heard during the period from 1915 to 1965 when behaviorism dominated psychology and education.

51. Walter Kintsch and Bonnie Meyer wrote compelling accounts of the structure of exposition that were translated by others (e.g., Barbara Taylor and Richard Beach) into instructional strategies. See Walter Kintsch, *The Representation of Meaning in Memory* (Hillsdale, NJ: Erlbaum, 1974); Bonnie J. F. Meyer, *The Organization of Prose and Its Effects on Memory* (Amsterdam: North Holland Publishing, 1975); Barbara M. Taylor and Richard Beach, "The Effects of Text Structure Instruction on Middle-grade Students' Comprehension and Production of Expository Text," *Reading Research Quarterly* 19: (134-146).

52. The most complete accounts of schema theory are provided by Rumelhart, "Schemata: The Building Blocks of Cognition," and Anderson and Pearson, "A Schema-Theoretic View of Basic Processes in Reading Comprehension."

53. Frederic C. Bartlett, *Remembering*. (Cambridge: Cambridge University Press, 1932).

54. It is not altogether clear that schema theory is dead, especially in contexts of practice. Its role in psychological theory is undoubtedly diminished due to attacks on its efficacy as a model of memory and cognition. See Timothy P. McNamara, Diana L. Miller, and John D. Bransford, "Mental Models and Reading Comprehension," *Handbook of Reading Research, Vol. 2*, eds. Rebecca Barr, Michael Kamil, Peter Mosenthal, and P. David Pearson. (New York: Longman, 1991): 490-511.

55. For early accounts of this perspective, see Joan Baratz and Roger Shuy, *Teaching Black Children to Read* (Washington, DC: Center for Applied Linguistics, 1969). William Labov, *Language of the Inner City*. (Philadelphia: University of Pennsylvania Press, 1972).

56. Baratz and Shuy, *Teaching Black Children to Read*.

57. See David Bloome and Judith Green, "Directions in the Sociolinguistic Study of Reading," *Handbook of Reading Research, Vol. 2*: 395-421.

58. Louise Rosenblatt, *Literature as Exploration*. (New York: Appleton Century Croft, 1936/1978). Louise Rosenblatt, *Reader, Text, and Poem* (Carbondale, IL: Southern Illinois University Press: 1978).

59. Rosenblatt credits the idea of transaction to John Dewey, who discussed it in many texts, including *Experience and Education* (New York: Kappa Delta Pi, 1938).

60. A very interesting, even provocative attempt to understand comprehension processes appears in Edward L. Thorndike, "Reading as reasoning: A study of mistakes in paragraph reading," *Journal of Educational Psychology* 8: 323-332. The classic reference for using tests to reveal the psychological infrastructure of comprehension is the first published factor analysis of reading comprehension by Frederick Davis, "Fundamental Factors of Reading Comprehension," *Psychometrika* 9 (1944): 185-197.

61. *Sixty-seventh Yearbook (1968), Part II, Innovation and Change in Reading Instruction*, edited by Helen M. Robinson.

62. Dolores Durkin published an infamous study in 1978 documenting the fact that what went on in the name of comprehension was essentially completing worksheets and answering questions during story discussions. She saw almost no instruction about how to engage in any sort of comprehension task—no modeling, no demonstration, no scaffolding. Dolores Durkin, "What Classroom Observations Reveal about Reading Instruction," *Reading Research Quarterly* 14: 481-533.

63. Among the most notable efforts at the Center were the classic work on reciprocal teaching: Annemarie Palincsar and Ann L Brown, "Reciprocal teaching of comprehension fostering and monitoring activities," *Cognition and Instruction* 1 (1984): 117-175; T. E. Raphael and P. D. Pearson, "Increasing students' awareness of sources of information for answering questions," *American Educational Research Journal* 22: 217-236; and explicit comprehension instruction as a general approach in P. D. Pearson and J. Dole, "Explicit comprehension instruction: A review of research and a new conceptualization of instruction," *Elementary School Journal* 88, no. 2: 151-165. P. D. Pearson, "Changing the face of reading comprehension instruction," *The Reading Teacher* 38: 724-738. This focus on comprehension and reasoning while reading continues even today at the Center with the work of Anderson and his colleagues.

64. The work of Paris and his colleagues is exemplary in the area of metacognitive training and comprehension monitoring (S. G. Paris, D. R. Cross, & M. Y. Lipson, "Informed strategies for learning: A program to improve children's reading awareness and comprehension," *Journal of Educational Psychology* 76: 1239-1252).

65. Michael Pressley, working in conjunction with a group of professionals in Montgomery County, Maryland, developed a set of powerful comprehension routines that, among other things, extended the four strategies of Reciprocal Teaching (questioning, summarizing, clarifying and predicting) to include more aspects of literary response (e.g., personal response and author's craft). The best resource on this line of pedagogical research is a 1993 volume of *Elementary School Journal* edited by Pressley, along with these articles, one of which is from that volume: M. Pressley et al., "Transactional instruction of comprehension strategies: The Montgomery County, Maryland, SAIL Program," *Reading and Writing Quarterly* 10: 5-19; M. Pressley et al., "Beyond direct explanation: Transactional instruction of reading comprehension strategies," *Elementary School Journal* 92: 513-555.

66. KWL, an acronym for a graphic organizer technique in which students chart, before and after reading, what they *know*, what they *want* to know, and what they *learned* is an interesting phenomenon because while it has attracted a great deal of curricular attention in basals, articles for practitioners and staff development materials, it is hard to find much research on its instructional efficacy. See Donna Ogle, "The K-W-L: A Teaching Model that Develops Active Reading of Expository Text," *The Reading Teacher* 39: 564-570.

67. Isabel Beck and Margaret McKeown have spent several years, in collaboration with a network of teachers perfecting this engaging practice which focuses on how and why authors put text together the way they do. The net result of this routine is that students learn a great deal about how to read critically (what is the author trying to do to me as a reader?) and about authors' craft (how do authors structure their ideas to achieve particular effects). See Beck et al., *Questioning the Author: An Approach for Enhancing Student Engagement with Text* (Newark, DE: International Reading Association, 1997).

68. Chall, in the 1991 edition of *Learning to Read*, documented this important increase in basal comprehension activities.

69. Chall devotes a section to individualized reading in her 1967 description of alternatives to the basal (pp. 41-42), but has little to say about it as a serious alternative

PEARSON   203

to basal, phonics, or linguistic approaches. In that same period, it is undoubtedly Jeanette Veatch who served as the most vocal spokesperson for individualized reading. She published professional textbooks describing how to implement the program in one's class (*Individualizing Your Reading Program* (New York: G. P. Putnam's Sons, 1959)). In the middle 1960s, Random House published a "series" of literature books that were accompanied (in a pocket on the inside cover) by a set of vocabulary and comprehension activities that look remarkably like basal workbook pages. The Random House materials remind one of the currently popular computer program, Accelerated Reader, which is similarly designed to manage some assessment and skill activity to accompany trade books that children read on their own.

70. Richard C. Anderson, Elfrieda Hiebert, Judith Scott, and Ian Wilkinson, *Becoming a Nation of Readers* (Champaign, IL: Center for the Study of Reading: 1984). Anderson and his colleagues reported several studies documenting the impact of book reading on children's achievement gains.

71. Nancie Atwell, *In the Middle: Writing, Reading, and Learning with Adolescents.* (Portsmouth, NH: Heinemann, 1987). While it is difficult to locate data to document these claims about Atwell's particular influence, the rise of literature in the middle school has been documented by changes in the teacher survey portion of the National Assessment of Educational Progress of Reading.

72. Hoffman and his colleagues painstakingly documented these sorts of changes in the early 90s basals. James V. Hoffman, Sarah J. McCarthey, J. Abbott, C. Christian, L. Corman, M. Dressman, B. Elliot, D. Matheme, and D. Stahle, "So what's new in the "new" basals," *Journal of Reading Behavior* 26 (1994): 47-73.

73. For a complete account of the Book Club movement, see *The Book Club Connection* by Susan I. McMahon and Taffy E. Raphael with Virginia Goatley and Laura Pardo (New York: Teachers College Press, 1997).

74. Two classic books by Donald Graves, *Writing: Teachers and Students at Work* (Portsmouth, NH: Heinemann, 1983) and *A Researcher Learns to Write* (Portsmouth, NH: Heinemann, 1984), were influential in leading the process writing movement at the elementary level, as was Lucy Calkins' classic, *The Art of Teaching Writing* (Portsmouth, NH: Heinemann, 1986).

75. Perhaps the most complete current reference on integrated curriculum is a new chapter in the third volume of the *Handbook of Reading Research* by James R. Gavelek, Taffy E. Raphael, Sandra M. Biondo, and Danhua Wang, "Integrated Literacy Instruction," in *Handbook of Reading Research*, Vol. 3, eds. Michael L. Kamil, Peter Mosenthal, P. David Pearson, and Rebecca Barr (Hillsdale, NJ: Erlbaum, in press).

76. In Chapter 10 of Huey's 1908 book on reading, two such programs, one at Columbia and one at the University of Chicago, were described in rich detail. It is Dewey's insistence that pedagogy be grounded in the individual and collective experiences of learners that is typically cited when scholars invoke his name to support integrated curriculum.

77. See Graves (1983) for an explication of his views on writing and Hansen (1987) for an account of how reading and writing support one another in an integrated language arts approach.

78. Frank Smith and Robert Tierney and P. David Pearson carried this metaphor to the extreme. All three used the reading "like a writer" metaphor in titles to papers in this period. Frank Smith, "Reading like a writer," *Language Arts* 60 (1983): 558-567; Robert J. Tierney and P. D. Pearson, "Toward a composing model of reading," *Language Arts* 60 (1983): 568-580; P. D. Pearson and Robert J. Tierney, "On becoming a thoughtful reader: Learning to read like a writer," eds. Alan Purves and Olive Niles, *Reading in the Secondary School*, National Society for the Study of Education 83rd yearbook (Chicago: National Society for the Study of Education), pp. 144-173.

79. Donald Holdaway, *The Foundations of Literacy*, summarizes this perspective and work.

80. The notion of significance here is intended to capture its impact, not its validity. Even those who question its validity would have difficulty discounting its influence on practice.

81. Patrick Shannon, *The Struggle to Continue* (Portsmouth, NH: Heinemann: 1990) provides a rich account of the curricular antecedents of whole language and other progressive and critical pedagogies. See also Yetta Goodman, "Roots of the Whole-language Movement," *Elementary School Journal* 90: 113-127. The phrase, the child as curriculum informant, comes from Jerome Harste, Carolyn Burke, and Virginia Woodward, *Language Stories and Literacy Lessons*. (Portsmouth, NH: Heinemann, 1984).

82. One cannot possibly name all the important leaders of the whole language movement in the United States, but surely the list will be headed by Ken Goodman, Yetta Goodman, and Jerry Harste, all of whom wrote important works explicating whole language as a philosophical and curricular initiative.

83. In the 3rd edition of *Learning to Read*, Chall makes the case that phonics instruction increased during the 1970s and began its decline in the middle 1980s at the time when comprehension became a dominant research and curricular issue. She also notes a further decline in phonics instruction in basals, based on the work of Hoffman et al., "So What's New in the New Basals" in 1993. On this issue, one should also consult Kenneth G. Goodman, Patrick Shannon, Yvonne Freeman, and Sharon Murphy, *Report Card on Basal Readers*. (Katonah, NY: Richard C. Owen, 1988).

84. My understanding of the primary focus of the opposition to basals is that whole language advocates regarded basals as a pernicious form of external control on teacher prerogative, one that would lead inevitably to the "de-skilling" of teachers. In 1988, several whole language advocates and supporters wrote a monograph documenting what they took to be these pernicious effects (Goodman, Freeman, Shannon, and Murphy, 1988).

85. See Hoffman et al., "What's New in the New Basals?"

86. Perhaps the most compelling sign of the backgrounding of skills was their systematic removal from the pupil books. In the middle and even late 1980s, basal companies featured skills lessons in the pupil books on the grounds that even teachers who chose not to use the workbooks would have to deal with skills that were right there in the student materials. By the early 90s, as I noted earlier, they were out of the student books.

87. One must keep in mind that I am discussing changes in published materials, not necessarily changes in classroom practice. Whether teachers changed their actual classroom practices in a matter consistent with, or at least proportional to, the basal practices is difficult to determine given our lack of broad-based data on classroom practices. One suspects that the pendulum swings of actual classroom practice are never quite as wide as the swings in the rhetoric of policy or even the suggestions in published materials.

88. P. David Pearson, "*RT* Remembrance: The second 20 years," *The Reading Teacher* 45 (1992): 378-385. This analysis documents the increasingly dominant force of whole language, literature-based reading and process writing in the discourse of elementary reading and language arts instruction.

89. Perhaps the best documentation for the resistance to, or at least a more critical acceptance of, whole language practices comes from studies of exemplary teachers who, it appears, never bought into whole language lock, stock, and barrel but instead chose judiciously those practices which helped them to develop rich, flexible, and balanced instructional portfolios. See Ruth Wharton-MacDonald, Michael Pressley, and J. M. Hampton, "Literacy instruction in nine first-grade classrooms: Teacher characteristics and student achievement," *The Elementary School Journal* 99 (1998): 101-128.

90. Leigh Ann Martin and Elfrieda H. Hiebert, *Little Books and Phonics Texts: An Analysis of the New Alternatives to Basals* (Ann Arbor: Center for the Improvement of Early Reading Achievement/University of Michigan, in press). This analysis of the basals adopted in the early 1990s in California suggests that the vocabulary load of many of these basals was so great that most first graders could gain access to them only if they were read to them by a teacher.

91. In the late 1970s, Marie M. Clay coined the term *emergent literacy* to signal a break with traditional views of readiness in favor of a more gradual view of the shift from novice to expert reader.

92. In my own case, it was the disdain that whole language seemed to spawn regarding the explicit teaching of skills and strategies, especially those that promoted the meaning-making goals of the movement—comprehension and metacognitive strategies. See Marie M. Clay, *Emergent reading behavior*. Unpublished doctoral dissertation, University of Auckland, Auckland, NZ (1966).

93. Elfrieda H. Hiebert and Barbara M. Taylor, eds., *Getting Reading Right from the Start: Effective Early Literacy Interventions* (Boston: Allyn and Bacon, 1994) describes several research-based interventions that balance skills instruction with authentic reading.

94. Interestingly, a recent piece in *The Reading Teacher* makes exactly this point about the comprehension strategy instruction of the 80s. See Sarah L. Dowhower, "Supporting a Strategic Stance in the Classroom: Comprehension Framework for Helping Teachers Help Students to be Strategic," *The Reading Teacher* 52(7), pp. 672-689.

95. Smith, "Learning to Read like a Writer" makes just this point.

96. For a compelling account of this "no text" phenomenon, watch for Ruth Schoenbach, Cyndy Greenleaf, Christine Cziko, and Lori Hurwitz, *Reading for Understanding in the Middle and High School* (San Francisco: Jossey-Bass, in press). In this account the staff developers and teachers of a middle school academic literacy course document the role of text in middle school as well as attempts to turn the tide.

97. Similar arguments have been made for the reform movements in mathematics, i.e., that the reforms got out ahead of the professional knowledge base; the results of the reform movement in mathematics have also been similar to the fate of the whole language movement. See Thomas Good and J. Braden, *Reform in American Education: A Focus on Vouchers and Charters* (Hillsdale, NJ: Erlbaum).

98. In 1989, a special interest group with the apocryphal label of Balanced Reading Instruction was organized at the International Reading Association. The group was started to counteract what they considered the unchecked acceptance of whole language as *the* approach to use with any and all students and to send the alternate message that there is no necessary conflict between authentic activity (usually considered the province of whole language) and explicit instruction of skills and strategies (usually considered the province of curriculum-centered approaches). For elaborate accounts of balanced literacy instruction, see Ellen McIntyre and Michael Pressley, *Balanced Instruction: Strategies and Skills in Whole Language* (Boston, MA: Christopher-Gordon, 1996); Linda B. Gambrell, Lesley M. Morrow, Susan B. Newman, and Michael Pressley, *Best Practices in Literacy Instruction*. (New York: Guilford Publications, 1999); P. David Pearson, "Reclaiming the Center," in *The First R: Every Child's Right to Read*, eds. Michael Graves, Paul van den Broek, and Barbara M. Taylor (New York: Teachers College Press, 1996).

99. Pearson details many of these concerns and arguments in "Reclaiming the Center."

100. As early as 1965, Kenneth Goodman had popularized the use of miscues to gain insights into cognitive processes. The elaborate version of miscue analysis first appeared in Yetta Goodman and Carolyn Burke, *Reading Miscue Inventory* (New York: Macmillan, 1969).

101. See Larry F. Guthrie and William S. Hall, "Ethnographic Approaches to Reading Research," and David Bloome and Judith Greene, "Directions in the Sociolinguistic Study of Reading," in *Handbook of Reading Research*, for an index of the rising momentum of qualitative research in the early 1980s.

102. As a way of documenting this change, examine the *Handbook of Reading Research*, volumes I (1984) and II (1991). Volume II contains only two chapters that could be construed as relying on some sort of interpretive inquiry. Volume II has at least eight such chapters. For an account of these historical patterns in non-quantitative inquiry, see Marjorie Siegel and Susana L. Fernandez, "Critical Approaches," in *Handbook of Reading Research*, Vol. 3, in press).

103. Starting in the mid 1980s and continuing until today, the pages of *Educational Researcher* began to publish accounts of the qualitative-quantitative divide. It is the best source to consult in understanding the terms of the debate.

104. For an account of the evolution of this line of inquiry, consult Reid Lyon, "Research initiatives in learning disabilities: Contributions from scientists supported by the National Institute of Child Health and Human Development," *Journal of Child Neurology* 10, 120-126 (1995) and Reid Lyon and Vinita Chhaba, "The current state of science and the future of specific reading disability," *Mental Retardation and Developmental Disabilities Research Reviews* 2, 2-9 (1996).

105. The most highly touted pedagogical experiment supported by NICHD was published in 1998; Barbara R. Foorman, David J. Francis, Jack M. Fletcher, Christopher Schatschneider, and Paras Mehta, "The role of instruction in learning to read: Preventing reading failure in at-risk children," *Journal of Educational Psychology* 90 (1998): 37-55. The NICHD work in general and the Foorman et al. piece in particular has been cited as exemplary in method and as supportive of a much more direct code emphasis, even in the popular press (e.g., *Dallas Morning News*, May 12, 1998; *Houston Chronicle*, May 17, 1998; *Minneapolis Star Tribune*, August 5, 1998).

106. Much is made in this new work of the inappropriateness of encouraging young readers to use context clues as a way of figuring out the pronunciations of unknown words. The data cited are eye-movement studies showing that adult readers appear to process each and every letter in the visual display on the page and, most likely, to then recode those visual symbols into a speech code prior to understanding.

107. Richard Allington and Haley Woodside-Jiron, "Thirty Years of Research in Reading: When Is a Research Summary Not a Research Summary?" in Kenneth S. Goodman, *In Defense of Good Teaching* (York, ME: Stenhouse, 1998). These writers document the manner in which Bonnie Grossen's unpublished manuscript *30 years of research: What we now know about how children learn to read* (Santa Cruz: The Center for the Future of Teaching and Learning Web document: http//www.cftl.org/30years/30years, 1997), which is an alleged summary of the research sponsored by NICHD, was used in several states as the basis for reading policy initiatives.

108. Classic references attesting to the importance of phonemic awareness are Connie Juel, "Beginning Reading," *Handbook of Reading Research, Vol. 2*, edited by Rebecca Barr, Michael Kamil, Peter Mosenthal, and P. David Pearson. (New York: Longman, 1991): 759-788; and Adams, *Beginning to Read*. More recently, it has been documented in Snow, Burns, and Griffith, *Preventing Reading Difficulties in Young Children*.

109. See Connie Juel, "Beginning Reading."

110. See Connie Juel, "Beginning Reading," and Adams, *Beginning to Read*.

111. The work of Linda K. Clarke, "Invented versus traditional spelling in first graders' writings: Effects on learning to spell and read," *Research in the Teaching of English* 22(3), 281-309 and Pamela Winsor and P. David Pearson, *Children at-risk: Their phonemic awareness development in wholistic instruction* (Tech. Rep. No. 556), Urbana: Center for the Study of Reading, University of Illinois) are most relevant on the issue of the various curricular routes to phonemic awareness development.

112. One entire issue of *American Educator* was devoted to the phonics revival in 1995 (the Summer issue: Vol. 19, no. 2). Authors of various pieces included those who would generally be regarded as leaders in moving phonics back onto center stage—Marilyn Adams, Isabel Beck, Connie Juel, and Louisa Moats, among others. A second issue was also devoted entirely to reading (Spring/Summer, 1998: Vol. 22, no. 1 and 2). The piece by Marilyn J. Adams and Maggie Bruck ("Resolving the Great Debate," *American Educator* 19 (1995), 7, 10-20.) is one of the clearest expositions of the modern phonics first position I can find.

113. See Connie Juel, "Beginning Reading," in 1991, and Gough and Hillinger, 1980.

114. One of the reasons for the continuation of the debate is that few people seek common ground. Researchers who come from the whole language tradition, were they to read Adams and Juel openly, would find much to agree with about in the common privileging of big books, writing, invented spelling, and the like. They would not even disagree with them about the critical role that phonemic awareness or knowledge of the cipher plays in early reading success. They would, however, disagree adamantly about the most appropriate instructional route to achieving early success; phonics knowledge and phonemic awareness are better viewed, they would argue, as the consequence of, rather than the cause of, success in authentic reading experiences.

115. These and other reading policy matters have been well documented in a series of pieces in *Education Week* by Kathleen Manzo Kennedy (1997, 1998, 1999).

116. Marilyn Adams (see *Beginning to Read* and Adams and Bruck, "Resolving the Great Debate") has consistently championed invented spelling.

117. Richard Allington and Hallie Woodside-Jiron, "Decodable text in beginning reading: Are mandates and policy based on research?" *ERS Spectrum*, Spring 1998, 3-11. Allington and Jiron-Ironside have conducted a pretty thorough analysis of the genesis of this "research-based" policy and concluded that it all goes back to an incidental finding from a study by Juel and Roper-Schneider in 1983. They could find no direct experimental tests of the efficacy of decodable text.

118. Learning First Alliance, *Every Child Reading* (Washington, DC: Learning First Alliance, 1999).

119. The war metaphor comes up time and again when the debate is portrayed in the public press. See, for example, Art Levine, "The Great Debate Revisited," *Atlantic Monthly*, December 1994.

120. Kathleen K. Manzo, "Study stresses role of early phonics instruction," *Education Week* 16 (24), March 12, 1997, pp. 1, 24-25; Kathleen K. Manzo, "New national panel faulted before it's formed," *Education Week* 17 (23), 1998a, p. 7; and Kathleen K. Manzo, "NRC panel urges end to reading wars," *Education Week* 17 (28), March 25, 1998, pp. 1, 18.

121. Several studies are relevant here. First is the work of Wharton-McDonald and Pressley, cited earlier. Also important is the work of Pressley and Allington, 1998, and Taylor, Pearson, Clark, and Walpole, in press.

122. See Pearson, DeStefano, and García, 1998, for an account of the decrease in reliance on portfolio and performance assessment.

123. An interesting aside in all of the political rhetoric has been the question of who is de-skilling teachers. As early as the 1970s, whole language advocates were arguing that canned programs and basal reader manuals were de-skilling teachers by providing them with preprogrammed routines for teaching. Recently, whole language has been accused of the de-skilling, by denying teachers access to technical knowledge needed to teach reading effectively. Elizabeth McPike, "Learning to Read: The School's First Mission," *American Educator* 19 (1995), 4.

124. Written from a somewhat centrist whole language position, Regie Routman's *Literacy at the Crossroads* (Portsmouth, NH: Heinemann, 1996) provides a compelling account of the political and pedagogical issues we confront in the current debates.

125. The *balance* label comes with excess baggage. I use it only because it has gained currency in the field. Balance works for me as long as the metaphor of ecological balance, as in the balance of nature, is emphasized and the metaphor of the fulcrum balance beam, as in the scales of justice, is suppressed. The fulcrum, which achieves balance by equalizing the mass on each side of the scale, suggests a stand-off between skills and whole language—one for skills, one for whole language. By contrast, ecological balance suggests a symbiotic relationship among elements within a coordinated system. It is precisely this symbiotic potential of authentic activity and explicit instruction that I want to promote by using the term, *balance*.

126. Adams and Bruck, "Resolving the Great Debate"; Marilyn Adams, *Beginning to Read: Thinking and Learning About Print* (Cambridge, MA: MIT Press, 1990); Jack Fletcher and G. Reid Lyon, "Reading: A research based approach," in *What's Gone Wrong in America's Classrooms?*, ed. W. Evers (Stanford, CA: Hoover Institution Press).

127. See the earlier cited studies by Clarke and Winsor and Pearson, as well as the review of phonemic awareness in Adams, *Beginning to Read*.

CHAPTER V

Elementary and Middle School Mathematics at the Crossroads

DOUGLAS A. GROUWS AND KRISTIN J. CEBULLA

As we near the turn of the century, there is considerable public discussion and frequent debate in the popular press and in scholarly journals about the quality of school mathematics programs. Many of the discussions center on how much mathematics American students know and are based on reports of studies of student achievement such as the National Assessment of Educational Progress (NAEP) and the Third International Mathematics and Science Study (TIMSS). The discussions have also focused on other issues including the latest set of recommendations from the National Council of Teachers of Mathematics (NCTM), *Principles and Standards for School Mathematics: Discussion Draft*.[1]

The ongoing debates focus not only on how much mathematics students learn in school but also what mathematics they learn and how they learn it. The fervor of these debates is reminiscent of the rancorous discussions of the late 1950s and 1960s when the United States was thought to be behind in the space race and American students were thought to be ill prepared in mathematics and science.

The current discussions and debates about mathematics education will likely lead to changes in mathematics education as they did in the 1960s. In the 1960s, for instance, elementary school mathematics textbooks became more formal in their treatment of many topics. This occurred in response to calls from reformers for more curricular attention to the structure and logic of the discipline of mathematics. Thus, students at the elementary school level began studying a curriculum that emphasized set ideas and the formal notation used to represent them.

Douglas A. Grouws is Professor of Mathematics Education at the University of Iowa. He was a Visiting Scholar at the Pacific Mathematics and Science Consortium at Pacific Resources for Education and Learning (PREL) when this chapter was written and he gratefully acknowledges their support. Kristin J. Cebulla is a Ph.D. student in mathematics education at the University of Iowa and a former teacher and research chemical engineer.

Attention to such ideas as intersection, union, and complement of sets and the related symbols of ∩, ∪, and X' became commonplace. These ideas in their formal form and with symbolic notation were new to students and parents alike and caused considerable frustration for both.

Although no one can predict with precision what changes will evolve from the current debates, nor how well the arguments put forth will endure the test of time, it is likely that the debates, or the "math wars" as some observers have referred to them, will result in significant changes in schools just as they did in the 1950s and 1960s. We expect this will happen because the new NCTM *Principles and Standards for School Mathematics: Discussion Draft* discusses in more detail the role and importance of basic computational skills than did its predecessor, the 1989 NCTM *Curriculum and Evaluation Standards for School Mathematics*.[2] No doubt one reason for this shift was the pointed criticism that the original Standards received for de-emphasizing the development of computational efficiency. Whether or not this criticism of the old NCTM Standards was valid, it is quite clear that many people perceived the recommendations to be at best a weak advocate for basic skills. For example, a parent group in California states, "The major problem with the 1989 National Council of Teachers of Mathematics (NCTM) Standards is their lack of balance. . . . The Standards say 'All mathematics should be studied in contexts that give the ideas and concepts meaning' (p. 67). This is a naive and unproved approach that is often interpreted by teachers to mean that they should *never* teach any skills directly. Some amount of drill is important for the math student, . . . This need should be clarified in the Standards."[3] Mathematician Kenneth Ross in a 1998 report to the American Mathematics Society states, "The NCTM Standards emphasize that children should be encouraged to create their own algorithms, since more learning results from 'doing' rather than 'listening' and children will 'own' the material if they create it themselves. We feel that this point of view has been over-emphasized in reaction to 'mindless drills.' Success in mathematics needs to be grounded in well-learned algorithms as well as understanding of the concepts. None of us advocates 'mindless drills.' . . . The challenge, as always, is balance."[4] A survey of teachers and principals in Georgia concerning their views of the NCTM Standards showed that most disagreed with the de-emphasis of procedural skills and computation.[5] We expect that in the near future greater attention will be given to establishing and maintaining student computational skills in textbooks than has been the case in the past decade.

One of the explicit concerns of the American Mathematical Society (AMS) is the extent to which technical skills are necessary for conceptual understanding, or, put more starkly, how far technical skills can be neglected before understanding and mathematical power also flag.[6] Although the new standards document is clear about the place of intuitive and student-generated computational algorithms and methods in the curriculum (they should be given attention), it is vague about how students should learn to use traditional computational algorithms and at what grade level students should be expected to be proficient in their use.

Whether the preceding prediction about increased attention to developing and maintaining computational skills materializes or not—see Anthony Ralston for an example of how some mathematicians are reacting very negatively to the possibility of such a change[7]—few scholars would disagree that it is critical that future discussions and decisions concerning mathematics teaching and curriculum reform be based to the greatest extent possible on solid research findings. We say "to the extent possible" because there are questions for which there is no conclusive research evidence available and there are issues that require value judgments rather than appeals to research.[8] Choosing standards, for example, is more a matter of making value judgments than conducting scientific investigations.

Our goal in this chapter is to provide an accurate characterization of the current state of elementary and middle school mathematics education in the United States and to highlight "crossroads" points where crucial reevaluations are needed. In order to promote a contextualized understanding of some of the current issues that confront mathematics education, we begin the chapter with an historical overview of the development of mathematics education during the twentieth century. Following the historical review, we report baseline data on the current state of mathematics learning at the elementary and middle school level. Next we provide our interpretation of this data, though, of course, the reader can examine the data and draw his or her own conclusions. Following our discussion of trends and comparisons in student mathematics performance, we examine the existing mathematics curriculum and the status of mathematics teachers. How the curriculum is implemented is then discussed with attention to such issues as time allocated to mathematics, issues regarding quality of instruction, and the difficulty level of the mathematical content that receives attention in the curriculum and the classroom. The chapter closes with a discussion of an interdisciplinary issue, the wisdom of integrating the teaching of mathematics and science, and, finally, some thoughts on the future direction of mathematics education.

Mathematics Education in Historical Perspective

Before considering the present state of mathematics education, we examine some of the trends and milestones in mathematics education over the past century in order to provide a context for understanding our discussion of the current status of mathematics education. Of course, it is beyond the scope of this chapter to provide an in-depth description of each of the preceding decades; instead we give a general overview of the major time periods with special attention to changing views regarding two topics of current interest: (1) the emphasis placed on applications of mathematics and the extent to which mathematics is linked to other content areas in the school curriculum; (2) the generally accepted view of "learning with meaning" during each historical time period and the degree to which instruction focused on teaching mathematics meaningfully. For convenience we have frequently broken the past century into discrete periods. This, of course, masks some of the overlap in the movements described and the ever-present counter movements within each time frame.

MATHEMATICS IN THE EARLY 1900S

At the turn of the twentieth century, the rationale for including mathematics as a school subject was based on two prevailing theories: classical humanism and mental discipline. For classical humanists, traditional mathematics was part of our cultural heritage and as such was an important school subject. The advocates of the mental discipline theory held that the mind, like any other muscle, needed practice and exercise to develop. Therefore, mathematics was valuable as a good mental exercise, crucial to improving one's general reasoning ability. This theory assumed that mathematical reasoning ability would transfer to other domains and improve general reasoning ability. Both the mental discipline theory and classical humanism provided a strong justification for teaching mathematics.[9] Mental discipline theory called for mathematics to be abstract in nature and focused on arithmetic. Very few practical applications were given attention and branches of mathematics (e.g., arithmetic, geometry) were not connected to each other in instruction. In the early 1900s, the secondary school mathematics curriculum was firmly established as the typical progression of courses: arithmetic, algebra, geometry, trigonometry. The courses were taught in isolation from one another with few connections made to science and other subjects.[10]

From 1890 to 1915 there was a call for mathematics reform from within the mathematics community, led by Eliakim Hastings Moore, a mathematician from the University of Chicago. In 1902, in a presidential address to the American Mathematical Society, Moore called for the unification of mathematics disciplines within mathematics as well as connecting mathematics to its applications, particularly those in science.[11] "He favored emphasizing to students the practical side of mathematics, the unity of pure and applied mathematics, and the connection between different areas of mathematics with subjects of interest to students."[12] Moore wanted mathematics to be more closely tied to natural science, particularly physics, and advocated combining algebra, geometry, and physics into one course.[13] He also recommended a laboratory method of instruction that required two consecutive class periods in which students worked in small groups on explorations involving physical models that required them to develop the mathematics themselves.[14] He asked, "Would it not be possible for the children in the grades to be trained in power of observation and experiment and reflection and deduction so that always their mathematics should be directly connected with matters of thoroughly concrete character?"[15] Moore advocated unification and inclusion of applications primarily as a motivational aid for students. Other mathematicians were also advocating unification of mathematics in secondary curriculum during this period.[16] The reform effort was not meant to eliminate the prevailing axiomatic (deductive) approach, but rather to include a balance of applications with the traditional approach.[17]

The advocated reform did not have a powerful effect for several reasons. First, there was a lack of commitment and agreement from other mathematicians, some of whom felt Moore's ideas would lead to a lack of rigor. Furthermore, with the decentralized American school system, it was difficult to have a significant standardizing impact. Scheduling problems also made two consecutive class periods difficult to implement. Probably the most important reason Moore's ideas did not take hold, however, was that a counter movement within general education circles, called the social efficiency movement, ultimately threatened the very existence of mathematics in schools.[18]

The social efficiency movement gathered momentum in the early twentieth century when several psychologists, most notably Edward L. Thorndike, obtained experimental evidence that seriously questioned the mental discipline theory. In several studies Thorndike demonstrated

that training in one domain does not readily transfer to another domain. In other words, practice in mathematics does not improve reasoning in other areas. Thorndike concluded that one cannot assume
that broad transfer of learning will occur. Instead one should train or
drill in the area where one wants learning to occur. He advocated teaching methods that used stimulus and response methods, a precursor to
behaviorism and wrote mathematics textbooks applying his teaching
theories. His research and textbooks had a profound effect on arithmetic teaching in the United States.[19] Mathematics became a drill-and-
practice subject based on a curriculum driven by behavioral objectives.
Thorndike also felt that every task in a mathematics curriculum must
have meaning to the student, that is, it must be of practical value.[20] His
definition of meaning, as having practical, everyday value, is very different from later definitions the term will take on.

MATHEMATICS EDUCATION AND THE SOCIAL EFFICIENCY MOVEMENT

Once the mental discipline theory fell into disfavor, educators
began to question the value of mathematics as a school subject. This
perspective became part of the social efficiency, or social utility, movement in education and spanned the period 1910 to 1940. Social utili-
tarians questioned the necessity of any content that was not directly
applicable to real life and required that all curriculum objectives reflect
something useful to the student in his or her everyday life. Since
Thorndike's research suggested that mathematics did not improve general reasoning and most people used very little mathematics in their
daily lives, mathematics became a much less important part of the
school curriculum. Mathematics requirements were removed from the
secondary school curriculum and the inclusion of mathematics at the
junior high school level was seriously questioned.[21]

Another factor contributing to the de-emphasis of mathematics in
school curricula during this period was the large increase in the number of students attending secondary school. As the United States
became more industrialized, more students began attending secondary
school. As enrollment increased, the new students were perceived as
being incapable of, or uninterested in, the type of mathematics that
was being taught in secondary schools.[22] These students needed to be
trained in how to work, not how to understand the world.

Not only were mathematics requirements affected by the social
efficiency movement, but course content was also changed to include
more applications of mathematics. Studies were performed to determine what businesses wanted students to know mathematically. Other

studies surveyed average Americans to determine what type and depth of mathematics they used in their daily lives. The results showed that the demand was for simple calculations with small numbers and simple fractions. Furthermore, there was no need for students to understand why algorithms worked or to understand how the realms of mathematics were connected, as there was no social utility in these skills.[23] Thus, the abstract unifications linking the parts of mathematics and the logical meaning of mathematics were eliminated from the curriculum.[24] Topics were arranged around units such as community interest, cost of living, and budgets. Students were taught specific algorithmic skills and how to solve specific types of problems that were deemed useful in everyday life. "Some of the generalists became so absorbed in the concept of social utility that they lost sight of the logical integrity of mathematics."[25]

Mathematicians and mathematics educators opposed the changes in mathematics education, but their opposition had little impact on mathematics education. Some questioned Thorndike's methods and his definition of transfer; others felt, as the humanists did, that mathematics had great value in and of itself, regardless of its direct practical value. They argued that Thorndike's notion of transfer was very limited and that concepts could transfer even if specific elements did not. They felt that transfer would occur if it was taught by teaching meaning and connections within and outside of mathematics. This argument about transfer generated a large body of research on how to teach so that students can transfer what they learn to new situations.[26]

In 1920, the National Council of Teachers of Mathematics was formed as a reaction to the threats to school mathematics.[27] In 1923, the Mathematical Association of America published the *Reorganization of Mathematics in Secondary Education* that focused on demonstrating the importance of mathematics. This document criticized current mathematics teaching practices for using too much drill and not focusing on teaching for understanding. It called for teaching more connections both within and outside of mathematics. Mathematics educators stressed that mathematics was an important way of thinking and understanding the world and not just a tool subject.

Unfortunately, the pleas from mathematicians and mathematics educators went unheeded and mathematics continued to suffer from neglect and de-emphasis through the 1930s.[28] Mathematics was taught primarily as a collection of isolated skills, devoid of underlying meaning or connections to other areas of mathematics. Practical applications were stressed, but not in a coherent, connected way. Instead, applications were taught through drill and practice, and problem solving was taught as the recognition of problems by types. The mathematical meaning behind algorithms was largely ignored. Teaching for meaning meant to teach mathematical content that was useful (i.e., meaningful in a social sense), and much class time was spent practicing mathematical skills.

WORLD WAR II AND THE POSTWAR ERA

World War II brought mathematics education to the forefront of the public's attention by demonstrating the value and usefulness of mathematics. Mathematics was seen as a prerequisite for success in wartime engineering and technical efforts, leading to a temporary widespread interest in mathematics. Educators worked toward ensuring that all students learned mathematics for the good of the country. Remedial and refresher courses in arithmetic, algebra, and trigonometry were developed for military recruits. In an effort to motivate students, school mathematics incorporated military examples and applications. Curriculum changes, however, were generally cosmetic in nature and there were few changes in the pedagogical methods or the underlying focus. But, for a time, the country was focused on mathematics and educators were focused on making sure students were learning mathematics.[29]

Since the increase in the importance of mathematics was linked to its usefulness as a wartime effort, when the war was over, so too was the heightened interest in mathematics. The optimistic view that all students could and should learn mathematics faded and mathematics fell prey once again to the social efficiency arguments of the 1920s and 1930s. There was a renewed call for the mathematics curriculum to be adjusted so that the content, level, and amount of mathematics was better suited to students' lives and their "realistic" educational goals. The prevailing view was that there was no need for students to study mathematics in depth unless they were planning on becoming scientists or mathematicians.[30]

Some within the mathematics community continued to voice disagreement with the social efficiency ideology's hold on mathematics education. One such voice was that of William A. Brownell, who called for mathematics instruction that included an emphasis on teaching for meaning while not discarding class time for students to practice skills. By "meaning" he was referring to an understanding of why algorithms worked and how mathematics builds on and connects to itself. He was not speaking of meaning in the social utility sense of having an immediate practical value for the student. As Brownell put it, "meaningful arithmetic, in contrast to 'meaningless' arithmetic, refers to instruction which is deliberately planned to teach arithmetical meanings and to make arithmetic sensible to children through its mathematical relationships."[31] He felt teaching isolated facts without understanding the underlying mathematics necessitated much more time for repetitive practice and led to low levels of student retention. Furthermore, in a direct challenge to Thorndike, he argued that arithmetic meaningfully taught provided a sound foundation for increasing a student's ability to transfer what was learned to new situations.[32]

THE "NEW MATH" MOVEMENT

In the early 1950s, members of the mathematics and science communities were growing concerned about the low mathematics achievement levels of college-bound students. Simultaneously, military personnel and business leaders began attacking American schools for ill preparing students.[33] These concerns were fueled by the 1957 Russian launch of the first satellite, Sputnik, and the fear that Americans were lagging behind in the space race. Although the concerns and reforms had begun before Sputnik, Sputnik acted as a catalyst, increasing public and government interest in school mathematics reform. Thus began the so called "modern math" or "new math" reform era (circa 1950-1970), which encompassed a variety of national and regional, federally funded, curriculum projects, most of which were led by mathematicians with some mathematics educators also involved.[34]

The modern mathematics movement focused on making school mathematics more rigorous by upgrading the content of the mathematics curriculum.[35] Mathematicians felt that if curricula focused on the foundations of mathematics and the underlying logical structure, students would develop a solid understanding which would allow them to be facile users of mathematics. Many of the new math curricula used set theory as the basis for mathematics and described arithmetic operations and algebraic concepts in formal ways as operations on sets. There was also a strong focus on precise mathematical language, symbol manipulation, and abstract conceptual understanding. New math reformers assumed that once students had an understanding of the unified foundation of mathematics and the abstract connections, they would naturally be able to apply the mathematics to new situations.[36]

Parts of the new math movement focused on making connections *within* mathematics. Curriculum developers felt that if they connected the different branches within mathematics, students would have a deeper understanding of mathematics. Thus there was a focus on teaching mathematics meaningfully and a de-emphasis on the direct application approach used in the social efficiency movement. Meaningful mathematics was defined as mathematics based on an understanding of the formal, logical foundations of mathematics. This definition of "meaningful" was quite different from the social efficiency movement's tendency to associate meaningfulness with practical value.

Although the new math reform movement began with the development of curricula for college-bound high school students, eventually the development efforts moved down to the elementary school curriculum. "The elementary school proved a much tougher arena for the reformers, and the ideas that appeared to work well with enthusiastic teachers and eager students in the high schools near universities often floundered when they were exported to less advantaged schools."[37]

The difficulty in describing the new math era is that there was great variety in the curriculum projects developed, variety in the content, the methodology, and the epistemological bases.[38] Reform efforts were based on such different and varied things as discovery learning, behaviorist theories, readiness-for-learning theories, and abstract mathematical foundations.[39] The unifying belief of all these projects, however, was that the current state of mathematics education was not adequate.

One vocal critic of the new math movement was Morris Kline, an applied mathematician. In his 1973 book *Why Johnny Can't Add: The Failure of the New Math*, Kline blasted the new math, as well as the traditional curricula. He claimed that a set theory basis for the mathematics curriculum was inappropriate for a school setting because the logical, deductive approach to mathematics deceives students by giving them a false sense of how mathematics is created. "In the creative work imagination, intuition, experimentation, judicious guessing, trial and error, the use of analogies even of the vaguest sort, blundering and fumbling enter. Deductive proof plays little if any role."[40]

Kline argued that mathematics grows out of real situations and applying mathematics is the primary purpose of learning mathematics; thus school mathematics should be centered around applications and real world situations. According to Kline, applications allow students to experience the real purpose of mathematics and act as a primary motivating tool. "Psychologically the teaching of abstractions first is all wrong. Indeed, a thorough understanding of the concrete must precede the abstract. Abstract concepts are meaningless unless one has many and diverse concrete interpretations well in mind. Premature abstractions fall on deaf ears."[41] Furthermore, he claimed the examples and problems used in the new math curricula were contrived, artificial, and pointless, sure to drive every student away from mathematics.

Kline recommended that mathematics be taught in an integrated manner with connections to other subjects. "What we should be fashioning and teaching, then, beyond mathematics proper, are the relationships of mathematics to other human interests—in other words, a broad cultural mathematics curriculum which achieves an intimate communion with the main currents of thought and our cultural heritage. Some of these relationships can serve as motivation; others would be applications; and still others would supply interesting reading and discussion material that would vary and enliven the content of our mathematics courses."[42] Kline believed that students would be more motivated and better understand mathematics if mathematics curricula made mathematics meaningful by using physical objects and real life experiences.[43]

THE "BACK TO BASICS" MOVEMENT

There were other critics of the new math movement and the 1970s became a decade of reaction to its perceived failure. Critics claimed the new math was too abstract, confusing, and impractical. Other critics were alarmed with the lack of applications in the curricula. Standardized test scores were in a period of decline and people attributed this to the new math reforms. The criticism of the new math movement and a major reduction in funding from the federal government precipitated what is now referred to as the "back to basics" movement. This movement called for a return to an emphasis on the procedural skills of algebra and arithmetic without attention to the theoretical foundations of mathematics and was strongly supported by parents and the general public. Basic skills were defined as the ability to do paper-and-pencil computation. Student work emphasized gaining proficiency with algorithms such as addition, subtraction, multiplication, and division, generally using numeric exercises rather than word problems and applications. This was also a decade of direct instruction, behavioral objectives, and an increase in the use of standardized achievements tests.

In the mid-1970s, although most schools readily retreated "back to the basics," not everyone was pleased with this movement. There was a growing concern among mathematics educators that back-to-basics was an overreaction to the new math reforms and had too narrow a focus. In 1975, the National Advisory Committee on Mathematical Education (NACOME) studied the state of mathematics education, the extent to which the new math reforms had been implemented, and the success of various programs. The NACOME report suggested that the new math reforms were more visible in high school curricula than in elementary curricula. "Despite presence in most text series, these topics are most often skipped in favor of more time to develop computational skills that are comfortable to and valued by elementary teachers."[44] The report also claimed that the impact of the new math reform efforts was modest and the decline in standardized test scores during that period could not therefore be attributed to the new math programs. "The overwhelming conclusion to be drawn from these findings is that mathematics teachers and classrooms have changed far less in the past 15 years than had been supposed. . . . If there are indeed declines in mathematics test scores, it is questionable that a large part of that decline can be attributed to 'new mathematics' since few of the reform movement's suggestions have been extensively implemented in the classroom."[45] The report recommended eliminating the false dichotomy of "new" versus "old" mathematics and called for a balanced curriculum for *all* children which focused on the logical structure of mathematics as well as concrete experiences and applications.

THE 1980S: REPORTS AND RECOMMENDATIONS

A major criticism of the back-to-basics movement from mathematics educators was that basic skills were too narrowly defined and should include more than just arithmetic and algebraic computation. In 1978, the National Council of Supervisors of Mathematics (NCSM) issued a paper outlining this position on basic skills. This position paper defined basic skills as problem solving, applying mathematics, and using number sense, as well as performing traditional computation skills. "There are many reasons why basic skills must include more than computation. The present technological society requires daily use of such skills as estimating, problem solving, interpreting data, organizing data, measuring, predicting, and applying mathematics to everyday situations."[46] The NCSM report also argued for use of a variety of teaching methods, not just drill and practice, a reduced emphasis on standardized tests, and broad, rigorous state minimum requirements in mathematics. Two years later, NCTM issued *An Agenda for Action* which called for similar changes in mathematics curricula with a strong recommendation that problem solving become the cornerstone of mathematics instruction. This report gave a broad definition of basic skills, called for the use of computers and calculators in school mathematics, and advocated evaluation of student learning that included more than conventional tests. The report promoted the notion that what is "basic" must change as society and technology change. "The full scope of what is basic should contain at least . . . problem solving; applying mathematics in everyday situations; alertness to the reasonableness of results; estimation and approximation; appropriate computational skills; geometry; measurement; reading, interpreting, and constructing tables, charts, and graphs; using mathematics to predict; and computer literacy."[47]

In 1983, the National Commission on Excellence in Education (NCEE) published *A Nation at Risk: The Imperative for Educational Reform*, a critical indictment of the state of America's educational system. *A Nation at Risk* cited declining SAT scores, lack of higher-order thinking skills, and an increase in remediation by colleges, businesses, and the military as indicators of the terrible state of education. Using vivid language, the report warned that the state of education "threatens our very future as a Nation and a people."[48] The report noted that the American school curriculum was diluted, unfocused, and much less demanding in both time and content than that of other industrialized nations. The report recommended that all students receive a demanding mathematics education, which includes an understanding of concepts, applications to real life, and estimation skills. *A Nation at Risk* summoned public attention to the poor state of education much as Sputnik had done twenty-five years earlier. This marshalled public support for the reforms already begun within the mathematics education community.[49]

At the same time as *A Nation at Risk* was generating public and government awareness of the state of American education, mathematics educators were busy preparing responses to the criticisms. *An Agenda for Action* was followed by several conferences in the mid-1980s designed to respond to *A Nation at Risk* and to make recommendations to correct the reported problems. Recent research in mathematics education and cognition suggested that children learn mathematics in a variety of ways besides the traditional direct-instruction method.[50] The research was used as a rationale for making changes in mathematics education and to support the changes called for by NCTM and NCSM.[51] The reform rhetoric of the 1980s called for an increased focus on problem solving, setting high standards, and making mathematics more accessible for all students.[52]

Another area of mathematics education research that received considerable attention in the 1980s was the notion of teaching for understanding. This was a renewal of interest in the meaningful mathematics defined by Brownell and was heavily influenced by research in cognition and the psychology of learning. As in the new math era, meaning again referred to comprehending the meaning behind concepts and algorithms and to understanding connections within mathematics. However, implications from research suggested that teaching for meaning should be done differently than in the new math era where teaching for understanding focused student attention directly and emphatically upon the underlying logical structure of mathematics. The new research suggested that understanding should be developed by allowing students to build for themselves connections often referred to as schemas or networks. This involved, in part, giving students opportunities to develop symbol systems and procedural algorithms that are linked to their personal representations of concepts and to manipulative materials they have used. The position advanced was that through using multiple representations students build mathematical networks, or schemas, which connect many procedures, concepts, and ideas. This was then referred to as developing conceptual understanding, with deep conceptual understanding associated with more complex networks of linkages in a learner's cognitive structure.[53]

THE NCTM STANDARDS

During the reform movement of the 1980s, NCTM, as a large professional organization of mathematics teachers, felt the need to clarify their position with regard to the mathematics curriculum. They believed that education policymakers, school boards, curriculum developers, and mathematics teachers would benefit from a comprehensive set of standards that represented the NCTM's considered position on mathematics reform. In 1989, NCTM published *Curriculum and Evaluation Standards for School Mathematics*. NCTM developed the Standards over a four-year period, and the project was funded entirely from within the organization without any government or external support.[54]

A standard was defined in the NCTM document as a statement about what is valued. "Inherent in this document [Standards] is a consensus that all students need to learn more, and often different, mathematics and that instruction in mathematics must be significantly revised."[55] The Standards emphasized that knowing mathematics means doing mathematics, and mathematics instruction should allow students to experience genuine real-life problem situations. Across all grade levels, the Standards included as central themes (1) mathematics as problem solving, (2) communication, (3) reasoning, and (4) mathematical connections. The document combined an emphasis on meaning with an emphasis on practical applications by advocating a balanced curriculum that uses applications and connections both within and outside of mathematics to build conceptual understanding. "A conceptual approach enables children to acquire clear and stable concepts by constructing meanings in the context of physical situations and allows mathematical abstractions to emerge from empirical experience. A strong conceptual framework also provides anchoring for skill acquisition."[56] The Standards also recommended that computers and calculators be used in all mathematics classrooms and that teachers de-emphasize paper-and-pencil computations and drill.

For each of the three grade bands (K-4, 5-8, 9-12), the Standards listed concepts and skills that should receive increased attention and those that should receive decreased attention. Areas recommended for increased attention included meaning behind operations, use of real-world problems, and statistics. Topics for decreased attention included two-column proof, computational skills such as long division, complex paper-and-pencil computations, and memorization of facts and procedures.[57] Thus, it has been argued that the skills traditionally known as "basic" were de-emphasized in the recommended curriculum.

The curriculum standards were followed by *Professional Standards for Teaching Mathematics* (1991), which outlined standards for mathematics teaching as well as standards for the professional development of mathematics teachers. Particularly noteworthy in this document was the call for moving from teachers stating procedures and concepts to students inventing their own methods and solutions, often while working in small groups. *Assessment Standards for School Mathematics* followed in 1995 and focused on multiple means of assessing student learning in mathematics.[58]

THE MATH WARS

The 1989 Standards can be thought of as marking the beginning of the current mathematics reform era, often referred to as "standards-based" reform. Critics have often called it "new New Math" or "fuzzy math." Most states revised their mathematics curriculum guides during the 1990s and many of these revisions were influenced by the NCTM Standards.[59] As educational policymakers, parents, teachers, and the mathematics education community became involved in this reform, heated debates arose about the focus, content, and pedagogical methods embodied in the new mathematics curricula that flowed from the NCTM Standards. Many misinterpreted de-emphasis in the Standards to mean elimination, and consequently attention to such things as proof and basic computational skills was greatly reduced in many curricula and completely eliminated in some classrooms.

As teachers shifted their attention away from these skills, critics and parents began to complain about a loss of mathematical content in the curriculum, content that some felt was fundamental to mathematics instruction. Proponents of reform mathematics, on the other hand, felt strongly that reform mathematics brought beneficial, necessary changes to instruction. Many refer to these debates as the "math wars" and in some parts of the country they have become vigorous politicized debates. For example, California embraced reform mathematics in the 1980s and early 1990s. The 1992 revision of the state curriculum guide was strongly influenced by the NCTM Standards. As the new curriculum was making its way into classrooms, results from the 1992 NAEP showed that fourth grade California students performed near the bottom of the distribution in mathematics, scoring only better than Mississippi, Guam, and the District of Columbia.[60] In 1995 and 1996, the California State Board of Education listened to emotional parents who complained bitterly that their children were not learning rudimentary computational skills. With pressure from these parent groups and other vocal critics of standards-based reform, the State Board revised the state curriculum guide in 1998 and returned to a much more traditional curriculum. It included a heavy emphasis on basic computation skills as well as explicit lists of competencies that students must master at the end of each grade level. It is too early to determine the effect the new curriculum will have on mathematics education in California, but with 5.6 million students and 12 percent of textbook sales, California has a strong influence on the rest of the country.[61]

Critics of standards-based mathematics claim that it does not prepare future mathematicians because it leads to a lack of rigor and a loss of mathematical precision, and it downplays the importance of formal proof.[62] Other critics claim that mathematics has not changed in the last thirty years and the basic skills taught in the past are still important skills. They believe that mathematics should focus on speed and accuracy of computational skills because one cannot use mathematical concepts without a grounding in facts through memorization and drill.[63]

Proponents of standards-based mathematics claim that a basic skills curriculum is obsolete, narrow, and mind-numbing. They claim that because of new technology and our changing society, being mathematically literate requires skills beyond traditional basic skills.[64] They believe students must learn skills such as problem solving, data analysis, and applying mathematics to new situations. The basic skills curriculum does little to teach these skills.[65]

STANDARDS 2000

In October 1998, NCTM released a draft of an updated version of the 1989 Standards, *Principles and Standards for School Mathematics: Discussion Draft* (*PSSM*). The intent is for this draft to be widely disseminated, actively discussed, revised, and then adopted and released in

April 2000. The *PSSM* document discusses more fully the issue of attention to paper-and-pencil skills than did the 1989 Standards but continues to advocate a balanced curriculum with time for both practice and discovery. There is a strong recommendation for allowing students to invent and use their own informal computational algorithms, although there is also recognition of the value of standard computational algorithms. When and how to get students from their own algorithms to standard algorithms is, however, left undetermined.

PSSM advocates using applications and connecting mathematics to other branches of mathematics and other subject areas,[66] a recommendation that has strong historical roots as we have seen. Representation of mathematical ideas is an added core standard in the new standards, bringing the total to five—the four original Standards plus representation. The final form that this standard will take, as well as the entire *PSSM* document, is unknown at this time as is the effect it will have on mathematics curriculum, instruction, and student learning.

The preceding discussion of historical milestones and movements in mathematics education shows that school mathematics is the product of on-going debates about the purpose and content of mathematics education. Various reform efforts and educational movements have affected school mathematics to different degrees. Some claim that mathematics classrooms have changed little in the past fifty years.[67] Others argue that most reform efforts are little more than fads.[68] Still others argue that reform is too strong a word for what is, at most, small continual changes in education.[69] What can be gleaned from our historical overview are the polarities of the debates which remain relatively constant in spite of changing times, especially the tension between the development of computational skills versus the development of understanding of mathematical concepts. Before considering the direction mathematics education should be heading, it is necessary to take a close look at the current state of student learning in mathematics, the mathematics curriculum, the qualifications of mathematics teachers, and the nature and quality of mathematics instruction.

What Do We Know About Student Learning in School Mathematics?

When considering the myriad issues that surround mathematics education in the United States, it is essential to focus on student learning. As elementary as such a focus may seem, it does not always happen. For example, adopting new teaching methods where students learn the value of working together or of enjoying mathematics may have merit provided mathematics learning is not sacrificed. *How much* mathematics students are learning and *what* mathematics they are learning should always be central questions. Some educators would also add that *how* a student learns mathematics is critical, because it often affects transfer of learning. We now consider each of these questions.

HOW PROFICIENT ARE AMERICAN STUDENTS IN MATHEMATICS?

Student performance data must be a central consideration in decision making in areas such as program evaluation, teacher accountability, curriculum development, and lesson planning, if improved ability in mathematics is our goal. Each of these areas might call for different types of performance data gathered in different ways. For example, data from representative samples of students may be satisfactory for program evaluation but not useful for daily lesson planning. Similarly, interview data from students having difficulties with mathematics may be more helpful for curriculum development than for program evaluation. These issues aside, there should always be an interest in data about how well students perform on measures that reflect large blocks of mathematical content and major commitments of learning time. The two best sources of such data that involve nationally representative samples are the National Assessment of Educational Progress (NAEP) and the Third International Mathematics and Science Study (TIMSS). The most recent NAEP mathematics data were collected in 1996, and the TIMSS data were collected in 1995. NAEP data in mathematics will be collected again in 2000 and there is another international data collection in mathematics and science, TIMSS-R, currently underway.

National Assessment of Educational Progress. NAEP is the most representative measure we have of American students' achievement in mathematics. NAEP has been reporting data on student performance for over a quarter of a century, most recently of mathematics achievement in 1990, 1992, and 1996. Each data collection follows a carefully planned multi-stage sampling design involving stratification over region, urbanization, percent minority enrollment, and median household income.[70] In 1996, over 20,000 students at grades 4, 8, and 12 were assessed. Students showed significantly improved performance in mathematics from 1990 to 1992 and from 1992 to 1996 across all three grade levels tested. (See Table 1.) At grade 4, the average mathematics scale score improved from 213 to 220 to 224 across the years 1990, 1992, and 1996, respectively. At grade 8, the average mathematics scale score increased from 263 to 268 to 272 from 1990 to 1992 to 1996.[71]

TABLE 1

AVERAGE NAEP MATHEMATICS SCORES BY ASSESSMENT YEAR AND GRADE LEVEL

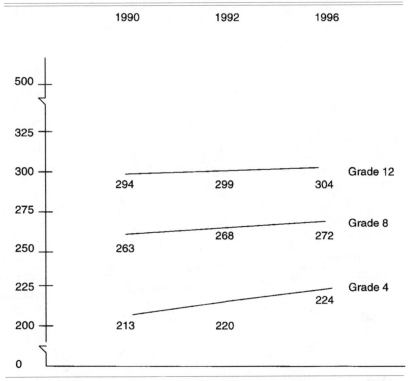

Source: National Center for Educational Statistics, National Assessment of Educational Progress (NAEP), 1990, 1992, 1996 Mathematics Assessments.

Although data from the 2000 NAEP assessment are not available at this time, and the gains shown in Table 1 are modest, the 1996 data argue strongly against the claims of some critics that student mathematics performance has been in a steady and precipitous decline over the past decade. There are, however, some disturbing aspects with respect to student performance in specific content areas and within certain socio-geographic contexts.

First, student mathematics performance shows considerable variation across geographic regions and socio-economic status (SES). Urban school systems enroll nearly one-half of all public school children in the nation. The 28 urban school systems in the United States which have the largest enrollment of K-12 students below the poverty line teach 5.5

million students.[72] Students in low SES settings and urban schools performed especially poorly on NAEP mathematics items. In 1996, for example, the average scale score for grade 4 students participating in Title I programs was 200, and for non-Title I students it was 231.[73] There was a similar significant difference at grade 8 (244 vs. 276) and at grade 12 (270 vs. 305). The magnitude of such differences can be thought of in terms of "the rule of thumb applied in many NAEP analyses of 10 proficiency scale points approximating a grade placement level."[74]

Another measure of student SES from the NAEP data is eligibility for the free or reduced-price lunch program. As shown in the line graph in Table 2, students at all three grade levels who were eligible for this program scored significantly lower than their classmates who were not eligible.[75]

TABLE 2

AVERAGE NAEP MATHEMATICS SCORES BY GRADE AND FREE/REDUCED LUNCH ELIGIBILITY

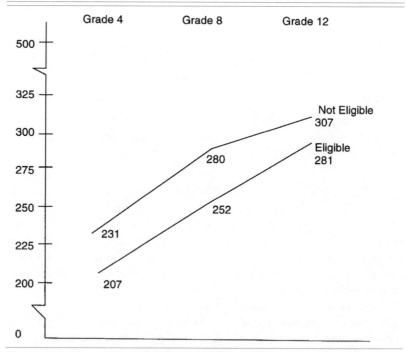

Source: National Center for Educational Statistics, National Assessment of Educational Progress (NAEP), 1996 Mathematics Assessment.

Note that these differences ranged in size from 24 to 28 scale points, equivalent to two to three grade levels behind their peers. The differences are also large when compared to the size of the increased performance differences for all students from 1990 to 1992 to 1996, which ranged in size from 4 to 7 scale points. (See Table 1.) This suggests that bridging the achievement gap may be a lengthy process.

When one considers schools in large urban areas, it is certainly not the case that all students are Title I participants or eligible for free or reduced-price lunch, although there are large numbers of these students in urban settings. When we look elsewhere for data on student achievement in urban settings, we consistently find cause for concern. For example, Maryellen Donahue reported that in the Boston public schools, "81 percent of eighth-graders scored at the lowest level on a national standardized achievement test, meaning that they had not reached the basic level of performance."[76]

Second, student performance in certain content areas and contexts suggests that there are important gaps in student learning that need attention. Problem solving is an arena where student ability to use mathematics is noticeably weak, even in situations where the computational requirements are minimal. For example, in the 1996 NAEP, more than 66 percent of fourth-grade students correctly answered a relatively straightforward, one-step verbal problem that involved whole number subtraction with renaming in a multiple-choice format, as shown in Table 3. In a more complex problem-solving situation involving a multi-step verbal problem with two- and three-digit numbers and not in a multiple-choice format, only 33 percent of grade 4 students and 76 percent of grade 8 students answered the item correctly. On the other hand, in numeric addition and subtraction situations, student

TABLE 3

GRADE 4 STUDENT PERFORMANCE ON A NAEP WHOLE NUMBER SUBTRACTION PROBLEM

ITEM	PERCENT RESPONDING GRADE 4
1. Kitty is taking a trip on which she plans to drive 300 miles each day. Her trip is 1,723 miles long. She has already driven 849 miles. How much farther must she drive?	
A. 574 miles	12
B. 874 miles*	64
C. 1,423 miles	10
D. 2,872 miles	12

*Correct Answer

Source: Kouba and Wearne (in press)

performance was better. On a simple numeric subtraction exercise like 852–38 (in vertical format), for example, 73 percent of grade 4 students answered the item correctly.[77] Thus, student problem-solving ability needs improvement, but student inability to do basic computation with whole numbers does not seem to be the principal limiting factor.

There are other important mathematical content areas where student performance is weak. Some of these areas, such as fractions and decimals, represent topics that are necessary for both successful functioning in everyday life and for future mathematics learning. Data from the 1996 NAEP mathematics assessment support the contention that there are knowledge deficiencies in some fundamental concepts. For example, among grade 4 students, only 50 percent responded correctly to a question about how many fourths make a whole and only 23 percent could use equivalent fraction concepts to solve a verbal problem.[78] Grade 8 student performance on the latter item was considerably better than at fourth grade, with 51 percent answering the question correctly. The important point is that the concepts of unit and equivalence are fundamental ideas in mathematics, and student performance on items that measure these ideas are well below a standard that meets even basic expectations.

Only 16 percent of fourth grade students were prepared to explain why one unit fraction is larger or smaller than another unit fraction when the situation was set in a context.[79] One might expect that the very gradual improvement of student performance over the last decade, the low performance of students in urban and low SES areas, and the difficulties students have in performing in some key mathematical areas portend that American students will rank unfavorably when compared to students of other countries. This is indeed true, as data from international studies of student mathematics achievement show.

Third International Mathematics and Science Study. TIMSS is the largest, most comprehensive, and most rigorous international comparison of education ever undertaken. In 1995, the study tested the mathematics and science knowledge of a half-million students from 41 different nations.[80] The study involved not only tests and questionnaires but also curriculum analyses, videotapes of teaching, and case studies.

In mathematics, data from TIMSS achievement tests show that in comparison to their age-group peers in other countries, American students at grade 4 perform at about the international average. At the grade 4 level, American students' mean score was 545, on a scale with mean of 500 and standard deviation of 100. This is slightly above the international average of 529 at this grade level. Table 4 shows how American students compared to students from the other 25 countries participating in the grade 4 part of the study.

TABLE 4

TIMSS Nations' Average Mathematics Performance at Grade 4

Country	Average	Country	Average
Singapore	625*	Israel	531
Korea	611*	Latvia	525*
Japan	597*	Scotland	520*
Hong Kong	587*	England	513*
Netherlands	577*	Cyprus	502*
Czech Republic	567*	Norway	502*
Austria	559*	New Zealand	499*
Slovenia	552	Greece	492*
Ireland	550	Thailand	490*
Hungary	548	Portugal	475*
Australia	546	Iceland	474*
United States	545	Iran	429*
Canada	532	Kuwait	400*

* Statistically different from United States average.

Source: Mullis et al. (1997) *Mathematics Achievement in the Primary School Years*. Table 1.1. Boston College: Chestnut Hill, MA.

At grade 8, the American student mean was 500, which was below the international average of 513. In a linear ranking of countries, American students at grade 8 ranked 26th among 41 countries (Table 5), whereas grade 4 students ranked 12th among 26 countries. Analyses of the TIMSS data also show that in a nation-by-nation comparison, American student performance declines from grade 4 to grade 8. For example, one can examine the 26 countries that participated at both the grade 4 and grade 8 levels. On this basis, 5 of the 6 countries with average scores similar to the United States at grade 4 have scores at grade 8 that are significantly higher than the average score for the United States. Likewise, 8 of the 12 countries with average scores below the United States at grade 4 have scores that are similar to the United States at grade 8. Put another way, the United States is the only country that falls above the international average at grade 4 and below the international average at grade 8.

A frequent reaction to international comparative data is that the best students in the United States do as well as or better than the top students in other countries. This, in fact, is not the case. Only 9 percent of fourth-grade students in the United States rank in the top 10 percent of all fourth-grade students that participated in the TIMSS

TABLE 5

TIMSS Nations' Average Mathematics Performance at Grade 8

Country	Average	Country	Average
Singapore	643*	Thailand	522
Korea	607*	Israel	522
Japan	605*	Germany	509
Hong Kong	588*	New Zealand	508
Belgium-Flemish	565*	England	506
Czech Republic	564*	Norway	503
Slovak Republic	547*	Denmark	502
Switzerland	545*	United States	500
Netherlands	541*	Scotland	498
Slovenia	541*	Latvia	493
Bulgaria	540*	Spain	487
Austria	539*	Iceland	487
France	538*	Greece	484
Hungary	537*	Romania	482
Russian Federation	535*	Lithuania	477*
Australia	530*	Cyprus	474*
Ireland	527*	Portugal	454*
Canada	527*	Iran, Islamic Republic	428*
Belgium-French	526*	Kuwait	392*
Sweden	519*	Colombia	385*
		South Africa	354*

* Statistically different from United States average.

Source: Beaton et al. (1996) *Mathematics Achievement in the Middle School Years.* Table 1.1. Boston College: Chestnut Hill, MA.

research;[81] only 5 percent of eighth grade students scored in the top 10 percent of students internationally.[82] Thus, we see again that American students perform at about international average level at grade 4 and at a below-average level at grade 8. Together the TIMSS data and the NAEP data suggest that American students don't *start* behind their international counterparts, they *fall* behind them.[83] Some reasons for this disappointing situation are discussed later when curriculum issues, teacher quality, and teaching practices are addressed.

Another hypothesis that is frequently put forward to explain why American average scores are low is that students from our large urban areas tend to pull down the average score for the United States. There may be some truth in this assertion, but the fact that only 5 percent of American eighth grade students placed in the top 10 percent internationally shows that there are deficiencies even among the highest-achieving American students. Still, it is worth noting that some high SES schools have been able to achieve high mean student performance levels on TIMSS mathematics achievement tests, scores that compare favorably with the mean scores of the highest-scoring nations. For example, fourth grade students in a consortium of 20 suburban Chicago school districts were tested using the TIMSS mathematics achievement test, and their mean was statistically equivalent to the mean fourth grade scores of four of the five top scoring nations. (See Table 4.) Their mean score was surpassed only by the fourth grade students from Singapore.[84]

What Role Does the Mathematics Curriculum Play?

The mathematics curriculum students study clearly influences what they learn. If students study a number-oriented curriculum exclusively, then one should not expect high student performance on geometry tasks. The notion of "what is studied or embodied in the tasks students do" is often referred to as "opportunity to learn." Historically, opportunity to learn has been cited as an important variable to consider when trying to understand and increase mathematics learning.[85] Differences in opportunity to learn sometimes occur among different mathematical content areas, and in these situations they can sometimes be studied by examining student performance on clusters of achievement test items organized around specific content topics (e.g., subtests, subscales). Opportunity to learn can also be investigated by examining the topics and activities included in textbooks and curriculum guides.

Mathematics content areas. TIMSS data are useful in looking for differences in student performance across content areas because they provide achievement data about six separate content areas for American fourth grade students in relation to their peers in 25 other countries. Of the six mathematics content areas surveyed by TIMSS at the fourth grade level, American students were slightly above the international average in three areas (whole numbers; fractions and proportionality; and patterns, relations, and functions), at the international average in two areas (geometry; data representation, analysis, and probability), and below the international average in one area (measurement, estimation, and number sense).[86] At the eighth grade level, students performed at about the international average in the content areas of algebra, fractions and number sense, and data representation, analysis, and probability.[87] In the areas of geometry, measurement, and proportionality they scored below the international average.

Another way to consider achievement data from a content area is to compare the percentage of items American students answered correctly with the percentage of items answered correctly by students in the top-ranking country in that content area. In this type of comparison, we find that in the area of algebra, eighth grade students answered 51 percent of the items correctly, whereas eighth grade students in Singapore answered 76 percent of the items correctly. Likewise, in geometry, students in the United States answered 48 percent of the items correctly, and students in Japan answered 80 percent correctly. The clear implication from these data is that at the end of elementary and middle grades, American students are far behind students in top-scoring countries in important areas of mathematics. The reason for this deficit may in part be related to the mathematics curriculum in place and the textbooks the students use.

Textbook and curriculum analyses. There is ample evidence that in the United States, mathematics textbooks determine to a large extent what is taught in elementary, middle, and high school classrooms. In 1990, Woodward and Elliott summarized several studies of textbook usage and concluded that "research evidence indicates that textbooks are ubiquitous and widely used in classrooms," and textbooks structure 75 to 90 percent of classroom instruction.[88] In mathematics, Fey claims textbooks together with the chalkboard form the predominant media.[89] This observation matches teacher self-report data from NAEP where 61 percent of grade 4 students and 72 percent of grade 8 students had teachers who indicated they use the mathematics textbook almost every day.[90] There is, however, some evidence from a small, in-depth study of four teachers that teachers are not slavishly tied to the textbook, but rather pick and choose material to fit their needs. Interestingly, one of the four teachers in this study used the textbook 51 percent of the time in reading and 98 percent of the time in mathematics.[91]

In summary, it may be true that some American teachers do not rely heavily on a basic textbook in implementing the mathematics curriculum and a few teachers use no textbook at all, but these situations are rare and certainly not representative of what happens in typical classrooms. Since textbooks play such an important role in how a mathematics curriculum is enacted in the classroom, we now review recent research on the content and structure of textbooks with an eye toward relating the findings to what we know about student mathematics learning. As with our examination of student achievement, we again rely heavily on a major component of TIMSS that analyzed the textbooks and curriculums of the participating countries,[92] and on a comprehensive national study of middle grade mathematics textbooks conducted under the auspices of the American Association for the Advancement of Science (AAAS).[93]

The TIMSS curriculum analysis examined the curricular aims and visions of almost 50 participating countries. The primary data sources were the textbooks and curriculum documents themselves, rather than the expert opinion and questionnaires that have characterized most large-scale curriculum analysis research in the past. Differences were found among the participating countries in the kinds of learning opportunities provided, in the mathematical content presented, in the typical expectations of student achievement, and in the organization and sequence of student learning opportunities.[94] The use of textbooks was common across the participating countries but there were considerable differences among countries in "curriculum flow"; that is, differences in when a topic is introduced, across how many grades it is developed, and at what grade level direct attention to it is completed.

Accumulating evidence from TIMSS and other research studies show that the mathematics curricula in place in the United States and the textbooks that support it lack a focus on central concepts, are overly repetitious in their attention to topics, and fail to promote instructional focus and pace that allow students to master a significant body of mathematical knowledge. For example, textbooks in the United States are far above the 75th percentile of the TIMSS countries in the number of topics covered.[95] American fourth and eighth grade textbooks, for instance, cover an average of 30 to 35 topics, whereas textbooks in Germany and Japan average 20 topics and 10 topics, respectively, at these grade levels. If the full span of the curriculum from first grade through eighth grade is examined, the intended curriculum in the United States contains more topics than the international average at every grade level. This lack of focus in American mathematics textbooks is also evident when the amount of attention to basic mathematical topics—those receiving most attention at a grade level—is examined. Among the fourth grade mathematics textbooks analyzed, the five topics receiving the most space accounted for an average of about 60 percent of the space in American textbooks but over 85 percent of the textbook space internationally.

In general, once a topic enters the curriculum in the United States it tends to stay there longer than in most other countries. Schmidt, McKnight, and Raizen report that the American practice is to add far more topics than other countries in grades one and two and then repeat these topics until grade seven. On average, mathematical topics remain in the composite curriculum for two years longer than the international median. In fact, only five countries have higher average duration. Because instructional time is limited, this means that American students tend to study less advanced topics than do their international peers as they move through the K-12 mathematics curriculum.

The picture that emerges from recent research is that the mathematics curriculum in American elementary and middle schools is overcrowded with topics, lacking in content emphasis, repetitious in nature, and low in expectations for what students can accomplish. In comparison to other countries, our curricula, textbooks, and teaching all are a mile wide and an inch deep.[96]

The TIMSS curriculum analysis was performed on textbooks being used by students in the early 1990s and thus, in almost every case, the textbooks were prepared prior to the publication of NCTM's 1989 *Curriculum and Evaluation Standards for School Mathematics*. Might the findings of the TIMSS curriculum analysis be different if more recent mathematics textbooks were examined or if a different type of curriculum analysis were performed? The American Association for the Advancement of Science (AAAS) Project 2061 textbook evaluation study provides partial answers to these questions. The study analyzed and compared 12 middle school mathematics textbook series—all with copyrights in 1994 or later—using the AAAS's Project 2061 curriculum framework. The textbook series evaluated included all the recently produced, reform-oriented, middle grade mathematics textbooks developed with major financial support from the National Science Foundation (NSF). All textbooks were judged against six content benchmarks, and selected activities from the textbooks were rated against 24 instructional criteria organized around seven broad categories: Identifying a Sense of Purpose, Building on Student Ideas about Mathematics, Engaging Students in Mathematics, Developing Mathematical Ideas, Promoting Student Thinking about Mathematics, Assessing Student Progress in Mathematics, and Enhancing the Mathematics Learning Environment. "[T]hese instructional criteria are not intended to espouse or reflect any particular theory or ideology of learning, beyond the principles and strategies that are supported by the available research evidence."[97]

The study found important similarities and differences among the textbooks with respect to how thoroughly they addressed the six content benchmarks. The textbooks in general did not differ greatly in their inclusion of number and geometry skills, but there were noticeable differences among the textbook series in the breadth and depth of their conceptual treatment of fractions, shapes, and equations. One textbook series addressed five of the six benchmarks in depth, four series addressed four benchmarks in depth, and the remaining series addressed only three or fewer benchmarks in depth. These results suggest that the broad and repetitious approach identified in the TIMSS curriculum analysis still pervades many middle grade mathematics textbook series in the United States.

In the AAAS curriculum analysis of textbook instructional strategies there were stark contrasts among the textbook series in the adequacy of instruction for the six content benchmarks. Four of the 12 textbook series compared were rated high for their engagement of students, development of mathematics concepts, and support of teachers. The other eight textbook series received mixed ratings on the instructional criteria. In summarizing the results of their analyses, the authors reported that only four of the 12 textbook series could be rated satisfactory.[98] Interestingly, the four highly rated series were all recently produced, and all had major grant support for their development from NSF. Unfortunately, none of the popular commercial textbooks was among the best rated.

In summary, the preceding curriculum analysis studies suggest that mathematics textbooks, which have a determining influence on the curriculum in almost all classrooms, may have serious deficiencies that could account in part for what is generally considered disappointing performance by American students on international comparisons of student achievement. This leads to the next important question: Are there well-qualified teachers teaching mathematics in elementary and middle schools who can successfully counteract the lack of coherence in the mathematics curriculum and the textbook deficiencies?

What is the Status of Our Teachers of Mathematics?

High-quality teachers can enhance students' mathematics learning. A good teacher, for example, can often compensate for an undemanding curriculum, overcome negative student attitudes, and refocus low expectations. Defining teacher quality, however, is complicated because teaching takes place in a complex social environment. In this environment, there are conditions that hinder learning, and some of these conditions are very difficult for a teacher to control. Student absenteeism is one example. Absenteeism rates in many schools greatly exceed what would normally be expected from illness, for example, and in instances of truancy teachers often have limited ability to improve the situation.

Nevertheless, there are many areas where teachers are the major decision makers and their decisions affect student learning. In general,

American teachers are experienced and well qualified. Nearly one-half of public school teachers (45%) hold master's degrees, and the average teacher has 15 years of teaching experience.[99] When more specific teacher qualifications and experience are examined, the data cause concern because they suggest that there may *not* be a well-qualified teacher teaching mathematics in many American classrooms.

"You can't teach what you don't know" is a common adage that seems to have research support. In a 1989 study comparing high-achieving and low-achieving elementary schools in New York, Armour-Thomas et al. found that differences in teacher qualifications accounted for more than 90 percent of the variance in student achievement in mathematics and reading.[100] Data analysis from the 1996 NAEP mathematics study showed teacher preparation in mathematics was one variable related to eighth grade student performance. Students of teachers with a major in mathematics had significantly higher NAEP average achievement scores (278) than did students taught by teachers with majors in education but not mathematics or mathematics education (269) or majors in some other field (267).[101] The relationship did not hold at grade 4, perhaps because the content taught was not as complex or demanding, or because the number of students who had teachers with a major in mathematics was too small (9%) to give a rigorous test of the relationship.

Unfortunately, we do not have a deep understanding of how teachers' knowledge of mathematics gets translated into the decisions they make in planning and conducting lessons. But there is research that suggests where the advantages of having a teacher with more mathematical knowledge may accrue. In a 1997 study of 9,000 seventh grade students in 33 matched schools, Mandeville and Liu hypothesized that the extent of a mathematics teacher's content area preparation would differentially affect student performance as a function of the level of difficulty of the mathematics tasks used to assess that performance. They compared the performance of students of secondary-mathematics-certified teachers and students of elementary-school-certified teachers on three cognitive levels of mathematics test items from the Stanford Achievement Test: knowledge and recognition (43 items), understanding (52 items), and thinking skills (23 items). They concluded that seventh grade students tend to perform better on higher-level thinking tasks in mathematics when their teachers have advanced certification in it. In particular, they found that the seventh grade students of teachers who had secondary mathematics certification scored better, statistically and practically, than students of teachers with elementary school certification.[102] Students below the seventh grade level seldom have teachers with secondary mathematics certification. For example, data from NAEP show that teachers of the large majority of fourth grade students (83%) have college majors in education rather than in mathematics or mathematics education.[103]

The relationship between teacher knowledge and student learning draws our attention to research on the quality and quantity of mathematical knowledge that teachers possess. We examine the extent of teacher knowledge in two ways. First, we report data about out-of-field teaching at the middle grade levels, primarily grades 7 and 8, because that is where students often begin to have different teachers for different subjects. Second, we summarize research on the mathematical knowledge of elementary teachers and how this knowledge is used in the daily teaching of mathematics.

OUT-OF-FIELD TEACHING

Out-of-field teaching, where teachers are assigned to teach subjects for which they have little preparation, is a major but often unrecognized problem in American schools, particularly in mathematics. Analyzing data from the Schools and Staffing Surveys conducted by the National Center for Education Statistics (NCES) in 1999, Richard Ingersoll found that out-of-field teaching in mathematics is alarmingly prevalent. He found that one-third of all secondary school teachers of mathematics have neither a major nor a minor in mathematics. Out-of-field teaching in mathematics occurs disproportionately in the lower secondary school grades. Almost one-half (48.8%) of all seventh grade public school students are taught by teachers without a major or a minor in mathematics.[104]

In 1999, Laurie Lewis et al. analyzed data collected in 1998 by NCES from a nationally representative sample of 4,049 full-time teachers in regular public elementary, middle, and high schools in the 50 states and the District of Columbia. Their data examined the relationship between the main teaching assignment of teachers (i.e., the field in which they taught the most courses) and their academic preparation. These analyses greatly underrepresented the magnitude of the mismatch between teacher assignment and teacher qualifications because they ignored situations where, for example, a physical education teacher teaches one or two mathematics courses but the rest of the teaching assignment is in physical education. Nevertheless, their data still show that 18 percent of full-time public school teachers in grades 7 through 12 who reported mathematics as their main teaching assignment did not have a major nor a minor in mathematics.[105]

Just as the excellent analysis by Ingersoll sheds light on the extent of out-of-field mathematics teaching in grades 7 and 8, the detailed analyses by Lewis and colleagues reveal another context where there is disproportionate out-of-field teaching: the classrooms of students in poverty. In low SES schools (i.e., schools with 60 percent or more students eligible for free or reduced-price school lunch), 31 percent of teachers in grades 7-12 whose main teaching assignment was mathematics reported that they had neither a major nor a minor in mathematics.[106] Recall that this percentage is an understatement of the extent of the problem. On the other hand, only 14 percent of the mathematics teachers (main assignment) in other schools (less than 60 percent eligible for free or reduced-price school lunch) reported not having a mathematics major or minor. The inequity of the distribution of qualified mathematics teachers between high and low SES schools is disturbing, especially when one considers that the disparity reported here might be substantially larger if the data analysis had compared the highest SES classes with the lowest SES classes, rather than splitting the entire distribution of teachers into two large blocks for comparison. This suggests that our most challenged students may be burdened with our least prepared teachers.

The concern that the preceding results raise is magnified by the fact that other studies that have investigated the relationship between variables related to teachers' knowledge of subject matter and student achievement have found that greater teacher knowledge is related to increased student performance. For example, in 1997 Goldhaber and Brewer analyzed data from the 1998 National Educational Longitudinal Study (NELS) to determine the effect of teachers' degree levels on student performance. They found that in mathematics and science, but not in English or history, subject-specific training had a significant impact on student test scores. In particular, a teacher with a B.A. or an M.A. in mathematics had a statistically significant positive impact on student achievement as compared to teachers without advanced degrees or with degrees in non-mathematics subjects.[107]

In summary, the research literature shows that out-of-field teaching in mathematics is a significant problem at the middle school level, and the magnitude of the problem is especially great in low socio-economic contexts. Further, other proxies for subject matter knowledge such as subject-specific degrees also seem to be related to increased student performance with more teacher knowledge associated with greater student learning. Although having a major or a minor in mathematics or a subject-specific degree does not guarantee teacher competence, having at least a minor in mathematics should be considered a minimal requirement for teaching mathematics at grades 7 and 8. The quality of the mathematical knowledge a teacher possesses is, of course, critical regardless of whether one has a major or a minor in mathematics. We now examine research that further investigates the quality of teachers' subject matter knowledge in mathematics at the elementary and middle school levels.

TEACHERS' SUBJECT MATTER KNOWLEDGE

"No one questions the idea that what a teacher knows is one of the most important influences on what is done in classrooms and ultimately on what students learn."[108] A growing research base shows that preservice elementary school teachers' knowledge of mathematics as they enter the teaching field is often shallow, rule-bound, and compartmentalized. In a 1990 study of 252 prospective elementary and secondary school teachers, Deborah Ball used questionnaires and interviews to examine the mathematical knowledge of prospective teachers as they entered preservice teacher education programs in five colleges and universities. Student understanding of division was explored by examining division of fractions. On the questionnaire, 217 preservice elementary and secondary teachers responded to a multiple-choice question that asked them to select an appropriate verbal problem representation for $4\ 1/4 \div 1/2$. In a follow-up study using an interview task, the preservice teachers (25 elementary and 10 secondary) were asked to show how they would divide $1\ 3/4$ by $1/2$ and then asked to provide an appropriate representation (picture, model, story, real-world representation) for the statement. Only 30 percent of the preservice elementary teachers and 40 percent of the secondary teachers selected a mathematically appropriate representation on the multiple-choice question. On the interview task, all of the preservice teachers were able to calculate the correct answer, but none of the preservice elementary teachers were able to generate an appropriate representation, and only 4 of the 10 secondary subjects were able to do so. Ball concluded, "[T]he mathematical understandings that prospective teachers bring are inadequate for teaching mathematics with understanding."[109]

It should be noted that representing division of fractions with a real-world situation may be a bit esoteric* and more difficult than representing

---

*It can be argued that most situations where one could divide fractions to solve a problem are solved using multiplication. For example, to halve a recipe that calls for 2/3 cup of flour, one would multiply by 1/2. Or to determine how many 1/3rds there are in $4\ 2/3$, one would think, "What multiplied by 1/3 gives $4\ 2/3$?"

other operations. Nevertheless, it is easy to argue that teachers who are going to teach division with meaning should be able to represent it; in fact, they probably should be able to represent it using a variety of representational modes. Further, research studies that examined other aspects of teacher knowledge of division found teachers' conceptual knowledge to be weak and insufficient to teach mathematics well.[110]

Teacher knowledge of other mathematical topics has also been shown to have weaknesses that may interfere with the development of mathematical ideas in the classroom in a meaningful and connected manner. Interestingly, data from NAEP show that over three-fourths of students at grade 4 and nine-tenths of students at grade 8 have teachers who report being "very well prepared" to teach both mathematical concepts and procedures.[111] The consequences of this mismatch between content knowledge and feelings of preparedness are unclear, but should be taken into account in teacher development activities.

What is Classroom Mathematics Instruction Like?

Are good things happening in mathematics classrooms? Are the conditions conducive to student learning? Clearly these questions cannot be answered with a simple yes or no. Case studies, including those conducted as part of the TIMSS study, help provide rich detail about what is happening in some mathematics classrooms. Although it is difficult to generalize across these studies, this should not deter the interested reader from perusing these descriptive reports. We have chosen to provide considerable detail in our portrait of classroom instruction with regard to matters that may be related to the underperformance of American students. We make this decision in the interest of stimulating discussion and sparking research interest and not to present an unduly negative picture of classroom instruction. We say that we will emphasize factors that "may be related to underperformance" because there is relatively little research in mathematics education that focuses on establishing cause-and-effect relationships. Much more of the research is correlational and qualitative in nature and from these studies we will only be able to look for patterns of results that show potential causal relationships.

TIME ALLOCATED TO MATHEMATICS INSTRUCTION

Time spent on mathematics can include time actually devoted to mathematics during the mathematics class period, time spent on homework, and mathematics-related thinking and procedures that are part of the study of other disciplines, such as science and social studies.

Probably the most important time devoted to studying mathematics is time spent in mathematics class because it is during this time that students regularly and directly interact with their teacher and other students about mathematics.

Many states have regulations and guidelines concerning the amount of time that should be allocated to mathematics during the school day. Typically, state guidelines call for between 45 and 60 minutes daily in the upper elementary grades and in middle schools, with somewhat less time required in the primary grades. Despite state recommendations and guidelines that are quite similar from state to state, data from NAEP teacher questionnaires show that there is considerable variation in the amount of time allocated to mathematics at grade 4 and at grade 8. Surprisingly, fourth grade students are likely to receive more hours of mathematics instruction per week than are eighth grade students in many situations. In 1996, 68 percent of fourth grade students had teachers who reported that they spent four or more hours on mathematics instruction per week, whereas only 33 percent of eighth grade students had teachers who reported spending that much time on mathematics instruction per week.[112] This result is especially puzzling since the complexity of the mathematics studied in the eighth grade is much greater than in the fourth grade.

Students who are getting the least amount of time allocated to mathematics instruction may not be provided with sufficient time to learn all the mathematics they are capable of learning. At the most worrisome extreme, the most recent NAEP study of mathematics found that 20 percent of students at grade 8 had teachers who reported that their time allocation for mathematics was less than or equal to 150 minutes per week, which means less than 30 minutes daily.[113] Given the sophistication of mathematical ideas that should be a part of the eighth grade curriculum, 30 minutes is not sufficient, regardless of how much time students are involved with mathematics in other ways, such as through homework. It would be interesting to know whether short time allocations are related to school organization patterns. In particular, are short time allocations to mathematics more prevalent in schools where there are not set time periods for classes than in schools that have a fixed bell schedule?

QUALITY OF INSTRUCTIONAL TIME

If time allocations for mathematics classes are short in many schools, then it is especially important that the instructional time be used wisely. One measure of the quality of mathematics time is the number of interruptions that occur for such things as students leaving the classroom, announcements over the loudspeaker, visitors entering the room, non-mathematics related activities such as lunch counts and attendance taking, and so forth. There are data from the TIMSS video-tape study of eighth grade classrooms in the United States, Japan, and Germany that relate to this issue. One lesson from each of 83 American, 100 German, and 100 Japanese (all teachers randomly selected) were analyzed—with striking results.

There were major differences, for example, in lesson focus and organization. In 28 percent of American lessons there was at least one interruption, whereas this occurred in only 13 percent of German lessons and never during a Japanese lesson.[114] The TIMSS video study also coded mathematics class time devoted to "other" activities unrelated to mathematics or to the current lesson. These unrelated activities occurred in 23 percent of American lessons, 9 percent of Japanese lessons, and 4 percent of German lessons. Although the total amount of time devoted to such activities is small in all countries, even a brief diversion can spoil the flow of a lesson, especially in an already short class period. Other evidence of the fragmented nature of mathematics lessons in the United States comes from an analysis of the number of topics and topic segments (i.e., points in the lesson where the topic shifts from one content area to another) per mathematics lesson. American lessons contained significantly more topics per lesson (1.9) and topic segments per lesson (2.3) than did Japanese lessons (1.3 and 1.3, respectively).[115]

Interruptions, unrelated activities, and proliferating topics and topic segments during class sessions are indicators of a lack of lesson focus and organization. Taken cumulatively they may portend a significant problem; namely, many mathematics lessons lack the coherence and structure needed for students to acquire mathematical knowledge in a meaningful way.

An interesting characteristic of mathematics instruction in the United States is how often concepts are developed as opposed to just being stated. Recent research in grade 8 classrooms has shown that, for almost 80 percent of the time, concepts are simply stated and not developed.[116] Concepts that are not developed in meaningful ways are unlikely to be used in problem-solving situations because students will not recognize the connections. Also, psychological research suggests that we can expect short retention of ideas that have been learned with little meaning attached to them.

Equally important is the nature and substance of the mathematics content. Learning is obviously restricted even in well-taught lessons if the content of the lesson is not new and challenging to the students.

MATHEMATICS CONTENT OF LESSONS

When the topics studied in videotaped mathematics lessons from eighth grade classrooms in the United States, Germany, and Japan were analyzed and compared with their average placement in the mathematics curricula of the 41 TIMSS countries, the results showed that lessons in the United States involved less challenging topics. When matched against the international scale, the average grade level for topics in the American lessons was mid-seventh grade level, in the German lessons it was the mid-eighth grade level, and for the Japanese lessons it was the beginning ninth grade level.[117]

NAEP data also suggest an emphasis on less challenging mathematical ideas during class time. For example, over 90 percent of the fourth grade students and about 80 percent of the eighth grade students had teachers who reported that they addressed facts and concepts as well as skills and procedures for routine problems "a lot." In contrast, at both grade levels only 52 percent concentrated frequently on developing reasoning and analytic ability to solve unique problems.[118]

Rates of inclusion of specific content ideas reveal findings similar to the general findings about the low level of the mathematics content in lessons. For example, when lessons were examined for instances of deductive reasoning in the TIMSS video study, no instances were found in the 83 eighth grade lessons from the United States, whereas such instances were found in 62 percent of the Japanese lessons.[119]

The TIMSS video study also had four mathematicians rate the overall quality of the mathematical content of each lesson on a three-point scale: high, medium, and low. Although a subjective measurement, there was a high degree of agreement among the raters. The results for American lessons were 0 percent high quality, 11 percent medium, and 89 percent low. For Germany the results were 28 percent high, 38 percent medium, and 34 percent low. For Japan, the ratings were 39 percent high, 51 percent medium, and 11 percent low.[120] In summary, there seems to be considerable evidence to support the claim that American lessons are less demanding in their mathematical content than are lessons in other countries.

LESSON FORMAT AND STRUCTURE

American mathematics lessons seem to have a very distinct style, a style that is quite different from that of Japanese lessons, for example. In 1996, James Hiebert and colleagues concluded that lessons in the United States follow what they call an acquisition/application script. In the acquisition phase, students are expected to learn how to solve a particular type of problem, often through watching a demonstration by the teacher. Frequently teachers work several problems at the board and then work several additional problems where students are asked to supply the steps in solving the problems. In the application phase, students are expected to practice what they have learned on a large number of similar types of problems, often working individually at their desks. Homework generally is assigned and usually consists of a number of exercises from the textbook which differ in only small ways from the problems solved in class.[121]

In contrast, the lessons of Japanese teachers make problem solving the central context in which competencies are developed and used. Typically, attention to only one or two problems unfamiliar to the students but related to previous work dominates an entire lesson. Generally, a teacher states a problem and then students work on it individually or in groups. As they work the teacher circulates around the room noting what methods students use to solve the problem, and later students share their methods with the class. Students are assigned homework problems that provide *extensions* of the main idea inherent in the problem(s) they solved in class.

Hiebert and colleagues imply that the Japanese teaching model is preferable to the American model. It may be, however, that the best choice is not to ask teachers to adopt uniformly an entirely different teaching method. Perhaps, instead, teachers should be encouraged to match their teaching methods to the instructional objectives of the lesson they are teaching. For example, the American model may have advantages when used in particular contexts and with certain objectives, such as developing traditional computational algorithms. Using the acquisition/application approach, even in such limited circumstances, would probably be dismissed as inappropriate by critics who argue for students inventing their own algorithms. It does seem, however, that a discovery phase could appropriately precede an acquisition/application phase in many lessons. Such a two-phased teaching approach for carefully chosen objectives is worthy of further study. However, as mentioned previously, the best way to get from invented algorithms to traditional, shared algorithms is not clear from extant research.

Issues

Many important questions need to be resolved in order for the mathematics learning of children in the twenty-first century to meet the expectations of society. Many of these issues are being widely discussed in the mathematics education community. Choosing from among many proposals, we target for discussion here the issue of integrated approaches to teaching mathematics because it is an idea that is more and more frequently being recommended for implementation in elementary and middle schools and because on the surface it seems to make educational sense. We concur with Thomas Good and his colleagues, however, that too often educational change merely reflects adopting the latest fad,[122] rather than taking a reasoned approach to change based on research and evaluated in terms of effects on students. Our concern is that one of the currently popular methods of integrating mathematics and science is a fad that does not take into account many potential shortcomings.

INTEGRATED DISCIPLINARY APPROACHES TO TEACHING MATHEMATICS

Implementation of an integrated curriculum often takes one of two distinct approaches. One approach is to integrate aspects of other disciplines into the teaching of each subject as it is taught during the school day. For example, in the teaching of music, related aspects of dance, the visual arts, and the dramatic arts are regularly incorporated into the teaching of fundamental concepts such as rhythm and pattern. The other approach is to reorganize the school day into larger blocks of time and to teach subjects together while emphasizing their interrelationships. For instance, in many schools, reading and language arts are taught in a single block. In some schools, mathematics and science are taught within a single time block, an arrangement that seems to be within the spirit of the recommendations of some professional organizations. One of the premises put forth by the AAAS, for example, is: "The common core of learning in science, mathematics, and technology should center on science literacy, not on an understanding of each of the separate disciplines."[123] More specifically, the rationale stated most often is that mathematics provides many of the tools needed to do science and that science provides interesting applications of mathematics in the real world. This synergy is thought to result in increased learning and appreciation of both disciplines.

Whatever the merit of integrating the teaching of elementary school subjects, there are several reasons why one should be cautious about implementing the large-time-block approach to instruction in mathematics and science. First, there is a fundamental difference in the nature of the two disciplines. Science derives new knowledge frequently from induction and often makes use of the "scientific method" of inquiry. Mathematics, on the other hand, establishes new knowledge through deductive means that do not always rely on real-world observations, though the real world often suggests interesting problems. This is a fundamental difference between mathematics and science. It is unclear how we can ensure that students acquire a valid sense of the nature of each subject when classroom instruction emphasizes their commonality.

Second, science depends on mathematics for its tools, but mathematics need not rely on science for applications. There are important real-world applications of mathematics in other fields, including economics, political science, psychology, sociology, philosophy, logic, art, and music. If mathematics and science are taught in a common block it is likely that non-scientific examples of mathematics in real world contexts would get little attention. This would be a disservice to students because it would likely limit their view of both the nature and usefulness of mathematics.

Finally, it is quite possible that in a fully integrated approach, mathematics would be lost among the many scientific concepts and applications studied. Students might learn a lot of science, but they might not acquire many fundamental mathematical ideas, ideas that would need to be abstracted from the many scientific examples and applications considered and given explicit attention in the classroom. In summary, rather than integrating the teaching of mathematics and science, it may be more prudent to incorporate aspects of science (and other disciplines) into the teaching of mathematics when applications of mathematics are being considered.

Future Directions

We live in a global society and the students of today will compete with students from across the world when they become adults. It is important that their knowledge of mathematics be sufficiently deep for them to compete effectively. Data from international studies show quite clearly that American students perform in mathematics at about an average level on an international scale. Although some may argue that in the United States student performance is above average in some content areas and at some grade levels, these arguments focus attention on the wrong questions in our opinion. The questions should be: How far are American students from being first in the world in their knowledge of mathematics? What do we need to do to get there? Americans do not settle for being average in business, technology, or sports. We should not settle for being mediocre in mathematics achievement, or be satisfied with small annual improvements. Elementary and middle school mathematics in the United States is at a crossroads. We can choose to proceed by continuing to make minor modifications in the present system, which will likely lead to continued small incremental improvements in student performance, or we can commit to making major systemic reforms that have the potential to greatly improve the depth and quality of learning.

Findings from international studies of mathematics achievement, national studies of student performance, and other mathematics education research suggest some of the impediments to accomplishing our goals. Simple solutions to our problems probably do not exist, but there are certain diagnosable problems that merit immediate attention. First, every student deserves a well-qualified mathematics teacher. Out-of-field teaching in mathematics needs to be eliminated. The long-standing recommendation by NCTM that subject matter specialists teach mathematics from grade 4 onward deserves a large-scale test to prove its merit. Teachers need to be better prepared. At a minimum, improved preparation must include a more thorough comprehension of the mathematics content to be taught in elementary and middle schools and a deeper understanding of the nature of mathematics and its power to make sense of real-world situations.

Second, the mathematics curriculum at the elementary and middle school levels must become more focused and more ambitious, and must be taught to more students. A basic skills curriculum oriented to computational procedures alone is inappropriate in this technological age for any student, regardless of SES status, school context, or past achievement. Attention to computational procedures is important, but cannot continue to dominate the elementary school curriculum in terms of textbook coverage and class time. Whether the problem here is one of fact or perception, it needs to be dealt with explicitly in order for other appropriate curriculum reforms to move forward.

Finally, too many mathematics lessons are too short, unorganized, interrupted, cluttered with unrelated activities, and, in general, lacking in focus. Mathematics lessons need to become more coherent, convey high expectations for students, and be aligned with important mathematical goals. It is open to debate whether this requires a wholly new methodology for teaching mathematics in American schools, different teaching methods for different types of instructional objectives, or a modification of existing teaching methods and techniques. This is an issue to be widely debated and discussed. Most important, it should be the basis for targeted research on instructional systems that take account of differences in content and objectives. Research resources equivalent to those now allocated for mathematics curriculum development and systemic reform are needed and should be supported by federal agencies and private foundations.

NOTES

1. National Council of Teachers of Mathematics (NCTM), *Principles and Standards for School Mathematics: Discussion Draft* (Reston, VA: National Council of Teachers of Mathematics, 1998).

2. National Council of Teachers of Mathematics, *Curriculum and Evaluation Standards for School Mathematics* (Reston, VA: National Council of Teachers of Mathematics, 1989).

3. Honest Open Logical Debate on Math Reform (HOLD), "Suggestions and Recommendations for Improvement of 1989 NCTM Standards," Available Online: [http://mathematicallycorrect/holdnctm.htm]

4. Kenneth A. Ross, "Doing and Proving: The Place of Algorithms and Proofs in School Mathematics," *American Mathematical Monthly* 105 (1998): 252-53.

5. Lynn Deal Futch and James C. Stephens Jr., "The Beliefs of Georgia Teachers and Principals Regarding the NCTM Standards: A Representative View Using the Standards' Belief Instrument (SBI)," *School Science and Mathematics* 97 (1997): 242-47.

6. Roger Howe, "The AMS and Mathematics Education: The Revision of the 'NCTM Standards'," *Notices of the AMS* 45 (1998): 245.

7. See Anthony Ralston, "Let's Abolish Pencil-and-paper Arithmetic," *Journal of Computers in Mathematics and Science* (in press) for an example of how some are reacting very negatively to the possibility of such a change.

8. James Hiebert, "Relationships Between Research and the NCTM Standards," *Journal for Research in Mathematics Education* 30 (1999): 3-19.

9. Jeremy Kilpatrick, "A History of Research in Mathematics Education," in *Handbook of Research on Mathematics Teaching and Learning*, ed. D. A. Grouws (New York: Macmillan, 1992), 3-38; George M. A. Stanic, "Mathematics Education in the United States at the Beginning of the Twentieth Century," in *The Formation of the School Subjects: The Struggle for Creating an American Institution*, ed. T. S. Popkewitz (New York: Falmer Press, 1987), 145-75; George M. A. Stanic, "The Growing Crisis in Mathematics Education in the Early Twentieth Century," *Journal for Research in Mathematics Education* 17 (1986): 190-205.

10. George M. A. Stanic and Jeremy Kilpatrick, "Mathematics Curriculum Reform in the United States: A Historical Perspective," *International Journal of Educational Research* 17 (1992): 407-17.

11. Eliakim Hastings Moore, "On the Foundations of Mathematics," (1902) Reprint, *Mathematics Teacher* 60 (1967): 360-74.

12. Sidney Ratner, "John Dewey, E. H. Moore, and the Philosophy of Mathematics Education in the Twentieth Century," *Journal of Mathematical Behavior* 11 (1992): 105-16.

13. Moore, "Foundations of Mathematics"; Stanic, "Mathematics Education in the United States."

14. Moore, "Foundations of Mathematics"; Ratner, "John Dewey, E. H. Moore, and the Philosophy of Mathematics Education."

15. Moore, "Foundations of Mathematics," 367.

16. Jeremy Kilpatrick and George M. A. Stanic, "Paths to the Present," in *Seventy-five years of progress: Prospects for school mathematics*, ed. I. M. Carl (Reston, VA: National Council of Teachers of Mathematics, 1995), 3-17.

17. Alan R. Osborne and F. Joe Crosswhite, "Forces and Issues Related to Curriculum and Instruction, 7-12," in *A History of Mathematics Education in the United States and Canada, NCTM Thirty-second Yearbook*, ed. P. S. Jones (Washington, DC: National Council of Teachers of Mathematics, 1970), 155-297.

18. Stanic, "Mathematics Education in the United States"; Stanic and Kilpatrick, "Mathematics Curriculum Reform."

19. Kilpatrick, "A History of Research."

20. Robert M. W. Travers, *How Research Has Changed American Schools: A History from 1840 to the Present* (Kalamazoo, MI: Mythos Press, 1983).

21. Stanic, "The Growing Crisis."

22. Kilpatrick, "A History of Research."

23. Stanic, "Mathematics Education in the United States."

24. Kilpatrick, "A History of Research."

25. Osborne and Crosswhite, "Forces and Issues," 192.

26. Kilpatrick, "A History of Research."

27. Kilpatrick and Stanic, "Paths to the Present."

28. Osborne and Crosswhite, "Forces and Issues."

29. Alan W. Garrett, "Mathematics Education Goes to War: Challenges and Opportunities During the Second World War" (paper presented at the Research Presession of the annual meeting of the National Council of Teachers of Mathematics, San Francisco, CA , April 1999).

30. Ibid.

31. William A. Brownell, "The Place of Meaning in the Teaching of Arithmetic," *Elementary School Journal* 47 (1947): 257.

32. Brownell, "The Place of Meaning"; William A. Brownell, "Meaning and Skill—Maintaining the Balance," (1956) Reprint, *Arithmetic Teacher* 34 (1987): 18-25.

33. Kilpatrick, "A History of Research."

34. Carol Findell, "Mathematics Education Then and Now: The Need for Reform," *Journal of Education* 178, no. 2 (1996):3-13; Kilpatrick, "A History of Research"; Osborne and Crosswhite, "Forces and Issues," 235-59.

35. Geoffrey Howson, Christine Keitel, and Jeremy Kilpatrick, *Curriculum Development in Mathematics* (Cambridge: Cambridge University Press, 1981), 131-39,187-97.

36. Michael J. Bossé, "The NCTM Standards in Light of the New Math Movement: A Warning!" *Journal of Mathematical Behavior* 14 (1995): 171-201; Findell, "Mathematics Education Then and Now"; Osborne and Crosswhite, "Forces and Issues," 235-97.

37. Stanic and Kilpatrick, "Mathematics Curriculum Reform," 413.

38. Bossé, "The NCTM Standards: A Warning!" 173.

39. Howson, Keitel, and Kilpatrick, *Curriculum Development in Mathematics*; Kilpatrick, "A History of Research."

40. Morris Kline, *Why Johnny Can't Add: The Failure of the New Math* (New York: St. Martin's Press, 1973), 48.

41. Ibid., 99.

42. Ibid., 146.

43. Kline, *Why Johnny Can't Add*; Morris Kline, "The New Math: A Passing Aberration," *Learning* 2, no. 5 (1974): 18-20.

44. National Advisory Committee on Mathematical Education (NACOME), *Overview and Analysis of School Mathematics Grades K-12* (Washington, DC: Conference Board of the Mathematical Sciences, 1975), 11.

45. Ibid., 77-78.

46. National Council of Supervisors of Mathematics (NCSM), "Position Statement on Basic Skills," *Mathematics Teacher* 71 (1978): 148.

47. National Council of Teachers of Mathematics (NCTM), *An Agenda for Action* (Reston, VA: National Council of Teachers of Mathematics, 1980), 6-7.

48. National Commission on Excellence in Education (NCEE), *A Nation at Risk: The Imperative for Educational Reform* (Washington, DC: United States Government Printing Office, 1983), 5.

49. Douglas B. McLeod et al., "Setting the Standards: NCTM's Role in the Reform of Mathematics Education," in *Bold Ventures*, vol. 3, *Case Studies of U. S. Innovations in Mathematics Education*, eds. S. A. Raizen and E. D. Britton (Dordrecht, The Netherlands: Kluwer Academic Publishers, 1996).

50. Thomas A. Romberg and Thomas P. Carpenter, "Research on Teaching and Learning Mathematics: Two Disciplines of Scientific Inquiry," in *Handbook of Research on Teaching*, 3rd ed., ed. M. C. Wittrock (New York: Macmillan, 1986).

51. McLeod et al., "Setting the Standards."

52. Kilpatrick and Stanic, "Paths to the Present."

53. James Hiebert and Thomas P. Carpenter, "Learning and Teaching with Understanding," in *Handbook of Research on Mathematics Teaching and Learning*, ed. D. A. Grouws (New York: Macmillan, 1992), 65-97.

54. For a detailed description of the creation of the 1989 NCTM *Standards* see McLeod et al., "Setting the Standards."

55. NCTM, *Curriculum and Evaluation Standards*, 1.

56. Ibid., 17.

57. Ibid., 20-21, 72-73, 126-127.

58. NCTM, *Professional Standards for Teaching Mathematics* (Reston, VA: NCTM, 1991); NCTM, *Assessment Standards for School Mathematics* (Reston, VA: NCTM).

59. Gretchen Vogel, "The Calculus of School Reform," *Science*, 29 August 1997, 1192-95.

60. Barbara Kantrowitz and Andrew Murr, "Subtracting the New Math," *Newsweek*, 15 December 1997, 62.

61. Ibid.; Vogel, "The Calculus of School Reform."

62. For a university mathematician's critique of standards-based mathematics reform see Hung-His Wu, "The Mathematics Education Reform: Why You Should Be Concerned and What You Can Do," *American Mathematical Monthly* 104 (1997): 946-954.

63. Wayne Bishop, "The California Math Standards: They're Not Only Right; They're the Law," *Phi Delta Kappan* 180 (1999): 439-440.

64. Lynn Arthur Steen, ed., *Why Numbers Count: Quantitative Literacy for Tomorrow's America* (New York: College Entrance Examination Board, 1997).

65. Ruth Cossey, "Are California's Math Standards Up to the Challenge?" *Phi Delta Kappan* 180 (1999): 441-443; Jeremy Kilpatrick, "Confronting Reform," *American Mathematical Monthly* 104 (1997): 955-962. The reader is encouraged to read the February 1999 (vol. 180) issue of *Phi Delta Kappan* for a thorough discussion of many of the arguments in the math wars.

66. NCTM, *Principles and Standards*.

67. See, for example, Hiebert, "Relationships Between Research" and Thomas C. O'Brien, "Parrot Math," *Phi Delta Kappan* 180 (1999): 434-438.

68. See, for example, Thomas L. Good, Sally N. Clark, and Donald C. Clark, "Reform Efforts in American Schools: Will Faddism Continue to Impede Meaningful Change?" in *International Handbook of Teachers and Teaching*, eds. B. J. Biddle et al. (Dordrecht, The Netherlands: Kluwer Academic Publishers, 1997), 1387-1427.

69. Kilpatrick and Stanic, "Paths to the Present."

70. Nancy L. Allen, Debra L. Kline, and Christine A. Zelenak, *The NAEP 1994 Technical Report*, NCES-97-897 (Washington, DC: National Center for Education Statistics, 1997).

71. Clyde M. Reese et al., *NAEP 1996 Mathematics Report Card for the Nation and the States* (Washington, DC: National Center for Educational Statistics, 1997).

72. National Science Foundation (NSF), *Systemic Initiative Capsule* (1999), Available Online: [http://www.ehr.nsf.gov/ehr/esr/portfolio.htm]

73. Reese et al., *NAEP 1996 Mathematics Report Card.*

74. John A. Dossey, "The State of NAEP Mathematics Findings: 1998," in *Results from the Seventh Mathematics Assessment of the National Assessment of Educational Progress*, eds. E. A. Silver and P. Kenney (Reston, VA: National Council of Teachers of Mathematics, in press).

75. Reese et al., *NAEP 1996 Mathematics Report Card.*

76. Office of Educational Research and Improvement (OERI), *What the Third International Mathematics and Science Study (TIMSS) Means for Systemic School Improvement* (ISBN 0-16-049826-0) Policy Brief from TIMSS Policy Forum, Washington, DC, October 6-7, 1997, (1998): 9.

77. Vicky L. Kouba and Diana Wearne, "What Do Students Know About Whole Number Properties and Operations?" in *Results from the Seventh Mathematics Assessment of the National Assessment of Educational Progress*, eds. E. A. Silver and P. Kenney (Reston, VA: National Council of Teachers of Mathematics, in press).

78. Ibid.

79. Ibid.

80. Lois Peak, *Pursuing Excellence: A Study of United States Eighth-Grade Mathematics and Science Teaching, Learning, Curriculum, and Achievement in an International Context*, NCES 97-198 (Washington, DC: National Center for Education Statistics, 1996).

81. Lois Peak et al., *Pursuing Excellence: A Study of United States Fourth-Grade Mathematics and Science Achievement in International Context*, NCES 97-255 (Washington, DC: National Center for Education Statistics, 1997).

82. Peak, *Pursuing Excellence: A Study of United States Eighth-Grade Mathematics.*

83. William H. Schmidt, Curtis C. McKnight, and Senta A. Raizen, *A Splintered Vision: An Investigation of U. S. Science and Mathematics Education* (Dordrecht, The Netherlands: Kluwer Academic Publishers, 1997).

84. Mark Hawkes, Paul Kimmelman, and David Kroeze. "Becoming 'First in the World' in Math and Science," *Phi Delta Kappan* 79 (1997): 30-33.

85. See, for example, Thomas L. Good, Douglas A. Grouws, and Howard Ebmeier, *Active Mathematics Teaching* (New York: Longman, 1983); Douglas A. Grouws and Kristin J. Cebulla, "Mathematics," in *Handbook of Research on Improving Student Achievement*, ed. G. Cawelti (Arlington, VA: Educational Research Service, in press); Andrew Porter, "A Curriculum Out of Balance: The Case of Elementary School Mathematics," *Educational Researcher* 18 (1989): 9-15; and Walter G. Secada, "Race, Ethnicity, Social Class, Language, and Achievement in Mathematics," in *Handbook of Research on Mathematics Teaching and Learning*, ed. D. A. Grouws (New York: Macmillan, 1992), 623-60.

86. Peak et al., *Pursuing Excellence: A Study of United States Fourth-Grade Mathematics.*

87. Peak, *Pursuing Excellence: A Study of United States Eighth-Grade Mathematics.*

88. Arthur Woodward and David L. Elliot, "Textbook Use and Teacher Professionalism," in *Textbooks and Schooling in the United States: Eighty-ninth Yearbook of the National Society for the Study of Education* (Chicago: University of Chicago Press, 1990), 178; Harriet Tyson and Arthur Woodward, "Why Students Aren't Learning Very Much from Textbooks," *Educational Leadership* 47 (1989): 14-17.

89. J. T. Fey, "Mathematics Education Research on Curriculum and Instruction," in *Research in Mathematics Education*, ed. R. J. Shumway (Reston, VA: National Council of Teachers of Mathematics, 1980), 222-223.

90. Douglas A. Grouws and Margaret S. Smith, "Findings from NAEP on the Preparation and Practices of Mathematics Teachers," in *Results from the Seventh Mathematics Assessment of the National Assessment of Educational Progress.*

91. Lauren A. Sosniak and Susan S. Stodolsky, "Teachers and Textbooks: Materials Use in Four Fourth-Grade Classrooms," *Elementary School Journal* 93 (1993): 249-75.

92. See Schmidt, McKnight, and Raizen, *A Splintered Vision* and William H. Schmidt et al., *Many Visions, Many Aims*, Vol. 1, *A Cross-National Exploration of Curricular Intentions in School Mathematics* (Dordrecht, The Netherlands: Kluwer Academic Publishers, 1997).

93. Gerald Kulm, Kathleen Morris, and Laura Grier, *Middle Grades Mathematics Textbooks: A Benchmarks-based Evaluation* (Washington, DC: American Association for the Advancement of Science, in press).

94. Schmidt et al., *Many Visions, Many Aims.*

95. Schmidt, McKnight, and Raizen, *A Splintered Vision.*

96. Ibid.

97. Kulm, Morris, and Grier, *Middle Grades Mathematics Textbooks.*

98. Ibid.

99. Laurie Lewis et al., *Teacher Quality: A Report on the Preparation and Qualifications of Public School Teachers*, NCES 1999-080 (Washington, DC: National Center for Educational Statistics, 1999), 10-11.

100. Eleanor Armour-Thomas et al., *An Outlier Study of Elementary and Middle Schools in New York City: Final Report* (New York: Board of Education, 1989).

101. Grouws and Smith, "Findings from NAEP on Mathematics Teachers."

102. Garrett K. Mandeville and Qiduan Liu, "The Effect of Certification and Task Level on Mathematics Achievement," *Teaching and Teacher Education* 13 (1997): 397-407.

103. Evelyn F. Hawkins, Frances B. Stancavage, and John A. Dossey, *School Policies and Practices Affecting Instruction in Mathematics: Findings from the National Assessment of Educational Progress*, NCES 98-495 (Washington, DC: National Center for Educational Statistics, 1998).

104. Richard M. Ingersoll, "The Problem of Underqualified Teachers in American Secondary Schools," *Educational Researcher* 28 (1999): 1-12.

105. Lewis et al., *Teacher Quality.*

106. Ibid.

107. Dan D. Goldhaber, and Dominic J. Brewer, "Evaluating the Effect of Teacher Degree Level on Educational Performance," in *Development in School Finance, 1996*, NCES 97-535, ed. W. Fowler, Jr. (Washington, DC: National Center for Education Statistics, 1997).

108. Elizabeth Fennema and Megan L. Franke, "Teachers' Knowledge and Its Impact," in *Handbook of Research on Mathematics Teaching and Learning*, ed. D. A. Grouws (New York: Macmillan, 1992), 147.

109. Deborah L. Ball, "The Mathematical Understandings that Prospective Teachers Bring to Teacher Education," *Elementary School Journal* 90 (1990): 464.

110. See, for example, Martin A. Simon, "Prospective Elementary Teachers' Knowledge of Division," *Journal for Research in Mathematics Education* 24 (1993): 233-54; and Rina Zazkis, and Stephen Campbell, "Divisibility and Multiplicative Structure of Natural Numbers: Preservice Teachers' Understanding," *Journal for Research in Mathematics Education* 27 (1996): 540-63.

111. Grouws and Smith, "Findings from NAEP on Mathematics Teachers."

112. Ibid.

113. Ibid.

114. James W. Stigler et al., *The TIMSS Videotape Classroom Study: Methods and Findings from an Exploratory Research Project on Eighth Grade Mathematics Instruction in Germany, Japan, and the United States*, NCES 99-130 (Washington, DC: National Center for Education Statistics, 1999).

115. Ibid.

116. Ibid.

117. James W. Stigler and James Hiebert, "Understanding and Improving Classroom Mathematics Instruction: An Overview of the TIMSS Video Study," *Phi Delta Kappan* 79 (1997): 16.

118. Grouws and Smith. "Findings from NAEP on Mathematics Teachers."

119. Stigler and Hiebert, "Understanding and Improving Classroom Mathematics."

120. Stigler et al., *TIMSS Videotape Classroom Study*.

121. James Hiebert et al., "Problem Solving as a Basis for Reform in Curriculum and Instruction: The Case of Mathematics," *Educational Researcher* 25 (1996): 12-21.

122. See Good, Clark, "Reform Efforts in American Schools."

123. American Association for the Advancement of Science (AAAS), *Benchmarks for Science Literacy* (New York: Oxford University Press, 1993), xii.

CHAPTER VI

Elementary School Social Studies: Yesterday, Today, and Tomorrow

JERE BROPHY, JANET ALLEMAN, AND CAROLYN O'MAHONY

This chapter focuses on social studies as taught in elementary schools in the United States. It addresses the purposes and goals of social studies, its evolution as a school subject, its present status, and possible future trends. Throughout the chapter, the term "elementary" is used to refer to the entire K-to-6 range, with "primary" referring to grades K to 3, "middle" to grades 4 to 6, and "upper" or "junior high" to grades 7 and 8.

The National Council for the Social Studies (NCSS) and most leaders in the field think of social studies (singular) as a coherent K-12 school subject organized to prepare young people for citizenship. However, some discipline-based organizations and leaders prefer to view social studies (plural) as an umbrella term for courses in history, geography, and the social sciences. Elementary teachers usually have only limited exposure to these debates, so their views of social studies tend to be shaped by state and district curriculum standards or guidelines and (especially) by the content covered in the textbooks used at their grade levels. Thus, for primary teachers social studies is units on holidays and on cultural universals studied in the context of family, neighborhood, or community; for middle grade teachers it is units on the state, on American history and geography, on geographical regions, and on past and present world cultures; and for secondary teachers it is courses on history, government, economics, or perhaps sociology, psychology, or anthropology.

Competing Visions of Social Studies as Citizen Education

Lacking a big picture perspective on social studies as a coherent K-12 subject, elementary teachers often are confused about its purposes

Jere Brophy and Janet Alleman are professors and Carolyn O'Mahony is a doctoral candidate, all in the Department of Teacher Education at Michigan State University.

and uncertain about how to teach it. This leads many of them to downgrade its importance in the curriculum or offer fragmented programs because they select activities for convenience or student interest rather than for their value as means of accomplishing clearly formulated social education goals.[1]

Such confusion is readily understandable. The history of social studies has been marked by ongoing debates over its nature, scope, and definition.[2] Curriculum developers disagree both on the general purposes of social education and on how to address agreed-upon goals. Consequently, social studies instructional materials differ considerably, not only in the general kinds of content included (history, geography, etc.), but also in their treatments of topics addressed in common (the tribes are covered in units on Native Americans, the countries included in units on geographical regions, the perspective(s) represented in treatments of history, etc.).

However, most competing points of view can be understood using a few basic ideas about the purposes and goals of social education. Once teachers understand these ideas, they can clarify their own positions, recognize the thinking behind social studies curriculum guides and instructional materials prepared by others, and if necessary adapt them to better serve their students' social education needs.

Most social educators accept the idea that social studies bears a special responsibility for citizen education.[3] However, their visions of the ideal curriculum conflict because they differ in their definitions of citizen education and in their assumptions about how to accomplish it.[4] Some of these disagreements are linked to curricular tensions observable in all school subjects, some reflect issues that are especially salient in social studies, and some reflect competition for curriculum space among disciplinary and special interest groups.

Herbert Kliebard[5] noted that curriculum debates in all school subjects reflect continuing struggles among supporters of four competing ideas about what should be the primary basis for K-12 education. The first group believes that schools should equip students with knowledge that is lasting, important, and fundamental to the human experience. This group typically looks to the academic disciplines, both as storehouses of important knowledge and as sources of authority about how this knowledge should be organized and taught. The second group believes that the natural course of child development should be the basis for curriculum planning. This group would key the content taught at each grade level to the interests and learning needs associated with its corresponding ages and stages. The third group works backwards from its adherents' perceptions of society's needs, seeking to design schooling to prepare children to fulfill adult roles in society. The fourth group seeks to use the schools to combat social injustice and promote social change; so it favors focusing curriculum and instruction around social policy issues. Many past and present curricular debates in social studies can be understood as aspects of the ongoing competition among these four general approaches to K-12 curriculum development.

In addition, competing approaches to social education reflect issues that are especially salient in social studies. Barr, Barth, and Shermis[6] identified three main traditions: (1) teaching social studies as citizenship transmission, with emphasis on inculcating traditional values; (2) teaching social studies as social science, with emphasis on disciplinary knowledge and data-gathering skills; and (3) teaching social studies as reflective inquiry, with emphasis on analyzing values and making decisions about social and civic issues. Research using this Three Traditions Model indicates that most teachers are eclectics rather than pure types. However, understanding the priorities that teachers favor helps us to understand what they do in the classroom.[7] For example, the citizenship transmission view fits well with textbook-based, lecture-recitation-seatwork approaches to teaching, whereas the reflective inquiry view fits well with constructivist approaches that emphasize reasoning and valuing processes. The social science view can fit with either teaching approach, depending on whether the teacher emphasizes content mastery or inquiry processes.[8]

John Haas[9] placed the Three Traditions into historical context. He noted that citizenship transmission has always been the mainstream approach in the elementary grades. It features support for the status quo, emphasis on western civilization, and uncritical celebration of, and inculcation into, American political values and traditions. Periodically, it is challenged by two reform approaches. Calls for the first reform approach typically come from academic historians and social scientists who want better coverage of disciplinary content and more preservation of the integrity of separate disciplines in the form of separate courses. The other recurring reform position calls for an emphasis on the process of thinking reflectively. Rooted in the ideas of John Dewey, this approach is associated with discussions of problems and issues that feature critical thinking, values analysis, and decision making.[10]

Peter Martorella[11] argued that both the evolution of social studies over time and the differences in current curricula can be understood in terms of differences in emphasis on five approaches (including the Three Traditions already described). All of these approaches agree that citizen education should be the major focus of social studies, but they differ in their perspectives on citizen education and their descriptions of how it should be played out in classrooms:

Perspective	Description
Social studies should be taught as:	*Citizenship education should consist of:*
1. Transmission of the cultural heritage	Transmitting traditional knowledge and values as a framework for making decisions
2. Social science	Mastering social science concepts, generalizations, and processes to build a knowledge base for later learning
3. Reflective inquiry	Employing a process of thinking and learning in which knowledge is derived from what citizens need to know in order to make decisions and solve problems
4. Informed social criticism	Providing opportunities for an examination, critique, and revision of past traditions, existing social practices, and modes of problem solving
5. Personal development	Developing a positive self-concept and a strong sense of personal efficacy

Although reasonable people disagree about what is needed to prepare students for current and future citizenship, there are many commonalities in the analyses by Barr and others, Haas, and Martorella. This indicates that most of the diversity observable in social studies is not random or chaotic, but results from competition among well-articulated alternative interpretations of its citizen education mission.

Evolution of the Social Studies Curriculum

Before social studies acquired its name and became established as a pandisciplinary school subject, it was represented in the form of courses or readings in history and civics. Citizen education had always been an important function of public schooling in the United States. This was reaffirmed during the late nineteenth and early twentieth centuries, when the nation was absorbing millions of immigrants and feeling the need to inculcate democratic traditions and values, especially in the elementary grades, which were the only schooling that most citizens experienced at the time. For example, a heroes-holiday-history curriculum became popular early in the twentieth century, reflecting recommendations of a committee appointed by the American Historical Association.[12] This curriculum involved studying Indian life, historical aspects of Thanksgiving, the story of Washington, and local history in grades 1 and 2; heroes of other times, Columbus, the Indians, and historical aspects of Independence Day in grade 3; biographical approaches to American history in grades 4 and 5; European backgrounds of American history in grade 6; and chronological study of American history paired with civics instruction that focused on the state and national governments in grades 7 and 8. However, the influence of the American Historical Association and other groups dominated by professors in determining the content of the elementary curriculum gradually receded in favor of organizations dominated by school teachers and administrators.[13]

The emergence of social studies as a pandisciplinary school subject is often credited to an influential committee report issued by the National Education Association in 1916,[14] although the term "social studies" and the key ideas advocated in the report have been traced to earlier sources.[15] The 1916 report called for establishing a curriculum strand to be called "social studies." Social education would be its primary purpose; its content would be informed by history, geography, and several social science disciplines; and selection of this content would be based on its personal meaning and relevance to students and its value in preparing them for citizenship. These same themes are still emphasized today by leading social studies educators and organizations. For example, the NCSS defined social studies as "the integrated study of the social sciences and humanities to promote civic competence." It added that "the primary purpose of social studies is to help young people develop the ability to make informed and reasoned decisions for the public good as citizens of a culturally diverse, democratic society in an interdependent world."[16]

Elementary social studies (grades K-6) did in fact develop along the lines envisioned in the 1916 report. Its curriculum drew from history, geography, civics, and economics, and later from sociology, anthropology, and psychology. Its content was taught as pandisciplinary social studies organized by topic, rather than as school-subject versions of the academic disciplines taught as separate courses. Gradually, the *expanding communities* approach became the dominant framework for structuring the curriculum. Also known as the expanding horizons or the expanding environments approach, this framework begins with the self and then gradually expands the purview to the family and school, the neighborhood, the community, the state, the nation, and the world.

Secondary courses (grades 7-12) also are taught within a social studies curriculum strand that includes responsibility for preparing students for citizenship. However, most secondary courses are school-subject versions of history or one of the social sciences, in which content is addressed primarily within the single discipline rather than through pandisciplinary treatment of topics.[17] There have been exceptions to this general trend: contemporary ones include courses in law-related education, global education, environmental studies, and conflict resolution. For the most part, though, secondary courses feature titles such as United States History, economics, or American government.

THE "NEW SOCIAL STUDIES" OF THE 1960s

In the 1950s and 1960s, social studies came under criticism for having moved too far in the direction of life adjustment goals and strayed too far from the underlying disciplines. Consequently, "new social studies" programs were developed in the 1960s around conceptual organization structures and modes of inquiry stressed in the disciplines. They featured inductive teaching and discovery learning; use of original documents and the methods of historians and social scientists; attempts to develop cumulative, sequential learning; the notion that any idea can be taught successfully in some form to any student of any age; content drawn from the newer social sciences; case studies; and post-holing (focusing on one topic or situation in depth).[18]

Perhaps the best known of these programs was *Man: A Course of Study* (MACOS), an anthropology-based curriculum for the middle grades that was influential among social educators for its innovative instructional techniques and activities but controversial among the general public because of its content. Other "new social studies" programs included the *Family of Man*, Hilda Taba's *Concepts and Inquiry*, the *Our Working World* program in economics education, and *Museum Materials and Activities for Teachers and Children* (MATCH).

These new programs generated a great deal of scholarly interest and approval, but they never became established in the schools. Some were limited to just one or two grades or were based on content not typically taught. These programs could not easily be assimilated into the established curriculum, yet did not offer full-scale alternatives that could replace it. Resources often were confined to a manual and a few simple unit plans, creating unrealistic demands on teachers to assemble appropriate materials. Also, proper implementation typically required a much deeper social science background than most elementary teachers possessed.[19] Finally, the social and political ferment of the 1960s provided more powerful citizen education material than the intellectualized analysis of discipline-based concepts that these programs offered. Thus, the student as academic inquirer was replaced by the student as social activist.[20]

Engle and Longstreet[21] offered an even more fundamental critique of discipline-based approaches, noting that most of the decisions we make in our daily lives are neither referred to nor guided by the disciplines. They went on to point out that the disciplines concern themselves with intentionally isolated segments of existence, producing knowledge that is fragmented, abstract, and theoretical. Others have argued that disciplinary knowledge is suitable for teaching to older students who are capable of appreciating its value, but elementary students need a topical approach that is better adapted to the realities of human situational learning and to what these students are able to comprehend and appreciate. Considering a topic in all of its aspects (rather than addressing only those aspects that fit within a particular discipline) and within the context of its implications for personal decision making should cause students to find social studies instruction relevant and meaningful.

THE 1970S AND 1980S

Beginning in the late 1960s, the emphasis in social studies classes shifted to personal development and citizen education accomplished through class discussion and projects concerned with values conflict and moral dilemmas, social and political issues (racism, sexism, Vietnam, Watergate), and non-traditional topics such as career education, consumer education, urbanization, environmental studies, and futurism. Games and simulation activities became popular, along with discussion and values analysis activities. In the elementary grades, there was also an emphasis on learning centers, hands-on activities, and other methods associated with the open education movement. However, criticisms developed suggesting that social studies had begun to place too much emphasis on process and not enough on establishing a coherent content base.[22] These criticisms have continued through the present, where they form part of the rationale used to justify calls for more systematic teaching of history and geography.

Another concern was that social studies had moved too far away from civic issues toward more individual issues of personal adjustment and morality. This led to a developing consensus among social educators that citizen education should be reaffirmed as the transcendent purpose of the social studies. The kind of citizen education envisioned was to be centered around preparation for informed social and civic decision making, and the purview was to be multicultural and global rather than monoculturally American. Curriculum and instruction would be informed by the disciplines of history, geography, and the social sciences, but guided more by beliefs about the needs of students and of society than by current formulations of knowledge within these disciplines. Content also would be drawn from the arts and humanities, current events, and value and policy debates.

Growing consensus on reaffirmation of citizen education as the transcendent purpose of social studies set the stage for the development of more balanced and integrated approaches that would combine the best elements of the traditional emphasis on social education accomplished through cultural transmission with the best elements of the newer social science/inquiry and values analysis/decision-making approaches.[23] However, progress was slowed by the "back to basics" movement, with its emphasis on the teaching and testing of basic reading and mathematics skills. This had the effect of reducing the time allocated to social studies, to the point that it was virtually pushed out of the curriculum in many elementary schools. Also, related pressures on publishers led to social studies textbook series designed with as much emphasis on language arts goals as on social education goals. Many of the activities in these texts called for such tasks as identifying the main idea in a paragraph rather than applying its social science concepts or considering its citizen action implications. Prominent in the early 1980s, these series have receded in favor of series that once again focus on social education goals, although overemphasis on and questionable selection and use of children's literature is a problem in some recent series.[24]

Contemporary Social Studies Curriculum Debates

Debates over the ideal social studies curriculum continued throughout the 1990s. In addition to competition among alternative positions on the purposes and goals of social education, these debates reflected renewed competition among the disciplines for curricular "air time." Organizations representing history, geography, and the social sciences issued policy statements concerning how their respective disciplines should be represented in K-12 social studies. Economics educators produced a set of scope-and-sequence guidelines for teaching economics outlining basic concepts to emphasize,[25] followed by a set of national content standards.[26] Associations representing geographers and geographic educators identified five main themes to emphasize in teaching geography,[27] and subsequently published more detailed guidelines and suggested activities for developing these.[28] Eventually they produced a set of 18 standards, elaborated for implementation in grades K to 4, 5 to 8, and 9 to 12.[29] The Center for Civic Education published the *CIVITAS* document suggesting reforms in civic education.[30] It emphasized knowledge of law and political processes, examination of public issues, and involvement of students in civic participation activities. This was followed by a shorter statement on national standards for teaching civics and government.[31] The National Center for History in the Schools produced three documents suggesting opportunity-to-learn standards for history teaching: one on history for grades 1 to 4, one on United States history for grades 5 to 12, and one on world history for grades 5 to 12.[32] Following a storm of criticism of these volumes from traditionalists concerned that they were multicultural and politically correct to a fault, a revised version was published containing revised standards and omitting most of the previously included suggestions for teaching and class activities.[33] Sourcebooks containing ideas for teaching United States history[34] and world history[35] were published separately.

These statements from disciplinary groups contain helpful summaries of powerful ideas and suggestions about teaching methods and activities. However, they also imply that each respective discipline ought to be taught much more extensively than it is now. Teachers rightly view each set of standards taken individually, and especially the entire set taken as a whole, as projecting unrealistic expectations about the time available to teach social studies, the teaching/learning that can be accomplished within a given time frame, or both.[36] The authors usually do not identify what might be reduced in the curriculum if space for their discipline were to be increased, although history advocates have attacked the educational value of other disciplines, which they believe have supplanted history as the core of the social studies curriculum.

History-oriented reform proposals call for a return to a curriculum focused primarily on history, supported by geography and civics. Social science content would be included, but within history courses. Its advocates argue that history is the naturally integrative focal point for social studies because it allows for comprehensive coverage of each topic—not only its historical aspects but also its geographical, civic, cultural, economic, and social aspects. Reform models based on these ideas include the Bradley Commission's *Historical Literacy: The Case for History in American Education*[37] and the curriculum guidelines for history and social science teaching published by the California State Department of Education.[38]

History-centered reform proposals have not been received warmly by social studies opinion leaders and professional organizations. They argue that the social sciences offer important insights about how the social world functions that all citizens ought to understand and be able to bring to bear in their civic decision making. Some of them also disparage the value of history as a basis for citizen education, arguing that knowledge about the past has limited application to the complexities of the contemporary world.[39] Finally, social studies scholars fault history-centered reform proposals for embodying an overly traditional approach to citizen education, that is, knowledge- and values-transmission. They would like to see social studies curricula be more global and multicultural in purview, more critical of traditions, and more focused on current and future issues than on the past.

Neither history advocates' calls for more history teaching nor their attacks on the supposed deficiencies of other social studies content are based on research, and their claims do not stack up well against the research that is available.[40] Evidence does not support the charge that history has "lost out" to other disciplines or that the essentials of history are not being taught,[41] and there is little reason to believe that social education goals would be accomplished better through an even heavier focus on history teaching, especially if this involved coverage of many more historical details studied in strictly chronological order. Studies indicate that, after two or three exposures to United States history, most students remain indifferent to and ill-informed about it.[42] Also, debates are not just over how much history should be taught, but whose history and how it should be represented. History advocates[43] have been promoting an approach to history that leading social educators have criticized as overly conservative and insufficiently attuned to diverse points of view.[44]

Reforms Suggested for Elementary Social Studies

For the most part, the reform proposals issued by discipline-based organizations and special commissions are focused on the secondary grades. They usually have little to say about elementary social studies, especially about the primary grades. However, some reform proposals have focused specifically on the elementary grades or included them within plans for alternative K-12 programs.

E. D. Hirsch, Jr.[45] and others have proposed cultural literacy as the basis for developing curricula for social studies (and other subjects). The early grades would be devoted to teaching traditional cultural knowledge and related values and dispositions to equip students with a common base of prior knowledge to inform their social and civic decision making. Critics of Hirsch tend to agree with him that a shared common culture is needed, but to view his lists of ostensibly important knowledge as dubiously extensive and detailed. Furthermore, because they are long lists of specifics, they lead to teaching that emphasizes breadth of coverage of disconnected details over depth of development of networks of connected knowledge structured around powerful ideas. Hirsch's ideas conflict with an emerging consensus[46] about what is involved in teaching school subjects for understanding, appreciation, and life application. (See Table 1.)

TABLE 1

TEACHING FOR UNDERSTANDING, APPRECIATION, AND LIFE APPLICATION:
TEN KEY FEATURES

1. The curriculum is designed to equip students with knowledge, skills, values, and dispositions that they will find useful both inside and outside of school

2. Instructional goals emphasize developing student expertise within an application context and with emphasis on conceptual understanding of knowledge and self-regulated application of skills

3. The curriculum balances breadth with depth by addressing limited content but developing this content sufficiently to foster conceptual understanding

4. The content is organized around a limited set of powerful ideas (basic understandings and principles)

5. The teacher's role is not just to present information but also to scaffold and respond to students' learning efforts

6. The students' role is not just to absorb or copy input but also to actively make sense and construct meaning

7. Students' prior knowledge about the topic is elicited and used as a starting place for instruction, which builds on accurate prior knowledge and stimulates conceptual change if necessary

8. Activities and assignments feature tasks that call for critical thinking or problem solving, not just memory or reproduction

9. Higher order thinking skills are not taught as a separate skills curriculum. Instead, they are developed in the process of teaching subject-matter knowledge within application contexts that call for students to relate what they are learning to their lives outside of school by thinking critically or creatively about it or by using it to solve problems or make decisions

10. The teacher creates a social environment in the classroom that could be described as a learning community featuring discourse or dialogue designed to promote understanding

Adapted from Thomas Good and Jere Brophy. *Looking in Classrooms*, 7th Ed., New York: Longman 1997 (pp. 408-409).

A second approach to reform is advocated by proponents of the academic disciplines that inform social studies. These critics favor abandoning social studies as a subject designed to pursue citizen education goals using integrated content. Instead, they would offer separate courses in the academic disciplines, simplified as needed but designed to pursue the goals of history, geography, and the social sciences rather than the goals of citizenship education. This was the approach taken by "structures of disciplines" advocates who developed the "new social studies" programs in the 1960s and 1970s. These programs never caught on in the schools for a variety of reasons, including the perception that they were not effective for addressing broad citizenship education goals and that they focused young children on relatively narrow and specialized disciplinary concerns prematurely, before they had acquired a basic social education.

More recently, Kieran Egan,[47] Diane Ravitch,[48] and others have advocated a variation of this approach that calls for replacing the expanding communities content of the early social studies curriculum with a heavy focus on history and related children's literature (not only historical fiction but myths and folktales). Critics of this approach tend to agree that K-3 children can and should learn certain aspects of history, but also to believe that they need a balanced and integrated social education curriculum that includes sufficient attention to powerful ideas drawn from geography and the various social sciences. They do not believe that children's social education needs are well served by replacing most social science content with history content.

Similarly, they acknowledge that certain forms of children's literature (e.g., historical fiction, stories of life in other cultures) are useful social education tools, but do not see much social education value in replacing reality-based social studies with myth and folklore likely to create misconceptions, especially during the primary years when children are struggling to determine what is real and enduring (versus false/fictional or transitory/accidental) in their physical and social worlds. Our sense is that whatever value the study of myth and folklore may have will be realized primarily within the language arts curriculum. Allocating significant social studies time to myth and folklore, and for that matter to most forms of children's literature, amounts to an extension of the language arts curriculum at the expense of attempts to develop a coherent social studies curriculum focused on citizen education goals. Proponents of this approach have made no attempts to test it empirically, and exemplary elementary teachers whom we have interviewed do not favor it.[49] Finally, our own and others' analyses of curriculum guidelines (California's *History and Social Science Framework*) and textbooks (the Houghton Mifflin series) that are based on this approach have identified some important problems with it.[50]

A third approach to reform has been suggested by those who believe that social studies should deemphasize providing students with information and instead engage them in inquiry and debate about social policy issues.[51] The NCSS has published a handbook containing chapters that elaborate this rationale and illustrate its implementation.[52] Supporters of this approach note that it incorporates principles emphasized in the past by John Dewey and more recently by social constructivist learning theorists. They also argue that debating social and civic issues is the most direct way to develop dispositions toward critical thinking and reflective decision making in our citizens. Critics of the approach typically agree that critical thinking, decision making, and other higher order applications should be emphasized in teaching social studies at all grade levels, but also believe that a heavy concentration on inquiry and debate about social policy issues is premature for elementary students, especially K-3 students whose prior knowledge and experience relating to the issues often are quite limited.

THE EXPANDING COMMUNITIES FRAMEWORK

The expanding communities framework and the scope and sequence of content associated with it eventually became almost universal in American elementary schools, to the point that Naylor and Diem[53] called it the de facto national curriculum. The following topics are typically included:

> **Kindergarten: Self, home, school, community.** Discovering myself (Who am I? How am I alike and different from others?), school (my classroom, benefits of school), working together, living at home, community helpers, children in other lands, rules, and celebrating holidays.
>
> **Grade One: Families.** Family membership, recreation, work, cooperation, traditions, families in other cultures, how my family is alike and different from others, family responsibilities, the family at work, our school and other schools, and national holidays.
>
> **Grade Two: Neighborhoods.** Workers and services in the neighborhood, my role within the neighborhood, neighborhoods and communities in other cultures, farm and city life, and protecting our environment.
>
> **Grade Three: Communities.** Communities past and present, different kinds of communities, changes in communities, community

government and services, communities in other countries, cities, careers, urban problems, business and industry, and pioneers and American Indians.

Grade Four: Geographic regions. World regions, people of the world, climatic regions, physical regions, population, food. Also, *state studies*. Our state government, state history, people of our state, state laws, state workers, communities past and present. [Note: Textbook series typically cover geographic regions in their fourth grade texts, but state policies often lead local districts to omit purchase or minimize use of these texts and instead devote fourth grade to study of the state. This used to be done using locally produced materials, but the major publishers now supply state studies texts for each state.]

Grade Five: United States history and geography. The first Americans, exploration and discovery, Colonial life, revolution and independence, westward movement, the Civil War, immigrants, the Roaring 20s, lifestyles in the United States, values of the American people, and the United States as world power. Some fifth-grade texts also include units on regions in the United States, and Canada and Mexico.

Grade Six: World cultures/hemispheres. Political and economic systems, land and resources, people and their beliefs, comparative cultures. Western hemisphere: Early cultures of South America, the major contemporary South American countries, Central American countries, Canada, Mexico, historical beginnings of the western world. Eastern hemisphere: Ancient Greece and Rome, Middle Ages, Renaissance, Middle East, Europe, Africa, India, China, and Japan.

This content is drawn from various sources and blended to center on each unit's topic rather than organized according to the separate disciplines. The basic framework can accommodate most emerging topics (environmentalism, multicultural education, etc.), as well as contrasting approaches to curriculum and instruction that represent quite different mixtures of the five emphases described by Martorella.[54] It also can be taught with different degrees of emphasis on across-subjects integration, causal explanation, life applications, and associated skills and dispositions.

Paul Hanna[55] rationalized the expanding communities approach as being both logical in starting with the family and then moving outward toward progressively wider human communities and convenient in allowing for a holistic, coordinated approach to the study of people living in societies. He recommended that students study the ways in which people in each community carry out basic activities such as providing for their physical needs, transporting goods and people, communicating with one another, and governing their societies. Hanna's arguments are well taken, but they speak only to the feasibility of the expanding communities framework, not to its necessity. Most social educators believe that except for certain aspects of geography and economics, social studies content is not inherently hierarchical. Degree of difficulty resides more in the levels of depth and sophistication with which topics are addressed than in the topics themselves. Difficulty tends to increase as one moves from the concrete to the abstract, from easily observable and familiar situations to phenomena less rooted in experience, and from an emphasis on facts to an emphasis on concepts, generalizations, principles, and theories.

Concepts differ among themselves in level of difficulty.[56] Those with straightforward definitions or structures that are observable in clear illustrations are easier to learn than those with "if-then" or relational structures. Thus, goods, services, producers, and consumers are simpler economic concepts to learn than opportunity cost, scarcity, or comparative advantage. Subordinate and coordinate concepts are easier to learn than superordinate and relational concepts.

Jean Fair[57] suggested the following generalizations about content difficulty:

1. The sheer quantity of things to be dealt with simultaneously makes for increased difficulty level (it is harder to compare or interpret three things than two things).
2. More abstract content is more difficult than less abstract content.
3. Fine distinctions are more difficult than gross ones.
4. Relying solely on print as the source for input makes for greater difficulty than using a multimedia approach.
5. It is easier to develop skills in thinking about matters that students see as closely related to their own lives than about other matters.
6. Providing structure, cues, and props makes thinking easier.

Elementary social studies curricula usually reflect these ideas. The primary grades tend to concentrate on universal human experiences occurring within families and local communities, with content drawn heavily from psychology, sociology, and anthropology. In the middle grades, the focus shifts to geography, economics, civics, and history, and students begin to study states and nations of the past and present and to address some of the more conceptual and abstract aspects of the content.

The idea that social studies involves abstractions that are not well grasped until at least the fourth grade caused some to argue that social studies instruction should not begin until that time, and many to argue that history should not be taught until the secondary grades. However, subsequent debate and data collection led to the rejection of these arguments. It is now generally accepted that elementary students can understand general chronological sequences (e.g., that land transportation developed from walking to horse-drawn carriages to engine-powered vehicles) even though they may still be hazy about particular dates, and that they can follow age-appropriate representations of people and events from the past (especially narratives built around central characters with whom the students can identify, depicted as pursuing goals that the students can understand) even though they might not be able to follow analytic treatments of abstract historical topics or themes.[58]

Controversy over what is suitable for elementary grade children to learn continues, but its focus has shifted. Arguments (based on skill hierarchies or Piagetian stages) that elementary students are not ready for certain topics have receded in favor of the idea that the difficulty level of content resides primarily in the manner and depth with which it is approached, so that even the strange and abstract can be learned meaningfully if instruction emphasizes schemas that are familiar and concrete to the students (e.g., historical narratives built around the goals and motives of central characters; cultural comparisons focused on food, clothing, shelter, and other cultural universals). The focus is on content that is meaningful because it can be linked to students' social experiences, especially content that they find interesting because it engages their emotions or provides opportunity for identification with key persons in a narrative. Current arguments center less on what it is possible to teach children in the early grades than on what is worthwhile, why it is more worthwhile than alternatives, and how it can be taught effectively.

There is nothing inherently necessary about the scope and sequence of topics typically included within the expanding communities curriculum. Piaget's cautions against getting too far away from children's experience base to the point of trying to teach abstractions that will yield "merely verbal" learning are well taken. However, his ideas about what children are capable of learning at particular ages are too pessimistic and too focused on the learning of logical-mathematical structures through self-initiated exploration of the physical environment. More recent neo-Vygotskian research on teaching in the zone of proximal development indicates that children can learn a great many things earlier and more thoroughly if guided by systematic instruction than they would learn on their own. Also, contemporary information-processing and schema-development research has shown that children can use situational schemas built up through prior knowledge and experience as templates for understanding information about how people in other times and places have responded to parallel situations. Thus, there is no need to start with the child in the here and now and move linearly backwards in time or outwards in physical space and scope of community. Children can understand historical episodes described in narrative form with emphasis on the motives and actions of key individuals, and they can understand aspects of customs, culture, economics, and politics that focus on universal human experiences or adaptation problems that are familiar to them and for which they have developed schemas or routines.

Even so, the expanding communities approach clearly is a feasible framework for sequencing the elementary social studies curriculum. If it were implemented as Hanna envisioned, it would produce systematic instruction structured around powerful ideas. However, critics portray a very different picture of what typically occurs in social studies classes.

CRITICISM OF THE EXPANDING COMMUNITIES FRAMEWORK

Much of this criticism has been directed at the expanding communities framework itself. Some critics claim that primary-grade children are interested in stories about heroes, the exotic, and the "long ago and far away," so that primary curricula should concentrate on these topics rather than on familiar aspects of the family, neighborhood, and community.[59] Others who want students to develop a global rather than a more narrowly American purview note that television now brings non-Western lands and cultures into the home early, so that if one waits until the sixth grade to begin teaching world geography and cultures with an emphasis on human commonalities, it may be too late to overcome ethnocentrism that has developed in the meantime.[60]

Expanding communities curricula also have been criticized for being too age-grade oriented; being too traditional and middle-class oriented in their treatment of families and communities; being sequenced according to adult rather than child logic (for example, a state is just as abstract a concept as a nation, so there is no reason why children must study their state before studying the nation); fragmenting the curriculum so that students do not get enough opportunity to see relationships that exist across communities; and failing to integrate skills instruction with instruction in content.[61] Nevertheless, the expanding communities approach remains entrenched. It is familiar to teachers and so far has proved adaptable enough to incorporate new content and respond to common criticisms without changing its basic structure.

CRITICISM OF SOCIAL STUDIES TEXTBOOK SERIES

Whether or not the expanding communities framework is identified as the culprit, there is widespread dissatisfaction with its associated curriculum content and instructional materials. Few elementary teachers have sufficient knowledge about social education to allow them to develop well-articulated positions on social studies purposes and goals that they can use to guide their curriculum planning, so most of them rely on local resources and the curriculum materials supplied by the major publishers.[62] Local resources may be quite helpful in districts that have developed connections with museums or detailed social studies curriculum guides, especially if these are supplemented by collections of specialized instructional materials (such as kits containing selections from children's literature and historical artifacts for use in units on Native Americans or frontier life).

Unfortunately, few teachers have access to such rich resources. This leaves most of them heavily dependent on the publishers of instructional materials, especially the major textbook series. These series are attractively packaged and presented so as to suggest that they are complete curricula that have been carefully developed by experts and revised to meet the needs of students at each grade level (and recently, to suggest that use of the series will enable students to meet state standards). However, the series are not written by the kinds of experts that teachers envision. A "writing team" composed of social studies professors and teachers develops outlines for the materials and provides feedback about early drafts. Most of the actual writing, however, is done by employees of the publishing company who are not recognized experts in either child development or social studies education.

Also, these textbook series are not painstakingly developed and revised through successive field testings. Usually there is no systematic classroom testing at all—just revisions in response to the comments of reviewers. The publishers are interested in feedback from teachers,

but their efforts are driven primarily by the textbook adoption guidelines established by the states. Unfortunately, these guidelines tend to
feature long lists of disconnected knowledge and skills objectives. This
creates coverage pressures, and publishers have responded by producing texts that say less and less about more and more. Instead of providing networks of connected knowledge structured around important
ideas, the texts offer parades of disconnected facts, seemingly random
questions, and isolated skills exercises. Teachers who are not prepared
to do otherwise tend to rely on such texts. Unfortunately, this creates
a dreary routine of reading the text, answering questions during
recitations and on assignments, taking tests, and then forgetting most
of what was "learned."

It also demotivates students (and teachers). Even though social
studies is about people and therefore should be highly interesting, students consistently rate it as their least favorite among the major school
subjects. Heavy emphasis on memorization and regurgitation of miscellaneous facts is usually given as the reason.[63]

Some of the problems with social studies series reflect generic
problems rooted in the economics and politics of the textbook industry: The texts attempt to cover too many topics, yet treat even important topics superficially, so that readers would have to know a great
deal about the topic already in order to make sense of the material; the
writing is dry and wooden, reflecting misguided attempts to "dumb
down" texts or alter them so that they will produce lower scores on
"readability" indexes; information about minorities and women is often
tacked on rather than integrated into the content flow; and excessive
space is allocated to pictures and graphics that are unrelated to the
text.[64]

Several additional criticisms focus specifically on social studies
series. One is that not enough content is included in the texts for the
primary grades, and much of what is included does not need to be
taught. Ravitch[65] dismissed much K-3 social studies content as "tot
sociology." She viewed it as a collection of mostly boring information
that students have no interest in and do not need to be taught anyway
because they learn it through normal experiences outside of school.
Similarly, Larkins, Hawkins, and Gilmore[66] argued that much of the
K-3 curriculum is "hopelessly noninformative" because children
already know that families contain parents and children or that people
live in houses, wear clothes, and eat food. They added that much of
the content of K-3 texts is needlessly redundant (children already possess the knowledge), superfluous (children will acquire it without

instruction), text-inappropriate (it should be taught more directly than through reading about it in texts), sanitized (purged of anything that might offend anyone), biased (presented from a single viewpoint when multiple viewpoints are appropriate), or aimless (not clearly related to important social education goals).

Whereas critics of K-3 texts typically find them thin and redundant, critics of social studies texts for grades 4 to 6 typically complain that they are too thick yet not redundant enough (or, more specifically, lacking in coherence and reader friendliness). Texts for grades 4 to 6 emphasize breadth of coverage over depth of development of ideas, so that they contain disconnected parades of facts rather than networks of connected content structured around powerful ideas. Beck and McKeown[67] argued that, in order to promote student understanding, texts must be high in coherence—the extent to which the sequence of ideas or events makes sense and the relationships among them are made apparent. Coherent content is selected in a principled way, guided by ideas about what students should gain from studying the topic. Failure to do this leads to three problems observed in fifth-grade history texts: (1) lack of evidence that clear content goals were used to guide text writing (so that texts read as chronicles of miscellaneous facts rather than as narratives built around connecting themes), (2) unrealistic assumptions about students' prior knowledge (so that key elements needed to understand a sequence often were merely alluded to rather than explained sufficiently), and (3) inadequate explanations that failed to clarify connections between actions and events (in particular, causal relationships). Beck, McKeown, and, Gromoll[68] found similar coherence problems in fourth grade geography texts. Subsequent work by McKeown and Beck[69] showed that texts rewritten to make them more coherent and engaging to students produced better recall, and especially more connected learning of key ideas, than the original texts.

A third set of criticisms of social studies series focuses on their skills components. Most series do a good job of introducing and developing map skills, but their programs for developing other skills (finding, synthesizing, and using information; reading critically; conducting inquiry; formulating and justifying value or policy positions) tend to be uneven in scope and quality.

Arthur Woodward[70] identified three primary problems in the way that skills are handled in the series. First, more is promised in the introductions to the teachers' editions and the scope-and-sequence charts than is actually delivered in the lessons. Mere mention of a skill

is often treated as sufficient for it to be cited in the charts, when in-
spection of the lesson reveals that it calls for use of the skill but does
not actually develop it. Second, skills that are most easily measured,
such as map and globe skills, are repeated unnecessarily throughout the
series, whereas inadequate attention is given to information gathering,
report writing, critical thinking, decision making, value analysis, and
other higher-order application skills. Third, despite publishers' claims
to have integrated knowledge and skills teaching, the skills content is
typically separated from the knowledge content so that students end up
learning and practicing skills in isolation instead of using them to
process, construct, or apply the knowledge content they are learning.

Our own analyses of elementary social studies series reaffirmed the
problems identified by other investigators and pointed to several additional ones: Not only was there insufficient structuring of content
around key ideas, but the identified key ideas often were trite; suggested questions concentrated on miscellaneous facts and lacked
sequential flow or provision for critical thinking or decision making;
most of the provided worksheets or suggested activities emphasized
reinforcement but not extension or application of knowledge; little
information was provided to help teachers understand the program as a
whole and relate particular units or lessons to the big picture; there was
little use of data-retrieval charts or other mechanisms for analyzing and
synthesizing content in ways that promote understanding; many of the
suggested activities did not promote progress toward significant social
education goals or were unnecessarily time-consuming or complicated;
and most of the activities ostensibly intended to promote integration
across subjects lacked significant social education value.[71] The problems with the activities suggested in these series led us to develop a set
of principles for use in designing, selecting, or adapting learning activities so as to maximize their potential for helping students accomplish
instructional goals.[72]

Our most recent analyses indicate that many of the problems seen
in the 1986-1988 series continue. Some of the series published in the
1990s feature inserted literature selections and more emphasis on extended writing assignments and cooperative learning activities. They
are less likely to call for practice of language arts skills such as alpha-
betizing, but they still reveal a lack of goal-oriented integration of
knowledge and skills components. Many of the inserted literature
selections and the questions and activities associated with them have
little connection to major social education goals, and some of them
foster misconceptions or even undermine the big ideas supposedly

being developed. Suggestions for cooperative learning sometimes are applied to activities that do not lend themselves well to the cooperative format. Thus, the publishers are still making piecemeal responses to miscellaneous coverage pressures rather than offering coherent social education curricula. Such problems are likely to continue unless there is a shift of focus from lists of topics and skills to be covered to more general social education goals as the major force driving content selection, a shift from broad but shallow coverage to deeper development of limited networks of connected information structured around powerful ideas, and a shift from separation of the skills strands from the knowledge strands to development and use of skills as strategies for applying the knowledge.[73]

Gloria Alter studied the 1991 versions of the six major elementary textbook series (with only minor modifications, these were substantially the same series available in 1998). She noted the same problems identified by previous investigators but focused on the extent to which textbooks took a multicultural or global purview and were useful in helping develop caring citizens free of stereotypical and prejudiced views of others. She found that the texts typically lacked diverse perspectives and recognition of multicultural and global realities, avoided rather than confronted controversial issues, and tended to skirt value-laden content and activities by focusing on traditional and noncontroversial facts. However, the Houghton Mifflin series had begun to make progress along these lines.[74]

It should be noted that elementary teachers often are more satisfied with social studies textbooks than professors of social studies education are.[75] Many of these teachers may not notice or may not be concerned by the texts' content emphasis and coherence problems because they are more oriented toward teaching students than subject matter. They typically favor a citizenship training emphasis, teaching of a broad range of facts, and inculcation of traditional and locally favored values. In contrast, professors tend to emphasize concepts and generalizations drawn from the disciplines, addressing less content in greater depth and with more emphasis on application, and a critical stance toward values and traditions (but with acceptance of democratic core values of justice, equality, responsibility, freedom, diversity, and privacy).

Scholars tend to criticize teachers for relying too much on textbooks, teaching isolated facts and skills without enough emphasis on coherent structures and application opportunities, being overly accepting of textbook content as valid, teaching in ways that inculcate blindly positive attitudes toward the nation and the status quo, and being overly pessimistic about what students are capable of learning. Teachers tend to criticize scholars for being too academic and middle class in their orientation, overemphasizing generalizations from the disciplines while underemphasizing humanistic or value elements and content that is important in the students' lives or currently in the news, underemphasizing the need for direct teaching and a strong base of concepts and factual information before undertaking problem solving, and overemphasizing experimentation, inquiry/discovery, or other approaches to teaching that are either impractical for classroom use or not worth the time and trouble that they require.[76] It seems obvious to us that social studies needs both better texts and better preparation of teachers for adapting currently available texts and using them in combination with other content sources.

We have noted that the textbook series fail to articulate social studies as a coherent subject designed to develop connected sets of fundamental understandings about the social world and to move students toward clearly identified social education goals. As a result, most elementary teachers view (and teach) social studies as a collection of disconnected content and skills clusters, rather than as a coherent goals-driven curriculum composed of connected networks of knowledge, skills, values, and dispositions to action. These concerns have led to calls for more substantive and coherently organized content for elementary social studies.

We agree that much of the content taught in the primary grades is trite, redundant, and unlikely to help students accomplish significant social education goals. However, we believe that the problem lies not with the topics addressed within the expanding communities framework, but with the way that these topics have been taught. Many of the topics—families, communities, food, clothing, shelter, government, occupations, transportation, and communication, among others—provide a sound basis for developing fundamental understandings about the human condition. They tend to be cultural universals—basic human needs and social experiences found in all societies, past and present. We have argued that if these topics are taught with appropriate focus on powerful ideas, students will develop a basic set of connected understandings of how the social system works, how and why it got to be that way over time, how and why it varies across locations and cultures, and what all of this might mean for personal, social, and civic decision making.[77] Also, because all students have direct experience with cultural universals in their home lives, the instruction can build on existing prior knowledge and include opportunities for immediate application, regardless of the students' social or cultural backgrounds.

Recent NCSS Standards Statements

Through the years, the National Council for the Social Studies has occasionally published official policy statements reflecting the organization's stance on curriculum, instruction, assessment, teacher education, and other issues. Prior to the 1990s, perhaps the best-known and most influential NCSS policy documents were the curriculum guidelines released in 1979 and the "essentials of the social studies" statement released in 1981. The curriculum guidelines reaffirmed that "the basic goal of social studies education is to prepare young people to be humane, rational, participating citizens in a world that is becoming increasingly interdependent."[78] The guidelines went on to differentiate the social studies from the social sciences, indicating that the social studies would be pandisciplinary in their content base and focus primarily on citizenship education rather than induction into the disciplines. The "essentials" statement reaffirmed this and identified four main clusters of social studies goals, construed in terms of student outcomes: knowledge, democratic beliefs and values, thinking skills (data gathering, reasoning, decision making, construing social situations), and participation skills (working with others as a group member or citizen).[79]

Recognizing that even people who agree on citizenship education as the overarching purpose of social studies disagree about the ideal curriculum for accomplishing this purpose, and believing that local schools or districts ought to make their own decisions about curriculum, the NCSS has always refrained from endorsing any single scope and sequence.[80] However, in the 1990s, it released two definitive position statements, one on curriculum standards and one on powerful teaching and learning. The curriculum standards are built around ten themes that form a framework for social studies. (See Table 2.) The standards statement elaborates on each theme in separate chapters for the early grades, the middle grades, and the secondary grades, listing performance expectations and potential classroom activities that might be used to develop the theme. For example, the following is said about developing the "culture" theme in the early grades: Social studies programs should include experiences that provide for the study of *culture and cultural diversity*, so that the learner can:

   a. explore and describe similarities and differences in ways groups, societies, and cultures address similar human needs and concerns;

   b. give examples of how experiences may be interpreted differently by people from diverse cultural perspectives and frames of reference;

   c. describe ways in which language, stories, folktales, music, and artistic creations serve as expressions of culture and influence behavior of people living in a particular culture;

   d. compare ways in which people from different cultures think about and deal with their physical environment and social condition;

   e. give examples and describe the importance of cultural unity and diversity within and across groups.[81]

The document then describes primary-grade classroom activities relating to this standard, such as comparing how families meet their basic food, clothing, and shelter needs in five communities around the world. Note that the ten thematic strands of the NCSS curriculum standards call for drawing relevant content from history, geography, and the social sciences, but are construed as strands in a pandisciplinary K-12 social education. This makes them more suited to curriculum planning in social studies than the standards statements published by organizations representing separate disciplines or special interest groups. The NCSS subsequently sponsored publication of a collection of readings illustrating how the ten strands might be addressed in elementary social studies teaching[82] and a survey of children's literature published in the 1990s that relates to these strands.[83] Also available are collections of standards-related teaching ideas for grades K-6[84] and grades 5-12.[85]

   The NCSS also released a position statement identifying five key features of powerful social studies teaching and learning. (See Table 3.) Social studies teaching is viewed as powerful when it helps students develop social understanding and civic efficacy. Social understanding is integrated knowledge of the social aspects of the human condition: how these aspects have evolved over time, the variations that occur in different physical environments and cultural settings, and emerging trends that appear likely to shape the future. Civic efficacy is readiness and willingness to assume citizenship responsibilities. It is rooted in social studies knowledge and skills, along with related values (such as concern for the common good) and dispositions (such as an orientation toward confident participation in civic affairs).[86]

   Along with publishing the powerful teaching statement, the NCSS has made available two multimedia teacher education resources. The

TABLE 2

TEN THEMATIC STRANDS

Ten themes serve as organizing strands for the social studies curriculum at every school level (early, middle and high school); they are interrelated and draw from all of the social science disciplines and other related disciplines and fields of scholarly study to build a framework for social studies curriculum design.

I. Culture

Human beings create, learn, and adapt culture. Human cultures are dynamic systems of beliefs, values, and traditions that exhibit both commonalities and differences. Understanding culture helps us understand ourselves and others.

II. Time, Continuity, and Change

Human beings seek to understand their historic roots and to locate themselves in time. Such understanding involves knowing what things were like in the past and how things change and develop-allowing us to develop historic perspective and answer important questions about our current condition

III. People, Places, and Environment

Technological advancements have insured that students are aware of the world beyond their personal locations. As students study content related to this theme, they create their spatial views and geographical perspectives of the world; social, cultural, economic, and civic demands mean that students will need such knowledge, skills, and understandings to make informed and critical decisions about the relationship between human beings and their environment.

IV. Individual Development and Identity

Personal identity is shaped by one's culture, by groups and by institutional influences. Examination of various forms of human behavior enhances understanding of the relationships between social norms and emerging personal identities, the social processes which influence identity formation, and the ethical principles underlying individual action.

V. Individuals, Groups, and Institutions

Institutions exert enormous influence over us. Institutions are organizational embodiments to further the core social values of those who comprise them. It is important for students to know how institutions are formed, what controls and influences them, how they control and influence individuals and culture, and how institutions can be maintained or changed.

VI. Power, Authority, and Governance

Understanding of the historic development of structures of power, authority, and governance and their evolving functions in contemporary society is essential for the emergence of civic competence.

VII. Production, Distribution, and Consumption

Decisions about exchange, trade, and economic policy and well being are global in scope and the role of government in policy making varies over time and from place to place. The systematic study of an interdependent world economy and the role of technology in economic decision making is essential.

VIII. Science, Technology, and Society

Technology is as old as the first crude tool invented by prehistoric humans, and modern life as we know it would be impossible without technology and the science which supports it. Today's technology forms the basis for some of our most difficult social choices.

IX. Global Connections

The realities of global interdependence require understanding of the increasingly important and diverse global connections among world societies before there can be analysis leading to the development of possible solutions to persisting and emerging global issues.

X. Civic Ideals and Practices

All people have a stake in examining civic ideals and practices across time, in diverse societies, as well as in determining how to close the gap between present practices and the ideals upon which our democracy is based. An understanding of civic ideals and practices of citizenship is critical to full participation in society.

Source: Pat Nickell (1995). Pullout feature: Thematically organized social studies. *Social Studies and the Young Learner*, 8, 1-8. National Council for the Social Studies.

TABLE 3

FIVE KEY FEATURES OF POWERFUL SOCIAL STUDIES TEACHING AND LEARNING

Meaningful

The content selected for emphasis is worth learning because it promotes progress toward important social understanding and civic efficacy goals, and it is taught in ways that help students to see how it is related to these goals. As a result, students' learning efforts are motivated by appreciation and interest, not just by accountability and grading systems. Instruction emphasizes depth of development of important ideas within appropriate breadth of content coverage.

Integrative

Powerful social studies cuts across disciplinary boundaries, spans time and space, and integrates knowledge, beliefs, values, and dispositions to action. It also provides opportunities for students to connect to the arts and sciences through inquiry and reflection.

Value-Based

Powerful social studies teaching considers the ethical dimensions of topics, so that it provides an arena for reflective development of concern for the common good and application of social values. The teacher includes diverse points of view, demonstrates respect for well-supported positions, and shows sensitivity and commitment to social responsibility and action.

Challenging

Students are encouraged to function as a learning community, using reflective discussion to work collaboratively to deepen understandings of the meanings and implications of content. They also are expected to come to grips with controversial issues, to participate assertively but respectfully in group discussions, and to work productively with peers in cooperative learning activities.

Active

Powerful social studies is rewarding but demanding. It demands thoughtful preparation and instruction by the teacher, and sustained effort by the students to make sense of and apply what they are learning. Teachers do not mechanically follow rigid guidelines in planning, implementing, and assessing instruction. Instead, they work with the national standards and with state and local guidelines, adapting and supplementing these guidelines and their instructional materials in ways that support their students' social education needs.

The teacher uses a variety of instructional materials, plans field trips and visits by resource people, develops current or local examples to relate to students' lives, plans reflective discussions, and scaffolds students' work in ways that encourage them to gradually take on more responsibility for managing their own learning independently and with their peers. Accountability and grading systems are compatible with these goals and methods.

Students develop new understandings through a process of active construction. They develop a network of connections that link the new content to preexisting knowledge and beliefs anchored in their prior experience. The construction of meaning required to develop important social understanding takes time and is facilitated by interactive discourse. Clear explanations and modeling from the teacher are important, but so are opportunities to answer questions, discuss or debate the meanings and implications of content, or use the content in activities that call for tackling problems or making decisions.

Source: Janet Alleman and Jere Brophy. (1995). National Council for the Social Studies social studies standards and the elementary teacher. *Social Studies and the Young Learner,* 8, 4-8.

first is a videotape showing lessons that illustrate the key features of powerful teaching being implemented in classrooms.[87] The second is a professional development program that includes print materials and videotapes for use by district-level staff developers working with teachers to revitalize local social studies programs.[88]

Martorella[89] also produced a list of key features of good social studies teaching based on similar theoretical principles and related research. He identified the following as characteristics of exemplary elementary social studies teachers:

Planning characteristics: Have clearly formulated purposes, goals, and objectives; have acquired a well-grounded social studies knowledge base; select subject matter and activities that will interest and challenge students and intersect with meaningful aspects of their lives; emphasize coverage of a small number of topics and key ideas in depth, rather than a superficial coverage of many; strike a balance among knowledge, skills, and values and social participation goals in the curriculum; identify a variety of instructional resources; incorporate authentic ways to assess what students learn; and provide adequate time for social studies teaching.

Instructional characteristics: Relate new knowledge to students' existing knowledge; engage students in analyzing important social issues and values; present students with intriguing questions and anomalies as a way to engage them in inquiry; afford students frequent opportunities to engage actively in constructing and applying social knowledge; develop skills in the context of solving problems or answering questions; emphasize relationships among ideas, people, places, and events; provide frequent opportunities for students to work cooperatively in small groups; and encourage students' oral and written communications relating to social data.

Values and Moral Education

Throughout most of this chapter, we have focused on the knowledge component of the social studies curriculum because this has been the focus of most debate. However, the values component also has been controversial in at least two respects. First, there is disagreement about the degree to which the curriculum should address value-laden issues. Many members of the general public, and even a few prominent social educators, believe that public schools should concentrate on teaching knowledge and skills, leaving values education to the family and the church.[90] In contrast, the vast majority of state and curriculum guidelines and of position statements by leading social studies organizations and scholars call for values education as a basic component of the social studies curriculum. The latter position has been emphasized more in recent years, when several sources of influence have converged on the notion that schooling in general, and social studies in particular, should address issues of morality, ethics, and social responsibility.

One influence has been the conservative or traditionalist side in the "culture wars," which has called for a renewed emphasis on teaching children virtues such as diligence, sincerity, personal accountability, honesty, courage, and perseverance. Other influential popular and scholarly sources have included feminist writers emphasizing the notion of caring and communitarian writers emphasizing the importance of establishing communal bonds and a sense of responsibility for subordinating personal agendas to the common good. Additional influences have developed out of research on the moral and social aspects of child development, especially studies of parent or teacher influences on children's thinking and behavior related to caring, empathy, justice, and other social values.

Most social educators believe that social studies should include values education designed to prepare students to make the kinds of value-based decisions about social and civic issues that they will need to make throughout their lives. However, their elaborations on this idea highlight a second area of controversy: whether the values education component should be limited to public "core" values or should also include private "personal morality" values.

NCSS policy statements typically refer to concepts such as justice, equality, responsibility, freedom, diversity, and privacy. R. Freeman Butts, whose writings heavily influenced the *CIVITAS* framework for civic education, advocated educating students in two sets of values: six values that comprise key rights of citizenship (freedom, diversity, privacy, due process, property rights, and international human rights) and six other values that comprise key obligations of citizenship (justice, equality, authority, participation, truth, and patriotism).[91] Naylor and Diem listed the following as core values embedded in the legal system: human dignity and the worth of the individual; equality and respect for the rights of all people; the consent of the governed, majority rule, and protection of the rights of minorities; the rule of law and fair treatment under law; freedom of religion, thought, conscience, assembly, and expression; sanctity of life; privacy and the right to be secure in one's possessions and in one's own home; respect for property and the rights of private property; the importance of the common good; and the right to pursue happiness.[92]

Almost all social studies curriculum guidelines and materials emphasize these American Creed values. Some also call for emphasis on personal and social values (the Golden Rule, honesty, caring, respect for the dignity of others). These personal and social values are likely to be emphasized in texts and instructional materials developed for use in the primary grades and in the writings of social educators who believe that social studies should address interpersonal relationships in addition to civic policy issues. Personal and social values have been receiving increasing emphasis lately, for the reasons described previously and because they are involved in preparing students to engage in currently popular cooperative learning methods.

Most social educators stress the importance of addressing values, not only as objects of study but as considerations to be taken into account when making social or civic decisions. Views on how the values component of the curriculum should be handled have ranged from a pure inculcation approach that indoctrinates students in a fixed set of values to a pure values clarification approach in which students are made aware of the values that underlie their decisions but no attempt is made to argue that some of these values are preferable to others.

The inculcation approach has been dominant historically, especially in the elementary grades, even though most scholarly leaders believe either that inculcation is counterproductive and should be minimized or that it is a useful component, but only one component, in a more complete program. Currently, the inculcation approach is represented by the values socialization embedded in most of the textbooks and much of the children's literature used in social studies classes, as well as in versions of the character education movement that call for training children in the classically emphasized virtues.[93] (Other versions of character education are more eclectic.[94])

Past alternatives to the inculcation approach have included values clarification[95] and moral reasoning.[96] These approaches call for leading the students in discussions of moral dilemmas or policy issues, but with emphasis on analyzing the values or moral reasoning underlying decisions rather than the appropriateness of the decisions themselves. Values clarification and moral reasoning approaches were never implemented very widely because they were seen as insufficiently rooted in core values (taught as such). Also, these approaches were seen as too focused on hypothetical situations that were far removed from students' lives instead of dealing with more realistic social and civic decision-making contexts and analyzing reasoning instead of values.[97]

More commonly recommended by social educators is the values analysis (or values inquiry) approach that guides students in examining the warrants for values themselves (not just the linkages between their decisions and their underlying values) and deciding which positions and values are most justified. Values analysis approaches typically include instruction in the common values found in the nation's basic social contracts—the Declaration of Independence, the Constitution, and the Bill of Rights.[98] Instead of complete moral relativism, these approaches teach students to project the probable consequences of decisions and justify them as consistent with core values, not with the student's own narrower self-interests.[99] They include not only direct teaching about values but also role-play and simulation activities, decision-making activities, and discussions of controversial issues.

In recent years, values and moral education have taken on a communal aspect, fueled by interest in developing dispositions such as caring[100] and in forging classes of students into communities of learners who interact respectfully and collaborate in constructing knowledge.[101] In the primary grades, much of the values component of social education focuses on peer relationships (caring about others, being a good friend) and behavior in groups (fulfilling your responsibilities, participating actively, listening and trying to understand others' point of view in addition to putting forth your own). In later grades, the purview expands from immediate social contexts to larger civic contexts (learning and practicing the values involved in being a good citizen of the neighborhood, community, state, nation, and world).

Social educators who have reviewed the limited research on approaches to values and moral education tend to agree that the most powerful approach is a comprehensive one that includes elements from most of the various models that have been suggested. A complete program would raise students' consciousness of the value-related aspects of social and civic decision making and teach students to make such decisions (and follow through in subsequent behavior) by engaging in reasoning rooted in core values.[102] Instructional methods would include direct teaching of core values, modeling of value-based reasoning and decision making, developing dispositions toward caring about others and considering the common good in social and civic participation, and discussing moral issues and social or civic policy issues with an eye toward developing defensible positions that square with core values. This direct focus on values, whether it occurred within or outside of social studies, would be supplemented by attention to value-related issues in teaching all school subjects.

Research in Elementary Social Studies

Social education scholars have produced many useful ideas concerning rationales for social education, general purposes and goals for social studies, and general approaches to accomplishing them, but have not yet produced an extensive empirical knowledge base. Most of what is available, particularly research on the teaching and learning of history, geography, the social science disciplines, global education, multicultural education, controversial issues, and values and moral education is reviewed in a handbook published almost ten years ago.[103] Space limitations will not allow us to revisit all of these topics, so we focus here on topics that have special relevance for elementary social education and highlight some recent trends that have emerged since publication of the handbook.

Not much research has been done in social studies classes, and most of it has focused on relatively narrow issues that are not unique to social studies (e.g., the effects of questioning students at primarily lower vs. higher cognitive levels, or the effects of advance organizers on learning from lectures). The paucity of research is especially noticeable at the elementary level. Prior to the 1990s there were just a few ethnographic studies focusing on how social studies instruction differs according to the socioeconomic status of the students,[104] descriptive studies focusing on the kinds of instructional methods and activities observed in social studies classes,[105] and evaluation studies of the effects of various special curricula (e.g., MACOS, values clarification, moral dilemma discussions) on selected student outcomes.

The findings of these studies, along with less direct indicators, were not encouraging with respect to the effectiveness of social studies in fulfilling its citizen education mission. Marker and Mehlinger summarized by stating that knowledge surveys indicated that American youth were relatively ignorant about basic historical, geographical, and governmental information; that skills studies revealed problems in critical thinking and decision making; that values education programs did not seem to have much impact on students' values or moral development; and that indicators such as falling voting rates and rising crime rates belied the effectiveness of attempts to accomplish the participation goals of social education. These authors suggested that social studies educators adopt more modest goals for which they could more reasonably be held accountable.[106] Most social educators, however, would argue that the main problems with social education are not in its citizenship education goals or its ideal curriculum models, but in the way that social studies is taught in most classrooms.

Most accounts of teaching and learning in social studies have painted a dismal picture of over-reliance on textbook-based reading and recitation followed by solitary work on fill-in-the-blank assignments.[107] Others have noted frequent absence of any social studies teaching.[108] However, researchers have begun to describe social studies teaching that reflects research-based principles for teaching for understanding within classroom learning communities. For example, Susan Stodolsky observed a wide range of instructional diversity occurring in 39 fifth-grade classrooms. In addition to reading and answering questions, students also engaged in peer work groups, simulations, and projects, including research using a range of resource materials. Higher-level thinking was stressed, along with social skills and problem-solving skills.[109]

Perhaps the best known and most influential work has been that of Fred Newmann and his colleagues on higher-order thinking and thoughtfulness in high school social studies classes.[110] Newmann described higher-order thinking as challenging students to interpret, analyze, or manipulate information in response to a question or problem that cannot be resolved through routine application of previously acquired knowledge. He argued that this definition of higher-order thinking implies that social studies instruction should both develop and reflect a set of student dispositions that together constitute thoughtfulness: a persistent desire that claims be supported by reasons (and that the reasons themselves be scrutinized), a tendency to be reflective by taking time to think through problems rather than acting impulsively or automatically accepting the views of others, a curiosity to explore new questions, and a flexibility to entertain alternative and original solutions to problems.

Newmann and his colleagues identified six key indicators of thoughtfulness:

1. Classroom discourse focuses on sustained examination of a few topics rather than superficial coverage of many.
2. The discourse is characterized by substantive coherence and continuity.
3. Students are given sufficient time to think before being required to answer questions.
4. The teacher presses students to clarify or justify their assertions, rather than accepting and reinforcing them indiscriminately.
5. The teacher models the characteristics of a thoughtful person (showing interest in students' ideas and their suggestions for solving problems, modeling problem-solving processes rather than just giving answers, acknowledging the difficulties involved in gaining clear understandings of problematic topics).
6. Students generate original and unconventional ideas in the course of the interaction.

Thoughtfulness scores based on these indicators distinguish class-rooms that feature sustained and thoughtful teacher-student discourse from two less desirable alternatives: (1) classrooms that feature lecture, recitation, and seatwork focused on low-level aspects of the content; (2) classrooms that feature discussion and student participation but do not foster much thoughtfulness because the teachers skip from topic to topic too quickly or accept students' contributions uncritically.

Teachers whose classroom observation data yielded high thoughtful-ness scores experienced content-coverage pressure primarily as external and tended to resist it by favoring depth over breadth. Other teachers experienced it primarily as internal and thus emphasized breadth of content coverage over depth of topic development. All teachers men-tioned that students are likely to resist higher-order thinking tasks, at least initially, but high-scoring teachers emphasized these tasks never-theless. This persistence paid off: the same students who initially re-sisted later described their classes as more difficult and challenging but also as more engaging and interesting.

Most of the ideas and methods observed by Newmann in high school classes also appear to be applicable in elementary classes. Thorn-ton and Wenger[111] reported observing lessons exhibiting many of the characteristics of thoughtfulness described by Newmann, and Stodolsky reported that the quality of students' task engagement was higher dur-ing more cognitively complex activities than during lower-level activi-ties.[112] In addition, Jane White described several case studies in which teachers set up contexts and arranged tasks to allow students to con-struct meaning interactively instead of relying on a low-level textbook/recitation approach.[113]

CASE STUDIES

The research literature on elementary social studies teaching and learning contains several other noteworthy case studies, especially on his-tory teaching. For example, Linda Levstik described a first-grade teacher who included a strong history component within an integrated approach to instruction. This teacher did not attempt to teach history chronologi-cally, but she provided her students with age-appropriate information and learning experiences designed to teach them worthwhile knowledge about life in the past and historically significant people and events. Her students participated in a variety of hands-on activities designed to make their historical learning more personalized and concrete.[114]

Brophy and VanSledright described the contrasting approaches of three fifth-grade teachers to instruction in United States history. The first teacher was primarily a storyteller. She sought to stimulate interest in history by initially communicating much of the content in the form of stories that she related to her students in an engaging manner. Then she helped her students to remember and connect key ideas by embedding them within narrative formats. She emphasized traditional historical accounts and socialization of traditional American values. The second teacher was more of a scientific historian, using her course to introduce history as an academic discipline. She taught her students how historians use evidence and engage in historical reasoning in order to construct defensible accounts of the past, and attempted to build appreciation for the importance of facts, details, and research in making claims about historical cause-effect relationships and generalizations. The third teacher was a reformer who approached history as a tool for developing understanding of and policy positions on current problems and social issues. She was less interested in teaching a detailed chronology of the past than in using selected historical content as a basis for helping her students to become critical readers and principled social activists.[115]

Other studies done in the elementary grades provide thick description of various approaches to curriculum and instruction, illustrate what can be accomplished by improving texts or supplementing them with other instructional materials, or shifting from traditional recitation and seatwork to more interactive forms of discourse.[116]

Several case studies have also been done at the high school level, and the findings of some of these appear to apply as well to the elementary and middle school levels.[117] For example, Hynd and Guzzetti described a conceptual-change approach to teaching high school students about Christopher Columbus. Different groups of students used different texts. One text presented a traditional view treating Columbus primarily as a hero; a second text presented a revisionist view that depicted him as a bumbling explorer and a cruel, greedy ruler who decimated peaceful and trusting natives; and a third text presented a postrevisionist view that refuted common misconceptions about Columbus, gave a balanced accounting of his good and bad qualities, and concluded that if he had not sailed west and changed the world, someone else would have. Interestingly, the balanced text was more effective than the one-sided texts in changing students' attitudes and reducing their misconceptions.[118]

STUDIES OF STUDENTS' KNOWLEDGE AND THINKING

Recent theory and research on powerful teaching has emphasized the importance of connecting with students' prior knowledge and engaging them in actively constructing new knowledge and correcting existing misconceptions. This "conceptual change" approach appears to have great potential in elementary social studies, providing more is learned about what children typically know (or think they know) about content commonly taught at their grade levels. So far, little such information exists about topics addressed in elementary social studies. Child development researchers have concentrated on cognitive structures and strategies that children acquire through general life experiences rather than on their developing understanding of knowledge domains learned primarily at school. Research in the Piagetian tradition has focused on mathematical and scientific knowledge, except for a few studies of stages in the development of economic, political, and social knowledge.[119]

Scholars concerned with curriculum and instruction in social studies also have not developed much information about students' knowledge or thinking. There have been occasional surveys of knowledge about particular social studies topics.[120] However, these have concentrated mostly on isolated facts such as names, places, or definitions, with reporting of findings limited to percentages of students able to answer each item correctly. To be more useful to educators, the research needs emphasize questions that probe children's understanding of connected networks of knowledge and analyses that focus on qualitative aspects of their thinking about the topic, including identification of commonly held misconceptions.

Significant progress has been made in studying children's developing knowledge of politics and government. For example, children are much more aware of the administrative than the legislative or judicial aspects of government and they tend to view Presidents as godlike figures notable for their power to get things done and their benevolence or caring about the needs of each individual citizen.[121] Research on knowledge of economics has begun to uncover stages in children's development of understanding of, as well as common misconceptions in their ideas about, such topics as the functions of banks and the operations of retail stores.[122]

Very little information is available concerning children's knowledge and misconceptions relating to the cultural universals emphasized in K-3 social studies curricula. However, Brophy and Alleman interviewed students in the spring of second grade on the topic of shelter. They found that the students did understand that shelter is a basic need, could talk about some of the formal aspects of different types of homes, and displayed at least tacit knowledge of certain norms (e.g., people need to pay for their shelter, and most people prefer home ownership over apartment rental). However, their ideas about these topics were not always accurate and were not embedded within elaborated structures that included connections and cause-effect relationships. Furthermore, they did not understand much about the historical, geographical, or cultural reasons for differences in housing styles, the economics of housing purchase or rental, or the mechanisms through which modern houses are supplied with utilities and other conveniences. The students' knowledge about shelter was limited and spotty, tacit rather than well articulated, comprised of loose collections of observations rather than well-integrated networks of understandings, and often distorted by inaccurate assumptions or outright misconceptions.[123]

These authors later launched a series of studies that involves interviewing K-3 students about food, clothing, shelter, communication, family living, transportation, and other cultural universals. Each study is showing that primary-grade students' knowledge and thinking about these topics is quite limited, mostly tacit rather than well articulated, frequently distorted by misconceptions, and scattered rather than well organized into coherent networks structured around big ideas (especially cause-and-effect connections that support meaningful understandings). These findings refute the unsupported assertions of Ravitch and others who claim that students do not need to be taught about cultural universals because they already know this information through everyday life experience. They indicate that primary-grade students do stand to profit from instruction about cultural universals, although they need much more coherent and powerful instruction than what is currently offered in the leading textbook series.

Several teams of investigators have studied children's historical learning.[124] This work has demonstrated, for example, that much of the historical knowledge of fifth graders is organized in narrative form, so that it tends to feature stories focused around a few hero figures rather than less personalized causal analyses of historical trends. The students' narratives also tend to compress time and space, sometimes depicting face-to-face interactions between people whose life spans did not overlap (e.g., Columbus and the Pilgrims). Children tend to know more about evolution in material culture and other aspects of social history than about political history, and they tend to interpret historical events in terms of the intentions and actions of individuals, to ignore or misunderstand the roles of government and economics, and to think of change in terms of abrupt transformations rather than more gradual evolutions.[125]

Teacher Education in Social Studies

We have noted that elementary teachers often do not have a clear understanding of social studies as a coherent school subject organized to accomplish the purposes and goals of citizen education. One reason for this is that most elementary teacher education programs place heavy emphasis on language arts and mathematics, so that many preservice elementary teachers take only a single course in science or social studies education. Also, many instructors of social studies education courses are in educational foundations or general curriculum and instruction and do not themselves possess strong backgrounds in social education. If they do research, their work often focuses on particular aspects of their own courses or the programs in which they teach.[126] This makes it difficult to discuss teacher education programs in social studies in a normative fashion, because there is so much variation both in the general characteristics of teacher preparation programs and in their social studies components.

There is a growing mismatch between the background characteristics of elementary teachers and their students. By 2020, about 45 percent of school-age children will be children of color, whereas the proportion of minority teachers is and probably will remain much lower than that.[127] This indicates that preservice teachers' attitudes toward diversity need attention across all components of teacher preparation programs, especially because research to date suggests that the attitudes and beliefs of these preservice teachers regarding diversity, teaching, and subject matter tend to be traditional and to remain stable over time.[128] This is of particular concern for social studies, where addressing issues of diversity and pluralism are explicit goals. It appears important to help prospective teachers become aware of possible differences between their life experiences and those of their students.

When they start to teach in classrooms, preservice teachers tend to rely on the traditional, teacher-centered, lecture-recitation-seatwork approach. This has been attributed to the lack of diverse effective teaching models in their K-12 experiences[129] and to the transmission mode of teaching commonly experienced in university classes. Even experienced teachers tend to use more formal methods of teaching when the material is unfamiliar to them than they do when they are teaching in their areas of expertise.[130]

Another concern is that much of the content of the social science courses typically taken by future elementary teachers does not relate directly to elementary social studies. Students may have a disciplinary specialty such as anthropology, for instance, but may not be able to translate what they have learned into lessons and activities suitable for elementary students. This disconnection occurs because academicians in the disciplines are constantly refining their areas of interest whereas elementary social studies teachers are trying to help students construct a broad picture of the human condition.

Those who advocate increasing preservice teachers' social science coursework assume that more disciplinary background will help them to become more effective teachers. However, this can only happen if professors teaching these courses provide students with insights into both content and pedagogical content knowledge usable in K-12 contexts. Increased professorial collaboration among academic and teacher education faculty is needed to develop courses that will provide preservice teachers with general knowledge of the disciplinary foundations of social studies education.

The range of academic and ideological backgrounds within the social studies professoriate is evidenced in the diverse range of suggestions posited for improving social studies education for preservice teachers. Recommendations include honing critical thinking skills and inquiry techniques; improving the level of content area knowledge and pedagogical skills; learning how to work with community resources; developing multicultural and global perspectives; promoting a critical stance; and acquiring technological skills. However, research on teacher education in social studies indicates that preservice teachers' attitudes and beliefs are unlikely to change as a result of the classes they take.

Few studies have been undertaken on inservice education. A recent survey of elementary teachers who were members of NCSS revealed their concern over the lack of support for curriculum development and resource awareness in the social studies.[131] Established teachers who are more confident in the classroom may be better placed to focus on curricular issues. Theories of adult learning and development suggest that the greatest potential for improving the quality of teaching and learning in elementary social studies may lie in improving the quality of inservice teacher education.[132]

Recent Trends and Issues

As the new millennium begins, we are seeing continuation of the classic struggles over the social studies curriculum, although with evolution in the concepts and the language used to frame them. The tension persists between those who favor pandisciplinary citizenship education and those who favor socialization into history, geography, and the social science disciplines. The latter position was argued forcefully throughout the 1990s (particularly by those who favor a greater emphasis on history), and the release of standards documents drew at least temporary attention to arguments in support of the various disciplines. However, these discipline-oriented standards statements are unlikely to have much effect because they are unrealistic about the availability of curricular "air time" and about the background preparation that can be expected from generalist elementary teachers. Perhaps this is why even the Houghton Mifflin textbook series and the California history-social science curricular guidelines have more in common with the traditional expanding-communities curriculum than with the curriculum models envisioned by the Bradley Commission.

The 1990s also saw the release of content and process standards by NCSS. These documents have greater potential for influencing elementary social studies curriculum developers and teachers, partly because most of these people still favor a pandisciplinary approach, but mostly because the NCSS standards are much shorter and easier to interpret and apply. The content standards are built around just ten thematic strands and the process standards are built around just five key features of powerful teaching and learning, so these standards are feasible as bases for planning and assessing curriculum and instruction.

The most powerful short-term influences on elementary social studies, however, are likely to be the standards, and especially the associated assessment programs, that recently have been or currently are being developed and implemented by the states (notwithstanding national-level activities such as National Assessments of Educational Progress in history, geography, and civics). The emergence of high-stakes state-level testing in social studies has focused more attention and energy on social education than the field has received in some time. Many positives are associated with this, including reaffirmation of social studies as a basic curriculum strand and proliferation of inservice teacher education activities in the subject. However, high-stakes testing can be counterproductive. If the tests emphasize miscellaneous bits of knowledge and low-level skills, and if teachers experience strong pressures to prepare their students for these tests, there will be a narrowing of the curriculum and an emphasis on rote learning.

Such problems are not inherent to state assessment efforts. Much depends on how the assessment is implemented. If a state's efforts in social studies begin with clarification of the primary purposes and goals of social education, then proceed to content and teaching standards, and next to development of assessment instruments aligned to these purposes, goals, and standards, the resulting assessment program might not only avoid narrowing the curriculum inappropriately but actually help teachers and students accomplish major social education goals. This is a big *if*, however.

Also likely to continue is the tension between emphasis on disciplinary content and inquiry skills and emphasis on social issues and the value and participation goals of social education. Debates about standards movements, curriculum reform proposals, equity concerns (gender, racial, cultural), cultural literacy, character education, and related value-based issues are stimulating social educators to take a new look at values education, issues-centered education, and social and civic justice. Movements have arisen for addressing at least some of these issues (ecology, hunger, equity, conflict management, etc.) in the elementary grades rather than postponing them until later. The rise of interest in social constructivist models of teaching and in the use of cooperative learning methods have fueled renewed interest in socializing students as group members and forging classes of students into communities of learners. The learning community idea appears to have special relevance for social studies, with respect to its implications both for communally focused classroom management and for discourse-focused instruction.

READINESS AND OTHER CURRICULUM ISSUES

Readiness issues also persist with reference to discipline-based content and skills. Cognitive development theory and research has shifted from emphasis on broad Piagetian stages to emphasis on domain-specific knowledge networks, so that readiness to learn is now seen as more dependent on prior knowledge and experience than on age or general developmental level. Related developments such as sociocultural models of learning and recognition that children can retain knowledge within narrative structures as well as Piagetian logical/mathematical structures have led to increased respect for and confidence in elementary students' capacities for learning content in history, geography, and social science meaningfully, even though the understandings they construct may differ from those possessed by most adults. Current notions about the capabilities of elementary students for learning the social studies are highly optimistic (although essentially untested).

Curricular debates cannot be resolved through empirical research exclusively because they include assumptions about what is most worth teaching, and these must be addressed primarily through value-based reasoning. However, curricular arguments also contain implied assumptions that can and should be tested empirically. These include readiness assumptions (that students at a given grade level are ready to learn particular content), immediate application assumptions (that mastery of the content will enable the students to handle certain life situations effectively), and long-term outcome assumptions (that mastering the content will make them better citizens in the future). By clarifying and testing these embedded empirical claims, social studies scholars can contribute important empirical input to curricular debates.

Movements toward global education, multicultural education, and related perspectives have broadened the purview of social studies curricula and led to inclusion of more diverse content and points of view. Despite political controversies surrounding the concept of multiculturalism, these trends seem likely to continue. Consequently, most social studies curriculum-and-instruction in the future is likely to reach either the additive or the transformation stages as described by James Banks.[133] This would stop short of the ultimate social action stage, but still represent progress beyond traditional Eurocentric curricula. Attempts to accommodate new content and more diverse points of view can be expected to persist, fueling continued tensions between efforts to integrate myriad specific agendas into a holistically organized social studies curriculum and efforts to splinter the curriculum by developing separate strands, units, or lessons relating to gender, race, ethnicity, the environment, social or civic values, decision making, etc.

CURRICULAR INTEGRATION

A more recently developed threat to the coherence of social studies is the movement to integrate the school's curriculum (or at least the language arts and social studies strands), especially in middle schools. Curricular integration has long been advocated based on arguments that it will reduce artificial subject-matter boundaries and allow teachers to address more topics in a fixed amount of time. More recently, fueled in part by ideas coming from the whole language movement and from constructivist theories of learning, arguments have been put forth that it allows for a better rounded treatment of topics that students will find more motivating and better suited to their learning needs.[134] So far, remarkably little research has been done on integrated curricula, so these arguments remain untested claims.[135] Our impression is that integration could have the effect of strengthening and extending the social studies curriculum if the integration were achieved by blending language arts content sources and skills applications into social studies in ways that support progress toward key purposes and goals in social education. However, if integration efforts proceed primarily by focusing on the purposes and goals of the language arts, with social studies represented mostly only in the topics addressed in reading and writing assignments, the social studies strand will lose its coherence and most of its focus on powerful ideas. Unfortunately, our impression is that most efforts to integrate the curriculum take the latter approach. For information and resources concerning integrating language arts and social studies, especially in middle schools, see Roland Case,[136] Richard Kellough et al.,[137] Bruce VanSledright and Lisa Frankes,[138] and Myra Zarnowski.[139]

TEACHING FOR UNDERSTANDING

Whatever the content of the social studies curriculum, we hope to see an increased emphasis on teaching for understanding by structuring the content around key ideas and developing these ideas in depth (in contrast to both an approach that emphasizes breadth of coverage over development of key ideas and an approach that emphasizes activities at the expense of thoughtfulness and thus becomes "hands-on" without being "minds-on"). Developments along these lines would imply an increase in the substantive content addressed in the primary grades but a reduction in the breadth of coverage of topics taught in the middle grades in order to allow for more depth of development of key ideas.

Recent theory and research on instructional methods have featured a shift in emphasis from transmission- to constructivist-oriented modes of instruction. This has led to more emphasis on discussion rather than lecture and recitation in whole-class contexts and more emphasis on small-group cooperative learning and partner learning rather than solitary seatwork as the context for practice and application activities. These shifts are attractive theoretically, based on notions of the need for active construction of knowledge and authentic learning activities. However, other notions (such as the need for adequate prior knowledge to support meaningful critical thinking and decision-making activities, or the greater efficiency of learning structured and scaffolded by an expert compared to unstructured efforts to learn by discovery or trial and error) suggest limits to the feasibility of these methods. There is a great need for research on what are appropriate combinations of transmission and constructivist approaches to teaching various content at different grade levels, to determine the degree to which students need to acquire a common base of information before assuming primary responsibility for constructing further understandings, to determine how to prepare students to apply their school learning to their lives outside of school, and so on. More research also is needed to determine what is involved in accommodating diversity of student capacity and prior knowledge. This question has special relevance for social studies because mainstreamed special education students are usually included in social studies classes.

VALUES AND MORAL EDUCATION

There are at least four levels of debates about the place of values and moral education in elementary social studies. Most fundamentally, there are debates about whether values and moral education ought to be addressed at all in the school's curriculum. Most social educators believe that they should be and include values among basic social education goals. However, some social educators and a vocal segment of the general public believe that the schools should concentrate on academic knowledge and skills, leaving values and moral education to the home (and to churches and other private institutions). Among those who favor values and moral education in the school's curriculum, there is debate over whether these goals ought to be pursued within the social studies strand. Most social educators accept this as basic to social education, but some believe that social studies would be better off if these responsibilities were addressed through a guidance strand or through some other arrangement that did not assign them to social studies.

The third level of debate concerns general approaches to pedagogy: To what extent should values and moral education emphasize character education or other approaches that are primarily based on inculcation, and to what extent should it emphasize moral reasoning, values analysis, or other approaches that encourage students to think and make decisions for themselves? Recent exchanges on this argument seem to be moving away from either-or positions toward acceptance of the need for a balanced approach. The fourth level of debate concerns readiness issues: What aspects of values and moral education are elementary students able to address meaningfully, and what instructional approaches are needed to help them do so?

TEACHER EDUCATION AND PROFESSIONAL DEVELOPMENT

Published models and case studies of good subject-matter teaching have increased recognition of the need for sufficient teacher knowledge of both content (in particular, possession of connected understandings of networks of content to be taught, including recognition of which are the most important ideas worth developing in depth) and pedagogy (which explanations, examples, analogies, etc. are most likely to be effective for communicating initial understandings to students, and which questions and activities are most likely to be effective in helping the students to elaborate on these and construct connected understandings of their own). The most serious disconnects between the ideals espoused in various reform schemes and the realities of elementary teaching and teacher education concern what is reasonable to expect elementary teachers to know and be able to do in their classrooms. The statements on standards put out by various discipline-based groups strike us as unrealistic for both teachers and students. Furthermore, in part due to lobbying by these groups, teacher education programs have begun to place more emphasis on courses in the disciplines and less on courses in social studies education. We view this as counterproductive for elementary teachers, because neither the content nor the pedagogy they encounter in advanced classes for disciplinary majors is likely to have much applicability in the elementary grades.

The standards and other documents produced by discipline-based groups often include model lessons. These are helpful in conveying the spirit of what these groups would like to see occurring in the classroom, although they do not help teachers think about how to respond to the unrealistic expectations for curriculum scope built into the same documents. Pending unforeseen (and unlikely) radical changes in preservice or inservice teacher education, the resources likely to be most useful to elementary teachers are the print materials and videotapes published or distributed by NCSS and, in certain states, the teacher education materials and programs developed to support implementation of revised social studies standards.

Another resource that is already important for many teachers and likely to become so for virtually all teachers is the Internet. Increasingly, teachers are making or maintaining contacts with geographically distant colleagues and resource people (and students with other students). Just a few years ago there were only a handful of social studies sites on the Internet, and these did not have much to offer teachers. Now, however, there are dozens of sites that offer social education information, standards, or model lessons, as well as hundreds of sites that may be accessed by teachers or students to view or download historical sources, maps, cultural artifacts, digests of information, or other material that may be used in social studies learning activities.

Many of the most valuable of these sources may be accessed through the NCSS site at http://www.ncss.org, the Social Studies Sources site at http://education.indiana.edu/~socialst, the ERIC Clearinghouse for Social Studies Education at http://www.indiana.edu/~ssdc/eric-chess.htm, or the World Wide Web Resources—Social Studies site at http://www.uky.edu/subject/social-sciences.html. For a useful guide to Internet and other technological resources in social studies, see Braun, Fernlund and White, and for topical updates see issues of *Social Education* and *Social Studies and the Young Learner* (NCSS publications).[140]

Looking Back, Looking Ahead

The "*e pluribus unum*" motto provides a useful lens for viewing the ways in which social studies in the United States has changed and yet remained the same over the last century. Social studies education has moved from a focus on the *unum*, the notion of a single American identity, to a focus on the *pluribus*, the consideration of multiple peoples who together make up the American nation as it moves into the new millenium. Evolution in social studies can be attributed to changes in the nature of the society in which our schools have operated, the structures of schooling, and the definition of social studies and its role in the curriculum. Across the last century, American society has changed drastically in its demographics, sociocultural blending, land use, economy, technology, and other factors that create the contexts within which schools operate and social studies is taught.[141]

Consider just one example of changes in the structure of schooling: A century ago, elementary school attendance was neither compulsory nor universal. Only a small and homogeneous proportion of the population even graduated from high school, let alone attended college. Social studies as we know it was not identified as a school subject. Instead, students studied geography and history and learned patriotism through recitation and ritual. Publicly funded schooling had become commonplace in urban areas, and administrators saw a need for standardization of resources and curricula to educate as American citizens a rapidly increasing population characterized by cultural and linguistic variety. Committees appointed by the National Education Association in the 1890s developed curriculum policy statements for elementary education, secondary education, and college entry requirements. These policy statements, with their focus on the role of the disciplines in education, shaped school curricula for generations to come.[142]

A century later, the nation was still addressing the same basic educational issues. However, the policy-making focus had shifted from committees composed of a primarily academic intellectual elite to a much broader range of participants in state and national politics. Interest in educational reform during the 1980s led to articulation of national educational goals by the National Governors' Association. In 1992 Congress passed the Goals 2000: Education America Act, which sanctioned the development of national educational standards as a way to encourage and evaluate student achievement. Instead of talking about social studies, these documents cited the same social sciences that had been cited in the 1918 *Cardinal Principles of Secondary Education:* civics and government, economics, geography, and history.[143] Thus, the disciplines have had an enduring presence as organizing structures for the discourse surrounding social studies education.

The purview has broadened, however. Whereas documents from the 1900s identified geography, history, civics, and economics as key contributors to the study of good citizenship, recent statements about social studies released by NCSS also make reference to anthropology, archaeology, economics, law, philosophy, political science, psychology, religion, and sociology, as well as "appropriate content" from the humanities and mathematics.

Broadening of purview can also be seen in definitions of good citizenship. The 1918 document promoted participation in local affairs and being an active citizen of the state and nation, but gave only passing mention to understanding international problems. This approach reflected a time when few citizens had regular contact with people outside of their local community and the United States typically took an isolationist stance toward foreign affairs. In contrast, the 1994 NCSS definition of social studies recognizes how closely today's societies are connected and articulates the need to prepare students to live in a world in which people are separated more by language, wealth, and ideology than by geography.

It has become increasingly important to adopt a global perspective on the topics addressed in social studies, as well as to adopt a multicultural perspective on aspects that are specific to the United States.[144] Thus, even as we continue to focus on *unum* by educating students in core values and a common culture, we also focus on *pluribus* by connecting these issues to multiple perspectives. This is fitting for a nation that continues to be a magnet for immigrants, but in a world that is far more interconnected and interdependent than the world of a century ago.

NOTES

1. Virginia Atwood, "Elementary social studies: Cornerstone or crumbling mortar?" in V. Atwood , ed., *Elementary school social studies: Research as guide to practice* (Bulletin No. 79) (Washington, DC: National Council for the Social Studies, 1986): pp. 1-13; Carole Hahn, "The status of the social studies in the public schools of the United States: Another look," *Social Education* 49 (1985): 220-223; Stephen Thornton, "Teacher as curricular-instructional gatekeeper in social studies," in James Shaver, ed., *Handbook of research on social studies teaching and learning* (New York: Macmillan, 1991): pp. 237-248.

2. Michael Lybarger, "The historiography of social studies: Retrospect, circumspect, and prospect," in Shaver, ed., *Handbook of research on social studies teaching and learning*, pp. 3-15; James Shaver, ed., *Handbook of research on social studies teaching and learning*; Stephen Thornton, "The social studies near century's end: Reconsidering patterns of curriculum and instruction," in Linda Darling-Hammond, ed. *Review of research in education* (Washington, DC: American Educational Research Association, 1994): Vol. 20, pp. 223-254.

3. Gerald Marker and Howard Mehlinger, "Social studies," in Philip Jackson, ed., *Handbook of research on curriculum* (New York: Macmillan, 1992): pp. 830-851; Peter Martorella, "Consensus building among social educators: A Delphi study," *Theory and Research in Social Education* 19 (1991): 83-94; Walter Parker and John Jarolimek, *Citizenship and the critical role of the social studies* (Bulletin 72) (Washington, DC: National Council for the Social Studies, 1984).

4. Peter Martorella, *Social studies for elementary school children: Developing young citizens* (New York: Macmillan, 1994).

5. Herbert Kliebard, *The struggle for the American curriculum 1893-1958* (New York: Routledge and Kegan-Paul, 1987).

6. Robert Barr, James Barth, and Samuel Shermis, *Defining the social studies* (Arlington, VA: National Council for the Social Studies, 1977).

7. Jere Brophy and Bruce VanSledright, *Teaching and learning history in elementary schools* (New York: Teachers College Press, 1997); William Stanley, "Recent research in the foundations of social education: 1976-1983," in W. Stanley, ed., *Review of research in social studies education: 1976-1983* (Washington, DC: National Council for the Social Studies, 1985): pp. 309-399; William Stanley, "Teacher competence for social studies," in Shaver, ed., *Handbook of research on social studies teaching and learning*, pp. 249-262.

8. Stephen Thornton, "The social studies near century's end."

9. John Haas, "Social studies: Where have we been? Where are we going?" *Social Studies* 70 (1979): 147-154.

10. William Stanley, *Curriculum for utopia: Social reconstructionism and critical pedagogy in postmodern era* (Albany: State University of New York Press, 1992).

11. Peter Martorella, *Social studies for elementary school children*.

12. Beverly Armento, "Reform revisited: The story of elementary social studies at the crest of the 21st century," in V. Wilson, J. Litle, and G. Wilson, eds., *Teaching social studies: Handbook of trends, issues, and implications for the future* (Westport, CT: Greenwood, 1993): pp. 25-44.

13. Gerald Marker and Howard Mehlinger, "Social studies."

14. National Education Association, *Social studies in secondary education: A six-year program adapted to the 6-3-3 and the 8-4 plans of organization* (Bulletin No. 28) (Washington, DC: United States Department of the Interior, Bureau of Education, 1916).

15. David Saxe, *Social studies in schools: A history of the early years* (Albany: State University of New York Press, 1991).

16. National Council for the Social Studies (NCSS), "A vision of powerful teaching and learning in the social studies: Building social understanding and civic efficacy," *Social Education* 57 (1993): 213-223.

17. David Jenness, *Making sense of social studies.* (New York: Macmillan, 1990); John Patrick, *Topics in the social studies curriculum, grades K-12.* In S*ocial studies curriculum research handbook* (Millwood, NY: Kraus International Publications, 1992): pp. 65-82.

18. Hazel Hertzberg, *Social studies reform: 1880-1980.* (Boulder, CO: Social Science Education Consortium, 1981); Gerald Marker and Howard Mehlinger, "Social studies."

19. James Banks and Walter Parker, "Social studies teacher education," in W. Houston, ed., *Handbook of research on teacher education* (New York: Macmillan, 1990): pp. 674-686.

20. Gerald Marker, "Why schools abandon 'new social studies' materials," *Theory and Research in Social Education* 7(4) (1980): 35-58.

21. Shirley Engle and Wilma Longstreet, *A design for social education in the open curriculum* (New York: Harper & Row, 1972). For similar views, see Donald Bragaw and H. Michael Hartoonian, "Social studies: The study of people in society," in R. Brandt, ed., *Content of the curriculum* (Reston, VA: Association for Supervision and Curriculum Development, 1988): 9-29.

22. Hertzberg, *Social studies reform*; Theodore Kaltsounis, *Teaching social studies in the elementary school: The basics for citizenship*, 2nd ed. (Englewood Cliffs, NJ: Prentice-Hall, 1987).

23. Ibid.

24. Jere Brophy and Janet Alleman, "Elementary social studies textbooks," *Publishing Research Quarterly* 8(4) (1992/93): 12-22.

25. National Council on Economic Education, *A framework for teaching basic economic concepts with scope and sequence guidelines, K-12* (New York: Author, 1995).

26. National Council on Economic Education, *Voluntary national content standards in economics* (Waldorf, MD: National Council for the Social Studies, 1997).

27. Joint Committee on Geographic Education, *Guidelines for geographic education: Elementary and secondary schools* (Washington, DC: Association of American Geographers and National Council for Geographic Education. 1984).

28. Geographic Education National Implementation Project, *K-6 geography: Themes, key ideas, and learning opportunities* (Skokie, IL: Rand McNally, 1987); Joseph Stoltman, *Geography education for citizenship* (Bloomington, IN: ERIC Clearinghouse for Social Studies/Social Science Education, 1990).

29. Geography Education Standards Project, *Geography for life: National geography standards* (Waldorf, MD: National Council for the Social Studies, 1994).

30. Center for Civic Education, *CIVITAS: A framework for civic education*, Bulletin No. 86 (Washington, DC: National Council for the Social Studies, 1991).

31. Center for Civic Education, *National standards for civics and government* (Waldorf, MD: National Council for the Social Studies, 1995).

32. National Center for History in the Schools, *National standards for history: Expanding children's world in time and space* (*grades K-4 expanded edition*) (Los Angeles: University of California, Los Angeles, 1994); National Center for History in the Schools, *National standards for United States history: Exploring the American experience* (*grades 5-12 expanded edition*) (Los Angeles: University of California, Los Angeles, 1994); National Center for History in the Schools, *National standards for world history: Exploring paths to the present* (*grades 5-12 expanded edition*) (Los Angeles: University of California, Los Angeles, 1994).

33. National Center for History in the Schools, *National standards for history (basic edition)* (Waldorf, MD: National Council for the Social Studies, 1996).

34. Kirk Ankeney, Richard Del Rio, Gary Nash, and David Vigilante, eds., *Bring history alive! A sourcebook for teaching United States history* (Waldorf, MD: NCSS, 1996).

35. Ross Dunn and David Vigilante, eds., *Bring history alive! A sourcebook for teaching world history* (Waldorf, MD: National Council for the Social Studies, 1996).

36. Robert Cohen, "Moving beyond name games: The conservative attack on the United States History standards," *Social Education* 60 (1996): 49-54; Murry Nelson, "Are teachers stupid?—Setting and meeting standards in social studies," *Social Studies* 89 (1998): 66-70.

37. Bradley Commission on History in Schools. *Building a history curriculum: Guidelines for teaching history in schools* (Washington, DC: Educational Excellence Network, 1988).

38. California State Department of Education, *History-social science framework for California public schools kindergarten through grade 12* (Sacramento: Author, 1997).

39. Shirley Engle and Anna Ochoa, *Education for democratic citizenship: Decision making in the social studies* (New York: Teachers College Press, 1988); Ronald Evans, "A dream unrealized: A brief look at the history of issue-centered approaches. *The Social Studies* 80 (1989): 178-184; Wilma Longstreet, "Alternative futures and the social studies," in R. Evans and D. Saxe, eds., *Issues centered education* (Waldorf, MD: National Council for the Social Studies, 1996): pp. 317-326; Stephen Thornton, "The social studies near century's end."

40. Ibid.

41. Rod Farmer, "Social studies teachers and the curriculum: A report from a national survey," *Journal of Social Studies Research* 11(2) (1988): 24-42; Gerald Marker and Howard Mehlinger, "Social studies."

42. Stephen Thornton, "The social studies near century's end"; Bruce VanSledright, "'I don't remember—the ideas are all jumbled in my head': Eighth-graders' reconstructions of Colonial American history," *Journal of Curriculum and Supervision* 10 (1995): 317-345; Paul Gagnon and the Bradley Commission on History in the Schools, eds., *Historical literacy*.

43. William Bennett, *First lessons: A report on elementary education in America* (Washington, DC: United States Department of Education, 1986); Paul Gagnon, "The plight of history in American schools," in P. Gagnon and the Bradley Commission on History in the Schools, eds., *Historical literacy: The case for history in American education* (New York: Macmillan, 1989): pp. 51-68; Diane Ravitch, "The plight of history in American schools"; in P. Gagnon and the Bradley Commission on History in the Schools, eds., *Historical literacy: The case for history in American education* (New York: Macmillan, 1989).

44. James Banks, "The canon debate, knowledge construction, and multicultural education," *Educational Researcher* 22(5) (1993): 4-14; Catherine Cornbleth and Dexter Waugh, *The great speckled bird: Multicultural politics and education policymaking* (New York: St. Martin's Press, 1995); Gloria Ladson-Billings, "Through the looking glass: Politics and the social studies curriculum," *Theory and Research in Social Education* 21 (1993): 84-92; Gary Nash, Charlotte Crabtree, and Ross Dunn, *History on trial: Culture wars and the teaching of the past* (New York: Knopf, 1997).

45. E. D. Hirsch, Jr., *Cultural literacy: What every American needs to know* (New York: Houghton Mifflin, 1987).

46. Linda Anderson, "Implementing instructional programs to promote meaningful, self-regulated learning," in Jere Brophy, ed., *Advances in research on teaching. Volume 1. Teaching for meaningful understanding and self-regulated learning* (Greenwich, CT: JAI,

1989): pp. 311-343; Jere Brophy, "Probing the subtleties of subject-matter teaching," *Educational Leadership* 49(7) (1992): 4-8; Richard Prawat, "Promoting access to knowledge, strategy, and disposition in students: A research synthesis," *Review of Educational Research* 59 (1989): 1-41; Lauren Resnick, ed., *Knowing, learning, and instruction* (Hillsdale, NJ: Erlbaum, 1989).

47. Kieran Egan, *Primary understanding: Education in early childhood* (New York: Routledge, 1988).

48. Diane Ravitch, "Tot sociology or what happened to history in the grade schools," *American Scholar* 56 (1987): 343-353.

49. Jere Brophy and Bruce VanSledright, *Exemplary elementary teachers' beliefs about social studies curriculum and instruction* (Elementary Subjects Center Series No. 93) (East Lansing: Michigan State University, Center for the Learning and Teaching of Elementary Subjects, 1993).

50. Janet Alleman and Jere Brophy, "Trade-offs embedded in the literary approach to early elementary social studies," *Social Studies and the Young Learner* 6(3) (1994): 6-8.

51. Shirley Engle and Anna Ochoa, *Education for democratic citizenship*; Ronald Evans, "A dream unrealized: A brief look at the history of issue-centered approaches. *The Social Studies* 80 (1989): 178-184.

52. Ronald Evans and David Saxe, editors, *Handbook on teaching social issues* (Bulletin No. 93) (Waldorf, MD: National Council for the Social Studies).

53. David Naylor and Richard Diem, *Elementary and middle school social studies* (New York: Random House, 1987).

54. Peter Martorella, *Social studies for elementary school children*.

55. Paul Hanna, "Revising the social studies: What is needed?" *Social Education* 27 (1963): 190-196.

56. Beverly Armento, "Learning about the economic world," in V. Atwood (Ed.), *Elementary school social studies: Research as guide to practice* (Bulletin 79) (Washington, DC: National Council for the Social Studies, 1986): pp. 85-101.

57. Jean Fair, "Skills in thinking," in D. Kurfman, ed., *Developing decision-making skills* (47th NCSS Yearbook) (Arlington, VA: National Council for the Social Studies, 1977): pp. 29-68.

58. Martin Booth, "Students' historical thinking and the national history curriculum in England," *Theory and Research in Social Education* 21 (1993): 105-127; Charlotte Crabtree, "History is for children," *American Educator* 13(4) (1989): 34-39; Matthew Downey and Linda Levstik, "Teaching and learning history," in James Shaver, ed., *Handbook of research on social studies teaching and learning*, 400-410; Linda Levstik and Christine Pappas, "New directions for studying historical understanding," *Theory and Research in Social Education* 20 (1992): 369-385; Stephen Thornton and Ron Vukelich, "Effects of children's understanding of time concepts on historical understanding," *Theory and Research in Social Education* 16 (1988): 69-82; C. James Willig, *Children's concepts and the primary curriculum* (London: Paul Chapman. 1990).

59. Kieran Egan, *Primary understanding*; Diane Ravitch, "Tot sociology or what happened to history in the grade schools," *American Scholar* 56 (1987): 343-353.

60. Charles Mitsakos, "A global education program can make a difference." *Theory and Research in Social Education* 6 (1978): 1-15.

61. James Akenson, "The expanding environments and elementary education: A critical perspective," *Theory and Research in Social Education* 17 (1989): 33-52; William Joyce and Janet Alleman-Brooks, "The child's world," *Social Education* 46 (1982): 538-541; Leo LeRiche, "The political socialization of children in the expanding environments sequence," *Theory and Research in Social Education* 20(2) (1992): 126-140; David Naylor and Richard Diem, *Elementary and middle school social studies*.

62. Howard Mehlinger, "Social studies: Some gulfs and priorities," in H. Mehlinger and O. Davis, eds., *The social studies (Eightieth yearbook of the National Society for the Study of Education, Part II* (Chicago: University of Chicago Press, 1981): pp. 244-269; James Shaver, "What should be taught in social studies?" in Virginia Richardson-Koehler, ed., *Educators' handbook: A research perspective* (New York: Longman, 1987): pp. 112-138; Stephen Thornton, "Teacher as curricular-instructional gatekeeper."

63. Virginia Atwood, "Elementary social studies"; Jere Brophy and Janet Alleman, *Powerful social studies teaching and learning* (Fort Worth, TX: Harcourt Brace, 1996); Joan Shaughnessy and Thomas Haladyna, "Research on student attitude toward social studies," *Social Education* 49 (1985): 692-695.

64. David Elliott and Arthur Woodward, eds., *Textbooks and schooling in the United States (Eighty-ninth yearbook of the National Society for the Study of Education, Part I)* (Chicago: University of Chicago Press, 1990); Harriet Tyson-Bernstein, *A conspiracy of good intentions: America's textbook fiasco* (Washington, DC: Council for Basic Education, 1988).

65. Diane Ravitch, "Tot sociology."

66. A. Guy Larkins, Michael Hawkins, and Allison Gilmore, "Trivial and noninformative content of elementary social studies: A review of primary texts in four series," *Theory and Research in Social Education* 15 (1987): 299-311.

67. Isabel Beck and Margaret McKeown, "Toward meaningful accounts in history texts for young learners," *Educational Researcher* 17(6) (1988): 31-39.

68. Isabel Beck, Margaret McKeown, and Erika Gromoll, "Learning from social studies texts." *Cognition and Instruction* 6 (1989): 99-158.

69. Margaret McKeown and Isabel Beck, "Making sense of accounts of history: Why young students don't and how they might," in G. Leinhardt, I. Beck, and C. Stainton, eds., *Teaching and learning history* (Hillsdale, NJ: Erlbaum, 1994): pp. 1-26.

70. Arthur Woodward, "Textbooks: Less than meets the eye," *Journal of Curriculum Studies* 19 (1987): 511-526.

71. Jere Brophy, "The de facto national curriculum in United States elementary social studies: Critique of a representative example." *Journal of Curriculum Studies* 24 (1992); 401-447; Jere Brophy and Janet Alleman, "Elementary social studies textbooks," *Publishing Research Quarterly* 8(4) (1992/93): 12-22; Jere Brophy, Susan McMahon, and Richard Prawat, "Elementary social studies series: Critique of a representative example by six experts," *Social Education* 55 (1991): 155-160.

72. Jere Brophy and Janet Alleman, "Activities as instructional tools: A framework for analysis and evaluation," *Educational Researcher* 20(4) (1991): 9-23.

73. Janet Alleman and Jere Brophy, "Trade-offs embedded in the literary approach to early elementary social studies," *Social Studies and the Young Learner* 6(3) (1994): 6-8; Brophy and Alleman, *Powerful social studies teaching and learning.*

74. Gloria Alter, "Transforming elementary social studies: The emergence of a curriculum focused on diverse, caring communities," *Theory and Research in Social Education* 23 (1995): 355-374. Also, for an analysis of innovations in the use of illustrations introduced by the Houghton Mifflin series, see James LaSpina, *The visual turn and the transformation of the textbook* (Mahwah, NJ: Erlbaum, 1998).

75. Jere Brophy, Richard Prawat, and Susan McMahon, "Social education professors and elementary teachers: Two purviews on elementary social studies," *Theory and Research in Social Education* 19 (1991): 173-188; Blythe Hinitz, *Teaching social studies to the young child: A research and resource guide* (New York: Garland, 1992); Gerald Marker and Howard Mehlinger, "Social studies."

76. James Leming, "The two cultures of social education," *Social Education* 53 (1989): 404-408; Howard Mehlinger and O.L. Davis, Jr., eds., *The social studies (Eightieth*

yearbook of the National Society for the Study of Education, Part II (Chicago: University of Chicago Press, 1981); James Shaver, "What should be taught in social studies?" pp. 112-138; William Stanley, "Recent research in the foundations of social education: 1976-1983," in William Stanley, ed., *Review of research in social studies education: 1976-1983* (Washington, DC: National Council for the Social Studies, 1985): pp. 309-399.

77. Brophy and Alleman, *Powerful social studies learning and teaching.*

78. National Council for the Social Studies, "Revision of the NCSS social studies curriculum guidelines," *Social Education* 43 (1979): 261-278.

79. National Council for the Social Studies, "Statement on essentials of the social studies" *Social Education* 45 (1981): 162-164.

80. William Joyce, Timothy Little, and Stanley Wronski, "Scope and sequence, goals, and objectives: Effects on social studies," in J. Shaver, ed., *Handbook of research on social studies teaching and learning* (New York: Macmillan, 1991): pp. 321-331.

81. National Council for the Social Studies, *Curriculum standards for social studies: Expectations of excellence*, Bulletin 89 (Washington, DC: Author, 1994).

82. Mary Haas and Margaret Laughlin, eds., *Meeting the standards: Social studies readings for K-6 educators* (Washington, DC: National Council for the Social Studies, 1997).

83. DeAn Krey, *Children's literature in social studies: Teaching to the standards* (Bulletin No. 95) (Waldorf, MD: National Council for the Social Studies, 1998).

84. Tarry Lindquist, *Ways that work: Putting social studies standards into practice* (Waldorf, MD: National Council for the Social Studies, 1997).

85. Margaret Laughlin and H. Michael Hartoonian, eds., *Succeed with the standards in your social studies classroom* (Waldorf, MD: National Council for the Social Studies, 1997).

86. National Council for the Social Studies (NCSS), "A vision of powerful teaching and learning in the social studies: Building social understanding and civic efficacy," *Social Education* 57 (1993): 213-223.

87. Minds on Powerful Social Studies (Videotape). (Waldorf, MD: National Council for the Social Studies, 1999).

88. David A. Harris and Michael Yocum, *Powerful and Authentic Social Studies: A professional development program for teachers* (Washington, DC: National Council for the Social Studies, 1999).

89. Peter Martorella, *Social studies for elementary school.*

90. Robert Fullinwider, "Philosophical inquiry and social studies," in J. Shaver, ed., *Handbook of research on social studies teaching and learning* (New York: Macmillan, 1991): pp. 16-26.

91. R. Freeman Butts, *The morality of democratic citizenship: Goals for civic education in the republic's third century* (Calabasas, CA: Center for Civic Education, 1988).

92. David Naylor and Richard Diem, *Elementary and middle school social studies.*

93. Jacques Benninga, ed. *Moral, character, and civic education in the elementary school* (New York: Teachers College Press, 1991); Edward Winne and Kevin Ryan, *Reclaiming our schools: A handbook on teaching character, academics, and discipline* (New York: Macmillan, 1993).

94. Thomas Lickona, *Educating for character* (New York: Bantam, 1991); *The Character Education Partnership, Character education in United States schools: The new consensus* (Alexandria, VA: Author, 1996).

95. Louis Raths, Merrill Harmin, and Sidney Simon, *Values and teaching*, 2nd ed. (Columbus: Merrill, 1978).

96. Lawrence Kohlberg, "Moral education for a society in moral transition," *Educational Leadership* 33 (1975): 46-54.

97. Ronald Harshman and Charles Gray, "A rationale for values education," *Theory and Research in Social Education* 11 (1983): 45-66.

98. Theodore Kaltsounis, *Teaching social studies in the elementary school: The basics for citizenship, 2nd ed.* (Englewood Cliffs, NJ: Prentice-Hall, 1987.)

99. James Banks and Cherry McGee Banks, *Teaching strategies for the social studies: Decision-making and citizen action, 5th ed.* (New York: Longman, 1999); Jack Fraenkel, *Helping students think and value* (2nd Ed.) (Englewood Cliffs, NJ: Prentice-Hall, 1980); James Shaver and William Strong, *Facing value decisions: Rationale-building for teachers* (New York: Teachers College Press, 1982).

100. Nel Noddings, *Caring: A feminine approach to ethics and moral education* (Berkeley, CA: University of California Press, 1984).

101. Jean Baker, Tara Terry, Robert Bridger, and Anne Winsor, "Schools as caring communities: A relational approach to school reform," *School Psychology Review* 4 (1997): 586-602; Victor Battistich, Daniel Solomon, Marilyn Watson, and Eric Schaps, "Caring school communities," *Educational Psychologist* 32(3) (1997): 37-151; Pearl Oliner, "Putting 'community' into citizenship education: The need for prosociality," *Theory and Research in Social Education* 11 (1983): 65-81; F. Clark Power, Ann Higgins, and Lawrence Kohlberg, *Lawrence Kohlberg's approach to moral education* (New York: Columbia University Press, 1989); Thomas Sergiovanni, "Building community in schools" (San Francisco: Jossey-Bass, 1994).

102. Sheldon Berman, *Children's social consciousness and the development of social responsibility* (Albany: State University of New York Press, 1997); James Leming, "Research on social studies curriculum and instruction: Interventions and outcomes in the socio-moral domain," in W. Stanley, ed., *Review of research in social studies education: 1976-1983* (Washington, DC: National Council for the Social Studies, 1985): pp. 123-213; Kathryn Scott, "Achieving social studies affective aims: Values, empathy, and moral development," in J. Shaver, ed., *Handbook of research on social studies teaching and learning* (New York: Macmillan, 1991): pp. 357-369.

103. James Shaver, ed., *Handbook of research on social studies teaching and learning* (New York: Macmillan, 1991).

104. Jean Anyon, "Elementary schooling and distinctions of social class," *Interchange* 12 (1981): 118-132.

105. Carole Hahn, "The status of the social studies in the public schools of the United States: Another look," *Social Education* 49 (1985): 220-223; Richard Jantz and Kenneth Klawitter, "Early childhood/elementary social studies: A review of research in social studies education: 1976-1983," in W. Stanley, ed., *Review of research in social studies education: 1976-1983* (Washington, DC: National Council for the Social Studies, 1985): Bulletin No. 75, pp. 69-88; Colin Marsh, "Implementation of a social studies curriculum in an Australian elementary school," *Elementary School Journal* 87 (1987): 475-486; Susan Stodolsky, *The subject matters: Classroom activity in math and social studies* (Chicago: University of Chicago Press, 1988).

106. Gerald Marker and Howard Mehlinger, "Social studies."

107. Larry Cuban, "History of teaching in social studies," in Shaver, ed., *Handbook of research on social studies teaching and learning*, pp. 197-209; John Goodlad, *A place called school* (New York: McGraw-Hill, 1984); Stephen Thornton, "Teacher as curricular-instructional gatekeeper."

108. Neil Houser, "Social studies on the back burner: Views from the field," *Theory and Research in Social Education* 23 (1995): 147-168; Walter Parker, *Renewing the social studies curriculum* (Alexandria, VA: Association for Supervision and Curriculum Development, 1991).

109. Susan Stodolsky, *The subject matters: Classroom activity in math and social studies* (Chicago: University of Chicago Press, 1988).

110. Fred Newmann, "Qualities of thoughtful social studies classes: An empirical profile," *Journal of Curriculum Studies* 22 (1990): 253-275; Joseph Onosko, "Comparing teachers' instruction to promote students' thinking," *Journal of Curriculum Studies* 22 (1990): 443-461; Robert Stevenson, "Engagement and cognitive challenge in thoughtful social studies classes: A study of student perspectives," *Journal of Curriculum Studies* 22 (1990): 329-341.

111. Stephen Thornton and R. Neil Wenger, "Geography curriculum and instruction in three fourth-grade classrooms," *Elementary School Journal* 90 (1990): 515-531.

112. Susan Stodolsky, *The subject matters.*

113. Jane White, "What works for teachers: A review of ethnographic research studies as they inform issues of social studies curriculum and instruction, in W. Stanley, ed., *Review of research in social studies education: 1976-1983* (Washington, DC: National Council for the Social Studies, 1985): Bulletin No. 75, pp. 215-307.

114. Linda Levstik, "Building a sense of history in a first-grade classroom," in Jere Brophy, ed. *Advances in research on teaching. Volume 4. Case studies of teaching and learning in social studies* (Greenwich, CT: JAI, 1993): 1-31.

115. Jere Brophy and Bruce VanSledright, *Teaching and learning history in elementary schools* (New York: Teachers College Press, 1997).

116. Mark Aulls, "Contributions of classroom discourse to what content students learn during curriculum enactment," *Journal of Educational Psychology* 90 (1998): 56-69; Keith Barton, *History is more than a story: Expanding the boundaries of elementary learning.* Paper presented to the College and University Faculty Assembly of the National Council for the Social Studies, Nashville, 1993, November); Douglas Carnine, Jennifer Caros, Donald Crawford, Keith Hollenbeck, and Mark Harniss, "Designing effective United States history curricula for all students," in Jere Brophy, ed., *Advances in research on teaching. Volume 6. Teaching and learning history* (Greenwich, CT: JAI, 1996): pp. 207-256; Gaea Leinhardt, Cathryn Stainton, and Salim Virji, "A sense of history," *Educational Psychologist* 29 (1994): 79-88; Linda Levstik and Dehea Smith, " 'I've never done this before': Building a community of historical inquiry in a third-grade classroom," in Jere Brophy, ed., *Advances in research on teaching. Volume 6. Teaching and learning history* (Greenwich, CT: JAI, 1996): pp. 85-114; Kathleen Roth, "Making learners and concepts central: A conceptual change approach to learner-centered, fifth-grade American history planning and teaching," in Jere Brophy, ed., *Advances in research on teaching. Volume 6: Teaching and learning history* (Greenwich, CT: JAI, 1996): pp. 115-182; Bruce VanSledright, "I don't remember"; Bruce VanSledright, "Studying colonization in eighth grade: What can it teach us about the learning context of current reforms?" *Theory and Research in Social Education* (1996): 107-145; Bruce VanSledright, "And Santayana lives on: Students' views on the purposes for studying American history." *Journal of Curriculum Studies* 29 (1997): 529-557; Bruce VanSledright and Christine Kelly, "Reading American history: The influence of multiple sources on six fifth graders," *Elementary School Journal* 98 (1998): 239-265; Jane White, "Teaching for understanding in a third-grade geography lesson," in Jere Brophy, ed., *Advances in research on teaching: Volume 4. Case studies of teaching and learning in social studies* (Greenwich, CT: JAI, 1993): pp. 33-69.

117. Stephen Thornton, "Toward the desirable in social studies teaching," in Jere Brophy, ed., *Advances in research on teaching. Volume 4: Case studies of teaching and learning in social studies* (Greenwich, CT: JAI, 1993): pp. 157-178; Bruce VanSledright, "Closing the gap between school and disciplinary history? Historian as high school history teacher," in Jere Brophy, ed., *Advances in research on teaching. Volume 6. Teaching and learning history* (Greenwich, CT: JAI, 1996): pp. 257-290; Samuel Wineburg and Suzanne Wilson, "Models of wisdom in the teaching of history," *Phi Delta Kappan* 70 (1988): 50-58; Samuel Wineburg and Suzanne Wilson, "Subject matter knowledge in the teaching of history," in Jere Brophy, ed., *Advances in research on teaching. Volume 2: Teachers' knowledge of subject matter as it relates to their teaching practice* (Greenwich, CT: JAI): pp. 305-347.

118. Cynthia Hynd and Barbara Guzzetti, "When knowledge contradicts intuition: Conceptual change," in C. Hynd, ed., *Learning from Text across Conceptual Domains* (Mahwah, NJ: Erlbaum, 1998): pp. 139-163.

119. Anna Berti and Anna Bombi, *The Child's Construction of Economics* (Cambridge: Cambridge University Press. 1988); Adrian Furnham and Barrie Stacey, *Young People's Understanding of Society* (New York: Routledge, 1991); Hans Furth, *The World of Grown-ups* (New York: Elsevier, 1980); Stanley Moore, James Lare, and Kenneth Wagner, *The Child's Political World: A Longitudinal Perspective* (New York: Praeger, 1985).

120. Charles Guzzetta, "Children's knowledge of historically important Americans," in W. Herman, ed., *Current research in elementary school social studies* (New York: Macmillan, 1969): pp. 392-400; Diane Ravitch and Chester Finn, *What do our 17-year-olds know? A report of the first national assessment of history and literature* (New York: Harper & Row, 1987); United States Office of Education, National Center for Education Statistics, *NAEP 1994 Geography: A first look* (Washington, DC: Author, 1995); United States Office of Education, National Center for Education Statistics, *NAEP 1994 History: A first look* (Washington, DC: Author, 1995).

121. R. W. Connell, *The child's construction of politics* (Carlton: Melbourne University Press, 1971); Fred Greenstein, *Children and politics*, revised ed. (New Haven: Yale University Press, 1969); Robert Hess and Judith Torney, *The development of political attitudes in children* (Chicago: Aldine, 1967); Stanley Moore, James Lare, and Kenneth Wagner, *The child's political world*; Olive Stevens, *Children talking politics: Political learning in childhood* (Oxford: Martin Robertson, 1982).

122. Anna Berti and Anna Bombi, *The child's construction of economics*; Gustav Jahoda, "The development of thinking about socioeconomic systems," in H. Tajfel, ed., *The social dimension*, Vol. 1 (Cambridge: Cambridge University Press, 1984): 69-88.

123. Jere Brophy and Janet Alleman, "Second graders' knowledge and thinking about shelter as a cultural universal," *Journal of Social Studies Research* 21 (1997): 3-15.

124. Roslyn Ashby, Peter Lee, and Alaric Dickenson, "How children explain the 'why' of history: The *Chata* research project on teaching history," *Social Education* 6 (pp. 17-21), 1997; Keith Barton, "Narrative simplifications in elementary children's historical understanding" in Jere Brophy, ed., *Advances in research on teaching*, Volume 6, pp. 51-83 (Greenwich, CT: JAI Press, 1996); Keith Barton and Linda Levstik, "'Back when God was around and everything:' The development of elementary children's understanding of historical time," *American Educational Research Journal* 33 (1996): 419-454; Jere Brophy and Bruce VanSledright, *Teaching and learning history in elementary schools*; Margaret McKeown and Isabel Beck, "Making sense of accounts of history: Why young students don't and how they might," in G. Leinhardt, I. Beck, and C. Stainton, eds., *Teaching and learning in history* (Hillsdale, NJ: Erlbaum): 1-26.

125. Keith Barton, "History—it can be elementary: An overview of elementary students understanding of history," *Social Education* (1997) 61, 13-16.

126. Susan Adler, "The education of social studies teachers," in Shaver, ed., *Handbook of research on social studies teaching and learning*, 210-221; Beverly Armento, "The professional development of social studies educators," in John Sikula, ed., *Handbook of research on teacher education, second edition* (New York: Macmillan, 1996): 485-502.

127. Aaron Pallas, Gary Natriello, and Edward McDill, "The changing nature of the disadvantaged population: Current dimensions and future trends," *Educational Researcher* (1989): 18, 16-22.

128. Kathy Carter, "Teachers' knowledge and learning to teach," in W. Robert Houston, Martin Haberman and John Sikula, eds., *Handbook of research on teacher education* (New York: Macmillan, 1990): 291-310.

129. Suzanne Wilson, "Parades of facts, stories of the past: What do novice teachers need to know?" in Mary M. Kennedy, ed., *Teaching academic subjects to diverse learners* (New York: Macmillan, 1991): 99-116.

312   ELEMENTARY SCHOOL SOCIAL STUDIES

130. William Carlsen, "Teacher knowledge and discourse control: Quantitative evidence from biology teachers' classrooms," *Journal of Research in Science Teaching* (1989): 30, 5, 471-481.

131. Mary Haas and Margaret Laughlin, "A contemporary profile of elementary social studies educators," *Journal of Social Studies Research* (1998): 22(2), 19-30.

132. Carl Glickman, Stephen Gordon, and Jovita Ross-Gordon, *Supervision of instruction: A developmental approach* (Boston: Allyn and Bacon, 1998).

133. James Banks, "Approaches to multicultural curriculum reform," in J. Banks and C. Banks, eds., *Multicultural education: Issues and perspectives*, 3rd ed. (Boston: Allyn and Bacon, 1997): 229-250.

134. Terrence Mason, "Integrated curricula: Potential and problems," *Journal of Teacher Education* 47 (1996): 263-270.

135. Arthur Ellis and Jeffrey Fouts, *Research on educational innovations*, 2nd ed. (Larchmont, NY: Eye on Education, 1997).

136. Roland Case, "Integrating the curriculum: Getting beyond the slogan," in R. Case and P. Clark, eds., *The Canadian anthology of social studies: Issues and strategies for teachers* (Burnaby, BC: Simon Fraser University, 1997): 329-338.

137. Richard Kellough, John Jarolimek, Walter Parker, Peter Martorella, Gail Tompkins, and Kenneth Hoskisson, *Integrating language arts and social studies for intermediate and middle school students* (Englewood Cliffs, NJ: Prentice-Hall, 1996).

138. Bruce VanSledright and Lisa Frankes, "Literature's place in learning history and science," in C. Hynd, ed. *Learning from text across conceptual domains* (Mahwah, NJ: Erlbaum, 1998): 117-138.

139. Myra Zarnowski, *Learning with biographies: A reading and writing approach* (Washington, DC: National Council for the Social Studies, 1990).

140. Joseph A. Braun, Phyllis Fernlund, and Charles S. White, *Technology Tools in the Social Studies Curriculum* (Wilsonville, OR: Franklin, Beedle, and Associates, 1998).

141. David Tyack and Larry Cuban, *Tinkering towards Utopia: A century of public school reform* (Cambridge, MA: Harvard University Press, 1995).

142. William Pinar, William Reynolds, Patrick Slattery, and Peter Taubman, *Understanding curriculum: An introduction to the study of historical and contemporary curriculum discourses* (New York: Peter Lang, 1995).

143. Commission on the Reorganization of Secondary Education, *Cardinal principles of secondary education* (Bulletin No. 35) (Washington, DC: Government Printing Office, 1918).

144. Merry Merryfield, "Pedagogy for global perspectives in education: Studies of teachers' thinking and practice," *Theory and Research in Social Education* (1998): 26, 3, 342-379.

CHAPTER VII

Achievement Testing in American Schools

JEROME V. D'AGOSTINO

Testing students to determine their learning has always been an important component in American schooling. But in 1845 in the Boston schools, a new breed of tests was introduced. Instead of teachers using their own tests to gauge learning, uniform tests in multiple subjects were administered to students in schools throughout the district. Modern versions of these standardized achievement batteries presently are in use in nearly every American school. Their popularity has grown dramatically over the last century and a half, but not without great controversy. They were first considered the scientific means of fairly and objectively measuring students and schools. At the turn of the century, progressive educational reformers anticipated that testing would lead to effective school reform. More recently, achievement testing has come under attack for being culturally and ethnically biased, and fostering poor curricular and instructional practices, such as pressuring teachers to teach to the tests, encouraging narrowed and superficial coverage of the curriculum, and fostering passive student learning styles.[1]

Whether achievement testing has negative consequences on classroom activities remains debatable, though, mainly because few empirically driven consequential validity studies have successfully isolated its impact on classrooms. Even though achievement testing occurs in nearly every school, it is difficult to locate comparison sites, and testing rarely serves as the sole mechanism to improve schools. The structure of testing often is shaped by the ideological beliefs of reform strategies that may be the "true" source of the impact. Nonetheless, many test advocates would agree that achievement testing has never fulfilled its potential to improve schools as envisioned by the progressives. As we

Jerome V. D'Agostino is an Assistant Professor in the Department of Educational Psychology at the University of Arizona, Tucson. He specializes in assessment, evaluation, and the study of programs for at-risk students. Darrell L. Sabers and Anthony J. Nitko of the University of Arizona contributed greatly to the development of this chapter.

reach the new millennium, what can be learned from the past to make achievement tests more constructive for schools in the next century? To contribute to this understanding, I present in this chapter some of the key events in the history of achievement testing in an attempt to determine why it has not lived up to its promise. Until the barriers and limitations of testing are understood better, it may never be pivotal in improving the quality of education in this country.

From their first use in the Boston schools, achievement tests have always been used as instruments of educational reform. Many efforts to improve schools have been implemented in the United States since achievement tests were introduced, but most of these efforts fall under one of two general reform strategies: the political and the professional model.[2] Testing serves a different function within each model of reform. Yet because reform efforts representing both models are at work in schools simultaneously, and because testing time is limited in schools, often one achievement battery is used to fulfill the information needs of both models. This situation commonly leads to misuse and misinterpretation of the tests, thus limiting the power of reforms to affect positive change. Fundamental flaws of both models in terms of how tests function to induce change further curtail the potential of reforms to promote school improvement.

The political reform model is founded on the logic of the democratic process. Schools are seen as institutions for educating citizens who can participate effectively in the electoral system. The curriculum of schools, therefore, should reflect what society deems necessary for informed citizenship. Thus, schools should be open to public scrutiny and should be administered and monitored by elected officials or those appointed by them. Advocates of the political model believe that school reform is best achieved by creating a system of rewards and sanctions to motivate teachers and other school personnel. These individuals are held accountable for student achievement, which is seen as a reflection of the quality of the school. In order for accountability to work, student achievement levels must be made publicly visible and presented in an easily interpretable manner. Mandates are established to reward those practitioners who perform well and to sanction those who perform below expectations.

Within the political model, tests are used for two main purposes: (1) to determine who is and who is not performing up to the desired level; and (2) to produce performance results that can be publicly displayed and interpreted. Therefore, the political model requires test results that allow for comparisons among schools or between schools and a desired standard. To make these comparisons, testing every student in a given school from year to year is unnecessary. Indeed, yearly student testing often is construed as "obtrusive" and financially unsound. The primary purpose of yearly testing is to track individual student learning over time, which is not required to evaluate schools, and it provides technical information that rarely is of interest to the public. Measuring learning and cognitive development is a difficult and complex endeavor that requires professional understanding and interest. Because test results must be easily interpretable to the public, policymakers, and administrators, it would be senseless to provide this audience with detailed information regarding the dynamics of students' mental change processes. Thus, the most useful tests, according to the logic of the political model, contain items that sample a smattering of subject matter and indicate students' mastery level of course material.

The professional model assumes that school improvement is possible when educators are free to function within a professional culture. To achieve such a culture, schools must attract and retain teachers who are intrinsically motivated to educate youth, and schools must minimize external regulations. Decisions made by those who have not been trained in the profession may conflict with the norms and values that define competent practice. Tests serve two fundamental purposes within this model. First, they represent a cultural artifact for teachers by symbolically highlighting the importance to the profession of student learning, thus appealing to teachers' beliefs about the goals of education. Second, tests serve as important professional tools. They provide teachers needed information to monitor student progress, diagnose students' strengths and weaknesses, place students in special programs, group students for instruction, and formatively evaluate curriculum and instructional practices. Information derived from tests is not publicized but stays within the educational institution for purposes leading to technical improvement. This model encourages the testing of all students in all grades, preferably at multiple time points within a school year. To make sound professional judgments, teachers require longitudinal test data on individual students so that instruction can be tailored to students' needs. Because teachers are in the profession of promoting student learning, test items taken together should define learning processes so teachers can assess students' academic development. In this model, tests are considered inadequate if they merely report how much students know about various topics.

Student assessment is vital in both reform models, but the vast majority of achievement testing in the United States has served the needs of the political model. Testing within the professional model has consisted mainly of teacher-made assessments. In the latter years of the twentieth century, reform initiatives within the professional model have called for teachers to rely more on performance-based and authentic assessments than standardized achievement tests to evaluate their students.[3] However, in the middle part of the twentieth century, efforts were made, primarily under the leadership of Ralph W. Tyler and Everet F. Lindquist, to use achievement test information to invoke teacher improvement from a professional model perspective. These efforts essentially failed for reasons that will become clear when the history of achievement testing is reviewed.

The Birth of Achievement Testing

Though mental measurement existed long before the United States became a country, achievement testing primarily flourished in the United States to meet the expanding needs of schools. The first known system-wide use of achievement tests in the United States occurred in the Boston Schools in 1845.[4] At that time, Boston schools were visited annually by authorities, but commonly the result of these visitations was a very nominal report on the general condition of the school and the number of students enrolled. School reformers, led by Horace Mann, who was the appointed Secretary of the Massachusetts State Board of Education, demanded more information than the visitations provided in order to properly judge the quality of the schools. Two special sub-committees developed standardized tests of history, geography, arithmetic, grammar, vocabulary, natural philosophy, and astronomy. Test items were grouped into three categories—memory or skill items, intermediate items, and thought items. Most items were of the first category, which were designed to assess students' acquisition of the material covered in their textbooks. The intermediate items were created to assess students' abilities to draw generalizations or summaries from the facts they had learned, and the thought items required students to apply their knowledge in novel ways.

The test results revealed that students did fairly well on the memory or skill items, but did much worse on the items from the other two categories. In written reports of the findings, Mann and the special committee members used this information to claim that teachers were not adequately preparing students. Apparently, they conceptualized "effective teaching" as the ability not only to impart the knowledge of the textbooks, but to teach students the skills necessary to apply the material effectively in novel situations. In a sense, these early educational reformers were using elements of the political model to call for greater teacher professionalization, at least in terms of developing distinct pedagogical skills.

But those in charge of the testing program did not produce results that teachers could use to improve their instructional skills. Not every student enrolled in the schools was tested. Only the most meritorious students, less than ten percent of the entire student body, were given the examinations. Individual student scores were not reported. Instead, tables were generated that displayed the percentages of correct answers of all students in the schools by subject test, making it impossible for a teacher to address the instructional needs of each student tested. Interestingly, the percentages of correct responses in each school were not computed by the three defined item categories, which vaguely represented a precursor to later taxonomies of instructional objectives. The test developers apparently did not consider that it was possible to group items to represent the degree to which students developed skills in the three defined areas, which might have been useful information for teachers who were deemed in need of improvement.

Many large school districts in the latter half of the nineteenth century began to administer written examinations mainly for student accountability purposes. The Chicago Public Schools used essay and short-answer test formats for student promotion beginning in 1856, and for admission to high school starting in 1857.[5] Efforts were made to assure confidentiality by using identification numbers, to make scoring as reliable and accurate as possible, and, in general, to treat the examinees fairly and objectively. In other districts, the use of tests for purposes of student accountability led to abusive practices. The first superintendent of the Portland, Maine schools, Samuel King, saw tests as a way to instill discipline and industry in students. During the 1870s, Portland students were forced to take extremely challenging tests that many failed. The names, schools, and scores of failing students were published in the local newspaper. To avoid such embarrassment, many parents removed their children from school immediately before the examination dates, and in 1877 public outcry forced King to resign. His successor, Thomas Crawford, continued to use the examinations but stopped the publication of individual students' scores.

Tests were also used at this time to determine graduation and promotion. The tests of the New York State Board of Regents were administered for the first time in 1865 for elementary students and in 1878 for high school students. Most diploma testing was sanctioned at the state level, but many districts engaged in this practice as well. At the end of the last century, the practice of using tests to promote elementary school students virtually ceased, but it is being revived today by many states.

Testing at the Beginning of the Century

In the early years of the twentieth century, most American schools were not professional environments by today's standards.[6] The use of physical punishment was common, and the majority of teachers did not have formal pedagogical training. The professional education of teachers was in its infancy in the early 1900s. In 1904, 80 to 85 percent of the teaching force had no specialized teacher preparation. Many teachers lacked high school diplomas. Teacher certification varied widely across states and counties. In Massachusetts and Connecticut, the old colonial system remained intact. Individuals were granted approval to teach by a committee of local community members who based their decisions on personal preference. In other states, teachers had to pass certification examinations administered by counties; in Alabama, teacher candidates, including graduates of normal schools, were required to pass state examinations.[7] The ease of becoming a teacher and the variation in certification requirements prevented the field from having a large body of professionally trained individuals. It can be assumed that very few teachers in the early 1900s were equipped to interpret students' test scores and use them to improve their classroom practices.[8]

Consequently, early twentieth century testing occurred within the political model of reform. The testing program of Joseph M. Rice perhaps is the quintessential example. Rice was a psychologist and former pediatrician who published a series of articles about the state of American education in *The Forum*. He administered to students in schools from Massachusetts to Minnesota standard tests in spelling, arithmetic, handwriting, and composition. Based on the results of his spelling test, he concluded that teacher competency, rather than other factors such as home environment and instructional methods, was the prime determinant of achievement differences across schools. Actually, Rice never measured teacher competency, so his conclusion was not supported with direct empirical evidence. He simply ruled out other factors, such as instructional methods, by claiming that equal proportions of test score variance existed within and between various levels of these other factors. Rice believed the only remaining explanation for test score differences among schools was variation in the ability levels of teachers. In mathematics, he detected more between-school variance, and employing his process-of-elimination tactic, he concluded that schools with higher achievement levels were those with principals who evaluated classrooms and worked cooperatively with superintendents.[9]

Rice's findings provided a basis for progressive administrators to call for more centralized school administration and the scientific management of schools.[10] These reformers saw schools as inefficient organizations that lacked a common goal. To be more productive, it was necessary for schools to adopt managerial principles that characterized successful corporations of the time. It was the responsibility of superintendents and principals to function as managers by defining school goals and supervising the work of teachers to obtain those goals. Without a specific action plan and a set of standards to judge teachers' work, school managers could not supervise effectively. Thus, tests were needed to set standards and define the expected final product for teachers. The progressive reformers relied on tests primarily developed by those in the new field of educational psychology to fulfill these needs.

Edward L. Thorndike and his students at Teachers College, Columbia University, had developed tests of speed and accuracy in several subjects including arithmetic, reading, handwriting, and composition. One of Thorndike's students, Stuart A. Courtis, developed perhaps the most sophisticated tests in a number of these subjects. For mathematics, he crafted a series of eight arithmetic tests that were used widely in schools at the beginning of the twentieth century. The eight tests, based on interval scales, included addition, subtraction, multiplication, division, figure copying, speed in identifying the operation needed to solve word problems, and one- and two-step problem solving. Courtis administered his tests to several thousand students in every grade to develop performance standards. For the primary grades, Courtis set the standard for each subject at the average score, but for grades three to eight, he set standards so that 30 percent of the students in each grade would score above expectations.[11] He used similar procedures to set standards in his tests of other subjects.[12]

Though Courtis apparently believed that innate ability contributed greatly to test score variation among students of identical ages, he felt that schools were responsible for assuring that all students attain the standard level of performance. Unlike Rice, he believed that test score variation among students persisted due to inefficient teaching methods. To improve mathematics instruction, he provided schools with graphic records of each individual student's progress through the grades on each of his eight mathematics tests. The graphs also included average performance levels for students across the city and within the school. He believed this information was useful for both teachers and administrators. For teachers, he thought his graphic displays of each student's growth over time were helpful in diagnosing learning problems and planning instruction. The average performance levels of students across classrooms and across the city were most useful for administrators as an aid to supervise teachers.

Many progressives believed that test results were most productively used when in the hands of administrators. By reviewing the test scores by classroom, principals could judge the efficiency of the teacher, and could decide whether it was necessary to remove those teachers who were behind their peers or offer them help. Principals could determine which teachers were making improvements and which utilized effective instructional methods by continually examining test results over successive years and between classrooms. Once principals identified the best methods, they were to inform the teachers of their findings. Most reformers recognized the value of test results for teacher self-judgment and self-improvement but subscribing to the principles of organizational management, they believed that scientific tools like testing belonged in the hands of supervisors.[13] Teachers were expected to understand basic research methods, but they were not expected to apply them to improve their practices. Science and practice were considered separate specializations within the organization. Thus, in a sense, the scientific management model precluded efforts to tailor test results primarily for teachers' own use toward self-improvement.

Not all educators at the time agreed with the use of achievement tests to judge schools and teachers. In the Fifteenth Annual School Report of the New York City Schools of 1913, Middlesex A. Bailey, Head of the Mathematics Department at New York Training School for Teachers, strongly questioned the validity of Courtis's tests. He cited Courtis's interpretation of the test results and then offered rebuttals to each of his claims. Bailey was critical of Courtis for drawing conclusions about the New York schools based on tests that were considered experimental, and for setting standards that had no connection to students' lives. One particular problem of the tests, according to Bailey, was the emphasis placed on speed over accuracy. He wrote, "Consider the standard of 70% accuracy for computations in addition, subtraction, multiplication, and division. Merchants would not tolerate clerks who get right footings to 7 bills out of 10 (70%) even if the work were done in a fraction of a second. The plea that inaccuracy should be off-set by speed is like the plea that taint in meat should be offset by extra weight."[14] Bailey also saw as potentially problematic Courtis's owner-ship of the tests and his argument to develop a citywide Bureau of Investigation and Appraisal to assay schools. He said, "No longer are superintendents, principals and teachers who are in close daily touch with children, and who know their real needs and conditions, to exer-cise initiative and judgment of their own, but they are to follow the instructions of a Bureau of Investigation and Appraisal who are in turn to be guided by the present system of tests already patented, or to a modified system to be patented in the future. *Suppose Mr. Courtis were to refuse permission to use his test!*"[15] Bailey ostensibly was arguing that teachers were likely to resist external testing because: (1) the tests did not provide information tailored to the needs of their students; (2) if the content of the tests could easily change, modifying instruction around test content was a risky endeavor; and (3) they were unlikely to develop a sense of ownership in the tests. Bailey's critique foreshadows some of the major limitations of using testing within the political model to facilitate school improvement.

The Professional Use of Achievement Testing

At the turn of the century, the small proportion of the teaching force who received professional training may have rendered attempts to make tests more teacher-centered an implausible reform tactic. Teachers as a whole simply may not have had enough training and skill to use tests effectively even if the tests were made primarily for them. Besides teachers' lack of formal training in assessment, other factors hindered the development of professionalism. As is the case today, women constituted the majority of the teaching force at the century's beginning. Because women's careers were considered of secondary importance to those of men, teaching was not viewed as a sophisticated endeavor. As David Tyack explained, under-educated females were prime targets for subordination under a male-dominated administra-tive system. They were expected to serve a subservient role within the managerial hierarchy. At one of the National Education Association meetings around the turn of the century, a superintendent claimed that it was worthless for teachers to read professional books because they looked to him for proper methods.[16]

Another reason for the impairment of teacher professionalism per-tained to the prevailing belief about the nature of human ability and the role education played in shaping the individual. Many administrative progressives did not share Courtis's beliefs that all students were capable of reaching the same academic standards. Many believed that biological factors explained individual test score differences. The purpose of education, therefore, was to identify children's innate abilities and provide them with the schooling most suited to their talents. Once students were placed in the correct track, the system could operate more efficiently, because it made little sense to provide a challenging curriculum to children who were not capable of learning from it. Accordingly, children from advantaged homes were placed in college preparatory tracks, while children from the lower and working classes, mainly from recent immigrant families, received vocational schooling. Many test developers of the time were proponents of the administrative progressive movement, so they tended to maintain these beliefs as well. Edward L. Thorndike epitomized the philosophy of the movement by stating, "The one thing that educational theorists of today seem to place as the foremost duty of the schools—the development of powers and capacities—is the one thing that schools or any other educational forces can do least,"[17] and, "Educational agencies . . . help society in general tremendously by providing it not with better men, but with the knowledge of which men are good . . . The schools always have and always will work to create a caste, to emphasize inequalities."[18]

The role of instruction, and therefore of teachers, was of secondary importance within this educational belief system. It was difficult for teachers to develop a sense of professionalism within a system that did not value their role in fostering students' intellectual skills. Once students were properly sorted into curricular tracks, teachers had little influence over the "natural" course of human ability. Thus, it made little sense to build teachers' assessment skills when the primary goals of testing were to supervise teachers and place students in appropriate academic tracks.

Teacher professionalism was not possible until social conditions and beliefs about schooling changed. During and after the Second World War, women established themselves in the workforce, and the importance of their contribution to the betterment of the American economy started to be recognized. Educational requirements for entry into teaching increased steadily from the turn of the century. By the 1940s, all states required teachers to hold bachelor's degrees to be certified. At about this time, too, behaviorism became the dominant model of psychology and education. Ironically, test development from a perspective of behaviorism later would be criticized for encouraging decontextual-ized and fragmented curriculums and for promoting the over-use of multiple-choice test items.[19] Yet it was the tenets of behaviorism that changed educators' views about the function of education. Within behaviorism, learning was defined as enduring changes in behavior made possible by altering environmental conditions. Structuring the conditions of learning in particular ways led to specific outcomes. Within this model, teachers had more power to modify instruction to develop students' skills. They also had the power to experiment with various classroom practices to determine which ones led to the most desirable outcomes. This approach to education gave teachers a greater sense of importance in the lives of students, and required them to have greater technical skills.

As Kenneth A. Strike has pointed out, for an occupation to be so-cially recognized as a profession, members of the field must possess a deep knowledge base that is distinct from that of other occupations, and it must take several years of training to master this knowledge. The knowledge base must include a series of processes with demonstrated effectiveness for reaching prescribed goals. Further, for a field to be considered professional, its members must govern and evaluate them-selves, because only they have the expertise to do so competently.[20]

Working from a perspective of behaviorism and at a time that was ripe for the growth of teacher professionalization, Ralph W. Tyler proposed a curriculum development plan that was premised on the tenets of the professional model of reform. Tyler believed the main role of tests was to help teachers evaluate and improve their curricu-lum. Tyler defined education as the process of changing the behavioral patterns of students so they can function in society. In order to de-velop curriculum, it was the responsibility of schools to articulate the behaviors that effective citizenship required. He called these terminal behaviors "objectives," which were best defined by two dimensions, subject matter and general mental skills. Defining objectives in terms of content elements alone was insufficient, according to Tyler, because it did not allow the teacher to explicate what the student was to do with the course matter in mental and behavioral terms. Likewise, Tyler believed it was not adequate to describe objectives as general mental skills without specifying the specific content element which the stu-dent was to process during learning. Tyler suggested that learning the-ories be used to guide the formation of objectives because they offer "an outline of the learning process nature, define how learning takes place, under what conditions, and what sort of mechanisms operate and the like."[21] He guided educators to adopt the particular learning theory that was most suited to their goals, but he seemed to like theories that viewed learning as "the development of a generalized mode of attack on problems" rather than as "the acquisition of specific subject matter skills."[22] Thus, although he argued that objectives are best defined by content and mental skills, he tended to believe the articulation of the latter dimension was most important.

Tyler's ideas about mental skill development greatly influenced the direction of learning theory and test development. Learning taxonomies, which depicted learning as a hierarchical process of obtaining increasingly more complex skills in any given subject, were based largely on his rules for crafting behavioral objectives.[23] Taxonomies were attempts to organize objectives into a system that depicted human learning. In test development, taxonomies facilitated a movement away from crafting test items based on lists of objectives, or without regard for domain representation, toward item selection that was more focused on developing coherent measures of student learning. Tyler's work also influenced the creation of criterion-referenced tests, which yielded richer information regarding students' learning than traditional norm-referenced comparisons.[24] Both of these influences on testing led to increasing the potential of achievement tests to aid teachers in the improvement of their practices.

Yet Tyler's model of curriculum development was never fully implemented in schools across the country due to a number of factors that limited its use. First, in order to carry out the model successfully, teachers had to engage in numerous planning activities. Schools were not structured to allow teachers the time to prepare curricular and instructional materials, develop tests, and conduct evaluations. Further, although the educational levels of teachers had increased overall, few teachers were adequately trained during their preservice programs or through staff development workshops to conduct all of the activities successfully. In a sense, Tyler's model demanded a level of professionalism that has yet to be realized up to this day.

Another limitation of the model, pointed out by Lee J. Cronbach, pertained to implementation problems.[25] In the model, teachers and other local educators were expected to craft educational objectives around their students' needs, and then develop tests to determine the extent to which students completed the tasks embodied in the objectives. But locally developed tests tended to cover course content more than general mental skills. Thus, Tyler may have unwittingly encouraged local educators to develop the types of tests that he found problematic.

Teachers rarely considered learning theories when crafting test items, and few teachers had the skills of transforming theoretical principles into objectives and items in the first place. Many teachers required staff development to cultivate those skills, but as Cronbach asserts, inservice professional training too often focused on test development as an end itself. The actual test results and their use in curriculum revision became less important than the act of creating tests, which defeated the primary purpose of testing within Tyler's model.

Cronbach's critique highlights a fundamental issue regarding achievement testing within the professional model. When teachers design tests to improve their instruction, they tend to focus on testing content over general intellectual skills, and they tend to develop tests that are tailored to their classes. Consequently, their information needs appear to leave little place for uniform, standardized achievement tests, which usually measure a wide range of content. Tyler clearly was aware of the discordance between teachers' needs and achievement test information. Nonetheless, he felt that achievement test results were valuable to teachers if schools had the option to weigh the results of various sub-tests based on the relative importance of each sub-test to the instructional objectives of the school.[26]

Like Tyler, Lindquist was critical of testing programs that focused on school and teacher comparisons, and that placed more emphasis on the testing of content than general mental skills. But unlike Tyler, he worked to improve testing by developing better and more useful standardized tests. Lindquist directed the Iowa Testing program at the University of Iowa. Originally called the Iowa Academic Meet, the testing program served as a statewide scholastic competition for high school students, similar to intramural athletic competitions. In the beginning of the program in 1929, high schools that wanted to compete administered end-of-year content-oriented tests to their students covering most school subjects. Top-scoring students at each school qualified for the next rounds that occurred at the university in the summer. About one thousand students took several two- to three-hour examinations that were scored overnight. Individual student awards were given at an awards banquet, the top ten scorers in each subject were honored, and schools with the highest weighted averages per subject received awards. The university administration saw the meet as a mechanism to attract some of the more proficient students in the state.[27]

Nearly from the beginning, Lindquist was concerned about the competitive nature of the program and how it seemed to encourage teachers to teach to the tests, which translated into an inordinate coverage of course content. In an interview conducted in the late 1960s, he said, "Well, I soon began to feel that there was too *much* emphasis upon competition, resulting in an overemphasis upon the teaching of informational content, factual information, and rote learning of facts, since that is what the teachers anticipated the students would need. We did everything we could to get away from that kind of testing. We tried to build tests which were concerned with what we then called reasoned understanding of broad units of comprehension, generalizations, trends, and that sort of thing. But, the teachers, you know, traditionally thought of an examination as concerned with fact finding, so they prepared for the kind of examination they expected it to be, with the result that they became more interested in the teaching of subject matter for its effect upon the program than in the overall development of the individual pupil."[28]

To mitigate these problems, schools were permitted to participate on either a competitive or non-competitive basis, and school personnel constantly were made aware that the tests emphasized thinking skills and provided useful information to improve instruction. The program was renamed the Iowa Every-Pupil Achievement Testing program, symbolizing that the test was for all students, not just the academic elite. In 1935, tests created for the middle grades became the foundation of the Iowa Tests of Basic Skills. Lindquist claimed that "here we did succeed in placing emphasis on development of skills and generalized abilities, as opposed to rote learning of subject matter content."[29]

With the advent of machine scoring in the 1950s, which Lindquist was instrumental in developing, the test was expanded to serve the elementary grades. In the 1940s, the original competitive program was dropped entirely, and the tests were administered in the fall instead of the spring. According to Lindquist, testing was moved to the fall to prevent teachers from teaching to the test and to provide them with information for planning instruction. Test manuals and materials were prepared for teachers "to place the emphasis, as much as possible, upon the uses of the tests to help the teacher become better acquainted with the pupil so that she might do a better job of individualizing instruction."[30] The goal from the beginning was to allow schools to choose the test level that was best targeted to students' proficiency levels, rather than creating a test system strictly based on grade levels. But it was not until the 1970s that breakthroughs in machine scoring allowed for the complete individualization of testing, where, for instance, a student more proficient in reading than mathematics would receive a more difficult test in the former subject. This system allowed for better tracking of individual growth in particular subjects and more accurate scoring. By the 1980s, about a third of the schools in Iowa opted for individualized student testing. Schools that did not choose the individualized approach gave as a reason that it complicated test administration and did not fit with their curriculum structure.[31]

The Impact of Title I on Achievement Testing

President Lyndon Johnson's War on Poverty in the 1960s ushered in a new purpose for testing—program evaluation. As part of Title I of the Elementary and Secondary Education Act of 1965, the federal government required school districts that received program funds to test participating students for evaluation purposes. The original Title I law of 1965 stated, "A local educational agency may receive a basic grant or a special incentive grant under this title for any fiscal year only upon application therefor approved by the appropriate State educational agency upon its determination . . . that effective procedures, including provision for appropriate objective measurements of educational achievement, will be adopted for evaluating at least annually the effectiveness of the programs in meeting the special educational needs of educationally deprived children."[32] Members of Congress, including Senator Robert Kennedy, insisted on the evaluation requirement because they feared that school districts would not target funds effectively to eligible students. Evaluation served to make schools accountable to parents, especially those who lacked a strong political voice.[33]

Shortly after Title I was founded, a three-tiered reporting system was created where districts were to submit their evaluation results to states, the states in turn were to compile the district reports into state documents, which were to be gathered by the United States Office of Education. Though the office stressed to states the importance of encouraging districts to use identical or comparable outcome measures, the quality of district reports varied greatly.[34] Consequently, Congress mandated the development of a uniform evaluation system in the 1974 program reauthorization. The RMC Research Corporation was contracted to design the evaluation model. To make the model flexible enough for diverse school districts, the company originally developed five design options, but reduced the number to three because of the difficulty of implementing certain models. Districts could either design a control-group comparison study, conduct a regression discontinuity study, or rely on norm-referenced achievement gain scores of participating students.[35] To implement the latter model, RMC developed normalized scores known as normal-curve equivalents (NCEs). Students from ineffective programs were expected to maintain the same relative achievement standing in the norm-group from year to year, which would be indicated by a yearly student NCE gain of 0. This hypothesis, known as the "equipercentile" assumption, served to judge the quality of programs under the norm-referenced model. For a program to be deemed effective, students had to post an average NCE gain that exceeded 0 units.

Using essentially the same structure of the three-tiered reporting model developed in the late 1960s, the federal government in 1979 enacted the Title I Evaluation and Reporting System (TIERS) that required districts and states to submit their evaluation evidence based on one of the three research designs. Few districts implemented regression-discontinuity or comparison-group designs, mainly because schools had to modify their programs considerably to fulfill design requirements, and few schools and districts had the technical expertise to conduct such studies. Most districts reported participants' NCE scores, and many districts decided to administer the same tests to all enrolled students. TIERS remained intact until 1994 when Title I testing requirements were altered. Because over ninety percent of school districts across the nation received Title I funds, the federal government's evaluation mandate thoroughly institutionalized achievement testing in American schools.

In 1974, Congress not only changed the structure of Title I testing, but changed its purpose as well. Up to that time, testing served to provide for a national summative evaluation of the program. Testing was not intended to offer schools pertinent information to improve their programs. Congress attempted to expand the role of evaluation through the 1974 amendments by encouraging schools to use their test results for program improvement purposes. But Congress did not alter Title I testing to match this new intention, leaving schools with little constructive information from test results to effect change. In the 1988 Hawkins-Stafford amendments, the role of evaluation expanded. Congress required participating schools that did not demonstrate substantial yearly progress to develop a Program Improvement Plan (PIP). A school had to submit a PIP to the district office if the average NCE gain of the school's Title I students was 0 or less. If a school did not demonstrate progress after two years, it had to enter into a joint improvement plan with the state educational office.

The Department of Education required schools to gauge progress on certain approved standardized measures or on tests that were equated to those measures. States could use other tests in addition to the approved ones, but they could not supplant the federally certified tests. In fact, the Jefferson County, Kentucky, school district asked the Department of Education for approval to use the state performance-based assessment system for evaluating Title I programs. The request was denied.[36]

Several educational researchers questioned the rationale of the Title I testing and program improvement models for technical and substantive reasons. A number of criticisms were leveled against the practice of using simple gains from norm-referenced tests as indicators of program quality. Some researchers demonstrated that differences between two schools' mean NCE gains could have occurred if students at the schools received different standardized tests, because NCE scores were not equivalent across tests.[37] Others argued that NCE scores did not allow for the direct comparison of Title I students' gains with those of an equivalent group.[38] Test norm groups consisted of all students, not just low-performing ones, and many low-performing students from norm groups may have received other types of compensatory education. These problems made it difficult to estimate the effect of the program. Furthermore, NCEs did not yield an interval scale, so gains at varying points of the achievement spectrum were not equivalent. This limitation of the NCE metric did not allow for an accurate comparison of school programs, given that schools' pretest means differed. A closely related problem pertained to regression effects, where initially low- and high-performing students tended to drift closer to the mean on the post-test. Consequently, research demonstrated that Title I schools with above-average pretest scores were more likely to be categorized in need of program improvement because their students posted smaller gains than students who had lower pretest scores.

Besides these technical problems, critics argued that Title I testing contributed to a narrowing of the curriculum and the implementing of instructional practices founded on a belief that students learn best by being passive recipients of knowledge.[39] It was commonly believed that most approved tests for Title I consisted of multiple-choice items that measured basic skills. Thus, Title I teachers tended to spend an inordinate amount of time remediating students in the basics, and less time teaching them how to solve problems, think critically, and engage in other advanced skills. Many felt the program was defeating its original intent by preventing disadvantaged students from developing higher-order thinking skills that were necessary if they were to catch up with their more advantaged peers. These criticisms, though, were not very helpful given that educators had been aware of these tendencies in American education for decades.

The inadequacies of the tests in fairly and accurately identifying schools for program improvement, for supporting effective classroom practices, and for providing school staff with constructive information for change led many school personnel to consider program improvement as a mere formality. Few schools committed the time, effort, and thought needed to better their programs.[40] In response to the problems of Title I testing, Congress altered the assessment policies of the program during the 1994 reauthorization. The new assessment system was based on a standards-driven reform model. States were required by the 2000-2001 school year to develop and implement assessments in at least mathematics and reading or language arts. The assessments were to be linked with each state's standards for content and for performance that all students, regardless of Title I eligibility, were expected to reach. Content standards had to: (1) be rigorous and coherent; (2) define what students were expected to know and be able to do; and (3) focus on advanced skills. Performance standards had to be aligned with the content standards and describe three levels of student achievement—partially proficient, proficient, and advanced. To alleviate the testing burden placed on Title I schools, the 1994 reauthorization required states to test students at three grade levels. States could choose to test one grade from 3 to 5, 6 to 9, and 10 to 12. The program improvement model that had been developed in the mid-1970s was retained in the 1994 legislation with some modifications. Instead of requiring states to use approved tests, the states had to use their assessments to determine program improvement. Further, states were responsible for determining what constituted "adequate yearly progress" on their standards-based assessments; so the 1994 legislation shifted away from the use of one uniform national criterion for program improvement.

The new Title I assessment and program improvement systems, though, did not entirely mitigate the problems of the prior legislation, and in some ways they created additional problems of equal magnitude. To date, most states have, or plan to develop, content standards, but few states have developed performance standards.[41] Without performance indicators, states will find it difficult to develop assessment systems that can measure the degree to which students meet academic standards. As of 1998, nearly half of the states planned to rely on conventional standardized achievement measures, the same tests that were approved for testing before 1994, as their standards-driven assessment devices.[42] The use of these tests for Title I assessment was criticized in the past because these tests tend to promote a passive view of learning and primarily emphasize basic skills. If states follow the regulations and develop content and performance standards based on higher-order skills, it is doubtful that conventional standardized measures will adequately operationalize the new standards. Because states were required to develop their own definitions of "adequate yearly progress," considerable variation exists among states in the identification of schools in need of improvement. In 1996-97, eighty percent of Title I schools were identified in New Mexico, whereas only one percent of Texas schools were identified.[43] Questions of equity, fairness, and accuracy inevitably will arise given such diverse outcomes across states, and program improvement will continue to be treated as a formality if schools discredit the identification procedures.

Furthermore, for test information to be most useful for teachers, students' scores should be reported on a yearly basis. Annual testing allows teachers to monitor each student's academic growth, but this testing schedule often is construed as burdensome from a political reform model standpoint. Consequently, the 1994 legislation mandated that students had to be tested in only one elementary, intermediate, and high school grade. This flaw in the logic of the new legislation is indicative of the problems of attempting to use tests to serve the goals of the political and professional reform models simultaneously.

Recent Standards-based Tests

At the beginning of the twenty-first century, Title I testing is the primary force behind the development of states' standards-based assessments. Given that Title I is funded presently at about eight million dollars annually, the risk of losing Title I funds is too great for any state to ignore the federal testing requirements. As I have indicated in my brief account of the history of achievement testing, standards are not new in education. Setting standards was a primary activity of early twentieth century test developers. Ironically, although standards-based testing mainly represents a political reform strategy, the recent resurgence of standards began within the professional community of mathematics teachers. Members of the National Council of Teachers of Mathematics (NCTM) felt a need to improve mathematics instruction in the early 1980s. They banded together to develop standards around the general notion of learning and cognitive development which offers teachers an instructional guideline rather than a set of regulations about when and how students must learn certain subject matter elements. The standards were disseminated through professional teacher networks and created in a manner that facilitated professional development.[44]

The success of the NCTM standards led the federal government to fund standard-setting committees in nearly every other school subject, but the representation of these committees did not consist of teachers alone. In fact, many members were not associated with education. Consequently, many committees did not produce standards that reflected student learning or current thinking in the teacher profession. Development of state standards has occurred in much the same manner, and teachers rarely, if ever, take the initiative to disseminate these standards. It is doubtful if most state standards, taken together, fully operationalize the dynamics of learning. Indeed, state standards, fueled by federal Title I monies, represent a political reform tactic to enforce curriculum at certain grade levels. The usefulness of these standards as a curriculum guide to foster instruction aligned with current pedagogical knowledge is questionable.

Other characteristics of state standards-based tests, which reflect political model testing, are discordant with teachers' formative evaluations. For instance, many states do not test students at every grade, so it is not possible for teachers to monitor individual student growth. Also, because many state standards systems do not represent student learning, the scores from these state tests are inadequate to quantify academic growth. With test scores from some students in selected grades, and an unclear meaning of the scores in terms of student learning, it is difficult to imagine how schools will use standards-based test results to improve instruction.

Conclusion

In many ways achievement testing has changed dramatically in American schools over the last century. Developments in psychometrics, learning theory, and technology have allowed for the creation of tests today that are much more sophisticated and efficient than tests in use in the early 1900s. Achievement testing has become a more established part of American schooling as well. In the early years of the century, tests were used by some, usually large, school districts as part of their school surveys. Few small districts had the resources to fund and operate testing programs. Today, it is difficult to locate schools where students do not take at least one standardized achievement battery. Testing no longer is a district-level activity only. In fact, most test development today is occurring at the state level. It is not uncommon for school children to take district- and state-supported tests in the same school year.

But in many other ways, achievement testing has come full circle over the last century. Uniform tests were administered at the start of the century to fulfill the aims of the political model. Tests were used to evaluate teachers and schools and to hold them accountable for student learning. In developing tests for this use, few concerns were raised as to how teachers were to use test score information to improve their practices. Strikingly, tests are used today to fulfill the same mission, and the morphology of tests reflects that lack of concern for providing teachers with constructive, formative information. Perhaps the only significant difference in testing today compared to the past is that all students are expected to learn at the same level of performance, whereas at the century's beginning, the predominant belief was to have different standards for children at different levels of innate ability.

This brief review of key events in the history of American achievement testing has revealed some fundamental limitations in the use of tests to effect change. Neither the political nor professional reform models use achievement tests effectively. Missing from the political model is teacher ownership of the tests and, consequently, the information tests yield. Few teachers are directly involved in test construction, leaving the great majority of teachers to view tests as the property of the district and state administrations. Without teacher buy-in, there is little to intrinsically motivate teachers to study what the tests purport to measure or to attend to test results. The primary motivation for teachers to use tests under the political model is the potential fear of being held publicly accountable for students' test scores, which leads teachers to resent tests and to perceive them as inaccurate indicators of student learning.

Another flaw in the logic of the political model pertains to the information provided by tests developed primarily for accountability purposes. If teachers and schools are to be held publicly responsible for students' test scores, the public must have some understanding of the skills tested. Further, tests that reflect on accountability must measure the skills the public believes are important for children to learn. When non-educators have a large voice in setting standards, the tests that result often measure subject matter in items that are not interconnected in a manner that reflects how children learn and think at various developmental stages.

Consequently, tests developed for accountability are inadequate for teachers who are deemed in need of improvement and are seeking constructive feedback about problems in their students' learning. Effective instructional modifications require teachers to know not only which topics their students did not learn well, but also the order in which topics should be taught, the cognitive processes students engage in to learn specific topics, and the sequence of mental operations that define a deeper understanding of material. In short, tests that are truly developed to improve teaching *should* provide information that the public finds esoteric or overly technical.

Because teachers tend to resent accountability testing, they frequently view tests as intrusions into their daily activities. In an effort to reduce teachers' pessimism toward testing, and because school evaluation does not require outcomes from all students, the number of grades tested and the frequency of test administrations are restricted. This testing and reporting schedule fails to promote an information feedback system designed to improve instruction.

Achievement testing within the professional model of reform has been equally disappointing, perhaps primarily because local teacher control over curriculum development and testing is discordant with uniform, external test content. If tests were developed based on contemporary theories of learning, cognition, and development, it is possible that uniform tests could provide useful information for teachers, even when focused on their students' unique needs. Yet there are barriers that prevent this notion from becoming reality. First, rarely are elements of these theories transformed into instructional methods and materials, so it is unclear how teachers would use theory-driven test results to plan instruction. Furthermore, because a grand theory that explains all of the nuances of learning does not exist, it is nearly impossible to construct one test to capture the complexities of learning.

Teachers' technical knowledge of achievement testing creates another barrier to useful implementation. Few inservice programs prepare teachers to interpret test score information or to develop integrated tests aligned with the instructional techniques they learn. Without a reason to attend to test score comparisons between classrooms and schools many teachers simply lack a desire to learn detailed psychometric properties and nomenclature. Many teachers are unsure what to do with the results of criterion-referenced tests, especially given that most of this information is irrelevant when it arrives at the end of a school year, and it is often presented in a manner that makes it difficult to interpret. Clearly, we need to increase teachers' capacities to use results from criterion-referenced tests, for it is this information from present achievement tests that is most in accord with the ideals of professionalism in teaching.

It is difficult to predict whether or not standardized achievement testing will ever live up to the expectations set by the progressives.

Perhaps a new form of testing will be needed that better meets the need of present reform models. Or, possibly, a new reform model will be developed that uses achievement tests more effectively. In either case, learning from the limitations of past and present testing will be a vital step in making tests more useful for schools of the future.

NOTES

1. George F. Madaus, "The Influence of Testing on the Curriculum," in *Curriculum: Selected Chapters from NSSE Yearbooks*, Ninety-eighth Yearbook of the National Society for the Study of Education, Part II (Chicago: University of Chicago Press, 1999), pp. 73-111.

2. Lorraine M. McDonnell, "Assessment Policy as Persuasion and Regulation," *American Journal of Education* 102 (August 1994): 394-420; Kenneth A. Strike, "Professionalism, Democracy, and Discursive Communities: Normative Reflections on Restructuring," *American Educational Research Journal* 30 (Summer 1993): 255-75.

3. See Bernard R. Gifford and Mary C. O'Connor, ed., *Changing Assessments: Alternative Views of Aptitude, Achievement and Instruction* (Boston: Kluwer Academic Publishers, 1992) for an example of testing within the professional reform model.

4. Otis W. Caldwell and Stuart A. Courtis, *Then and Now in Education, 1845-1923* (Yonkers-on-Hudson: World Book Company, 1924).

5. I. L. Kandel, *Examinations and Their Substitutes in the United States*, Bulletin No. 28 (New York: The Carnegie Foundation for the Advancement of Teaching, 1936).

6. David B. Tyack, *The One Best System: A History of American Urban Education* (Cambridge, MA: Harvard University Press, 1974).

7. See Ellwood P. Cubberley, "Introduction: Conditions: The Problem," in *The Certification of Teachers*, Fifth Yearbook of the National Society for the Scientific Study of Education, Part II (Chicago: University of Chicago Press, 1906), pp. 7-11, for an explanation of teacher certification requirements in the early 1900s.

8. See Henry L. Smith, "Plans for Organizing School Surveys," in *Plans for Organizing School Surveys*, Thirteenth Yearbook of the National Society for the Study of Education, Part II (Bloomington, IL: Public School Publishing Company, 1914), pp. 7-68, for an argument supporting teacher involvement in interpreting school surveys.

9. Joseph M. Rice, "The Futility of the Spelling Grind," *The Forum* 23 (1897): 163-72, 409-19; Joseph M. Rice, "Causes of Success and Failure in Arithmetic," *The Forum* 34 (1902): 437-52. See Edward L. Thorndike, *Mental Work and Fatigue and Individual Differences and Their Causes, Volume III, Educational Psychology* (New York: Teachers College Press, 1914), for a thorough explanation of Rice's findings and conclusions.

10. For an early account of the scientific management of schools, see Franklin Bobbitt, "Some General Principles of Management Applied to the Problems of City School Systems," in *The Supervision of City Schools*, Twelfth Yearbook of the National Society for the Study of Education, Part I (Chicago: University of Chicago Press, 1913), pp. 7-96. For an historical analysis of the administrative progressive movement, see Tyack, *The One Best System: A History of American Urban Education*.

11. Stuart A. Courtis, "Measurement of Growth and Efficiency in Arithmetic," *Elementary School Teacher* 10 (1909): 58-74, 177-99.

12. Stuart A. Courtis, "Standards in Rates of Reading," in *Minimum Essentials in Elementary School Subjects: Standards and Current Practices*, Fourteenth Yearbook of the National Society for the Study of Education, Part I (Bloomington, IL: Public School Publishing Company, 1919), pp. 44-58.

13. Bobbitt, "Some General Principles of Management Applied to the Problems of City-School Systems."

14. Middlesex A. Bailey, "The Courtis Tests in Arithmetic," in *The Fifteenth Annual Report of the City Superintendent of Schools to the Board of Education of the City of New York* (New York: Board of Education of the City of New York, 1913), pp. 505-38.

15. Ibid, p. 512.

16. Tyack, *The One Best System: A History of American Urban Education.*

17. Thorndike, p. 314.

18. Edward L. Thorndike, *Educational Psychology* (New York: Science Press, 1903), p. 96.

19. For an analysis of the influence of behaviorism on testing, see Lorrie A. Shepard, "Psychometricians' Beliefs About Learning," *Educational Researcher* 20 (October 1991): 2-15.

20. Strike, "Professionalism, Democracy, and Discursive Communities: Normative Reflections on Restructuring."

21. Ralph W. Tyler, *Basic Principles of Curriculum and Instruction* (Chicago: University of Chicago Press, 1949), p. 41.

22. Ibid.

23. Benjamin S. Bloom, Max D. Engelhart, Edward J. Furst, Walker H. Hill, and David R. Krathwohl, *Taxonomy of Educational Objectives* (New York: Longmans Press, 1956).

24. Peter W. Airasian, "The Impact of the Taxonomy on Testing and Evaluation," in *Bloom's Taxonomy: A Forty-Year Retrospective*, Ninety-third Yearbook of the National Society for the Study of Education, Part II (Chicago: University of Chicago Press, 1994), pp. 82-102.

25. Lee J. Cronbach, "Course Improvement Through Evaluation," *Teachers College Record* 64 (1963): 672-83.

26. Ralph W. Tyler, *Constructing Achievement Tests* (Columbus: Bureau of Educational Research, Ohio State University, 1934).

27. See Julia J. Peterson, *The Iowa Testing Programs* (Iowa City: University of Iowa Press, 1983).

28. William J. Feister and Douglas R. Whitney, "An Interview with Dr. E. F. Lindquist," *The University of Iowa Epsilon Bulletin* 42 (1968): 17-28.

29. Ibid, p. 19.

30. Ibid, p. 20.

31. Peterson, *The Iowa Testing Programs.*

32. Public Law 89-10, *Elementary and Secondary Education Act of 1965* (April 1965).

33. Milbrey W. McLaughlin, *Evaluation and Reform: The Elementary and Secondary Education Act of 1965, Title I* (Cambridge, MA: Ballinger Publishing Company, 1972).

34. Alan Davis, "Upping the Stakes: Using Gain Scores to Judge Local Program Effectiveness in Chapter 1," *Educational Evaluation and Policy Analysis* 13 (Winter 1991): 380-88.

35. Donald P. Horst, G. Kasten Tallmadge, and Christine T. Wood, "A Practical Guide to Measuring Project Impact on Student Achievement," *Monograph Series on Evaluation in Education 1* (Mountain View, CA: RMC Research Corporation, 1975). ED 106 376.

36. Mark Gittleman, *Chapter 1 Program Improvement and Innovation across the States: An Overview and State Profiles* (Washington, DC: Council of Chief State School Officers, 1992). ED 350 379.

37. Judith I. Anderson, "Using the Norm-referenced Model to Evaluate Chapter 1" (Paper presented at the annual meeting of the American Educational Research Association, Chicago, April, 1991). ED 350 315; Richard M. Jaeger, "The Effect of Test Selection on the Title I Project Impact," *Educational Evaluation and Policy Analysis* 1 (March-April 1979): 33-40.

38. Robert L. Linn, "Validity of Inferences Based on the Proposed Title I Evaluation Models," *Educational Evaluation and Policy Analysis* 1 (1979): 23-32.

39. Lorrie A. Shepard, "Chapter 1's Part in the Juggernaut of Standardized Testing" (Paper presented at the annual meeting of the American Educational Research Association, San Francisco, April, 1992). ED 354 260.

40. Abt Associates, *The Chapter 1 Implementation Study: Interim Report* (Cambridge, MA: Abt Associates, 1992).

41. U.S. Department of Education, *Promising Results, Continuing Challenges: The Final Report of the National Assessment of Title I* (Washington, DC: U.S. Department of Education, 1999).

42. Council of Chief State School Officers, *State Education Indicators with a Focus on Title I* (Washington, DC: Council of Chief State School Officers, 1998).

43. U.S. Department of Education, *The 1996-97 Title I Performance Report* (Unpublished tabulations, Washington, DC: U.S. Department of Education, n.d.).

44. Linda Darling-Hammond, "National Standards and Assessments: Will They Improve Education?" *American Journal of Education* 102 (August 1994): 478-510.

Name Index

N.B. The Notes at the end of each chapter have not been indexed.

Subject Index

N.B. The Notes at the end of each chapter have not been indexed.

RECENT PUBLICATIONS OF THE SOCIETY

1. The Yearbooks

99:1 (2000) *Constructivism in Education*. D. C. Phillips, editor. Cloth.

99:2 (2000) *American Education: Yesterday, Today, and Tomorrow*. Thomas L. Good, editor. Cloth.

98:1 (1999) *The Education of Teachers*, Gary A. Griffin, editor. Cloth.

98:2 (1999) *Issues in Curriculum*, Margaret J. Early and Kenneth J. Rehage, editors. Cloth.

97:1 (1998) *The Adolescent Years: Social Influences and Educational Challenges*. Kathryn Borman and Barbara Schneider, editors. Cloth.

97:2 (1998) *The Reading-Writing Connection*. Nancy Nelson and Robert C. Calfee, editors. Cloth.

96:1 (1997) *Service Learning*. Joan Schine, editor. Cloth.

96:2 (1997) *The Construction of Children's Character*. Alex Molnar, editor. Cloth.

95:1 (1996) *Performance-Based Student Assessment: Challenges and Possibilities*. Joan B. Baron and Dennie P. Wolf, editors. Cloth.

95:2 (1996) *Technology and the Future of Schooling*. Stephen T. Kerr, editor. Cloth.

94:1 (1995) *Creating New Educational Communities*. Jeannie Oakes and Karen Hunter Quartz, editors. Cloth.

94:2 (1995) *Changing Populations/Changing Schools*. Erwin Flaxman and A. Harry Passow, editors. Cloth.

93:1 (1994) *Teacher Research and Educational Reform*. Sandra Hollingsworth and Hugh Sockett, editors. Cloth.

93:2 (1994) *Bloom's Taxonomy: A Forty-year Retrospective*. Lorin W. Anderson and Lauren A. Sosniak, editors. Cloth.

92:1 (1993) *Gender and Education*. Sari Knopp Biklen and Diane Pollard, editors. Cloth.

92:2 (1993) *Bilingual Education: Politics, Practice, and Research*. M. Beatriz Arias and Ursula Casanova, editors. Cloth.

91:1 (1992) *The Changing Contexts of Teaching*. Ann Lieberman, editor. Cloth.

91:2 (1992) *The Arts, Education, and Aesthetic Knowing*. Bennett Reimer and Ralph A. Smith, editors. Cloth.

90:1 (1991) *The Care and Education of America's Young Children: Obstacles and Opportunities*. Sharon L. Kagan, editor. Cloth.

89:2 (1990) *Educational Leadership and Changing Contexts of Families, Communities, and Schools*. Brad Mitchell and Luvern L. Cunningham, editors. Paper.

88:1 (1989) *From Socrates to Software: The Teacher as Text and the Text as Teacher*. Philip W. Jackson and Sophie Haroutunian-Gordon, editors. Cloth.

88:2 (1989) *Schooling and Disability*. Douglas Biklen, Dianne Ferguson, and Alison Ford, editors. Cloth.

Order the above titles from the University of Chicago Press, 11030 S. Langley Ave., Chicago, IL 60628. For a list of earlier Yearbooks still available, write to the Secretary, NSSE, 5835 Kimbark Ave., Chicago, IL 60637.

2. The Series on Contemporary Educational Issues

This series has been discontinued.

The following volumes in the series may be ordered from the McCutchan Publishing Corporation, P.O. Box 774, Berkeley, CA 94702-0774. Phone: 510-841-8616; Fax: 510-841-7787.

Academic Work and Educational Excellence: Raising Student Productivity (1986). Edited by Tommy M. Tomlinson and Herbert J. Walberg.

Adapting Instruction to Student Differences (1985). Edited by Margaret C. Wang and Herbert J. Walberg.

Choice in Education (1990). Edited by William Lowe Boyd and Herbert J. Walberg.

Colleges of Education: Perspectives on Their Future (1985). Edited by Charles W. Case and William A. Matthes.

Contributing to Educational Change: Perspectives on Research and Practice (1988). Edited by Philip W. Jackson.

Educational Leadership and School Culture (1993). Edited by Marshall Sashkin and Herbert J. Walberg.

Effective Teaching: Current Research (1991). Edited by Hersholt C. Waxman and Herbert J. Walberg.

Improving Educational Standards and Productivity: The Research Basis for Policy (1982). Edited by Herbert J. Walberg.

Moral Development and Character Education (1989). Edited by Larry P. Nucci.

Motivating Students to Learn: Overcoming Barriers to High Achievement (1993). Edited by Tommy M. Tomlinson.

Radical Proposals for Educational Change (1994). Edited by Chester E. Finn, Jr. and Herbert J. Walberg.

Reaching Marginal Students: A Prime Concern for School Renewal (1987). Edited by Robert L. Sinclair and Ward Ghory.

Restructuring the Schools: Problems and Prospects (1992). Edited by John J. Lane and Edgar G. Epps.

Rethinking Policy for At-risk Students (1994). Edited by Kenneth K. Wong and Margaret C. Wang.

School Boards: Changing Local Control (1992). Edited by Patricia F. First and Herbert J. Walberg.

The two final volumes in this series were:

Improving Science Education (1995). Edited by Barry J. Fraser and Herbert J. Walberg.

Ferment in Education: A Look Abroad (1995). Edited by John J. Lane.

These two volumes may be ordered from the Book Order Department, University of Chicago Press, 11030 S. Langley Ave., Chicago, IL 60628. Phone: 312-669-2215; Fax: 312-660-2235.